The Complete NetWare Command Reference
Second Edition

Blaine Homer
Revised by Dorothy Cady

New Riders Publishing, Indianapolis, Indiana

NRP
NEW RIDERS
PUBLISHING

The Complete NetWare Command Reference, Second Edition

By Blaine Homer and Dorothy Cady

Published by:
New Riders Publishing
201 West 103rd Street
Indianapolis, IN 46290 USA

Warning and Disclaimer

Publisher	Don Fowley
Associate Publisher	Tim Huddleston
Product Development Manager	Rob Tidrow
Marketing Manager	Ray Robinson
Acquisitions Manager	Jim LeValley
Managing Editor	Tad Ringo

About the Authors

Blaine Homer is a technical editor for LAN Times. He writes previews, reviews, and product comparisons. His technical beats include: network hardware, Novell products, network management applications and tools, and network security. Before joining the LAN Times Testing Center, Blaine worked for Novell's internal network management team. He also worked for Novell's IS department repairing hardware and supporting the end user. Blaine also does private network installation and consulting. He has a B.S. degree from Brigham Young University's Marriott School of Management, with an emphasis in Information Systems.

Dorothy Cady is a Senior Technical Writer for Novell, Inc. She joined Novell in 1990 as a Team Leader for the Software Documentation Testing Team. Dorothy has worked with all versions of Novell NetWare since version 2.15c and has worked with Personal NetWare. As a freelance writer she has written several nonfiction books and magazine articles. Dorothy has an Associate of Arts degree in Accounting and is completing credits toward a Bachelor of Science in Computer Information Systems. She is a Certified Novell 3.1x Administrator, a Certified Novell 4.0 Administrator, a Certified Novell Engineer, a Certified Novell Instructor, and an Enterprise Certified Novell Instructor. Dorothy joined the Adjunct Faculty at Utah Valley State College, Department of Science in 1990. She lives in Arizona with her husband, Raymond, and their two children, Shana Michelle and Raymond.

Trademark Acknowledgments

All terms mentioned in this book that are known to be trademarks or service marks have been appropriately capitalized. New Riders Publishing cannot attest to the accuracy of this information. Use of a term in this book should not be regarded as affecting the validity of any trademark or service mark. NetWare is a registered trademark of Novell, Inc.

Product Development Specialist
Emmett Dulaney

Acquisitions Editor
Alicia Buckley

Senior Editor
Lisa Wilson

Copy Editors
Laura Frey
Stacia Mellinger
Cliff Shubs

Technical Editor
Roger Burt

Assistant Marketing Manager
Tamara Apple

Acquisitions Coordinator
Tracey Turgeson

Publisher's Assistant
Karen Opal

Cover Designer
Sandra Schroeder

Book Designer
Roger Morgan

Production Team Supervisor
Laurie Casey

Graphic Image Specialists
Dennis Sheehan
Clint Lahnen
Dennis Clay Hager

Production Analyst
Angela Bannan
Bobbi Satterfield
Mary Beth Wakefield

Production Team
Gary Adair, Angela Calvert, Nathan Clement, Dan Caparo, Kim Cofer, David Eason, Jennifer Eberhardt, Rob Falco, Kevin Foltz, David Garratt, Aleata Howard, Joe Millay, Erika Millen, Beth Rago, Gina Rexrode, Erich Richter, Karen Walsh, Robert Wolf

Indexer
Brad Herriman

Contents at a Glance

Part I: Command Reference

Introduction, 1
Command Reference, 7

Part II: Menu Utilities

Introduction, 349

Table of Contents

Table of Contents

Table of Contents

Table of Contents

Table of Contents

Table of Contents

Table of Contents

Table of Contents

Table of Contents

Table of Contents

Introduction

This book is designed to be used by system administrators and NetWare consultants who often work with multiple versions of NetWare. It provides a command reference to all command line utilities, and the most essential menu utilities.

How This Book Helps You

Versions 2.2, 3.11, 3.12, and 4.10 are covered in thorough detail, providing you with one source of information to replace the many version-dependent volumes you are used to carrying. This book is divided into two sections: command-line utilities and menu utilities. In each section, commands are listed in alphabetic order with thumb tabs along the outer margins of the book.

Appendixes provide listings of commands-at-a-glance, readily identifying which version each command works with and whether it was replaced by another utility. The appendixes also offer a reference to all variables used in NetWare and login scripts, as well as a breakdown of shortcut keys inside menu utilities.

Conventions Used in This Book

Several icons are used throughout the book to provide you with a quick reference as to functionality. These icons are as follows:

This utility works in NetWare version 2.2.

This utility works in NetWare on versions 3.11 and 3.12.

This utility works with NetWare version 3.12.

This utility works with NetWare version 4.10. In all practicality, it also works with 4.0 and 4.01.

This utility works at a functioning server console.

This utility works from a downed server console.

This utility works from an active, or logged in, workstation.

This utility works locally, or at a non-logged in workstation.

This denotes expansion on key points relevant to the utility being discussed.

A Different Look at Menus

So often, when menu utilities are discussed, screen shots are used to highlight the actions. In NetWare, as one proceeds through menus, however, new menus layer on top of old. Looking at a screen shot when you are three menus deep becomes confusing to a reader who is attempting to reach that point. In addition to screen shots, this book also employs illustrations to show the progression through menu choices to the desired action.

To find a user's login time with the FCONSOLE utility, for example, you first start FCONSOLE, then choose Connection Information from the menu that appears. Next, you choose the user for whom you want to see information and press Enter. Then select Other Information from the next menu, and the desired information appears. To express this information in a way that can be quickly understood, this book utilizes the following type of figure:

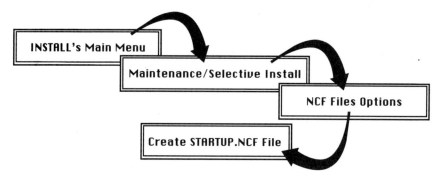

New Riders Publishing

The staff of New Riders Publishing is committed to bringing you the very best in computer reference material. Each New Riders book is the result of months of work by authors and staff who research and refine the information contained within its covers.

As part of this commitment to you, the NRP reader, New Riders invites your input. Please let us know if you enjoy this book, if you have trouble with the information and examples presented, or if you have a suggestion for the next edition.

Please note, though: New Riders staff cannot serve as a technical resource for NetWare or for related questions about software- or hardware-related problems. Please refer to the documentation that accompanies NetWare or to the applications' Help systems.

If you have a question or comment about any New Riders book, there are several ways to contact New Riders Publishing. We will respond to as many readers as we can. Your name, address, or phone number will never become part of a mailing list or be used for any purpose other than to help us continue to bring you the best books possible. You can write us at the following address:

New Riders Publishing
Attn: Associate Publisher
201 W. 103rd Street
Indianapolis, IN 46290

If you prefer, you can fax New Riders Publishing at (317) 581-4670. You can send electronic mail to New Riders at the following CompuServe address: 74507, 3713

NRP is an imprint of Macmillan Computer Publishing. To obtain a catalog or information, or to purchase any Macmillan Computer Publishing book, call (800) 428-5331.

Thank you for selecting *The Complete NetWare Command Reference, Second Edition*!

Part I

Command Reference

ABORT REMIRROR

Purpose: Stops the remirroring of a NetWare partition.

Syntax: `ABORT REMIRROR` `partition_number`

Options: Replace `partition_number` with the logical number of the NetWare partition for which you want to stop remirroring.

Rules and Considerations: By default, NetWare will automatically begin remirroring a mirrored partition that is out of sync once the disabled or damaged half of the mirrored pair is back online. This command halts the remirror process.

Important Messages: None

Examples: To stop remirroring for the second partition, type the following at the system console:

`ABORT REMIRROR 2`

Notes: Partition remirroring typically consumes over 70 percent of the CPU's time, so you might want to delay the remirroring process until disk activity is reduced.

See Also: REMIRROR PARTITION

A
B
C
D
E
F
G
H
I
J
K
L
M
N
O
P
Q
R
S
T
U
V
W
X
Y
Z

ACTIVATE SERVER

Purpose: Remirrors the disk from one SFT III server to another, and activates one of the servers as the primary. In the process, it loads the NetWare 4.1 SFT III system's MSEngine, synchronizes memory of both servers, and runs the MSSTART and MSAUTO NCF files.

Syntax: `ACTIVATE SERVER` *parameter...*

Parameter	Function
-na	Prevents MSAUTO.NCF file from running when loading the MSEngine, to allow you to change MSAUTO.NCF commands.
-ns	Prevents MSSTART.NCF from running when loading the MSEngine, to let you change the boot process.
-na and -ns	Prevents both MSAUTO.NCF and MSSTART.NCF from running when loading the MSEngine.

Rules and Considerations: MSERVER must be loaded before running ACTIVATE SERVER. Two servers running ACTIVATE SERVER at the same time may result in two separate and unsynchronized MSEngines being loaded, causing both servers to assume each was the primary server.

Be prepared to provide an IPX internal network number and MSEngine name if you run the ACTIVATE SERVER command without an accompanying MSAUTO.NCF file.

Example: To load the MSEngine, synchronize memory, and remirror disks without executing either the MSAUTO.NCF or MSSTART.NCF, type the following command lines at the file server's DOS prompt, and press Enter.

MSERVER

At the file server console prompt, type the ACTIVATE SERVER command, as follows, then press Enter:

ACTIVATE SERVER -na -ns

Important Messages: None

Notes: Exercise caution in putting ACTIVATE SERVER in the IOSTART.NCF file as synchronization problems can occur.

See Also: MSERVER

A
B
C
D
E
F
G
H
I
J
K
L
M
N
O
P
Q
R
S
T
U
V
W
X
Y
Z

ADD NAME SPACE

Purpose: Stores non-DOS files, such as Macintosh, on a NetWare volume. This command is available only at the file server console.

Syntax: ADD NAME SPACE *name* TO VOLUME *volumename*

Option	Description
Mac.NAM	Use for Macintosh files
OS2.NAM	Use for OS/2 files
NFS.NAM	Use for Unix files
FTAM	Use for Unix files

Rules and Considerations: To set up a volume for the storage of non-DOS files, make sure that the appropriate NetWare Loadable Modules (NLMs) for the non-DOS files have been loaded. Next, configure the volume for the new name space.

Before you can use this command, you must load the appropriate name space module. Extra server memory is required for each name space you add to a volume. Use the ADD NAME SPACE command once for each non-DOS naming convention you intend to store on a NetWare volume.

To use Macintosh files on your server, you must load INSTALL from the NW-MAC disk after you have added the name space.

Examples: To add Macintosh name space support to the NetWare volume SYS, type the following form of the command at the console:

ADD NAME SPACE MACINTOSH TO SYS

To see the name space support currently set up on your server, type the following command at the file server console:

ADD NAME SPACE

The screen displays the following message:

A

```
Missing name space name
Syntax: ADD NAME SPACE <name space name>
[TO [VOLUME]] <volumename>

Loaded name spaces are:
DOS
MACINTOSH
```

Important Messages: None

Notes: After you set up a NetWare volume to store non-DOS files, you can reverse the name space only by loading and running the VREPAIR utility and destroying all non-DOS file data.

You must use the ADD NAME SPACE command for every volume that needs to store non-DOS files.

See Also: VREPAIR

B

C

D

E

F

G

H

I

J

K

L

M

N

O

P

Q

R

S

T

U

V

W

X

Y

Z

ALLOW

Purpose: Enables you to change, view, or set the inherited rights mask (IRM) of a file or directory. The ALLOW command resides in the SYS:PUBLIC directory. In NetWare 4.10, the RIGHTS command is used to perform the same functions.

Syntax: ALLOW *path\filename rightslist*

Use the following rights in place of the *rightslist* variable. Except for ALL, use the first letter only.

Option	Function
ALL	Specifies all rights
No Rights	Specifies no rights, does not remove Supervisory
Read	Opens and reads files
Write	Opens and writes to files
Create	Creates and writes to files
Erase	Deletes a file or directory
Modify	Renames files or directories; modifies file or directory attributes
File Scan	Views files and directories
Access Control	Enables changes to security assignments

You can use the boldfaced letters instead of the entire word. Add a space between rights.

Rules and Considerations: You must change all of the IRM rights of a directory or file at the same time. Each time you use the ALLOW command to change the mask, it overrides the previous mask; you cannot change the mask incrementally.

You cannot remove the S (Supervisory) right from the IRM of a directory or file.

Examples: To change the IRM of SUBDIR1 to Read and File Scan, type the following:

`ALLOW SUBDIR1 R F`

To change the IRM of file1 in SUBDIR1 to Read, Write, and File Scan, type the following:

`ALLOW SUBDIR1\FILE1 R W F`

Important Messages: NetWare might display the following message when you issue the ALLOW command:

`No Entries Found!`

If this message appears, make sure that you specified a file or directory that exists and that you spelled it correctly. Also, make sure that you specified the correct path, and that you have File Scan rights in the directory.

The following message might appear if the Access Control right is not set correctly:

`Directory Name (mask) Not Changed.`

If this message displays with the name of your directory, make sure that the Access Control right is set in the directory.

Notes: When you change the IRM of a directory or file, you are changing the effective rights of all users in that directory or file.

See Also: RIGHTS

A
B
C
D
E
F
G
H
I
J
K
L
M
N
O
P
Q
R
S
T
U
V
W
X
Y
Z

ATOTAL

Purpose: The ATOTAL is designed to be used with Novell's Accounting feature. ATOTAL lists the following accounting totals:

♦ Connect time in minutes

♦ Service requests

♦ Blocks read

♦ Blocks written

♦ Disk storage in blocks per day

Syntax:

(2.2, 3.1x) **ATOTAL**

(4.10) **ATOTAL** Destination Option

Options	Functions	
Destination	The complete path and file name for saving the output to a file.	
Options	Replace with one of the following:	
	/C	Provides continuous scrolling of the output
	/?	Brings up online help
	/VER	Provides version number and list of files required by this utility to run.

Rules and Considerations: Before you run ATOTAL, make sure that NetWare's accounting feature has been installed. See SYSCON in 2.x and 3.x or NETADMIN and NWADMIN in 4.x for information on installing the accounting feature. This command must be run from the SYS:SYSTEM directory. In 3.x, it is in the sys:system. In 4.10 it is in sys:public.

ACCOUNTING SERVICES TOTAL UTILITY, Version 2.02

```
Unable to open sys:system\net$acct.dat
file not found. Perhaps accounting is not
enabled?
```

If this message appears, make sure that accounting has been installed on your file server. Also make sure that accounting has been running for at least half an hour and that you have logged out of the server and then logged back in.

Examples: To generate a summary list of the accounting services—from SYS:SYSTEM (or with a search drive mapped to SYS:SYSTEM)—use the following command:

```
ATOTAL
```

This displays the summary list on the workstation's screen.

Notes: ATOTAL generates a great deal of data, and you may not derive much value from simply displaying the data on-screen. A much more practical idea is to redirect the output data to a file using standard DOS redirection commands, and then print the file.

To redirect ATOTAL data to a file when running 2.2 or 3.1x, type the following:

```
ATOTAL > filename.ext
```

In this generic syntax, `filename.ext` is the name of the file in which you want to direct the ATOTAL data. To print the file, type the following:

```
NPRINT filename.ext
```

This command sends the ASCII text file `filename.ext` to the default print queue on your file server.

The DOS redirection procedure creates a standard ASCII file that you can import into a word processing or spreadsheet program for further processing.

For NetWare 4.10, to redirect ATOTAL data to a file, type the following:

```
ATOTAL path/filename
```

Replace *path/filename* with the exact path and name of the file into which the ATOTAL output is to be redirected.

See Also: NETADMIN, NPRINT, NWADMIN, SYSCON

A
B
C
D
E
F
G
H
I
J
K
L
M
N
O
P
Q
R
S
T
U
V
W
X
Y
Z

ATTACH

Purpose: Provides access to services provided by another file server after you have logged in to a file server.

ATTACH.EXE is stored in SYS:LOGIN\OS2, SYS:PUBLIC, and SYS:PUBLIC\OS2.

Syntax: ATTACH `fileserver_name/username /P /G`

Option	Description
`fileserver_name`	The name of the file server to which you want to attach.
`fileserver_name\username`	The file server name and user name for the file server to which you are attaching.
`private`	For OS/2 sessions only. This option enables you to attach to a server in single session.
`global`	For OS/2 sessions only. This option enables you to attach to a server in all sessions.

Rules and Considerations: The ATTACH command assigns a connection number to a workstation and attaches the workstation to an additional file server. ATTACH does not execute the system, user, or default login scripts. After you are attached, however, you have access to files, applications, and other resources. You can attach to as many as seven file servers other than the one you currently are using.

You can use the ATTACH command without entering the file server name or user name. After you type ATTACH, NetWare displays the message Enter server name to prompt for the file server name. NetWare then displays the message Enter user name to prompt for the user name. Enter the name of the user for that file server. If that file server requires a password, NetWare prompts for the password by displaying the message

`Enter your password.` When you enter the password, NetWare should display the following message:

`Your station is attached to server ` *`servername`*

If you do not know the name of the file server to which you want to attach, use the SLIST command to obtain a list of file servers that are available.

You can attach up to eight file servers at one time. Log in to the first file server and attach to seven others.

To automate attaching to other servers, add the following command to the system login scripts:

`attach fileserver_name/%LOGIN_NAME`

When executed from a system login script, you will not be prompted to enter any data provided the login name and passwords are the same on both servers. You will be prompted for a password if there is a difference. When placed in the user login script, you can leave out the /%LOGIN_NAME if username and password are the same.

Important Messages: If the ATTACH command fails, NetWare might display the following message:

`No response from file server.`

If this message appears, a bad connection might exist between the file server to which you are connected and the file server to which you are trying to attach.

If you are logged into a 2.2, 3.11, or 3.12 server, you can use the ATTACH command to connect to a 4.10 server. The 4.10 server must have Bindery emulation active.

Examples: To attach the user Jacob to the file server FS1, type the following command:

`ATTACH fs1\jacob`

Notes: If you try to attach to a ninth file server, NetWare displays the following message:

`The limit of 8 server connections has been reached`

If you already are attached to eight file servers and you want to attach to another one, you must first log out from one of the servers to which you are attached. Log out by issuing the following command:

A
B
C
D
E
F
G
H
I
J
K
L
M
N
O
P
Q
R
S
T
U
V
W
X
Y
Z

```
LOGOUT fileserver_name
```

You then can attach to another file server.

Too many file server attachments can affect your system's performance. If performance is slow, log out from the file servers whose services you do not need, then reattach when you need those services.

You also can use the MAP command to attach to another file server. Simply issue the MAP command and NetWare prompts you for the file server name, user name, and a password (if one is required for the user name you specify). NetWare runs the MAP command and attaches you to the file server at the same time.

One final way to attach to another server is to issue the CAPTURE or NPRINT commands with the */S=servername switch*. You will be asked for a user name and password if the user guest has a password or has been deleted.

See Also: LOGIN, LOGIN SCRIPTS, MAP, NLIST, SETPASS, SLIST, WHOAMI

BIND

Purpose: Links the LAN to a communication protocol and to a network board in the file server. The communication protocol must be linked to the board, or it will be unable to process packets. Each network board and protocol is bound separately.

Syntax:

BIND *protocol* to *board_name protocol_parameter*

or

BIND *protocol* to *LAN_driver [driver_parameters] protocol_parameter*

Option	Description
protocol	Normally, you would use IPX (Internetwork Packet Exchange) protocol although you may use other protocols such as IP.
LAN_driver	The name of the driver you loaded for the network board.
board_name	The board name you assigned when you loaded the driver, if any.
DMA=*number*	The DMA channel the network board is configured to use (if any).
FRAME=*name*	Frame type the driver is to use for this network board.
INT=*number*	The hardware interrupt the network board is configured to use.
MEM=*number*	The shared memory address the network board is configured to use (if any).
PORT=*number*	The I/O port address (in hex) the network board is configured to use.
SLOT=*number*	The slot in which the network board is installed (valid only for EISA and IBM Micro Channel equipped machines).

continues

A
B
C
D
E
F
G
H
I
J
K
L
M
N
O
P
Q
R
S
T
U
V
W
X
Y
Z

Option	Description
NODE=*number*	The 12-digit hexadecimal node address for the network board.
driver_parameter	You should include a driver_parameter when you have more than one network board of the same type in the file server.
NET=*number*	The unique IPX external network address number for the cabling system that is attached to the board.
protocol_parameter	Use for the parameters unique to the selected communications protocol. IPX has only one: NET.
ADDR=*number*	The unique IP address for that machine.

Refer to the documentation that comes with other third-party protocols for their specific protocol parameters.

Rules and Considerations: The following information applies when you load multiple network boards of the same type. When binding a protocol to a board name, you do not need to include the driver parameters because each board has a unique name that identifies its hardware settings.

The following example shows how to bind a protocol to a network board using a board name instead of a LAN driver. It assumes the assigned board name is ACCTNET:

BIND IPX to ACCTNET NET=105

If you choose not to name the boards, you must let the operating system know which protocol goes to which board. This is accomplished by binding the protocol to the LAN driver, then specifying which board to bind to by listing that board's hardware settings. These settings, or driver parameters, should be enclosed in square brackets.

If you loaded the driver with more than one frame type for a single network board, select a hexadecimal number that is different from all other network numbers (IPX internal network numbers and cabling systems).

Do not use the same number that was used for another frame type on the cabling system.

Before you use BIND, you must install the board and load the driver.

Unless a communication protocol has been linked (bound) to the network board, that board cannot process packets.

Bind a protocol to each LAN driver you load. If you load a LAN driver more than once, bind a protocol for each set of driver parameters.

NetWare 2.2 and previous versions use a frame type of ETHERNET_802.3 and NetWare 3.11 defaults to this as well. Starting with NetWare version 3.12 and 4.10, the default frame type is ETHERNET_802.2. The different Ethernet types will not communicate but a 3.x or above server can run both types. The workstations also must run the appropriate frame type. IPX.COM uses 802.3, the new VLM requester uses 802.2 or 802.3. Novell switched to the 802.2 frame type to enable additional security features like packet signatures.

Examples: To bind to the NE2000 LAN card, with a network address of 105, type the following:

```
BIND IPX to NE2000 NET=105
```

Repeat the process for each LAN driver in the file server.

To bind the IPX protocol to the NE2000 LAN card with a network address of 105, a port address of 340, an interrupt of 4, and a frame type of Ethernet_802.3, type the following command:

```
BIND IPX to NE2000 [PORT=340 INT=4 FRAME=ETHERNET_802.3] NET=105
```

You must issue this command each time the file server is booted; otherwise, you can place the command in the AUTOEXEC.NCF file. Include complete LAN-card configuration information in this file. Add the line after the LOAD LAN driver command.

Important Messages: To determine which LAN drivers need a protocol bound to them, type **CONFIG** at the file server console. Bind a protocol if the LAN driver information ends with the following message:

```
<C1>No LAN protocols are bound to this LAN board
```

Notes: If the network board is attached to an existing cabling system, NET=number must use that system's network address. Failure to comply results in router-configuration errors on other file servers and routers on the network.

NET=number is always required when binding the IPX protocol. If you fail to enter this parameter at the command line, the network operating system prompts for the network address.

See Also: CONFIG, INETCFG, IPX, LOAD, NET.CFG, PROTOCOL, ULOAD, UNBIND, VLM

A
B
C
D
E
F
G
H
I
J
K
L
M
N
O
P
Q
R
S
T
U
V
W
X
Y
Z

BINDFIX

Purpose: Helps solve problems with the NetWare bindery files. In 3.x, the bindery files are called NET$OBJ.SYS, NET$PROP.SYS, and NET$VAL.SYS. In 2.1x to 2.2, the bindery files are called NET$BIND.SYS and NET$BVAL.SYS. NetWare 4.10 uses the NDS (NetWare Directory Service) instead of binderies. To repair a corrupted NDS, use the DSREPAIR utility included with 4.10. Most symptoms occur in the SYSCON utility, and you might encounter one or several problems with the bindery, such as the following:

♦ You cannot change a user's password

♦ You cannot change or modify a user name

♦ You cannot modify a user's rights

♦ You receive the unknown server error message during printing, even when you are printing on the default file server

♦ At the file server console, you see error messages that refer to the bindery

BINDFIX.EXE and the bindery files are stored in the SYS:SYSTEM directory. Invoke the BINDFIX command from the SYS:SYSTEM directory.

Syntax: `BINDFIX`

Options: None

Rules and Considerations: Log in to the file server as user SUPERVISOR. Make sure that all other users are logged out of the file server. Before running BINDFIX, disable LOGIN at the file server console or in the FCONSOLE utility.

Important Messages: BINDFIX closes down the bindery files and then rebuilds them. After it rebuilds the files, it displays a list of the tasks it is performing. After it rebuilds the files, BINDFIX reopens them.

BINDFIX displays the following prompt:

```
Delete mail directories for users that no longer exist? (y/n):
```

If you answer Yes, BINDFIX deletes all corresponding mail directories for nonexisting users from the SYS:MAIL directory. BINDFIX then prompts as follows:

```
Delete trustee rights for users that no longer exist? (y/n):
```

If you answer Yes, BINDFIX scans all mounted volumes on the file server and deletes nonexisting users from all trustee lists.

BINDFIX renames the NET$OBJ.SYS, NET$PROP.SYS, and NET$VAL.SYS files to NET$OBJ.OLD, NET$PROP.OLD, and NET$VAL.OLD, and creates new NET$OBJ.SYS, NET$PROP.SYS, and NET$VAL.SYS files in 3.x. In 2.1x and 2.2, the NET$BIND.SYS and the NET$BVAL.SYS are renamed to NET$BIND.OLD and NET$BVAL.OLD. If the BINDFIX run on 2.x finishes successfully, the following message appears:

```
Please delete the files NET$BIND.OLD
and NET$BVAL.OLD after you have verified the
reconstructed bindery.
```

Notes: If you answered Yes to delete mail directories or trustee assignments and the workstation performing the bindfix hangs or loses its connection to the server data, loss may occur. This loss can include files and entire directory trees.

After BINDFIX reconstructs the bindery files, do not delete the OLD files from the SYS:SYSTEM directory. Keep these files so that you can restore the bindery if a problem arises with the newly constructed bindery files.

After all your users' groups and trustee assignments have been made with a new installation, you might want to execute BINDFIX to get an original backup copy of your bindery files. Copy OLD files onto a floppy disk for safe keeping. If BINDFIX is unable to reconstruct the bindery files, and if BINDREST is not restoring the bindery, copy the OLD files back into the SYS:SYSTEM directory and try BINDREST again.

See Also: BINDREST, BROADCAST, CLEAR STATION, DISABLE LOGIN, DSREPAIR, FCONSOLE, MONITOR, USERLIST

A
B
C
D
E
F
G
H
I
J
K
L
M
N
O
P
Q
R
S
T
U
V
W
X
Y
Z

BINDREST

Purpose: Reverses the effect of the BINDFIX command. The BINDREST command restores the backup bindery files created by BINDFIX. The backup bindery files are called NET$OBJ.OLD, NET$PROP.OLD, and NET$VAL.OLD in 3.x. In 2.1x and 2.2, the files are called NET$BIND.OLD and NET$BVAL.OLD. BINDREST returns these files to their original versions and names (NET$OBJ.SYS, NET$PROP.SYS, and NET$VAL.SYS in 3.x or NET$BIND.SYS and NET$BVAL.SYS). You only need to use BINDREST if BINDFIX fails. If you lose your bindery files and you have a backup copy of the bindery files on floppy disk, copy these files to the SYS:SYSTEM directory and execute BINDREST. NetWare 4.10 uses the DSREPAIR utility to perform similar functions.

Syntax: `BINDREST`

Options: None

Rules and Considerations: Before using the BINDREST command, log in to the file server as user SUPERVISOR and make sure that all other users are logged out of the file server. Use the FCONSOLE or USERLIST command to ensure all users are logged out of the file server. Use FCONSOLE or CLEAR STATION to clear all logged in users. Use DISABLE LOGIN to prevent users from logging in to the file server while BINDREST is running. If you invoke BINDFIX and then delete the OLD files after BINDFIX runs, you cannot use BINDREST to restore the bindery files.

If you deleted the old 3.x bindery files, when you run BINDREST NetWare displays a message similar to the following:

```
ERROR: File NET$OBJ.OLD does not exist.
ERROR: File NET$PROP.OLD does not exist.
ERROR: File NET$VAL.OLD does not exist.

          Unable to restore old bindery files.
```

If you have a backup of the OLD files on a floppy disk, copy them to the SYS:SYSTEM directory and rerun BINDREST.

Notes: Make sure that all users are logged out of the file server before you invoke the BINDREST. BINDFIX, BROADCAST, CLEAR STATION, DISABLE LOGIN, DSREPAIR (4.10), FCONSOLE, MONITOR, USERLIST.

BROADCAST

Purpose: Sends a message to all users logged in or attached to the file server or to a list of connection numbers. You must issue the BROAD-CAST command from the file server console.

Syntax: BROADCAST `"message"` to `username`

Option	Description
username	The user's login name.
connection number	The connection number for 2.2 and 3.x can be listed by the USERLIST command. For NetWare 4.10 use the NLIST USER /A command.
Press Space	Enter a space on the same line as the command to specify another user name or connection number. Place the space between user names or connection numbers.

Rules and Considerations: To determine a connection number, refer to Connection Information on the MONITOR screen of a 3.x or 4.10 file server console. From the workstation use FCONSOLE or USERLIST for 2.x and 3.x servers or NLIST for 4.10 based servers.

The message can be up to 55 characters long. If you do not specify the connection number or user name, NetWare sends the message to all attached users.

All logged in users receive the message, except the following:

♦ Users who have used the 2.x, 3.x command CASTOFF ALL

♦ Users who have used the 4.10 command SEND/A=N

♦ Users who logged in using an ACS or NACS

♦ Users who are logged in on a remote workstation

Some graphics applications that are being used will not show the message you received, but you will hear a beep. Press Ctrl+Enter to continue.

A
B
C
D
E
F
G
H
I
J
K
L
M
N
O
P
Q
R
S
T
U
V
W
X
Y
Z

Users who receive the message will see it appear on the 25th line of the screen when older workstation drivers are used the new drivers display the message on the first line. The message should not interfere with the screen display. The workstation locks and nothing happens until the user clears the message by pressing Ctrl+Enter.

Important Messages: None

Examples: Suppose that you want to send the message "Meeting in room 1A in 10 minutes" to all users. Issue the following command:

```
BROADCAST "Meeting in room 1A in 10 minutes"
```

You do not need to enclose the message in quotation marks when you are sending a message to all users.

If you want to send the same message to Tim, Jane, Jacob, and connection number 6, issue the following command:

```
BROADCAST "Meeting in room 1A in 10 minutes"
to Tim, Jane, Jacob and 6
```

Notes: A message received at a workstation prevents further work until the message is cleared from the screen.

Use the CASTOFF ALL command for 2.2 and 3.x NetWare at the workstation to prevent it from receiving messages, or use SEND /A=N for 4.x NetWare.

See Also: CASTOFF ALL, FCONSOLE, MONITOR, NLIST, SEND

CAPTURE

Purpose: Redirects printed output from applications not designed to run on a network or from the screen to a NetWare print queue. CAPTURE also can save printed data to a file.

Syntax: `CAPTURE` *options*

Options: The optional switches used by CAPTURE consist of one or more of the following. These options work with all versions.

Option	Description
/? (help)	Displays basic syntax help.
AU (AUtoendcap)	Automatically closes out a print job when you exit an application. Autoendcap is enabled by default.
NA (NoAutoendcap)	Requires the use of the ENDCAP utility to terminate the effects of CAPTURE. In NetWare 4.10, you can also use the TI= command to close the capture after the specified time. Use NoAutoendcap to move in and out of your applications without prematurely closing the print queue file(s) you are creating.
B (Banner)	A banner name can be any word or phrase up to 12 characters that you want to appear on the lower part of the banner page. To represent a space between words, use an underline character; the underline character does print. The default is LST.
NB (NoBanner)	Tells NetWare not to print a banner page.
C (Copies=*n*)	Replace n with the number of copies you want to print. The default is 1 copy. (4.10 allows up to 65,000 copies.)

continues

A
B
C
D
E
F
G
H
I
J
K
L
M
N
O
P
Q
R
S
T
U
V
W
X
Y
Z

Option	Description
CR (CReate=*filespec*)	Creates a print file for storage instead of sending the print job to a file server's print queue. *filespec* can be any legal DOS file name and can include path information; you can create the print file, however, only on a network drive. This option does not work with OS/2. It can only be used with TI=, AU, or NA options.
FF (FormFeed)	Sends a form-feed code to the printer at the end of each print job so that the next print job can start at the top of the next sheet of paper. If your application sends a form-feed code at the end of the print job, an extra page gets fed through the printer, wasting paper. Form feeding is enabled by default.
NFF (NoFormFeed)	Disables the sending of form-feed codes at the end of a print job.
F (Form=*formname* or *n*)	Replace *formname* with the name of the form on which you want your print job to print. Replace *n* with the form number onto which you want your print job to print. Use the PRINTDEF utility to define form names or numbers (or both) before using this option.
J (Job=*jobconfig*)	Replace *jobconfig* with the name of a pre-defined print job configuration you want to use. You must use the PRINTCON utility to define print jobs before using this option. In NetWare 4.10, you can use a print job located anywhere in the NDS tree if you have sufficient rights. Use as: CAPTURE J=jobconfig:context.
K (Keep)	Tells CAPTURE to keep all data it receives during a print capture, in case your workstation locks up or loses power while capturing data. This option is useful if you capture data over a period of several hours. If your workstation loses its connection to the file server, the server sends the data to the print queue after the server realizes your station is no longer connected to it.

Option	Description
L (Local=*n*)	Indicates which local LPT ports you want to capture. Valid choices are 1, 2, or 3. The default is 1. The local LPT ports defined here are "logical" connections, not "physical" ports. You can print to and capture from all three LPT ports even though your workstation might only have one physical LPT port installed. NetWare 4.10 can access up to 9 ports.
NAM (NAMe=*name*)	*name* can be any word or phrase up to 12 characters that you want printed on the upper part of the banner page. The default is the user name used when you logged in to the file server. The NoBanner option defeats the purpose of using this switch because no banner page is printed.
Q (Queue=*queuename*)	*queuename* is the file server queue name to which you want to send the print job. This option is useful if multiple queues are mapped to one printer. If you fail to specify a queue name, CAPTURE defaults to the queue to which spooler 0 has been assigned. In 4.10, this option should not be used with the P option.
S (Server=*name*)	*name* is the name of the file server to which you are sending the print job and the server on which the print queue is located. The default is the default server you first logged in to. Do not use for NetWare 4.10 print queues. In 4.10, the current server or current tree is the default.
SH (SHow)	Displays a list of the currently captured LPT ports. SH does not affect the capture status of an LPT port. It merely returns the currently active CAPTURE options (if any). You cannot use SH with other CAPTURE options.

continues

A
B
C
D
E
F
G
H
I
J
K
L
M
N
O
P
Q
R
S
T
U
V
W
X
Y
Z

Option	Description
T (Tabs=n)	Use this option only if your application program does not support print formatting, although most do. n is the number of characters in each tab stop, from 0 to 18. The default is 8.
NT (NoTabs)	Ensures that all tabs arrive at the printer unchanged. By default, this option also specifies the file to be a binary or "byte stream" file. Use this option only if your application program has its own print formatter. Most applications produce embedded printer-specific codes. This option ensures that those codes arrive at the printer intact.
TI (TImeout=n)	Enables you to print from an application without forcing you to exit from it. It sends the print data to the print queue in a specified number of seconds after the application finishes writing to the file or after waiting the specified number of seconds for additional print output. After the specified amount of time, CAPTURE begins again. For best results, TI should not be set to less than 5 seconds or greater than 60. In NetWare 4.10, the default is 0 (disabled). n = number of seconds, 1 to 1,000. Timeout is disabled by default.

The following options work in 3.1x and 4.10.

Option	Description
EC (End Capture)	Used in 4.10 only to terminate the redirection of data from the local parallel port to the NetWare printer, NetWare queue, or print file. If the L= option is not included to specify which parallel port to end capturing on, LPT1 is assumed, or ALL can be specified. Can also use with CA option to discard any captured data not yet printed.

Option	Description
NOTI (NOTIfy)	Causes the user to be notified when the print job has cleared the queue and is waiting in the output tray of the printer.
NNOTI (NoNOTIfy)	Will not notify the user when the print job has been printed. This is the default.

The following work in 4.10 only.

Option	Description
ECCA (EndCap CAncel)	Terminates the redirection of data from the local parallel port to the NetWare printer, NetWare queue, or print file and discards any partial data received thus far. If the L= option is not included to specify on which parallel port to end capturing, LPT1 is assumed. If the CR= option was included, the file is closed but still exists.
A (All)	When used in conjunction with the EndCap option, terminates the redirection of all local parallel ports. When used in conjunction with the /? option, displays all available help screens.
CA (Cancel)	When used in conjunction with the End Capture option, CA ends data being captured to LPT ports, and discards any data in the process of being captured but not yet printed.
D (Details)	Shows printing parameters and specifies whether a print job configuration is used.
/? or /H (Help)	Shows the Help screen for this command.
HOLD	Holds the print job in the queue until released using PCONSOLE or NetWare Administrator.

continues

Option	Description
P (Printer=*printername*)	*printername* is the 4.10 NDS printer object name. When specifying the printer name, you must either be in the printer's context or specify a complete or partial NDS name. For accuracy, a complete name is preferred but not required. Also, do not use the Q option if using the P option.
V (Verbose)	This displays more detailed information about the printer, print queue, and print job configuration than is presented through the standard Show option.
VER (Version)	Displays the utility's version number and a list of files required to run this utility.

You can list multiple options.

Rules and Considerations: The create=*filespec* switch must use a network drive.

The FormFeed switch might not be necessary on some laser printers that are installed as network printers. Many laser printers automatically issue a form feed at the end of a page or partial page of text.

You must use the PRINTDEF utility to define forms before you use the Forms switch.

You cannot use SH with any other CAPTURE option; it must be used alone.

If your TI setting is not long enough, you might experience printing problems, especially if you are printing graphics. Increase the TI setting if parts of files are being printed or if files do not print at all.

You can define commonly used CAPTURE options in PRINTCON as job configurations and use the Job option to indicate which configuration profile to use.

If you fail to specify options with the CAPTURE command, data is printed according to the default print job configuration defined in PRINTCON.

Output should be sent to print queues rather than printers. Printer numbers and print server names are not supported in CAPTURE.

The data you capture is not printed or sent to a file unless you end the CAPTURE command and send your data to a network printer or a file. This can be done by using either the AUtoendcap or TImeout switch, or by using the ENDCAP utility.

To use the ENDCAP utility effectively to send captured print jobs to the printer, disable AUtoendcap and TImeout in the CAPTURE command.

Important Messages: None

Examples: To capture print jobs to the queue called Laser on the file server Training Solutions, type the following:

```
CAPTURE S=TRAINING_SOLUTIONS Q=LASER_Q NB TI=5 NFF
```

The job does not print a banner, the time-out is five seconds, and no form feed follows the print job.

For best results, and to prevent your workstation from possibly hanging, use the CAPTURE command in your login script.

If you use the CAPTURE command at the DOS prompt, it overrides the command issued in your login script, unless you merely issue a CAPTURE SHow.

Notes: Use AU to save several different screen prints or printouts from the same application to a single print-queue file. AU does not automatically terminate the capture of an LPT port. To terminate an active LPT capture, you must issue the ENDCAP command.

If you experience problems (such as half-completed pages) when printing from your application, increase the value of TI until the problem stops or until you reach 60, whichever comes first. It is extremely rare when an application, even an intense database query, will pause longer than 45 seconds between print output bursts.

Your workstation might hang if you press Shift+Print Screen when none of your LPT ports is captured and no local printers are attached to your workstation. To prevent this, include the following line in the NET.CFG file on your boot disk:

```
LOCAL PRINTERS = 0
```

You can save data in a print file to a server to which you are not attached. If you specify a server to which you are not attached, CAPTURE attaches you as the user GUEST unless GUEST requires a password, or GUEST has no effective rights to any of the servers' print queues or disk space. You cannot create a file or send a file to a queue without rights.

A
B
C
D
E
F
G
H
I
J
K
L
M
N
O
P
Q
R
S
T
U
V
W
X
Y
Z

A

B

C

D

E

F

G

H

I

J

K

L

M

N

O

P

Q

R

S

T

U

V

W

X

Y

Z

It often is preferable to capture to a print file when you are plotting from CAD packages in the NetWare environment. This usually causes far fewer problems than trying to capture the plot output to a file server queue. After the plot file has been created, you can use the NPRINT utility to send the plot file to the queue.

CAPTURE cannot redirect print jobs to serial (COM) ports.

See Also: ENDCAP, NET.CFG, NPRINT, SPOOL

CASTOFF

Purpose: Prevents messages sent from the file server console or other workstations from reaching your station and interrupting operations (such as printing or compiling). NetWare 4.10 incorporates the functions of the CASTOFF command into the SEND command.

Syntax:

`CASTOFF`

or

`CASTOFF ALL`

Option	Function
A or ALL	Blocks messages from both the file server console and other workstations on the network

Rules and Considerations: The CASTOFF command blocks messages sent by other workstations. CASTOFF ALL blocks all messages, including those sent from the file server console.

Before starting any process that can run unattended (such as compiling, printing, remote LAN hookup, and so on), you should use CASTOFF ALL to prevent messages from interrupting the unattended process.

Important Messages: None

Examples: `CASTOFF ALL`

Notes: To enable your station to receive incoming messages again, use the CASTON utility.

See Also: BROADCAST, CASTON, SEND

CASTON

Purpose: Enables workstation to resume receiving messages if you used the CASTOFF utility to block incoming messages. NetWare 4.10 incorporates the functions of the CASTON command into the SEND command.

Syntax: `CASTON`

Options: None

Rules and Considerations: When a workstation receives a message, the station cannot continue processing until the user acknowledges the message by pressing Ctrl+Enter.

Important Messages: The following message appears on-screen after CASTON is invoked:

`Broadcast messages from the console and other stations will now be accepted.`

See Also: BROADCAST, CASTOFF, SEND

CD

Purpose: Used to monitor and administer a NetWare CD-ROM volume.

Syntax: `CD` *option*

Options	*Functions*
CHANGE	Switches from one to another media in the CD-ROM drive.
DEVICE LIST	Provides a list of CD-ROM devices.
DIR	Displays the contents of a CD-ROM volume, starting at the volume's root.
DISMOUNT	Removes a CD-ROM volume from user access.
GROUP	Lists or assigns group numbers.
HELP	View online help for this utility.
PURGE	Erases any hidden index files so they can no longer be recovered.
RENAME	Changes the name of a CD-ROM volume.
VOLUME LIST	Lists all CD-ROM volumes.
MOUNT	Makes a CD-ROM volume available to network users. To use it, type **CD MOUNT** followed by appropriate parameters including:
	Number or name for the volume
	/name space supported
	/supported options including:
	/R Rebuild index file.
	/I Mount even with import errors.

continues

A
B
C
D
E
F
G
H
I
J
K
L
M
N
O
P
Q
R
S
T
U
V
W
X
Y
Z

Options	Functions
/X	Exclude specified directories.
/G	Default volume group access rights. Must include a group number.

Rules and Considerations: When using the CD MOUNT command, you do not need to use the /I option if you want the CD-ROM volume to be mounted with the parameters you originally specified. If, however, you accidentally corrupted the CD-ROM volume by enabling block suballocation or turning on file compression, this option rebuilds the volume's index file.

Examples: To rename a CD-ROM volume that has first been dismounted, type the following:

`CD RENAME /D=1 APPS`

To see the contents of a root directory on a dismounted CD-ROM volume, type the following:

`CD DIR USERVOL`

Important Messages: None

Notes: None

See Also: CDROM

Scsi bios Ext @ boot

CDROM

Purpose: When loaded from the console, enables management of CD-ROM volumes on the server.

Syntax: `LOAD CDROM`

Options: None

Rules and Considerations: Required drivers for the SCSI board and CD-ROM drive must be loaded prior to loading CDROM. These drivers vary with board and CD-ROM drive manufacturer and model number.

The disk driver for the CD-ROM's controller or host bus adapter must be loaded prior to loading the CDROM NLM.

Some disk drivers require additional NLMs to function correctly or mount CD-ROMs as volumes. Refer to the documentation for your controller or host bus adapter for more information.

Important Messages: None

Notes: Loading CDROM enables the following commands:

♦ CD DEVICE LIST displays all CD-ROM devices with the following information for each:

DEVICE NAME

DEVICE NUMBER

MEDIA VOLUME NAME (IF FOUND)

VOLUME MOUNT STATUS

♦ CD VOLUME LIST displays all CD-ROM volumes with the following information for each:

DEVICE NUMBER

VOLUME NAME

DEVICE NAME

♦ CD DISMOUNT [*device number*][*volume name*] dismounts the CD-ROM with the device number or volume name that is specified.

A
B
C
D
E
F
G
H
I
J
K
L
M
N
O
P
Q
R
S
T
U
V
W
X
Y
Z

A

B

C

D

E

F

G

H

I

J

K

L

M

N

O

P

Q

R

S

T

U

V

W

X

Y

Z

◆ CD DIR [*device number*][*volume name*] displays a directory of the CD-ROM with the device number or volume name that is specified. The volume need not be mounted to display a directory.

◆ CD MOUNT [*device number*][*volume name*] mounts a CD-ROM with the device number or volume name that is specified.

◆ The /R switch can be used with CD MOUNT to reduce mounting time by reusing existing directories.

◆ CD CHANGE [device number][volume name] initiates a change sequence for a CD-ROM with the device number or volume name that is specified.

◆ CD HELP displays the syntax for the CD command.

Examples: To allow a CD-ROM attached to an Adaptec AHA-1540 SCSI host bus adapter to be mounted as a shared NetWare volume, type the following commands at the System Console:

```
LOAD ASPITRAN (C: W/SERVER down)
LOAD AHA1540 PORT=330 INT=B DMA=5
LOAD ASPICD - Startup
LOAD CDROM - Autoexec
```

Notes: To ensure remounting of CD-ROMs after the server has been shut down, all necessary commands should be placed in the STARTUP.NCF and AUTOEXEC.NCF file(s).

NetWare 4.10 supports ISO 9660 and High Sierra, but not Apple HFS formats. Also, NetWare 4.10 requires that the NWPA.DSK NPA driver be loaded before CDROM to provide the Media Manager interface.

In NetWare 4.10, do not enable block suballocation or file compression for a CD-ROM being used as a NetWare volume. It will corrupt the volume index.

See Also: MAGAZINE, MEDIA, SCAN FOR NEW DEVICES, LIST DEVICES, VOLUMES

CHKDIR

In NetWare 4.10, the functions of the CHKDIR command have been incorporated into the NDIR command.

Purpose: Lists information about directories and volumes. When invoked, CHKDIR displays the following types of information:

♦ Directory space limitations for the file server, volume, and directory

♦ The volume's maximum storage capacity in kilobytes, and the directory's maximum storage capacity (if the directory has a space restriction in effect)

♦ Kilobytes currently in use on the volume and in the specified directory

♦ Kilobytes available on the volume and in the specified directory

Syntax: `CHKDIR` *path*

Option	Description
path	The directory path leading to and including the path you want to check

Rule and Considerations: The path option must be a legal DOS path name. You can substitute NetWare volume names for DOS drive letters.

Important Messages: None

Examples: Suppose that you want to see information about a directory named SYS:DATA, type the following command:

```
CHKDIR SYS:DATA
```

NetWare displays information similar to the following:

```
Directory Space Limitation Information For:
TRAINING_SOLUTIONS/SYS:DATA
```

A
B
C
D
E
F
G
H
I
J
K
L
M
N
O
P
Q
R
S
T
U
V
W
X
Y
Z

```
Maximum        In Use          Available
631,600K       452,693K        178,907K Volume Size
38,776K        178,907K \DATA
```

See Also: CHKVOL

CHKVOL

Purpose: Shows the amount of space currently in use and the amount of space available on the volume. The CHKVOL command displays volume space in bytes, the byte count taken by files, the number of bytes available on the volume, and the number of directory entries left. You can view this information on all volumes and all file servers to which you are attached.

Syntax: `CHKVOL` `fileserver_name\volume_name`

Option	Description
`fileserver_name`	The name of the file server's volume to view
`volume`	The name of the volume to view
`*`	Specifies all file servers you are attached to, or all volumes

Rules and Considerations: The use of CHKVOL is not limited by security; you can view CHKVOL to view volume information for any file server to which you are attached.

Important Messages: The CHKVOL command displays information similar to the following:

```
Statistics for fixed volume TRAINING_SOLUTIONS/SYS:

Total volume space:              640,048 K Bytes
Space used by 7,105 files:       152,672 K Bytes
Space remaining on volume:       487,376 K Bytes
Space available to username:     487,376 K Bytes
Directory entries available      2,121
```

Directory entries available does not refer to the number of directories you still can create on this volume. One directory entry is used by a DOS file, subdirectory, and trustee list. Macintosh files use two directory entries.

Examples: To check the volumes called SYS on all file servers to which you are attached, issue the following command:

`CHKVOL */SYS`

A
B
C
D
E
F
G
H
I
J
K
L
M
N
O
P
Q
R
S
T
U
V
W
X
Y
Z

You can express wild cards in many different ways. If you want to see volume information for all the volumes on the file server named TRAIN-ING, for example, type the following command:

`CHKVOL TRAINING/*`

If you want to see information about all volumes on all the file servers to which you are attached, type the following command:

`CHKVOL */*`

You also can specify drive letters that are mapped to volumes that you want to view.

Notes: If NetWare displays the message `The specified volume not found`, either you mistyped the volume name or the volume does not exist. Check the volume name and try again.

See Also: ATTACH, FILER (Volume Information), WHOAMI

CLEAR MESSAGE

Purpose: Clears the messages at the bottom of the file server's display when you are using the MONITOR command.

Syntax: `CLEAR MESSAGE`

Options: None

Rules and Considerations: The CLEAR MESSAGE command clears a message from the bottom of the file server's display. The command does not clear the entire screen and does not affect the MONITOR screen.

The CLEAR MESSAGE command is coded into the operating system.

Important Messages: None

See Also: BROADCAST, SEND

A
B
C
D
E
F
G
H
I
J
K
L
M
N
O
P
Q
R
S
T
U
V
W
X
Y
Z

CLEAR STATION

Purpose: Removes all file server resources from the specified workstation, and breaks the link between the file server and the workstation.

Syntax: `CLEAR STATION station_number`

Options: None

Rules and Considerations: The CLEAR STATION command is coded into the operating system. When you invoke CLEAR STATION, all the workstation's open files are closed and the communication link to the file server is broken. If the workstation had drive mappings to other file servers, the user can continue working on those file servers' drive mappings. If no drive mappings exist to other file servers, however, the user must reboot the workstation and reload IPX and NETx before accessing any file server.

Important Messages: None

Examples: To clear station number two, type the following command:

`CLEAR STATION 2`

To view a list of station numbers, you can issue the MONITOR command at the 3.x and 4.10 file server console or use USERLIST at a workstation. The connection number is listed in the screen's left margin.

Notes: Because the CLEAR STATION command closes open files, data might be lost when you use the command. CLEAR STATION normally is used when a workstation locks up and leaves open files on the file server.

See Also: FCONSOLE, MONITOR, NLIST (4.10), USERLIST

CLIB

Purpose: Provides NetWare Loadable Module (NLM) developers with a set of global functions and routines that an NLM can utilize. This global library of C routines and functions should be used if you are using an NLM, such as the BTRIEVE NLM or the PSERVER NLM, which relies on CLIB to function properly.

CLIB is not fully functional unless the STREAMS NLM is loaded. If you fail to load STREAMS prior to loading CLIB, the NetWare operating system attempts to load STREAMS for you.

Syntax: `LOAD` *path* `CLIB`

Option	Description
path	The full path name to the directory that contains the CLIB NLM. The path name can begin with either a valid DOS drive letter or a valid NetWare volume name. If you do not specify a path, NetWare attempts to locate and load the NLM from the SYS:SYSTEM subdirectory.

Rules and Considerations: NetWare sets a time zone for CLIB when the utility loads. By default, NetWare uses the Eastern Standard time zone. Use the SET TIMEZONE command to set the time zone so that it is appropriate for your geographical area.

Be sure to save the command in the AUTOEXEC.NCF file so that CLIB is loaded and the appropriate time zone is set each time the file server is rebooted.

Important Messages: If using third-party NLMS and an error message displays indicating that low-priority processes cannot be run, reload the NLM with the CLIB option (including the parenthesis) as follows:

```
LOAD NLM_NAME (CLIB_OPT) /Y
```

Examples: To load the CLIB utility, type the following command:

```
LOAD CLIB
```

A
B
C
D
E
F
G
H
I
J
K
L
M
N
O
P
Q
R
S
T
U
V
W
X
Y
Z

To make sure that the additional modules necessary for CLIB to operate are loaded at boot time, add the following commands to the server's AUTOEXEC.NCF file:

```
LOAD STREAMS
LOAD CLIB
```

This example assumes the STREAMS and CLIB NLMs are located in the SYS:SYSTEM subdirectory.

Notes: You must load the CLIB NLM before you load any NLM that requires CLIB. If you want, you can place the STREAMS and CLIB NLMs on the DOS partition of the file server's hard disk. In NetWare 4.10, loading a module that requires CLIB usually causes CLIB to be loaded automatically.

The CLIB NLM is just one example of a loadable function library module. Some NLMs depend on other NLMs to function properly. To improve system performance and reliability, Novell recommends that you load the following NLMs in addition to CLIB. If you are using non-Novell supplied, third-party NLMs that are incompatible with the current version of NetWare 3.x and 4.10, these additional NLMs prevent the offending NLM from loading and corrupting the network operating system. It is strongly recommended that you load these NLMs in the following order:

LOAD STREAMS

LOAD CLIB

LOAD MATHLIB

LOAD TLI

LOAD IPXS

LOAD SPXS

To automatically load these NLMs at boot time, edit your AUTOEXEC.NCF file to include these commands.

See Also: LOAD, SET TIMEZONE

CLS

Purpose: Clears the file server's console screen.

Syntax: `CLS`

Options: None

Rules and Considerations: The cleared screen shows only the command prompt and the cursor.

Important Messages: None

See Also: OFF

A
B
C
D
E
F
G
H
I
J
K
L
M
N
O
P
Q
R
S
T
U
V
W
X
Y
Z

COMCHECK

Purpose: Tests the communication between network stations, file servers, and routers. The command does not require the file server or router to be running. Use COMCHECK to help locate possible cable problems, duplicate node addresses, and potential problems with cable linking devices. COMCHECK checks the entire communications path before the network is up and running.

Syntax: COMCHECK

Options: None

Rules and Considerations: Before you execute COMCHECK, make all cable connections to workstations, file servers, routers, and cabling devices. IPX must be loaded first. COMCHECK uses IPX to communicate to each cabled node on the cable system. Each node requires a unique ID. As you execute COMCHECK on the node, the utility prompts for a unique ID. You can use any name, such as NODE1, FILESERVER1, ROUTER3, and so on.

Examples:

```
IPX
COMCHECK
```

COMCHECK prompts you to enter a unique node name to identify the station. You can find the COMCHECK program on the disk labeled WSGEN. If you experience problems loading IPX, make sure that IPX is configured for the LAN card you are using, and that the setting on the LAN card matches that of IPX. The following message should appear on the screen:

```
NetWare Communication Check v2.00 Friday
October 30, 1991 2:00 pm
Network      Node        Unique User    Yr Mo Dy Hr Mn Sc *
00000000     000000F3    Node1          91/10/30 02:09:21 *
00000000     00001A34    File Server    91/10/30 02:14:12
00000000     000000BF    Node2          91/10/30 02:18:01
```

- ◆ **Network.** Displays 0s if the shell is not loaded.

- ◆ **Node.** Displays the node ID of the LAN card installed.

- ◆ **Unique User.** Displays the unique name you gave to this node.

- ◆ **Yr Mo Dy Hr Mn Sc.** Shows the time and date. The time is updated every 15 seconds to show that the node is communicating.

- ◆ ***.** Indicates that this is the current workstation.

COMCHECK from one of these previous versions can be used on a 3.12 or 4.10 network.

For workstations using either the ODI or VLM drivers you must have a frame type set to 802.3.

If the station does not show any of this information after 15 seconds, check all cabling, connectors, cabling devices, and LAN cards. Make sure that each of the nodes has a unique node ID.

You can change the broadcast delay period by pressing Esc and selecting Broadcast Delay from the menu. This is specified in seconds, and tells the system the number of seconds or broadcasts from a particular station. The default setting is 15 seconds.

The Dead Timeout Period specifies the amount of time COMCHECK waits after a workstation does not send out packets and then declares the node dead. This time period must be at least 10 seconds greater than the broadcast delay period. A workstation that is declared dead will appear on the other workstations as a bold entry. The default Dead Timeout Period is 60 seconds.

See Also: IPX

A
B
C
D
E
F
G
H
I
J
K
L
M
N
O
P
Q
R
S
T
U
V
W
X
Y
Z

COMPSURF

Purpose: Performs a low-level format and surface analysis (or integrity test) on standard MFM, RLL, ARLL, ESDI, and SCSI hard disks and prepares them for use under Novell NetWare.

Syntax: `COMPSURF`

Options: None

Rules and Considerations: The COMPSURF utility can require several hours to test each hard disk properly. Be sure to allow sufficient time.

You must install hard disks before you execute the COMPSURF utility.

You should use COMPSURF to reformat disks only as a last, extreme measure to attempt to correct major disk drive problems and only after you have tried VREPAIR (such as when it has become impossible to write and read data to and from the disk). COMPSURF destroys all data contained on a hard disk.

Do not execute COMPSURF on NetWare Ready drives because any NetWare ready information on the disk will be erased.

New hard disks no longer require testing with COMPSURF. The INSTALL command prepares new hard disks by using the ZTEST (track zero test) utility rather than COMPSURF.

Most hard disks are shipped with a manufacturer's bad block table that identifies, by head and cylinder number, any media defects (such as bad blocks) found by the manufacturer prior to shipment. If the hard disk you will be formatting (or reformatting) with COMPSURF has a manufacturer's bad block table, you should enter the bad blocks from this list prior to running COMPSURF.

If you are using SCSI hard disks, you also must run DISKSET, or an equivalent third-party utility, to configure the Host Bus Adapters (HBA) connected to any installed SCSI disk subsystems.

Important Messages: The following message appears when you issue the COMPSURF command:

`The COMPSURF command destroys all data on the hard disk!`

Make sure that you have a backup of the disk's data before you execute the command.

Examples: You can run the COMPSURF utility by typing the following command:

COMPSURF

Prepare to execute the COMPSURF utility by backing up the existing disk files and downing the file server. This step is required only on existing NetWare installations.

Locate the disk manufacturer's test printout. This will contain a list of media defects (such as bad blocks) detected by the manufacturer at the time of assembly. You are prompted to enter these blocks after you enter the COMPSURF utility. The manufacturer's bad block list usually is printed on a sticker attached to the hard disk housing. Often the list will be duplicated on a paper printout shipped with the disk.

If you do not have a hard copy printout of the bad block table, you might have to remove the cover from the file server or disk subsystem to locate the bad block table sticker on the hard disk housing. These defects should be entered into COMPSURF to enable COMPSURF to map out known media defects and prevent their use under NetWare. This will ensure greater data integrity.

If you want a printout of the media defects detected by COMPSURF, prepare and install a parallel printer. The printer must be connected to the first parallel port (LPT1) on the file server. You will be given an opportunity to print the media defect list before exiting COMPSURF.

COMPSURF can run without a parallel printer attached. If you run COMPSURF without a printer, however, you must refrain from selecting any option that indicates printing test results. If you do select a print option when no printer is attached, COMPSURF might hang up the computer.

Before executing COMPSURF on a problem disk, you should try to copy as many data files as possible to a disk that is operational.

Be sure you have correctly identified all network hard disks in your server's hardware configuration, including disks both inside the file server and inside external disk subsystems. If necessary, execute DISKSET to identify SCSI hard disks in external disk subsystems or inside the file server, or run the SETUP (or similar) utility supplied by the computer manufacturer to identify internal disk drives.

A
B
C
D
E
F
G
H
I
J
K
L
M
N
O
P
Q
R
S
T
U
V
W
X
Y
Z

A
B
C
D
E
F
G
H
I
J
K
L
M
N
O
P
Q
R
S
T
U
V
W
X
Y
Z

Before executing COMPSURF, make sure that you can identify the disk drive on which you want to run COMPSURF by channel number, controller address, and drive number.

If needed, refer to the documentation accompanying your hardware for information on how to determine controller addresses and drive numbers.

If you are using a disk that is defined in the CMOS of your computer, most likely you will be using the ISADISK driver. If this is true, this unit functions on Channel 0.

You can low-level format and test only one hard disk at a time. Execute COMPSURF on each disk you want to be low-level formatted and tested.

Start COMPSURF by locating the program. Under NetWare 2.1x, it usually is located on the UTILEXE disk. Under NetWare 2.2 and NetWare 3.11, it is located on the SYSTEM-2 disk.

To load and execute COMPSURF, insert the appropriate disk into drive A, and type **COMPSURF** at the DOS prompt.

The Comprehensive Surface Analysis header appears on the screen, along with a list of the hard disk drives COMPSURF can find attached to the file server.

Select the hard disk you want to test. Do not be concerned if the head, cylinder, and sectors-per-track values displayed on the screen do not correspond to the actual values for the disk. Certain types of disk drives do not supply this information, and COMPSURF uses default values for these disks.

Select the appropriate program operational parameters for the drive you have selected. The parameters that appear depend on the type of disk you are testing and whether it has been previously formatted with COMPSURF. For most disks, the list will be similar to the following:

- ♦ Specify whether to format the disk
- ♦ Specify whether to keep the current bad block list
- ♦ Specify if you want to enter the media defect list
- ♦ Select the number of passes for the sequential read/write test
- ♦ Select the number of reads and writes to be performed in the random test
- ♦ Confirm the operation parameters you have just selected

A more detailed discussion of each prompt follows:

♦ **Format the disk.** This prompt appears only when you are retesting a disk that has previously been low-level formatted by COMPSURF. Any hard disk that has never been low-level formatted or tested with COMPSURF will be formatted automatically. If you answered Yes to the Format disk prompt and if the hard disk you have selected requires an interleave factor value, select the appropriate interleave factor. Interleave should be selected based on the following criteria:

1. For internal hard disks in all NetWare file servers and IBM PC/AT-type file servers that run off original IBM or Western Digital 1003 series controllers, use the default interleave value of 2.

2. For internal hard disks in all IBM PC/AT and 100-percent compatible NetWare file servers that run off Western Digital 1006 series controllers (or 100-percent compatibles), select an interleave value of 1.

3. For internal hard disks in all IBM PC/AT and 100 percent compatible NetWare file servers that run off Western Digital 1007 series ESDI controllers (or 100 percent compatibles), select an interleave value of 1.

4. For internal hard disks in an IBM PS/2 file server, select an interleave value of 1.

5. For other types of hard disks (such as embedded SCSI or third-party external disks), check with the disk supplier to determine the appropriate interleave value.

6. For internal hard disks in all IBM PC/AT and 100-percent compatible NetWare file servers that run off controllers not listed above, check with the controller manufacturer to determine the appropriate interleave value.

♦ **Current bad block list.** Each hard disk drive maintains a list of media defects. These media defects are areas of the disk that are physically unable to hold data reliably. This list is sometimes referred to as the bad block table. Answer Yes if you want COMPSURF to keep the current list of bad blocks or rebuild a new bad block table. If you answer No, the media defect list is cleared.

♦ **Media defect list.** The media defect list also is known as the bad block list. If the disk you are testing was not shipped with a manu-facturer's media defect list, answer No to the prompt and go on to

A

B

C

D

E

F

G

H

I

J

K

L

M

N

O

P

Q

R

S

T

U

V

W

X

Y

Z

A
B
C
D
E
F
G
H
I
J
K
L
M
N
O
P
Q
R
S
T
U
V
W
X
Y
Z

the next section. If the disk was shipped with a manufacturer's media defect list, enter the bad block list manually at the file server's keyboard when prompted.

The bad blocks you enter from this list, as well as any additional bad blocks found by the COMPSURF utility, will be written to the disk's bad block table. It is important to enter the manufacturer's bad block list, if possible, to ensure that these blocks are included in the NetWare-compatible bad block table stored on the disk. This will prevent NetWare from using these potentially unreliable areas of the disk to store your valuable data.

♦ **Sequential Test.** This COMPSURF routine writes and reads various patterns to the disk sequentially to analyze the integrity of the disk's surface. Any bad blocks that are found during this process are added to the disk's bad block table so that the file server will not attempt to store data in them.

Each pass of the sequential test takes roughly 30 to 45 minutes for the average 20 MB hard disk—and longer for hard disks with larger storage capacity.

You can specify that the sequential test be performed from zero to five times. The COMPSURF criteria used to determine the reliability of the disk is based on three passes of the sequential test, however. It is strongly recommended that you not skip this section of COMPSURF.

♦ **Random Test.** This COMPSURF routine writes and reads data patterns to random locations on the disk to locate additional bad blocks. This procedure also will test the head positioning mechanics of the disk. As with the sequential test, any bad blocks that are found are included in the disk's bad block table so that the file server will not attempt to store data on them.

The default number of write/reads (I/Os) shown in the prompt is the recommended minimum number of random I/Os to ensure an adequate sampling of the disk's head-positioning mechanism. You can increase or decrease this number of I/Os.

It takes approximately 3 minutes for the random test to perform 1,000 I/Os. As an example, a random test performed on an average 20 MB hard disk would require 16,000 random I/Os and would take 45 to 50 minutes.

♦ **Enter the bad block list.** If the COMPSURF OPERATIONAL
PARAMETERS window shows that media defects will be entered by
hand, you must enter the manufacturer's bad block list from the file
server's keyboard. An empty bad block window appears on the
screen.

Bad blocks are identified by head and cylinder number. Each hard
disk has a specific number of read/write heads and cylinders. The
number of heads and cylinders for the currently selected disk should
be displayed on the second line of the COMPSURF screen header.

Media defects can be added to the list by performing the following:

1. Press Ins. The following prompt should appear:

   `Enter head number:`

2. Type the head number of one of the bad blocks on the
   manufacturer's bad block list. Heads usually are numbered
   starting with zero (such as zero relative). If your disk has
   seven heads, for example, they are numbered from zero to six.

3. After you have typed the head number, press Enter. The
   following prompt should appear:

   `Enter cylinder:`

4. Type the cylinder number of the bad block as it appears in the
   manufacturer's list. Like heads, cylinders also are numbered
   starting with zero (such as zero relative).

5. After you have typed the cylinder number, press Enter. The
   head and cylinder numbers should be displayed in the list on
   the screen. If you make a mistake and type an incorrect head
   or cylinder number, you can correct it by highlighting the
   incorrect entry and pressing Del.

6. Repeat these steps until you have entered all of the bad blocks
   on the manufacturer's bad block list.

7. Confirm the bad block list. After you have entered all the bad
   blocks from the manufacturer's bad block list, press Esc. If you
   need to add or delete bad blocks to or from the table, answer
   No and return to the Enter the bad block list prompt. If the
   table is complete and correct, answer Yes to the prompt and
   continue.

A
B
C
D
E
F
G
H
I
J
K
L
M
N
O
P
Q
R
S
T
U
V
W
X
Y
Z

- **Format and test the disk.** You do not need to make any more keyboard entries until the COMPSURF testing process is complete, but you should monitor the progress of the test as outlined in the process that follows. The information for each test assumes that you selected the recommended COMPSURF operational parameters, such as low-level formatting of the disk and repeating the sequential surface analysis three times.

- **Formatting the disk.** While the disk is being low-level formatted, the following message should appear on the screen:

```
The Drive is Being Formatted
Please Wait
```

The formatting process can last anywhere from a few minutes to several hours, depending on the storage capacity and the type of hard disk being tested. The average 20 MB hard disk, for example, takes roughly 15 to 25 minutes to low-level format.

After the disk has been successfully low-level formatted, the track zero integrity test begins. This test ensures that track zero on the selected disk is 100-percent free from any media defects. Any defects on track zero would render the drive unbootable under NetWare, and might render the drive unusable altogether.

During this test, the screen displays information in a format similar to the following:

```
Track Zero Test
Block #     Pattern     Pass      BadBlocks
0           a5a5        1/20          0
```

As the track zero test progresses, the numbers displayed in each column change to reflect what is occurring on the drive. This test will make 20 passes of track zero, writing and reading various binary patterns to ensure that it has no media defects.

When the track zero test is successfully completed, the sequential test begins. This test searches the entire disk surface for media defects (such as bad blocks). Media defects are defined as blocks on the disk that cannot reliably store data.

The disk's bad block table consists of both bad blocks that you entered by hand and those discovered during the sequential test sequence. While the sequential test is running, you should see a screen similar to the following:

```
Sequential Test
Block #     Pattern      Pass      BadBlocks
0           a5a5         1/20         0
```

The Block # column indicates the block currently being tested. This number counts down to zero for each of the five binary data patterns.

The Pattern column indicates the binary data pattern currently being written to the disk.

The Pass column indicates the number of passes of the sequential test that have been completed out of the total number of passes specified in the program operational parameters.

The Bad Blocks column indicates the number of bad blocks on the disk. This number is a total of those entered by hand and those located during the sequential test. This number might increment during the sequential test.

You can interrupt the sequential test at any time to view or to print a list of the bad blocks that have been located so far. You also can turn off the screen update to slightly speed up the execution of the program.

♦ **Display the bad block table.** This information appears on the screen in a format similar to the following. Do not worry about duplicate entries in the list; this is common and results from the fact that one track can have one or more bad blocks:

```
Head       Cylinder

1          234
2          476
```

Program execution continues while you view the list.

♦ **Print the bad block table.** If you have attached a parallel printer to the first parallel printer port (LPT1) on the file server, you can print a list of the bad blocks found so far. After the testing process is complete, you will have another opportunity to print the complete bad block list.

Do not select the `Print the bad block table` option if you have not attached a parallel printer to the file server. The computer will disconnect if you do, resulting in the loss of all located bad blocks and requiring you to restart COMPSURF from scratch.

A
B
C
D
E
F
G
H
I
J
K
L
M
N
O
P
Q
R
S
T
U
V
W
X
Y
Z

- ◆ **Turn off the screen update.** Turning off the screen update enables the sequential test to proceed without constantly refreshing the screen display. This can marginally reduce the time required to complete the sequential test. You can exercise this option at any time during the sequential test. Updates to the screen information cease until you reenable screen updating.

- ◆ **Turn on the screen update.** Resumes updates to the various columns on the screen.

- ◆ **Run the Random Test.** After the sequential test successfully completes, the random test automatically begins. If you specified zero passes of the sequential test, a random test initialization procedure will be executed before the actual random test begins. This initialization procedure prepares the disk's data storage area to prepare for the random I/O test.

  As with the sequential test, you can interrupt the random test at any time to view or to print a list of the bad blocks that have been located so far. You also can turn off the screen update to marginally speed up the operation of the program.

- ◆ Record the final bad block table. When all the COMPSURF formatting and testing procedures have successfully concluded, a message similar to the following appears:

  ```
  Surface Analysis Completed disk passed.

  Display Bad Block Table
  Print Bad Block Table
  ```

  If the disk did not successfully pass the COMPSURF testing series, this also is indicated on the screen. Failure to successfully pass a COMPSURF test requires replacing the hard disk.

  After completing the COMPSURF testing, press Esc to exit the program. You can display the bad block table on the screen and record the information by hand if you want, or, if you have a parallel printer attached to the file server, you can print a hard copy of the final bad block table.

  You should maintain a permanent record of the disk's bad block table. If you do not, you will be unable to reenter the bad block table should it ever be deleted.

Notes: Some manufacturers ship hard disk drives with the designation "NetWare Ready." You do not need to use the COMPSURF utility on the drives. In addition, advances in NetWare 2.2 and NetWare 3.11 hot fix techniques, as well as the ZTEST utility in NetWare 2.2, have made the COMPSURF utility somewhat unnecessary.

Beginning with NetWare 2.2, COMPSURF supports formatting the hard disk with a 1:1 interleave.

See Also: DISKSET, INSTALL

A
B
C
D
E
F
G
H
I
J
K
L
M
N
O
P
Q
R
S
T
U
V
W
X
Y
Z

CONFIG

Purpose: Lists the following information about the file server:

♦ File server name; internal network number (NetWare 3.x and 4.10).

♦ Loaded/linked LAN drivers.

♦ Hardware settings on network boards.

♦ Node (station) addresses (ID) of network boards.

♦ Communication protocol bound to the network board (NetWare 3.x and 4.10).

♦ Network number of the cabling scheme for a network board.

♦ Frame type assigned to the board (NetWare 3.x and 4.10). Ethernet and Token-Ring boards can have more than one.

♦ Board name assigned (NetWare 3.x and 4.10).

♦ Number of File Server Processes (NetWare 2.x).

♦ Linked active disk driver and settings (NetWare 2.2).

♦ Directory Tree and Bindery context for this server (NetWare 4.10)

Syntax: CONFIG

Options: None

Rules and Considerations: Use the CONFIG command to view a list of hardware settings on network boards before installing additional memory cards, network adapters, or disk coprocessor boards in the server. This will help you avoid conflicts before installation.

Under NetWare 2.x, use CONFIG to list the number of file server processes.

Use CONFIG to list all assigned network numbers and node addresses.

Under NetWare 3.x and 4.10, use MODULES and MONITOR to display information about NetWare Loadable Modules (NLMs) linked to the core operating system.

Under NetWare 3.x and 4.10, use INSTALL to display configuration information about disk drivers (look in either the STARTUP.NCF or AUTOEXEC.NCF file).

Under NetWare 3.x and 4.10, use DISPLAY NETWORKS to list all network numbers being used by other file servers on your network. This will help avoid router errors and internal IPX network number conflicts.

Important Messages: None

Examples: To use CONFIG, type the following command at the console:

```
CONFIG
```

Under NetWare 2.2, CONFIG displays information similar to the following:

```
Hardware Configuration Information for Server TRAINING_SOLUTIONS

Number of File Server Processes: 7

LAN A Configuration Information:
Network Address: [19910ACE] [ 32]
Hardware Type: NetWare RX-Net
Hardware Settings: IRQ = 9, I/O = 2E0, RAM Buffer at D000:0

LAN B Configuration Information:
Network Address: [19910ACE] [01A034845D1B]
Hardware Type: Novell NE1000
Hardware Settings: IRQ = 3, I/O = 300, No DMA or RAM
```

Under NetWare 3.x and 4.10, CONFIG displays information similar to the following:

```
File server name: TRAINING_SOLUTIONS386
IPX internal network number: BADCAFE

NE-2000 LAN Driver V3.10 (900308)
 Hardware setting: I/O Port 300h to 31Fh, Interrupt 3h
 Node address:00001B0280A3
 Frame type: ETHERNET_802.3
 Board name: BACKBONE
 LAN protocol: IPX network 00000001
```

See Also: DISPLAY NETWORKS, FCONSOLE, INSTALL, MODULES, MONITOR

A
B
C
D
E
F
G
H
I
J
K
L
M
N
O
P
Q
R
S
T
U
V
W
X
Y
Z

CONLOG

Purpose: Captures console messages to a file. The file can be specified, or the default of SYS:\ETC\CONSOLE.LOG may be used.

Syntax: `LOAD CONLOG` *parameters*

Options	Functions
FILE=*name*	Specify a different file if you do not want to use the default file and path. Also, if running SFT III servers, use this parameter to specify different files for each of the three engines.
SAVE=*backup*	Specify a file name to be used for saving the current console log, so that AUTOEXEC.NCF does not overwrite the existing log.
MAXIMUM=*SIZE*	Specify, in kilobytes, the maximum size the log file can become before it is deleted (or renamed if SAVE=backup is used.)
ENTIRE=YES	Save lines already displayed on the screen to the log file.
HELP	Display descriptions of each command parameter.

Rules and Considerations: The log can be edited using any text editor.

You can place the LOAD CONLOG command in the AUTOEXEC.NCF file to automate its loading each time the file server boots.

Examples: To start capturing console screen output to the log beginning with information currently displayed on the console screen, type the following at the console prompt:

`LOAD CONLOG ENTIRE=YES`

To view details about the command's parameters, type the following at
the console prompt:

`CONLOG HELP`

Important Messages: None

Notes: If INETCFG is loaded, do not use the EDIT NLM to edit this log
file.

A
B
C
D
E
F
G
H
I
J
K
L
M
N
O
P
Q
R
S
T
U
V
W
X
Y
Z

CONSOLE

Purpose: Switches a nondedicated file server or router to the Console screen. Once in the console screen, you can issue console commands.

Syntax: `CONSOLE`

Options: None

Rules and Considerations: After using the CONSOLE command to switch the file server or router to console mode, use the DOS command to switch back to the work station mode.

Important Messages: None

See Also: DOS

CX

Purpose: To view or change your current context within the NetWare Directory Service (NDS) tree structure. You also can view the containers and leaf objects in the tree.

Syntax: `CX [new context] [/R] [/T ¦ /CONT ¦ /A] [/C] [/?] [/VER]`

Option	Function
`new context`	Specifies the context where you would like to be placed in the Directory tree
`/R`	Lists all containers from the root level or changes you to the root
`/T`	Lists all containers below the current context or the specified context
`/CONT`	Lists all containers at the current context or the specified context
`/A`	Lists all objects at or below the current context when used with a /T or /CONT
`/C`	Scrolls display continuously
`/?`	Displays help
`/VER`	Provides version information and a list of files needed by this utility in order to run

Rules and Considerations: Using the CX command in the directory tree is similar to the CD command in the DOS file structure. The CX command enables the navigation through the tree.

The CX command also is similar to the DIR DOS command in that you can display container and objects in a tree format.

A
B
C
D
E
F
G
H
I
J
K
L
M
N
O
P
Q
R
S
T
U
V
W
X
Y
Z

A
B
C
D
E
F
G
H
I
J
K
L
M
N
O
P
Q
R
S
T
U
V
W
X
Y
Z

When using CX to navigate, add one period (.) to the end of CX to move up one level. Add an additional dot for every level that you wish to move up. When moving down a level, simply specify the CX command and the level that you want to move to.

Using the CX command with no parameters will display your current context.

CX does not recognize spaces in any object names. If spaces exist in object names, add double quotes around the name when using CX or replace spaces with underscores.

Examples: To change your current context from
SALES.TRAINING_SOLUTIONS.GENDREAU_ENT to
ENGINEERING.TRAINING_SOLUTIONS.GENDREAU_ENT, type the following:

CX ENGINEERING.TRAINING_SOLUTIONS.GENDREAU_ENT

To display your current context, type the following:

CX

To move up two levels in the tree, type the following:

CX ..

To change to the root of the tree, type the following:

CX /R

To show all containers in the current context, type the following:

CX /CONT

Important Messages: None

Notes: The CX command only works when logged in to NetWare Directory Services and not Bindery Emulation.

DCONFIG

Purpose: Changes the configuration of IPX.COM file or NET$OS.EXE operating system file for 2.2. Also changes the configuration of ROUTER.EXE, the executable file for an external router. Enables you to modify the IPX.COM to match the configuration setting of the network board in the workstation should it require change after generation. Also enables modification of various parameters in the NET$OS.EXE operating system file after generation.

Syntax: DCONFIG *filename options*

You can specify more than one option on a command line.

Option	Function
`i volume/drive: filename`	Uses input from specified file. This option is valid for IPX.COM only.
`SHELL: node address, configuration #;`	Valid for IPX.COM only.

Rules and Considerations: You cannot use the DCONFIG command to insert or delete network card drivers from NET$OS.EXE, or to change the network card for which IPX.COM was originally generated.

When you issue DCONFIG with just the file name (such as IPX.COM or NET$OS.EXE), NetWare displays a list of the adjustable parameters' current settings.

If you type DCONFIG alone (with no options) on the DOS command line, NetWare displays a brief list of the available options.

Although the SHELL option shown previously lists a node address option, this is seldom used. Most network cards used today determine the node address automatically.

If you do not want to change part of an option (such as net address), leave that field blank.

Important Messages: None

A
B
C
D
E
F
G
H
I
J
K
L
M
N
O
P
Q
R
S
T
U
V
W
X
Y
Z

A
B
C
D
E
F
G
H
I
J
K
L
M
N
O
P
Q
R
S
T
U
V
W
X
Y
Z

Examples: To change the configuration of the LAN adapter used by IPX.COM to option 2, type the following:

```
DCONFIG IPX.COM SHELL:, 2;
```

To change the configuration of the LAN adapter used by NET$OS.EXE to option 3, type the following:

```
DCONFIG NET$OS.EXE A: ,,3;
```

To change the IPX.COM file at the workstation, change to the directory containing the boot files. To view the current configuration for the IPX.COM file, type the following:

```
IPX I
```

NetWare should display an informational screen similar to the following:

```
Lan Option: NetWare Ethernet NE2000 V1.00EC
(801004)
Hardware Configuration:IRQ=3, I/O Base=300h,
no DMA or RAM
```

You also can type DCONFIG IPX.COM to receive an informational screen similar to the following:

```
 Shell Driver: NetWare Ethernet NE2000 V1.00EC
(801004)Node address is determined automatically.
 * 0: IRQ = 3, I/O Base = 300h, no DMA or RAM
 1: IRQ = 3, I/O Base = 280h, no DMA or RAM
 2: IRQ = 3, I/O Base = 2A0h, no DMA or RAM
 3: IRQ = 3, I/O Base = 2C0h, no DMA or RAM
 4: IRQ = 4, I/O Base = 300h, no DMA or RAM
 5: IRQ = 4, I/O Base = 2A0h, no DMA or RAM
 6: IRQ = 4, I/O Base = 2C0h, no DMA or RAM
 7: IRQ = 5, I/O Base = 300h, no DMA or RAM
 8: IRQ = 5, I/O Base = 280h, no DMA or RAM
 9: IRQ = 5, I/O Base = 320h, no DMA or RAM
 10: IRQ = 7, I/O Base = 280h, no DMA or RAM
```

The asterisk (*) indicates that the configuration option in IPX.COM is active, and displays the other options and the option numbers associated with each setting. To change IPX.COM to a different option number, such as option 4, type the following:

```
DCONFIG IPX.COM SHELL:,4
```

Following are examples of common changes made to NET$OS.EXE using the DCONFIG utility:

```
DCONFIG NET$OS.EXE BUFFERS:xxx
```

The *xxx* variable represents the desired number—150 is the maximum you can select in NETGEN. You can add more here. INSTALL in 2.2 enables you to use up to 1,000 communications buffers.

To change a LAN adapter to another available configuration, use the following command:

```
DCONFIG NET$OS.EXE A:,,xx
```

The *xx* variable represents the desired configuration number for LAN A Adapter configuration, and the network address can be changed simultaneously if you want.

Notes: Type **DCONFIG** *filename.ext* to display the current configuration of the selected file (IPX.COM or NET$OS.EXE). Before making any changes to the file, use this option and redirect it to a printer to create a handy reference. For the OS, this command would be DCONFIG NET$OS.EXE > LPT1.

If you want to make temporary changes to the IPX.COM configuration, you also can use the O# option in NET.CFG or SHELL.CFG, or load IPX.COM using the desired option number on the command line (such as IPX O#4). After the correct option is selected, you can use the ADCONFIG utility to make it permanent.

See Also: INSTALL, NET.CFG, NETGEN, ROUTEGEN, SHELL.CFG, WSGEN

A
B
C
D
E
F
G
H
I
J
K
L
M
N
O
P
Q
R
S
T
U
V
W
X
Y
Z

DISABLE LOGIN

Purpose: Prevents users from logging in to the file server.

Syntax: `DISABLE LOGIN`

Options: None

Rules and Considerations: The DISABLE LOGIN command does not affect users who already are logged in to the file server. It only prevents a user from logging in after you issue the command at the file server console.

To perform system maintenance you should be logged in before issuing the command.

Important Messages: After you issue the DISABLE LOGIN command, NetWare should display a message similar to the following:

```
Login is now disabled.
```

This confirms that the command has worked.

See Also: ENABLE LOGIN, FCONSOLE (Status), LOGIN

DISABLE TRANSACTIONS

Purpose: Manually disables the NetWare Transaction Tracking System (TTS). This command is used primarily by application developers who need to test transactional applications while TTS is disabled.

Syntax: `DISABLE TRANSACTIONS`

Options: None

Rules and Considerations: The NetWare TTS uses only 40 bytes of memory; it can, however, use as much as 400 KB of memory if it is handling extremely large records. TTS is an integral part of the file server operating system that protects the bindery and other files that have been flagged as transactional from becoming corrupted. TTS remains disabled until you issue the ENABLE TRANSACTIONS command or reboot the file server.

Disabling transactions is not an effective way to increase memory at the file server. The protection TTS provides is worth the additional memory used at the file server.

Important Messages: None

See Also: ENABLE TRANSACTIONS, FCONSOLE (Status), FLAG, SETTTS

DISABLE TTS

Purpose: Manually disables the NetWare Transaction Tracking System (TTS). This command is primarily used by application developers who need to test transactional applications while TTS is disabled.

Syntax: DISABLE TTS

Options: None

Rules and Considerations: The NetWare Transaction Tracking System uses only 40 bytes of memory; it can, however, use as much as 400 KB of memory if it is handling extremely large records. TTS is an integral part of the file server operating system that protects the bindery and other files that have been flagged as transactional from becoming corrupted. TTS remains disabled until you issue the ENABLE TTS command or reboot the file server.

Disabling transactions is not an effective way to increase memory at the file server. The protection TTS provides is worth the additional memory used at the file server.

Do not use DISABLE TTS with NetWare 4.1 as it prevents all NetWare Directory Services replicas from being updated.

Important Messages: None

See Also: ENABLE TTS, FCONSOLE (Status), FLAG, SETTTS

DISK

Purpose: Monitors and displays the status of network disk drives. Shows which disks and disk channels are functioning normally and which ones are not.

Syntax:

```
DISK volumename
```

or

```
DISK *
```

Option	Function
volumename	Causes DISK to display information specific to the volume you specify
*	Displays an overview of disk volumes

When you issue the DISK command alone (without switches), NetWare displays information about all known disks and disk channels installed in the server.

Rules and Considerations: You must issue the DISK command from the file server console.

Important Messages: None

Examples: The following three examples demonstrate the use of the DISK command by itself, with the * switch, and with a specific volume name.

If you want to check the status of all the disks on your system, issue DISK by itself, as follows:

```
DISK
```

NetWare displays information about all the system's disks, as follows (your system information may be different from the example shown here):

A
B
C
D
E
F
G
H
I
J
K
L
M
N
O
P
Q
R
S
T
U
V
W
X
Y
Z

A
B
C
D
E
F
G
H
I
J
K
L
M
N
O
P
Q
R
S
T
U
V
W
X
Y
Z

```
PHYSICAL DISK STATUS AND STATISTICS
      cha  con  drv   stat   IO Err  Free  Used

00     1    0    0     OK       0     699    8
01     1    0    1     OK       0      0     8
02     2    0    0   NO HOT     0      0     0
03     2    0    1    OFF       0      0     0
```

The preceding table includes the following types of information:

Column	Description
First column	The physical drive number.
cha	The channel number on which the interface board is installed.
con	The address of the controller for that disk.
drv	The disk address (as seen by the controller).
stat	The disk's operational status; the following values are possible:
	OK — Drive is set for Hot Fix and not mirrored.
	NO HOT — Hot Fix turned off for this drive (reinstall Hot Fix as soon as possible; the drive will shut down automatically).
	DOWN — Drive is out of service or not operating (repair if possible, or remove from system if necessary).
	M *xx* — Drive is part of a mirrored pair; *xx* is the number of the other drive in the pair.
	D *xx* — Drive was originally set up for mirroring, but is now dead (repair or replace drive and remirror).
IO Err	The number of input/output errors that have occurred on this drive.
Free	The number of unused blocks in the Hot Fix redirection area.
Used	The number of used blocks in the Hot Fix redirection area (Hot Fix uses 6 blocks by default).

If you want to see a list of all the file server's installed volumes, use the *
switch, as follows:

```
DISK *
```

NetWare displays the following information (your list might be different
from the one shown in this example):

```
        FILE SERVER VOLUMES

Volume Name    Phy Drv    Mir Drv
SYS              00          01
VOL1             02
ACCT             03
```

This table includes the following types of information:

Column	Description
Volume Name	The name assigned to each file server volume
Phy Drv	The physical drive number assigned to each drive
Mir Drv	The physical drive number of the secondary drive in a mirrored-pair set

If you want to see information about a specific volume, include the
volume's name with the DISK command. In the following example, the
volume is named SYS:

```
DISK SYS
```

NetWare displays the following information:

```
Information For Volume SYS
Physical drive number       : 00
Physical drive type         : ISA Disk type 09
IO errors on this drive     : 0
Redirection blocks available : 223
Redirection blocks used     : 9
Mirror physical drive number : 01

Other volumes sharing these
physical drive(s) :
VOL1
```

A
B
C
D
E
F
G
H
I
J
K
L
M
N
O
P
Q
R
S
T
U
V
W
X
Y
Z

A

B

C

D

E

F

G

H

I

J

K

L

M

N

O

P

Q

R

S

T

U

V

W

X

Y

Z

NetWare first displays information about the unmirrored or primary disk on the controller that contains the requested volume. If the disk is part of a mirrored pair, NetWare also reports information about the secondary disk.

Notes: In the preceding examples, the physical drive numbers are the drive numbers assigned to each disk by the operating system.

DISKSET

Purpose: Loads identification information about hard disks attached to a Novell Disk Coprocessor Board (DCB) into the DCB's EEPROM (Electronically Erasable and Programmable Read Only Memory) chip.

You can load DISKSET at any time on a downed file server to perform the following functions:

♦ Place configuration information about the hard disks attached to the DCB into the DCB's EEPROM chip. This configuration information enables the file server to communicate with the attached hard disks through the DCB.

♦ Back up the NetWare Ready configuration information from a NetWare Ready drive to a floppy disk.

♦ Restore NetWare Ready configuration information from a backup floppy disk to the NetWare Ready drive.

Syntax:

Use the following syntax for versions 2.2, 3.x, 4.10 for DISKSET.EXE:

```
A:>DISKSET
```

Use the following syntax for versions 3.x and 4.10:

```
LOAD DISKSET
```

Options: None

Rules and Considerations: If you are running version 2.2, the file server must be downed and in DOS before running the disk setup program.

If you are running version 3.x or 4.10, the file server must be up and running to load the disk setup program. The disk controller's driver should be loaded and no volumes should be mounted.

Important Messages: None

Examples:

```
A:DISKSET
```

A
B
C
D
E
F
G
H
I
J
K
L
M
N
O
P
Q
R
S
T
U
V
W
X
Y
Z

In this example, the DISKSET utility loads from a DOS disk in drive A. When the utility is loaded, DISKSET prompts you to specify the address of the controller you want to use. The system then presents a screen similar to the following:

```
Choose Controller Address
    1
    2
    3
    4
    5
    6
    7
```

After you select the DCB, you are ready to select a disk and controller type from the menu list. The screen should look similar to the following:

```
Select a DISK/CONTROLLER
CDC WRENIII HALF-HEIGHT
CDC WRENIII/EMBEDDED SCSI
FJ-M2243/A4000
FJ-M2243/A4000 , FJ-M2243/A4000
Fujitsu M2246AS/EMBEDDED SCSI
Generic SCSI
Generic SCSI , Generic SCSI
MAXTOR-1140/A4000
MAXTOR-1140/A4000 , MAXTOR-1140/A4000
MAXTOR-1140/A4070
MAXTOR-1140/A4070 , MAXTOR-1140/A4070
MAXTOR-3280/EMBEDDED SCSI
MINISCRIBE 4020
MINISCRIBE 4020 , MINISCRIBE 4020
Pyxis 27/A4000
NETWARE READY/EMBEDDED SCSI
Pyxis 27/A4000 , Pyxis 27/A4000

Toshiba MK56/A4000
Toshiba MK56/A4000 , Toshiba MK56/A4000
Toshiba MK56/A4070
Toshiba MK56/A4070 , Toshiba MK56/A4070
Vertex V150/A4000
Vertex V150/A4000 , Vertex V150/A4000
```

```
Vertex V150/A4070
Vertex V150/A4070 , Vertex V150/A4070
Vertex V170/A4000
Vertex V170/A4000 , Vertex V170/A4000
Vertex V170/A4070
Vertex V170/A4070 , Vertex V170/A4070
Vertex V185/A4000
Vertex V185/A4000 , Vertex V185/A4000
Vertex V185/A4070
Vertex V185/A4070 , Vertex V185/A4070
```

If you have a NetWare Ready or other generic embedded SCSI hard disk, select NetWare Ready/Embedded SCSI or Generic SCSI from the list of options.

Repeat the preceding steps to configure the remaining hard disks and DCBs installed in your system.

Notes: The drive list is accessed from a ROM on the DCB, different revisions of the ROM have different drives listed. Newer versions of NetWare (especially NetWare 3.x and later) require specific versions of this ROM to operate properly. For more information, contact your Novell reseller or Novell's After Market Products division. If you have revision E or older, you will definitely have problems.

The DISKSET program for NetWare 2.x will be located on the SYSTEM-1 disk. The DISKSET NLM for 3.11 is located on the SYSTEM-2 disk and for versions 3.12 and 4.10 is in the DISKDRV subdirectory on the CD-ROM.

The controller address (for Novell's DCB) is controlled by a PAL chip on the board. If you require a different setting, you must contact your Novell reseller or Novell's After Market Products division to purchase different PAL chips.

The Novell DCB is controlled by an 80188 CPU chip, which is located on the board. This chip loads instructions from ROM that also are contained on the DCB.

A
B
C
D
E
F
G
H
I
J
K
L
M
N
O
P
Q
R
S
T
U
V
W
X
Y
Z

DISMOUNT

Purpose: Dismounts a NetWare volume, rendering that volume unavailable to users. Once dismounted, a volume can be repaired using VREPAIR. If all volumes connected to a disk controller are dismounted, the disk controller's drivers can be upgraded.

Syntax: `DISMOUNT` *volumename*

Option	Function
volumename	The name of the volume you want to take out of service

Rules and Considerations: Use the BROADCAST console command to inform users that you are dismounting the volume before you actually take the volume out of service. This warning will enable users who are using that volume to close any files they have in use.

If you have a NetWare volume that is not used often, dismount it until you need it. Mounted volumes take up memory and reduce overall system performance.

You can use the UNLOAD command to dismount all volumes on a disk channel by unloading its disk driver. The following command will dismount all volumes on the DCB before unloading the driver from memory:

```
UNLOAD DCB
```

To dismount a CD-ROM volume in NetWare 4.10, use the CD DISMOUNT command.

Important Messages: If you dismount volume SYS of a 2.2 or 3.1x server, the binderies will be shut down and all users will lose their connections to the server. If the TTS backout volume is dismounted, TTS will be shut down.

Examples: Suppose that you want to dismount a NetWare volume named VOL1. To take the volume out of service, use DISMOUNT as follows:

```
DISMOUNT VOL1
```

This command enables you to service the drive or change disk drivers.

See Also: BROADCAST, CD (4.10), MOUNT, UNLOAD

DISPLAY NETWORKS

Purpose: When entered at the server console, the DISPLAY NETWORKS command displays the following information on the server console's screen:

♦ Network numbers, both cable and internal IPX. Internal IPX is displayed for NetWare 3.x and 4.x servers only.

♦ The number of *hops* (networks crossed) required to reach the network (0 hops is the server at which you issue the command). On 2.x servers the network addresses for LAN B, C, and D networks cards are always one hop away from their server.

♦ The estimated time in *ticks* (each tick equals 1/18 second) required for a packet to reach the other network.

♦ The total number of networks recognized by the internal router.

Syntax: `DISPLAY NETWORKS`

Options: None

Rules and Considerations: You must issue DISPLAY NETWORKS from the file server console.

Important Messages: None

Examples: To make sure that your file server can read all the network numbers, type the following command at the file server console:

`DISPLAY NETWORKS`

This command displays the total number of networks recognized by the internal router.

Notes: On a Novell NetWare network, each file server maintains an internal router tracking table. This table lists the network and node addresses of each file server, router, and service that this server recognizes. If you have trouble using the LOGIN and ATTACH commands, try using the DISPLAY NETWORKS command to determine whether the address for the network in question is visible to the other servers and routers on the network. The TRACK ON command will show the router tracking table being built.

See Also: DISPLAY SERVERS, RESET ROUTER, TRACK OFF, TRACK ON

A
B
C
D
E
F
G
H
I
J
K
L
M
N
O
P
Q
R
S
T
U
V
W
X
Y
Z

DISPLAY SERVERS

Purpose: When entered at the server console, the DISPLAY SERVERS command displays the following information on the server console's screen:

♦ The file servers recognized by the internal router

♦ The directory service tree names (4.10) and network addresses recognized by the server

♦ The number of hops (networks that must be crossed) required to reach the server

Syntax: DISPLAY SERVERS

Options: None

Rules and Considerations: You can issue the DISPLAY SERVERS command only at the file server's console.

Important Messages: None

Examples: If you are having trouble attaching to a file server, you can issue the DISPLAY SERVERS command as follows, to determine whether all the system's file servers recognize one another:

DISPLAY SERVERS

Notes: On a Novell NetWare network, each file server maintains an internal router tracking table. This table lists the network and node addresses of each file server, router, and service that this server recognizes. If you have trouble using the LOGIN and ATTACH commands, try using the DISPLAY SERVERS command to determine whether the internal router table recognizes the server in question.

See Also: DISPLAY NETWORKS, RESET ROUTER, TRACK OFF, TRACK ON

DOMAIN

Purpose: Enables a protected memory domain (called rings) in which NLMs can be run and tested without fear of crashing the entire server. DOMAIN provides server memory protection. Using the OS_PROTECTED memory domain to load NLMs until they have proven to be stable and non-disruptive prevents new or unproven NLMs from causing problems on your NetWare file server.

Syntax: `LOAD` [*path*]`DOMAIN` [/E]

Options: Replace *path* with the complete NetWare path to the DOMAIN.NLM. By default, NetWare will look in the same partition and directory as SERVER.EXE.

Use the /E option to load *misbehaved modules* (modules which have not been sufficiently tested and proven reliable, and which may cause the server to crash) so they have access to any data in the code segment of memory. Use this option cautiously because it also gives access to the code segment of memory to any other NLMs subsequently loaded into the OS_PROTECTED domain.

Loading the DOMAIN.NLM adds a new console command called DOMAIN to the existing list of console commands. The syntax for the DOMAIN command is as follows:

DOMAIN	Displays the current loader domain and a list of loaded modules in each domain.
DOMAIN HELP	Displays online help information.
DOMAIN domainname	Changes the domain into which NLMs will be loaded (the current loader domain) to domainname. Valid options for domainname are OS and OS_PROTECTED.

Rules and Considerations: The DOMAIN.NLM must be loaded in the STARTUP.NCF file.

NLMs that are run in the OS_PROTECTED domain will suffer a 15–20 percent performance degradation.

A
B
C
D
E
F
G
H
I
J
K
L
M
N
O
P
Q
R
S
T
U
V
W
X
Y
Z

Important Messages: None

Examples: To set up a NetWare 4.0 server for memory protection, the DOMAIN.NLM must be loaded in the STARTUP.NCF file. The following is an example of a STARTUP.NCF file that configures the server to support memory protection:

```
LOAD DOMAIN
LOAD IDE PORT=1F0 INT=E
LOAD ASPITRAN
LOAD AHA1540 PORT=330 INT=B DMA=5
LOAD ASPICD
```

Notes: Memory protection through the DOMAIN.NLM is based on Intel's memory protection scheme, which uses a four-ring system (0 through 3). Under Novell's implementation, OS and OS_Protected domains are created in these rings when DOMAIN is loaded. Therefore, ring numbers have no realistic effect on NLMs, their protection level, or their performance characteristics. Currently all NLMs loaded into OS_Protected domain suffer a 15–20 percent performance degradation.

NetWare versions 3.11, 3.12, and 4.10 by default load NLMs into ring 0 for high performance. With new or untrusted NLMs, use the DOMAIN.NLM and load them into a protected ring for testing. After an NLM becomes "trusted," it should be moved to ring 0 for better performance.

Any other NLMs, such as CLIB, required by the NLM need to be loaded into the same ring.

DOMAIN cannot be loaded on a NetWare for OS/2 server.

Loading DOMAIN also loads NWTIL.NLM and NWTILR.NLM. After the server is up and all NLMs are loaded, you can reclaim some memory by unloading NWTIL.NLM.

See Also: CLIB, LOAD

DOS

Purpose: This command switches a nondedicated file server or router from console mode to DOS mode.

Syntax: DOS

Options: None

Rules and Considerations: This command is valid only at a file server that is running NetWare 2.2 in nondedicated mode. NetWare 3.x and 4.10 file servers cannot run in nondedicated mode.

If the workstation session (or task) hangs, the file server or router task also might hang, breaking any and all connections maintained by the file server or router. The loss of connection causes users to lose files and access to their applications, printers, disk storage, and other services.

If a nondedicated file server or router hangs when in DOS or console mode, ask all users to try to save their work (to a local disk, if necessary) and log out. Then try using FCONSOLE to down the server. Bring the nondedicated machine up again to see if the problem is corrected.

Even if the nondedicated file server or router is still operating and functional, you must reboot the computer to return the workstation task to normal operation. As a result, however, the nondedicated file server or router will go down. Try to down the server using FCONSOLE status before rebooting the server.

Important Messages: None

Examples: After you have issued console commands, you might want to switch back to the DOS session and continue using your applications. To move back to the DOS session, issue the DOS command at the nondedicated file server or router console, as follows:

DOS

Notes: On a nondedicated file server running NetWare 2.2, the DOS session has the highest service priority. Virtually all other service requests generated by other users are serviced after the nondedicated DOS session. Further, because the DOS session is polled (not interrupt-driven, as are the network adapter cards), this overhead exists even if no programs are executed in the DOS session. If at all possible, you should change your server to run in dedicated mode.

If you are running your NetWare 2.2 file server in nondedicated mode, you are sacrificing approximately 30 percent or more of your server's performance. You can determine the system's minimum performance sacrifice by switching the file server to console mode (with all users logged out) and observing the server's utilization. The utilization data is displayed in monitor mode. The percentage displayed represents the amount of overhead required just to maintain the DOS session on your nondedicated file server.

The DOS session is run in real mode; the server session is run in protected mode on the Intel processor. The system switches between these modes by issuing an internal command to the processor similar to the command issued when you press Ctrl+Alt+Del. The processor will issue this command approximately 30 times per second. Servers running a 286-based processor will hang more often than the faster processors.

If the file server locks up and its keyboard does not respond, go to another workstation on the network and log in as Supervisor. When you are in the system, run FCONSOLE and select Down The Server. This command shuts down the server in an orderly fashion and should help avoid the corruption of files that might have been left open. *This procedure can take several minutes.*

See Also: CONSOLE, FCONSOLE, MONITOR

DOSGEN

Purpose: DOSGEN creates a boot image file called NET$DOS.SYS in the SYS:LOGIN directory. NET$DOS.SYS is a copy of the files on the system's book disk. This file enables diskless workstations to boot from remote boot image files, which reside on the server's hard disk.

Syntax:

DOSGEN *source filename* (2.2, 3.1x)

or

DOSGEN */?* */VER* (4.10)

Option	Definition
source	The drive in which DOSGEN can find the boot disk. If you omit this drive indicator, NetWare assumes that you want to use drive A.
filename	The output file name. If you do not specify an output file name, NetWare uses the name NET$DOS.SYS.
/?	Displays online help.
/VER	Displays version information and lists files needed by this utility to run.

Rules and Considerations: For proper operation, DOSGEN requires you to map two drives, as follows:

```
MAP F:=SYS:SYSTEM
```

```
MAP G:=SYS:LOGIN
```

If your network has several servers, copy the remote boot image files onto each server that may come up as the remote boot station's default server. Then, if the default server is busy when a remote boot station boots, the next available server becomes the default server.

A

B

C

D

E

F

G

H

I

J

K

L

M

N

O

P

Q

R

S

T

U

V

W

X

Y

Z

For 4.10, RPL must be loaded on the server and bound to the network board before running DOSGEN.

Important Messages: If NetWare displays the `Error opening boot disk image file` error message, you probably are attaching to another file server that does not contain the remote boot image file. Either log in to the other possible default file servers as Supervisor and run DOSGEN on each, or copy the SYS and BAT files in SYS:LOGIN from the default file server to the other file servers on the network.

If you receive the `Batch file missing` error message, make sure that the AUTOEXEC.BAT file is in SYS:LOGIN for every file server to which you can attach.

Examples: The following form of the DOSGEN command should be run from drive F. This example retrieves the boot files from drive A and uses the files to create a remote boot image file called NET$DOS.SYS in the LOGIN subdirectory:

```
F:DOSGEN A:
```

To use this command to create a remote boot image file, complete the following steps:

1. Boot a suitable workstation from a floppy or hard disk, and log in as supervisor (2.2 or 3.1x), ADMIN, or a user name with ADMIN equivalent rights (4.10).

2. Insert the configured boot disk for the remote boot workstation into drive A.

3. Map drive F to SYS:SYSTEM. (This must be a search drive for 4.10.)

4. Map drive G to SYS:LOGIN. (Any NetWare drive letter can be used for 4.10.)

5. Change to SYS:LOGIN by making the mapped drive current.

6. To run DOSGEN, type **F:DOSGEN A:**, as shown earlier. During the program's execution, your screen should contain the following information:

```
Floppy Type f9 = Quad Density, 15 Sectors per track

Total Floppy Space 2400 Sectors

Setting Up System Block.

Setting Up FAT Tables.
```

```
Setting Up Directory Structures.

Traversing Directory Structures.

Processing IBMBIO  COM

Processing IBMDOS  COM

Processing CONFIG  SYS

Processing COMMAND COM

Processing IPX     COM

Processing NET3    COM

Processing AUTOEXECBAT

Processing NET     CFG

Transferring Data to NET$DOS.SYS
```

7. Copy the AUTOEXEC.BAT file from the boot disk in drive A into the SYS:LOGIN subdirectory. NetWare might display the Batch file missing error message when you log in, if the AUTOEXEC.BAT file is not copied to SYS:LOGIN and the default user directory.

8. Copy the AUTOEXEC.BAT file from the boot disk to the default directory specified in the user's login script (usually the user's home directory).

9. Flag the NET$DOS.SYS file in SYS:LOGIN Shareable Read/Write.

The next example, which also should be run from drive G, assumes that you will be creating several remote boot image files. Like the first example, this form of the DOSGEN command retrieves the needed files from a disk in drive A, and uses the data to create a remote boot image file in the LOGIN subdirectory. This form of the DOSGEN command, however, names the new file ARCNET.SYS.

```
F:DOSGEN A:ARCNET.SYS
```

To use this command to create a remote boot image file, complete the following steps:

1. Boot a suitable workstation from a floppy or hard disk, and log in as supervisor.

2. Insert the configured boot disk for the remote boot workstation into drive A.

A
B
C
D
E
F
G
H
I
J
K
L
M
N
O
P
Q
R
S
T
U
V
W
X
Y
Z

A

B

C

D

E

F

G

H

I

J

K

L

M

N

O

P

Q

R

S

T

U

V

W

X

Y

Z

3. Map drive F to SYS:SYSTEM. (Must be a search drive for 4.10.)

4. Map drive G to SYS:LOGIN.

5. Change to SYS:LOGIN by making drive G current. (Any NetWare drive letter can be used for NetWare 4.10.)

6. For example, to run DOSGEN, type **F:DOSGEN A:ARCNET.SYS**, as shown earlier. During the program's execution, your screen should contain the following information:

```
Floppy Type f9 = Quad Density, 15 Sectors per track

Total Floppy Space 2400 Sectors

Setting Up System Block.

Setting Up FAT Tables.

Setting Up Directory Structures.

Traversing Directory Structures.

Processing IBMBIO   COM

Processing IBMDOS   COM

Processing CONFIG   SYS

Processing COMMAND COM

Processing IPX      COM

Processing NET3     COM

Processing AUTOEXECBAT

Processing NET      CFG

Transferring Data to ARCNET.SYS
```

7. Copy the AUTOEXEC.BAT file from the boot disk in drive A to the SYS:LOGIN subdirectory. NetWare may display a Batch file missing error when you log in if the AUTOEXEC.BAT file has not been copied to SYS:LOGIN and the default user directory. In the example, the AUTOEXEC.BAT file should contain only the name of a second batch file. This second batch file should contain the true desired contents of a boot AUTOEXEC.BAT. Because you are configuring for several remote boot image files, give a unique name and BAT extension (such as ARCNET.BAT) to each AUTOEXEC.BAT file from each boot disk, and copy them all into the SYS:LOGIN subdirectory.

When each Remote Boot workstation boots, the operating system reads the AUTOEXEC.BAT file and goes to the renamed batch file to execute the desired boot commands.

8. Copy the renamed AUTOEXEC.BAT file from SYS:LOGIN to the default directory specified in the user's login script (usually the user's home directory).

9. Flag the ARCNET.SYS file (use the actual file name you used when you originally created this file instead of ARCNET.SYS as used in this example) in SYS:LOGIN Shareable Read/Write.

10. Record the network number and node address of the station that will use the remote boot image file you just created. You will need this information when you create the BOOTCONF.SYS file.

When you create multiple remote boot image files, you also need a BOOTCONF.SYS file in the SYS:LOGIN directory. The BOOTCONF.SYS file lists the names of all the custom remote boot image files (except the default NET$DOS.SYS file), and the network and node address of each station that uses the customized remote boot image file. It is nothing more than an ASCII text file in the SYS:LOGIN subdirectory that routes the correct remote boot image file to the correct workstation. Take the following steps to create the BOOTCONF.SYS file:

1. Move to the SYS:LOGIN directory.

2. Use a DOS text editor (such as EDLIN) to create the BOOTCONF.SYS file in the SYS:LOGIN directory. The file should contain a line for each remote boot image file you created. Use the following format for entering the required information:

0x (the number zero plus x)

The network address

A comma (,)

The node or station address

An equal sign (=)

The remote boot image file name

Following this format, your file should look something like this:

```
0xBADCAFE,02F=ARCNET.SYS
```

This example is for an ARCnet workstation. An Ethernet workstation would have a much longer node address.

A
B
C
D
E
F
G
H
I
J
K
L
M
N
O
P
Q
R
S
T
U
V
W
X
Y
Z

3. To complete the setup, flag the SYS and BAT files in SYS:LOGIN as Shareable Read/Write. For example:

```
FLAG *.SYS SRW

FLAG *.BAT SRW
```

Notes: If one user can successfully log in, but other users are unsuccessful when trying at the same time, verify that the *.SYS files were flagged Shareable Read/Write. You also may need to grant users the Modify right to the SYS:LOGIN subdirectory.

Use the TRACK ON command at the server console and watch for GET NEAREST SERVER REQUESTS from the workstation. This will give you an idea as to whether the boot ROM on the workstation is successfully sending packets to the file server.

Load MONITOR at the file server console and see if the diskless workstations are opening the BOOTCONF.SYS file, the NET$DOS.SYS file, or other boot disk image files.

If a workstation using a boot ROM does not boot, and you have another workstation with a disk drive configured the same as the first workstation (that is, if both have the same type of network board using the same configuration options), see if the second station will boot with the boot disk you used during DOSGEN. By booting with the boot disk in the second workstation, the booting procedure should execute in the same manner as booting from the server with the Remote Boot image file on the first workstation.

If you upgrade your server from one version of NetWare to another version, you might have to replace the boot ROM on the workstations network card. Check with the manufacturer before upgrading your server.

See Also: MONITOR, TRACK OFF, TRACK ON

DOWN

Purpose: The DOWN command shuts down the NetWare operating system so that you can safely turn off the file server. When you issue the DOWN command, the following events occur:

♦ All cache buffers are written to disk

♦ All open files are closed

♦ All directory and file allocation tables are updated (if **appropriate**)

♦ All volumes are dismounted

♦ All user connections are terminated

Syntax: `DOWN`

Options: None

Rules and Considerations: Make sure that all users are logged out before you issue the DOWN command. You can use the SEND command to warn all users to close files and log out. Use the MONITOR command at the server console or FCONSOLE, USERLIST, NLIST from a workstation to make sure that all users have logged out and all files are closed.

Do not issue the DOWN command or turn off the server if database or word processing files are still open. Close these files from within the appropriate application, and then use DOWN.

On NetWare 4.10 servers, after using the DOWN command, if you do not use the EXIT command and return to the DOS prompt, you can reload the server using the RESTART SERVER command.

Important Messages: None

Examples: Before you can perform any type of hardware maintenance to the file server, you must turn it off. Before turning off the server, issue the DOWN command, as follows:

`DOWN`

When you issue the command, NetWare should display a message similar to the following:

A

B

C

D

E

F

G

H

I

J

K

L

M

N

O

P

Q

R

S

T

U

V

W

X

Y

Z

```
Server Training-Solutions has been shut down. Please reboot to
restart.
```

Notes: If you fail to use the DOWN command before turning off the file server, you will corrupt any files that may be open. Further, you may cause irreparable damage to the File Allocation Table (FAT) and Directory Entry Table (DET) on the hard disks. If the FAT and DET become corrupted, you probably will not be able to reboot the server and access your data.

Any changes to data files remain in cache buffers and are not written to disk until a minimum time (the default is three seconds) has elapsed or the files are closed. These changes are lost if you do not use DOWN before turning off the file server.

If the MONITOR screen shows a list of the files that are still open, it also should display the station connection numbers that opened them. If files remain open after all users have logged out, you can close these files from the server by using the CLEAR STATION command. You should use this procedure, however, only as a last resort. If the files are not closed by the application that opened them, they may become corrupted.

Downing a server but not exiting to DOS allows the server to remain connected to the network and to continue to receive packets. It also allows you to run other console commands such as TRACK ON and TRACK OFF.

See Also: BROADCAST, CLEAR STATION, EXIT, FCONSOLE, MONITOR, NLIST, RESTART SERVER, USERLIST

DOWNLOAD

Purpose: Enables NetWare 2.2 configuration (.CFG) and linking (.LNK) files, and the file server-specific utility files to be transferred to the working copies of the SYSTEM-1, SYSTEM-2, and OSEXE disks to later be loaded on the actual file server.

Syntax: DOWNLOAD *drive*

Options: Replace *drive* with the drive letter where the working disks are located.

Rules and Considerations: DOWNLOAD is used to generate multiple file servers from one NetWare directory. To use DOWNLOAD, log in to the NetWare file server and change to the NETWARE directory. Run DOWNLOAD from the NETWARE directory.

Important Messages: None

Examples: To run DOWNLOAD, insert the first working disk into drive A, then from the file server NETWARE directory, use the following command:

DOWNLOAD A

See Also: INSTALL, UPLOAD

A
B
C
D
E
F
G
H
I
J
K
L
M
N
O
P
Q
R
S
T
U
V
W
X
Y
Z

DSMERGE

Purpose: Enables two NDS [root] objects to be merged together into a single NDS tree structure.

Syntax: `LOAD [ path ]DSMERGE`

Options: Replace *path* with the complete NetWare path to the DSMERGE NLM. By default NetWare will look in the SYS:SYSTEM directory.

Once DSMERGE is loaded, you can check servers in this tree, check time synchronization, merge two trees, or rename trees by choosing the specific option from the list. You can also view the server name, version, and the status of servers in the tree.

Rules and Considerations: DSMERGE must be loaded on the source tree's server. It then will ask you for a target tree with which to merge your NDS tree.

When you merge trees, the objects in the source tree become subordinate objects in the target tree. The target's [root] becomes the [root] object for the entire newly created NDS tree.

Replicas are removed and reassigned during DSMERGE. The source tree server's master replica of the source tree is replaced with a replica of the target tree's root partition. Objects below the root object in the source tree are split into separate partitions.

Back up both the source and target trees before beginning a DSMERGE. If a power failure occurs while merging the two NDS trees, you might lose information in the source tree.

Important Messages: None

Examples: To merge two NDS trees, type the following at the source server's System Console:

`LOAD DSMERGE`

Notes: DSMERGE does not support a "prune and graft" feature. It can only be used to merge entire tree structures. Neither containers nor leaf objects can be merged separate from the tree structure.

See Also: None

DSREPAIR

Purpose: Enables the system to repair problems with the NDS database.

When you use DSREPAIR, the following events occur:

♦ The file server's local database is repaired

♦ Tools for repairing replicas, replica rings, and server objects are made available

♦ Synchronization errors are analyzed and can be viewed

♦ Replica information is written to a log

♦ The damaged database is compressed into a dump file and can be repaired

♦ A list of remote server identification numbers is provided so they can be verified and modified if needed

♦ Local database objects can be located and synchronized

Syntax: LOAD [*path*]**DSREPAIR** [-U] [-L *logfilename*]

Options: Replace path with the complete NetWare path to the DSREPAIR NLM. By default NetWare will look in the SYS:SYSTEM directory.

Options	Functions
-U	Tells DSREPAIR to run without user intervention.
-L	Tells DSREPAIR to log errors found to the log file specified by *logfilename*.

Rules and Considerations: DSREPAIR locks the NDS database while it rebuilds and repairs it. No changes or logins on this copy of the NDS database are allowed until you exit DSREPAIR.

DSREPAIR is a menu driven utility, with much the same type of interface as VREPAIR.

Important Messages: None

A
B
C
D
E
F
G
H
I
J
K
L
M
N
O
P
Q
R
S
T
U
V
W
X
Y
Z

A
B
C
D
E
F
G
H
I
J
K
L
M
N
O
P
Q
R
S
T
U
V
W
X
Y
Z

Examples: To repair an NDS database, type the following at the server's System Console:

LOAD DSREPAIR

Notes: DSREPAIR changes objects that do not have information in the mandatory fields into Unknown objects, which you can delete.

If the NDS database is stored on multiple servers, you must run DSREPAIR on all servers to repair the entire database.

See Also: VREPAIR

ECHO OFF

Purpose: Prevents commands executed from NCF files from displaying at the System Console.

Syntax: `ECHO OFF`

Options: None

Rules and Considerations: This command, if used, should be used only after the NCF file has been tested and debugged. This command will prevent anyone from seeing the commands executed and their sequence at the server console, thus making NCF troubleshooting extremely difficult.

Important Messages: None

Examples: To prevent commands from displaying in an NCF file simply include the ECHO OFF command at or near the top of the file. The sample NCF file below loads the MONITOR and SERVMAN NLMs:

```
ECHO OFF
LOAD MONITOR
LOAD SERVMAN
```

Notes: None

See Also: ECHO ON

A
B
C
D
E
F
G
H
I
J
K
L
M
N
O
P
Q
R
S
T
U
V
W
X
Y
Z

ECHO ON

Purpose: Enables commands executed from NCF files to be displayed at the System Console.

Syntax: `ECHO ON`

Options: None

Rules and Considerations: When ECHO ON is placed in an NCF file, all commands are shown as they execute at the server console from an NCF file.

Important Messages: None

Examples: To enable commands to be displayed in an NCF file after ECHO OFF had been issued, simply include the ECHO ON command at some point in the file. The sample NCF file below loads the MONITOR and SERVMAN NLMs with ECHO set to OFF, then reenables ECHO to display the execution of the VERSION command:

```
ECHO OFF
LOAD MONITOR
LOAD SERVMAN
ECHO ON VERSION
```

Notes: None

See Also: ECHO OFF

ECONFIG

Purpose: The ECONFIG command lists Ethernet configurations, configures workstation shells to use the Ethernet II protocol standard, and
embeds NetWare's unique protocol number (8137) in the workstation
shell file IPX.COM.

Syntax: *drive1:* **ECONFIG** *drive2:* **IPX.COM SHELL:***packet protocolnumber*

Options	Function
drive1:	Indicates the location of the ECONFIG.EXE file.
drive2:	Indicates the location of the IPX.COM file.
packet	Specifies the data that is to be transmitted, and its form of transmission. A packet can be one of the following:
	NetWare — Use N if the driver is to use the IEEE 802.3 standard frame format.
	Ethernet II — Use E if the driver is to use the Ethernet standard frame format.
protocolnumber	Specifies the Ethernet protocol number. By default, this is Novell's IPX protocol number (8137). You can specify any number currently registered with your server.

Important Messages: Not needed when the workstation is using ODI or
VLM drivers.

Examples: This example assumes that the WSGEN disk (which contains
ECONFIG.EXE) is in drive A, and that the IPX.COM file is in drive B. The
following form of the command lists the current Ethernet configuration
for IPX.COM:

```
A:ECONFIG B:IPX.COM
```

A
B
C
D
E
F
G
H
I
J
K
L
M
N
O
P
Q
R
S
T
U
V
W
X
Y
Z

A

B

C

D

E

F

G

H

I

J

K

L

M

N

O

P

Q

R

S

T

U

V

W

X

Y

Z

If the shell file is Ethernet-configurable, but has not yet been configured, you should see the following information on your screen:

```
SHELL: Novell Ethernet (IEEE 802.3 compatible)
```

If the shell file already has been configured with ECONFIG, you should see the following information:

```
SHELL: Ethernet Typefield: 8137 (Assigned Novell type constant)
```

To embed NetWare's protocol number 8137 into the IPX.COM file, type the following form of the ECONFIG command:

A:ECONFIG B:IPX.COM SHELL:E

NetWare displays the following information:

```
SHELL: Ethernet Typefield: 8137 (Assigned Novell type constant)
```

EDIT

Purpose: The EDIT command creates or modifies an ASCII text file from the NetWare file server console.

Syntax: `LOAD` *path* `EDIT`

Option	Function
path	Determines the full path to the directory containing the EDIT module. You may begin with either a DOS drive letter or a NetWare volume name. If you do not specify a path, the operating system looks for EDIT in SYS:SYSTEM. You can use the SEARCH command to set up additional paths for automatic searching.

Rules and Considerations: You may find EDIT particularly useful when you want to create NCF batch files that automatically execute file server commands. Although you can edit such files in the INSTALL NLM, EDIT provides an alternative means to create or edit them.

You can use EDIT with ASCII text files on either DOS or NetWare partitions. The EDIT NLM can edit ASCII files up to 8 KB.

Important Messages: You cannot edit files from a DOS partition if DOS has been removed from the file server's memory with either the SECURE CONSOLE or REMOVE DOS commands.

Examples: To load the editor at the file server, issue the EDIT command as follows:

```
LOAD EDIT
```

At the File to Edit prompt, enter the complete directory path for the ASCII file that you want to create or edit. After you create or edit the file, press Esc to exit from EDIT. When the confirmation box appears, select Yes to save the file with the changes you have made during this editing session. Otherwise, you can select No to abort and exit without saving the changes.

See Also: INSTALL, REMOVE DOS, SEARCH, SECURE CONSOLE

EMSNETX.COM or EMSNETX.EXE

Purpose: The EMSNETX command loads the NetWare shell driver and moves most of the commands in NETX.COM from DOS memory to LIM expanded memory. This arrangement frees approximately 34 KB of the DOS 640 KB base memory. About 6 KB must remain in conventional memory to handle various interrupts and some data.

Syntax: EMSNETX

Options	Function
-I	Enables you to see which version of the shell driver you are using, without actually loading it into memory
-U	Unloads the shell driver from memory, but must be the last TSR program loaded for this to function properly

Rules and Considerations: IPX.COM must be loaded before you attempt to load EMSNET*x*.EXE.

Older versions used the *x* to represent the version of DOS you are running at the workstation; for example, MS-DOS 5 requires you to issue the command as **EMSNET5**.

All NET*x*.COM parameters in the shell configuration files SHELL.CFG and NET.CFG work with the expanded memory shell.

Important Messages: Novell is discontinuing support of DOS shells (NETX, EMSNETX, XMSNETX). You should switch to the DOS requester (VLM).

Examples: Issue the following form of the command to load the shell driver into expanded memory:

EMSNETX

Notes: For ease of use, copy the EMSNETX.EXE (or COM) file to the workstation's boot disk and include the file name (EMSNETX) in the

AUTOEXEC.BAT file. This automatically loads the shell driver when you boot your workstation.

The expanded memory shell works with all NetWare versions and operates under the same conditions as the regular NetWare DOS shell 3.01 and later.

The expanded memory shell replaces the current NETX.COM shell option and is intended for use by users who have LIM expanded memory.

You can use the following parameter in the SHELL.CFG or NET.CFG file to determine the number of times you can reenter the expanded memory shell:

ENTRY STACK SIZE

See Also: NETX, VLM, XMSNETX

A
B
C
D
E
F
G
H
I
J
K
L
M
N
O
P
Q
R
S
T
U
V
W
X
Y
Z

ENABLE LOGIN

Purpose: After you have used the DISABLE LOGIN command or a user's login has been disabled through the intruder detection function, you must use ENABLE LOGIN to enable the system's users login. ENABLE LOGIN must be used to enable the NetWare 4.10 administrator's login, before the administrator can log in to the file server.

Syntax: `ENABLE LOGIN`

Options: None

Rules and Considerations: The ENABLE LOGIN function is built into the file server's operating system.

When you disable login and then down the file server, you do not need to issue ENABLE LOGIN. The command is issued automatically when you reboot the file server.

Important Messages: None

Examples: To reverse the DISABLE LOGIN command, type the following:

`ENABLE LOGIN`

See Also: DISABLE LOGIN, FCONSOLE (Status), LOGIN

ENABLE TRANSACTIONS

Purpose: If the NetWare Transaction Tracking System (TTS) has been disabled—either automatically or manually—you must manually reenable TTS by using the ENABLE TRANSACTIONS command.

Syntax: `ENABLE TRANSACTIONS`

Options: None

Rules and Considerations: ENABLE TRANSACTIONS is a part of the operating system. During normal operation, TTS is enabled. The file server automatically disables TTS if the TTS backout volume (usually SYS) becomes full, or if the file server does not have enough memory to run TTS. You also can manually disable TTS by using the DISABLE TRANSACTIONS command. Transactions that were initiated while TTS was disabled cannot be backed out after TTS is reenabled.

If the file server is rebooted while TTS is disabled, TTS is automatically reenabled when the file server is rebooted.

Important Messages: None

Examples: If you have disabled TTS and want to reenable it, type the following command:

`ENABLE TRANSACTIONS`

See Also: DISABLE TRANSACTIONS, FCONSOLE (Status), SETTTS

ENABLE TTS

Purpose: If the NetWare Transaction Tracking System (TTS) has been disabled—either automatically or manually—you must manually reenable TTS by using the ENABLE TTS command.

Syntax: `ENABLE TTS`

Options: None

Rules and Considerations: ENABLE TTS is a part of the operating system. During normal operation, TTS is enabled. The file server automatically disables TTS if the TTS backout volume (usually SYS) becomes full, or if the file server does not have enough memory to run TTS. You also can manually disable TTS by using the DISABLE TTS command. Transactions that were initiated while TTS was disabled cannot be backed out after TTS is reenabled.

If the file server is rebooted while TTS is disabled, TTS is automatically reenabled when the file server is rebooted.

Important Messages: None

Examples: If you have disabled TTS and want to reenable it, type the following command:

`ENABLE TTS`

See Also: DISABLE TTS, FCONSOLE (Status)

ENDCAP

Purpose: Use the ENDCAP command to terminate the capturing of one or more of your workstation's LPT ports. Always use the CAPTURE command before using the ENDCAP command. In 4.10, it was incorporated into CAPTURE.

Syntax: `ENDCAP` *option*

Options: ENDCAP ends capturing to LPT1, unless you enter one of the following options:

Option	Function
Local *n*	Indicates the LPT port from which you want to end capturing. Replace n with the number of the desired parallel port, such as 1, 2, or 3.
ALL	Ends the capturing of all LPT ports.
Cancel	Ends the capturing of LPT1 and deletes the data without printing it.
Cancel Local *n*	Ends the capturing of the specified LPT port and deletes data without printing it. Replace n with the number of the desired parallel port, such as 1, 2, or 3.
Cancel ALL	Ends the capturing of all LPT ports and deletes the data without printing it.

Rules and Considerations: Use the ENDCAP command only after having issued the CAPTURE command.

Important Messages: `LPTx set to local mode` indicates that port LPTx (LPT1, 2, or 3) has been set to local operation and the CAPTURE function has been canceled.

Examples: To end capturing to LPT1, issue the following command:

`ENDCAP`

A
B
C
D
E
F
G
H
I
J
K
L
M
N
O
P
Q
R
S
T
U
V
W
X
Y
Z

To end capturing to LPT2, issue the following command:

```
ENDCAP L=2
```

To end capturing to LPT1 and delete the print job without printing it, issue the following command:

```
ENDCAP CL=1
```

See Also: CAPTURE

EXIT

Purpose: Returns the file server console to DOS after you have used the DOWN command. EXIT enables you to access files on the DOS partition, or to reload SERVER.EXE with new parameters.

Syntax: EXIT

Options: None

Rules and Considerations: If you use the console commands REMOVE DOS or SECURE CONSOLE to remove DOS from memory, you cannot use the EXIT command to return to DOS. You will have to reboot the server after issuing a DOWN command.

Important Messages: None

Examples: After you have shut down the file server, you can return to the DOS prompt by issuing the following command:

EXIT

Notes: You can use EXIT or RESTART SERVER (4.10) to warm boot the file server if you have issued the REMOVE DOS command.

See Also: DOWN, REMOVE DOS, SECURE CONSOLE, RESTART SERVER

A
B
C
D
E
F
G
H
I
J
K
L
M
N
O
P
Q
R
S
T
U
V
W
X
Y
Z

FILE SERVER NAME

Purpose: Defines the file server in the AUTOEXEC.NCF file. This will not change the current name of a server from the console.

Syntax: `FILE SERVER NAME` *fileservername*

Options: Replace *fileservername* with the name you want for this file server.

Rules and Considerations: This command can only be issued in the AUTOEXEC.NCF file.

If this command is not found in the server's AUTOEXEC.NCF file, or the server does not have an AUTOEXEC.NCF file, or SERVER.EXE is started using the -NA switch to prevent execution of the AUTOEXEC.NCF file, the file server name will be prompted for by the operating system.

The file server's name is limited to 47 characters and cannot contain spaces.

Important Messages: None

Examples: Typically this command will be one of the first commands in the server's AUTOEXEC.NCF file and will look like the following:

`FILE SERVER NAME = TRAINING_SOLUTIONS_TEMPE`

Notes: Underline characters can be used as an effective substitute for spaces in the file server's name.

Uppercase, lowercase, or both may be used in the file server's name. But when executed, the file server's name will be converted to uppercase.

File server names should be short and descriptive; remember you will be typing this name a lot.

A
B
C
D
E
F
G
H
I
J
K
L
M
N
O
P
Q
R
S
T
U
V
W
X
Y
Z

FLAG

Purpose: Displays or changes files and directory attributes. In NetWare 4.10 the functions of the FLAGDIR command have been added to the FLAG command.

FLAG can also be used to modify a file's or directory's owner, or to modify how search drives are used to find executable files.

Syntax: FLAG *path flaglist options*

Options: In the following table, 4.10 at the beginning of the description indicates for NetWare 4.10 only.

When the FLAG command is used without parameters, the attribute status of files is displayed for the current directory.

Option	Function	
path	Designates directory path that leads to the name of the file you want to view or change.	
flaglist	Specifies one or more of the following attributes (use the bold character to express the attribute):	
	Shareable	Enables a file to be opened by more than one person at a time. Shareable is often used in conjunction with Read Only and also is used to mark application programs (that is, EXE or COM files). In 4.10, use SH.
	Read **O**nly	Prevents you from writing to, deleting, or renaming a specified file. The Read Only flag often is used in conjunction with Shareable on application program files.
	Read/**W**rite	Specifies the file as a data file, which means that data can be written to it. This is a default setting for files.
	Normal	Specifies the Nonshareable and Read/Write flags together. All files loaded on the network are set this way by default.

Option	Function
Transaction	Specifies the file is transactional tracking. This Tracking flag is designed to be used with NetWare's Transaction Tracking feature, which prevents database corruption in case of system failure. The Transaction Tracking System ensures that when a file is modified, either all changes are made or no changes are made, thus preventing data corruption.
Indexed	Forces NetWare to keep a special File Allocation Table to speed data access. Used with data files using more than 64 cache blocks. Automatic in 3.1*x* and 4.10.
Hidden	Prevents a file or directory from displaying when a DOS DIR command is executed. The file will appear, however, if you have the File Scan right in that directory, and you use the NDIR command. You cannot copy or erase Hidden files.
SYstem	Flags a file as a system file and is used for the system function. A system file does not appear when you use the DOS DIR command, but it will appear when you use the NetWare NDIR command if you have the File Scan right. You cannot copy or delete system files. In 4.10, SYstem prevents the copying, deleting, and displaying of a file using DOS commands.
Archive	Attaches automatically to all files that have been modified since the last backup was performed.
Execute Only	Allows the program file to execute, but prevents it from being copied. This special flag is attached to COM and EXE files. Files with this flag set are not backed up, nor can this flag be removed. In 4.10, use X instead of XO. The file must be deleted and reinstalled to remove this attribute. This attribute can be set only by the supervisor in the FILER utility.
Purge	When the file directory is deleted, they will be purged immediately.

continues

A
B
C
D
E
F
G
H
I
J
K
L
M
N
O
P
Q
R
S
T
u
V
W
X
Y
Z

A
B
C
D
E
F
G
H
I
J
K
L
M
N
O
P
Q
R
S
T
U
V
W
X
Y
Z

Option	Function
SUBdirectory	Displays or changes file attributes in the specified directory and its subdirectories.
Copy Inhibit	Prevents DOS stations from copying Mac files and can only be applied to Mac files.
Can't Compress	(4.10) Indicates system could not compress this file due to insufficient space.
COmpressed	(4.10) Indicates this is a compressed file.
Migrated	(4.10) Indicates this file has been migrated to another storage medium.
Don't Migrate	(4.10) The directory file will not be moved to a secondary storage media regardless of what the volume default is set to.
Don't Compress	Prevents the file from being compressed even if the volume or directory is compressed.
Delete Inhibit	The file cannot be copied over or deleted.
Immediate Compress	(4.10) Compresses a file or directory as soon as the operating system can process the request.
Rename Inhibit	Prevents the renaming of a file.
All	(4.10) Affects files and directories and causes all available attributes to be assigned to them. For files, they will be assigned Ro, SH, A, H, Sy, T, P, Ci, Di, Ri. For directories, they will receive H, Sy, P, Di, Ri.
Don't Suballocate	(4.10) Prevents suballocation of a file even when suballocation is on for the system.
/M=mode	(4.10) Uses specified search mode of executable files. Options available for this switch are numbers 0-7. Specify one or more of the following options:
	0 The default for all executable files. The executable file will look for information in the NET.CFG.

Option		Function
	1	Has the executable file search the path that is specified within itself or the default directory and all search drives.
	2	Has the executable file search the path that is specified within itself or just the default directory.
	3	The same as 1 except that if an open request is Read Only, then the file searches the search drives.
	4	Reserved.
	5	Has the executable file search the path that was specified and then all search drives. If there is no path specified, it then searches the default directory and all search drives.
	6	Reserved.
	7	Has the executable file search the specified path and if the open request is read only, it also will search the search drives. If no path was specified, it then searches the default directory and all search drives.
/C		Causes the screen to scroll continuously through the screen output.
/S		(4.10) Causes the command to affect files and directories in the current path and any subdirectories below.
/NAME ¦ GROUP =name		(4.10) Modifies the owner of a file or directory.
/OWNER=name		(4.10) Displays all files or directories owned by that user.
/FO		(4.10) Displays or modifies only files in the specified path, not the directories.

continues

A
B
C
D
E
F
G
H
I
J
K
L
M
N
O
P
Q
R
S
T
U
V
W
X
Y
Z

A
B
C
D
E
F
G
H
I
J
K
L
M
N
O
P
Q
R
S
T
U
V
W
X
Y
Z

Option	Function
/DO	(4.10) Displays or modifies only the directories in the specified path, not the files.
/?	Displays a help screen.
/D	Displays detailed output in 4.10 only.
/VER	(4.10) Provides information about the version of this utility, as well as a list of files this utility needs in order to run.

Rules and Considerations: You must be attached to the file server before you can view or change file attributes of files on that server.

You cannot change file attributes in a directory unless your effective rights in that directory include the Read, File Scan, and Modify privileges.

Use the – or + constants to add or delete all file attributes except Normal and SUBdirectory. When attributes are added or deleted in the same command, keep the + attributes separate from the – attributes.

Important Messages: None

Examples: If you want to flag as Shareable Read Only every file on the CDI server in the MS-DOS 5.00 directory under Public, type the following command:

```
FLAG CDI\SYS:PUBLIC\IBM_PC\MSDOS\V5.00\*.* SRO
```

Notes: PC/MS-DOS files should be flagged as Shareable Read Only.

If you type the command FLAG /?, a help screen is displayed.

The file name parameter in the syntax also supports standard DOS wild-card characters.

Use the Execute Only flag with extreme care. Some application programs will not execute correctly if they are flagged with this option. If you are going to use this flag, make sure you have a copy of the EXE or COM file before you set this flag. *The only way to remove this flag is to delete the file.*

See Also: FILER, FLAGDIR, NDIR, RIGHTS, TLIST

FLAGDIR

Purpose: Lists or changes the attributes of directories and subdirectories. The functions of FLAGDIR were added to the FLAG command in 4.10.

Syntax: `FLAGDIR` *path flaglist*

Option	Function	
path	Specifies the path to the directory you want to view or change.	
flaglist	Specifies one or more of the following attributes (use the bold character to specify the attribute):	
	Normal	Cancels all other directory attributes. Normal is automatically overridden if you include any other option.
	Hidden	Prevents a directory from listing when the DOS DIR command is used. The directory will appear if you have the File Scan right and you use the NetWare NDIR command. With these privileges, you can access a hidden directory, but you cannot copy or delete hidden directories.
	SYstem	Flags a directory as a System directory, which stores the network's operational files. A directory flagged as System will not appear when you use the DOS DIR command. A System directory will appear if you use the NetWare NDIR command and if you have the File Scan right.
	Private	Protects data from casual directory browsers. You can use the Private option to hide the directory names of all directories below the flagged directory. Although you cannot see any files on the system because you have no rights, you can see directories and use the DOS CD command to move through the directory structure. Can be used only in 2.2.

continues

A
B
C
D
E
F
G
H
I
J
K
L
M
N
O
P
Q
R
S
T
U
V
W
X
Y
Z

A
B
C
D
E
F
G
H
I
J
K
L
M
N
O
P
Q
R
S
T
U
V
W
X
Y
Z

Option	Function
Delete Inhibit	Prevents users from erasing a directory even if they have Erase rights for that directory. Can be used only in 3.11 and up.
Rename Inhibit	Prevents users from renaming directories even if they have Modify rights for that directory. Can be used only in 3.11 and later.
Purge	Marks files that you want to purge immediately after deletion. These files cannot be recovered by using SALVAGE. Can be used only in 3.11 and up.
Help	Displays the FLAGDIR help text.

Rules and Considerations: You cannot set attributes on local drives.

You cannot copy or delete system directories.

Important Messages: None

Examples: To flag the TGEN subdirectory as private and to prevent other users from seeing the subdirectories under it when they use the DOS DIR command, type the following:

```
FLAGDIR TRAINING_SOLUTIONS\SYS:USERS\TGEN P
```

See Also: FILER, FLAG

GRANT

Purpose: Grants trustee rights to a user or a group.

Syntax:

GRANT *rightslist* FOR path TO USER *username*

or

GRANT *rightslist* FOR path TO GROUP *groupname*

Option	Function
rightslist	Represents one or more of the following options (use the bold character to express the desired option):
All	Grants all rights except Supervisory rights.
Create	Enables users to create directories and files but not write to them after they are closed.
Erase	Enables users to delete or erase files and directories.
Modify	Enables users to modify file and directory names or attributes.
Access Control	Enables a user or a group to control access to the directory or file by changing trustee assignments and inherited and maximum right masks.
Read	Enables users to read a file in the directory.
File Scan	Enables users to see file and directory names during a DOS DIR command.
Write	Enables users to write to files.
Supervisor	Gives all available rights to user; 3.x.
No Rights	Revokes all rights except Supervisory.
ALL BUT or ONLY	Switches that you can use before the *rightslist* option.

Option	Function
path	Specifies the path for granting trustee rights.
username	Specifies the name of a valid user on the file server to whom you want to grant trustee rights.
groupname	Specifies the name of a valid group on the file server that is to be granted trustee rights.

Rules and Considerations: You must be attached to a server before you can grant Trustee rights on the server.

Before you can grant rights to a user (or group), the user must exist on the network.

If you elect to grant rights to a user, you can grant rights to only one user at a time with each GRANT command.

If you revoke trustee rights, the user remains a trustee of the directory unless the user is removed from the trustee list.

When using more than one option in the *rightslist*, the options must be separated by a space.

Important Messages: None

Examples: The following example grants the Read, Write, File Scan, and Modify rights to the user TGENDREAU for the PUBLIC subdirectory on the file server TRAINING_SOLUTIONS:

```
GRANT R W F M FOR
TRAINING_SOLUTIONS\SYS:PUBLIC TO TGENDREAU
```

See Also: ATTACH, MAP, NETADMIN, REMOVE, REVOKE, RIGHTS, SECURITY, SESSION, SYSCON, TLIST

HALT

Purpose: To down an SFT III IOEngine, leaving the other IOEngine up and running.

Syntax: HALT

Rules and Considerations: Can only be used when the SFT III servers are mirrored or before SFT III servers are activated.

Examples: To run this command, type the following at the system prompt:

HALT

Important Messages: You will receive the Unknown command error message if you run this command from the MSEngine instead of from the IOEngine.

You will receive the following message if the primary and secondary servers are not mirrored before executing this command:

WARNING!!! Not every disk is remirrored. Answering yes may cause some volumes to dismount and open files to be lost. Are you sure you want to halt the primary server?"

Notes: None

A
B
C
D
E
F
G
H
I
J
K
L
M
N
O
P
Q
R
S
T
U
V
W
X
Y
Z

HCSS

Purpose: See list of *High Capacity Storage System* (HCSS) commands, and to view or change their current settings. Settings are case sensitive. Some settings also remain in memory until reset. The settings which are persistent (remain in memory) are as follows:

Upper Threshold

Lower Threshold

Migrate to Lower Threshold Hour

Migrate to Lower Threshold Minute

Polling Frequency

Marking Frequency

Syntax: HCSS *option = setting*

Options	Functions
Eject Media Override	Prevents ejection of the media in the jukebox. Set to either ON or OFF. OFF is the default.
Delete Through	Lets you specify that file deletions be placed in the queue immediately (OFF), or that you be notified of a successful deletion completed through the media (ON).
Migrate Unarchived Files	Lets you specify to migrate unarchived files (ON) or not (OFF).
Migrate Compressed Files Only	Lets you specify to migrate compressed files or files that cannot be compressed (ON) or not (OFF).
Minimum Time In Drive	Indicates minimum number of seconds one side of the media is active before it's switched to the other side. Default is 20. Range is 0 to 3,600.

Options	Functions
Maximum Time In Drive	Indicates maximum number of seconds one side of the media is active before it's switched to the other side. Default is 30. Range is 0 to 3,600.
Request Idle Time	Specifies length of time HCSS waits before switching from one side of the media from the drive to the other side. Default is 2. Can use any fraction of difference between Maximum and Minimum Time in Drive settings.
Migration	Sets migration ON or OFF.
Upper Threshold	Sets maximum total percentage of volume space used before files are migrated to magneto-optical disk. Default is 80. Range is 1 to 100. If set to 40, for example, migration starts when 60 percent of space remains.
Lower Threshold	Sets total percent of volume space used at which files are no longer migrated. Default is 50. Range is 0 to 99.
Migrate to Lower Threshold Hour	Specifies a time for files to be automatically migrated, regardless of the threshold. Default is 3 (the equivalent of 3 am). Range is 0 to 23.
Migrate to Lower Threshold Minute	Specifies the minute of the hour set in Migrate Lower Threshold Hour. Default is 0. Range is 0 to 59. Use to migrate at other than the exact hour.
Remaining Capacity Before Warning	Sets the remaining percentage of available disk space at which a notice that volume is getting full will be sent. Default is 20 (20 percent full). Range is 10 to 100.
Polling Frequency	Specifies how frequently HCSS checks all set thresholds. Default is 1 (minute). Range is 1 to 34,560 (minutes).
Marking Frequency	Sets frequency with which list of least recently used (LRU) directories managed by HCSS is created. Default is 30 (minutes). Range is 1 to 34,560.

continues

Options	Functions
Warning Frequency	Sets frequency of warning to be displayed for upper capacity threshold. Default is 2 (minutes). Range is 1 to 34,560.
Marked Files Limit	Sets limit on number of migratable files to be scanned for LRU lists. If zero (0), all migratable files are scanned, even if they are already migrated. Default is zero (0). Maximum is same as current number of files flagged as migratable.

Rules and Considerations: Enter the settings using the proper case.

Examples: To view the current list of HCSS parameters and their current settings, type the following at the system console prompt:

HCSS

To improve security by requiring notification of any files deleted through to the media, type the following at the system console prompt:

HCSS Delete Through=ON

Important Messages: None

Notes: You can see a current list of HCSS parameters and settings by entering the HCSS command with no options.

HELP

Purpose: Enables you to view online information about NetWare. HELP provides information on NetWare concepts, system messages, and utilities. You can use HELP to search for information in databases that are called *infobases*. The help system is based on Folio Corporation's product called VIEWS.

Syntax: HELP *command*

Option	Function
command	Specifies the command that you would like more information about

Rules and Considerations: The HELP utility is placed in the SYS:PUBLIC directory during NetWare installation. Use the cursor keys to move around in HELP, or use the following keys:

+ or -	Rotates windows without closing them
Tab	Moves the cursor to the next link
Shift+Tab	Moves the cursor to the previous link
Esc	Closes windows, exits a search, or exits the help utility

If your workstation has graphics support, you can use the left- and right-arrow keys to access graphics screens. If you have a mouse, point and click on the menu name. If you use a keyboard, access the menus with the following keystrokes:

Alt+S plus arrow keys	Enables you to scan menus
Alt+F	Accesses the file menu
Alt+D	Activates menus at the top of the screen

Following Links: Links are used to connect related information from different parts of the infobase. Use the Tab and Shift+Tab keys to position

A
B
C
D
E
F
G
H
I
J
K
L
M
N
O
P
Q
R
S
T
U
V
W
X
Y
Z

the cursor on the link symbol, and then press Enter. A new window will display the information. The link symbol is displayed as a triangle with the point facing down.

Searching for Words or Phrases: When the cursor is in a window and not under a link, press the spacebar. The search window appears and the query window will be active. Type the word or phrase you want to find (enclose phrases in quotation marks), and then press Enter. A new window appears displaying the segments of the infobase where the searched words occur. You can use the Tab or Shift+Tab keys to move through the information. If you want to see where the information appears in the complete infobase, press Enter at the marker.

The following operands illustrate the different types of searches you can specify. These operands can be typed in upper- or lowercase letters.

- **AND.** Use the AND operator to search for combinations of words. You can use a space between each word to represent the AND operator. For example, to search for all occurrences of print and queues together in a segment, type **print queues**.

- **OR.** Use the OR operator to search for occurrences of words either together in the segment or separately. Use the forward slash character (/) to represent the OR operator. For example, to search for all occurrences of the word print or queues or both in the same segment, type **print/queues**.

- **NOT.** Use the NOT operator to search for all occurrences of a word except when it is used with another specific word. Use the circumflex symbol (^) to represent the NOT operator. For example, to search for all occurrences of the word print, except when it is used with the word queues, type **print^queues**.

- **Wild-card character.** Use the asterisk (*) and question mark (?) to search for variations or words. To search for all words that begin with prin followed by more than one unspecified character, for example, type **prin***.

You also can perform a proximity search in a specific order to search for words that occur within a certain number of words from each other. Place the words that you want to search inside quotation marks, followed by the number of words that you want to search within. For example, to search for the words print and queues within four words, type **"print queues" 4**.

You can use the ampersand (&) symbol to perform a proximity search in any order. For example, to search for the words print and queues within five words in any order, type **"print queues"&5**.

You can print the information you find in HELP in several ways. Follow these steps to print information:

1. Press Ctrl+B to begin blocking text.

2. Use the cursor keys or a mouse to group the text together.

3. Press Ctrl+Printscrn after you block the text.

4. Select PRINT, highlight the desired settings, and then press Enter.

The block of text will print.

Blocks of information also can be sent to a file and printed later by choosing the menu option Redirect document to:.

Examples:

```
HELP NPRINT
```

Important Messages: None

Notes: If you need help using the HELP utility, press the F1 key inside the HELP window. There is an online instruction manual about the help system, see NFOLIO to access.

See Also: NFOLIO

A
B
C
D
E
F
G
H
I
J
K
L
M
N
O
P
Q
R
S
T
U
V
W
X
Y
Z

A
B
C
D
E
F
G
H
I
J
K
L
M
N
O
P
Q
R
S
T
U
V
W
X
Y
Z

HELP

Purpose: Displays help for the NetWare 4.0 internal console commands.

Syntax: HELP[*command*¦ALL]

Options: Replace command with the name of the console command for which you want help.

Including the ALL keyword causes HELP to display help information on all the commands one at a time.

Rules and Considerations: If no option is included, HELP will display a list of valid console commands.

Important Messages: None

Examples: To see a list of valid console commands, type the following at the System Console:

HELP

To get help on the BIND command, type the following at the System Console:

HELP BIND

To get help on the VERSION command, type the following at the System Console:

HELP VERSION

To get help on all the console commands, type the following at the System Console:

HELP ALL

Notes: None

HOLDOFF

Purpose: Enables you to close a file that you have been using so that other users can access it. HOLDOFF reverses the effects of the HOLDON command.

Syntax: `HOLDOFF` *`filename.ext`*

Options: None

Rules and Considerations: You do not need to use the HOLDOFF command unless you previously used the HOLDON command.

Examples:

```
HOLDOFF LOTUS.COM
```

The preceding example reverses the effects of the HOLDON command that was issued on the file LOTUS.COM.

Important Messages: None

See Also: HOLDON

HOLDON

Purpose: Holds a file open to prevent other users from changing it. Use of single user programs by more than one simultaneous user can cause program execution errors or data loss. Use HOLDON to lock files open, thus preventing multi-user access.

Syntax: HOLDON *filename.ext*

Options: None

Important Messages: None

See Also: HOLDOFF

INITIALIZE SYSTEM

Purpose: To enable multiprotocol router configuration by running and executing commands in the system NETINFO.CFG file. This command is usually run from the INITSYS.NCF file when the server is started.

Syntax: `INITIALIZE SYSTEM`

Rules and Considerations: Do not run this command if the system has already been initialized as errors will be displayed when the system attempts to rerun commands that have already been run.

Examples: None

Important Messages: None

Notes: None

A
B
C
D
E
F
G
H
I
J
K
L
M
N
O
P
Q
R
S
T
U
V
W
X
Y
Z

INSTALL

Purpose: Enables you to install the Novell operating system on a file server's hard disk drive(s). INSTALL is used to load the SYSTEM and PUBLIC files onto the file server; format and mirror hard disks; and create NetWare partitions, volumes, and file server boot files. In 4.10, it can also be used to modify the server's configuration, and to perform server maintenance. Use the F1 key for help while the install utility is active. Press F1 twice for an overview of the installation process.

Syntax: LOAD *path* **INSTALL**

Option	Function
path	Specifies the path or drive letter that the computer uses to load the install utility

Rules and Considerations: When installing NetWare 2.2, place the SYSTEM-1 disk into the disk drive before typing INSTALL. A menu with the following four options appears:

♦ Basic Installation

♦ Advanced Installation

♦ Maintain existing system

♦ Upgrade from NetWare 2.x

If you choose Advanced installation, you are prompted to provide information about the operating system mode, number of communication buffers, whether or not this machine will be the file server, if core printing is to be included, and information about network boards and disk channels.

For NetWare 3.1x and 4.10, before you can use the INSTALL command, you must execute the SERVER program from DOS to bring up the file server. The SERVER program can be found on the SYSTEM-1 disk. To execute the server command, insert the SYSTEM-1 disk in drive A and type SERVER. After you press Enter, information similar to the following appears on the screen:

```
Novell NetWare 386 v3.11
Processor speed: 265
(Type SPEED at the command prompt for an explanation of the speed
rating)
Total server memory: 8 Megabytes
Copyright 1988, 1990 Novell, Inc. All Rights Reserved.
File server name:
```

Give the file server a unique name from 2 to 47 characters. The name cannot contain a period or spaces. After you name the file server, you will be asked to enter an internal network number. The internal network number must differ from all other internal network numbers and network numbers assigned to all network card protocols and frame types. The internal network number is a hexadecimal number (base 16) that uses 0-9 and A-F. The number can be 1 to 8 digits long.

Next, load the appropriate disk driver modules. Type **LOAD** *path disk driver*. Your disk driver could be either an ISADISK for AT type controllers, DCB for Novell Disk Coprocessor Boards, PS2ESDI, PS2MFM, or PS2SCSI for PS/2 type controllers. The manufacturer of the disk controller you are using will provide you with these drivers. Consult your controller and disk drive documentation for more detailed information. Early versions of the ISADISK driver did not correctly support IDE drives. If your server won't recognize your drives, get newer drivers from your reseller or from NETWIRE. You also can find them on a CD-ROM called Novell Support Encyclopedias Professional, also known as NSEPRO. NSEPRO contains electronic copies of Novell manuals, technical bulletins, other Novell publications, and patch files. The NSEPRO CDs are updated monthly and available from Novell as a yearly subscription.

Now you are ready to load the INSTALL utility. To do so, insert the SYSTEM-2 disk in drive A in the file server and type **LOAD INSTALL** at the prompt.

NetWare 4.10 INSTALL lets you choose between a Basic or Custom installation when running the Install program.

A
B
C
D
E
F
G
H
I
J
K
L
M
N
O
P
Q
R
S
T
U
V
W
X
Y
Z

A
B
C
D
E
F
G
H
I
J
K
L
M
N
O
P
Q
R
S
T
U
V
W
X
Y
Z

Examples:

```
INSTALL
```

(or)

```
LOAD A:INSTALL
```

The first example runs the NetWare 2.2 Installation program. The second example loads INSTALL.NLM from drive A (see INSTALL in the "Essential Menu Utilities" section).

Important Messages: None

See Also: BIND, DISKSET, DISPLAY NETWORKS, LOAD, TRACK ON

IPX

Purpose: The Novell IPX (Internetwork Packet Exchange) driver is a peer-to-peer communication protocol that creates, maintains, and terminates connections between network devices, such as workstations, file servers, and routers. IPX.COM was replaced by IPX.EXE; both files combine the protocol driver and NIC's (network interface card) hardware driver into one file. Novell has discontinued support of these files (see VLM and IPXODI for more information on their replacement).

Syntax: **IPX** *options*

Option	Function
I	Enables you to see how the IPX file is configured. The I option does not load IPX into memory

Additional switches for the version 3 IPX include the following:

Option	Function
D	Displays hardware options
Onum	Loads IPX using the hardware option (num)
C=path filename	Use an alternate configuration file
?	Displays this help screen

Rules and Considerations: At each workstation, two components in combination often are called the shell.

The first component is the *Internetwork Packet Exchange/Sequenced Packet Exchange (IPX/SPX)* interface. This interface provides the protocol and the hardware communications routines that enable the workstation to communicate with its installed network card. The network card communicates with other network devices such as file servers.

The other component, called NETX, the actual shell, monitors DOS calls from the application that is running on the workstation. DOS calls are requests from an application to DOS for service, for example, read from a file. NETX determines whether the DOS calls are for the file server or the local PC. NETX is the component that connects the workstation to a server.

Important Messages: IPX is created by the WSGEN menu utility. A different IPX file must be created for each type of network card and each hardware option used on the network.

Notes: The following message appears if you type IPX after you loaded the IPX file at the workstation:

```
IPX/SPX already loaded
```

Each version of a network card requires its own driver. The drivers usually are supplied with the network card when you purchase it.

See Also: EMSNETX, IPXODI, NETX, PROTOCOLS, VLM, WSGEN, XMSNETX

IPX INTERNAL NET

Purpose: Defines the IPX address of the file server's internal (virtual) IPX network.

Syntax: `IPX INTERNAL NET` *networkaddress*

Options: Replace *networkaddress* with a hexadecimal number. The number can be a maximum of eight digits in length. If you use less than eight digits, the server will insert leading zeros to make this an eight digit number.

Rules and Considerations: This command can only be issued in the AUTOEXEC.NCF file.

The IPX internal network address must be a unique hexadecimal number between 0h and FFFFFFFFh. It cannot be 0h or FFFFFFFFh; these are reserved.

If this command is not found in the server's AUTOEXEC.NCF file, or the server does not have an AUTOEXEC.NCF file, or SERVER.EXE is started using the -NA switch to prevent execution of the AUTOEXEC.NCF file, the IPX internal network address will be prompted by the operating system during start-up.

Important Messages: None

Examples: Typically this command will be one of the first commands in the server's AUTOEXEC.NCF file and will look like this:

```
IPX INTERNAL NET BADCAFE
```

Notes: A little forethought in address selection can go a long way to creating a series of internal network addresses that is not only expandable, but easy to remember, too. Suggestions include such words as ACE, BEEF, CAFE, DAD, ETC, FEED, FACE, F0E, or others which can be created using the letters A through F, or the number zero (0) as if it were the letter o, as internal addresses and numbers as cable addresses. This helps make troubleshooting much easier because internal and cable addresses are easily identifiable.

A
B
C
D
E
F
G
H
I
J
K
L
M
N
O
P
Q
R
S
T
U
V
W
X
Y
Z

A
B
C
D
E
F
G
H
I
J
K
L
M
N
O
P
Q
R
S
T
U
V
W
X
Y
Z

A valid hexadecimal number may contain numbers 0-9 and letters A-F. Hexadecimal or hex is base 16 numbering system and the standard decimal numbering is a base 10 system. The following table shows the relation between the two systems.

Hexadecimal	Decimal
0	0
1	1
2	2
3	3
4	4
5	5
6	6
7	7
8	8
9	9
A	10
B	11
C	12
D	13
E	14
F	15

See Also: BIND, INSTALL

IPXODI.COM

Purpose: Provides the IPX protocol routines for both the Open Datalink Interface (ODI) DOS shell and the VLM DOS requester. Unlike IPX.COM or IPX.EXE, the ODI drivers and the VLMs separate the protocol from the hardware driver allowing multiple protocols to be used at the workstation. The use of ODI is in keeping with the Open Systems Interconnect (OSI) standard setup by the International Standards Organization (ISO).

Syntax: `IPXODI`

Options: None

Rules and Considerations: IDXODI is one of several programs that must be loaded to connect a workstation to the network. They are as follows:

LSL	Link Support Layer (LSL) is the intermediary between the protocol and the network card's driver.
LAN DRIVER	The LAN driver is the software that makes the link between hardware and software. The driver loaded is card specific. NE2000.COM is the LAN driver for a Novell NE2000 16-bit Ethernet card.
IPXODI	The IPX/SPX protocol stack file.
SHELL	The DOS shell is NETX.COM or NETX.EXE.
	or
REQUESTER	The DOS requester is VLM.

Important Messages: When possible, use the DOS requester VLM, which is replacing the DOS shell NETX and provides backward compatibility.

Examples: To load the ODI with DOS shell support, type the following commands:

```
LSL
NE2000
IPXODI
NETX
```

A
B
C
D
E
F
G
H
I
J
K
L
M
N
O
P
Q
R
S
T
U
V
W
X
Y
Z

To load ODI with DOS requester support, type the following commands:

```
LSL
NE2000
IPXODI
VLM
```

Notes: The VLM DOS requester must be used for access to 4.10 through the Directory Services. By using the ODI drivers, additional protocols can be loaded other than IPX.

See Also: IPX, BIND, LSL, NETX, VLM, WSGEN

IPXS

Purpose: Used by loadable modules that require STREAMS-based IPX protocol services.

Syntax: `LOAD` *path* `IPXS` [IPXSPX.CFG]

Option	Functions
path	Defines the full directory path to the directory that contains the loadable module. You can use DOS drive pointers such as A: or B:, or use a NetWare volume name. If no path is specified, the operating system assumes that the loadable module is in the SYS:SYSTEM subdirectory.
[IPXSPX.CFG]	Defines the SAP filtering, SAP and RIP timers, and any IPX configuration parameters that the user wishes to become defaults.

Rules and Considerations: Before you unload a protocol-stack NL, such as IPXS, unload all other loadable modules that might potentially use IPXS.

If your loadable module requires STREAMS-based IPX protocol services, load the following additional modules in the order listed before you load IPXS:

1. The STREAMS module

2. The CLIB module

3. The TLI module

Important Messages:

`LOAD IPXS`

The preceding example loads STREAMS-based IPX protocol services.

Notes: None

See Also: STREAMS

A
B
C
D
E
F
G
H
I
J
K
L
M
N
O
P
Q
R
S
T
U
V
W
X
Y
Z

KEYB

Purpose: Changes the keyboard type for the server's console.

Syntax: LOAD [*path*] **KEYB** [*options*]

Options: Replace path with the NetWare path to the NLM. By default NetWare will look in SYS:SYSTEM.

Replace options with the keyboard language type you want to use.

KEYB supports the following keyboard language types:

BELGIAN

CANADIAN FRENCH

DANISH

ENGLISH (United States)

FRENCH

GERMAN

ITALIAN

LATIN AMERICAN

NETHERLAND

NORWEGIAN

PORTUGESE

RUSSIAN

SPANISH

SWEDISH

SWISS FRENCH

SWISS GERMAN

UNITED KINGDOM

A
B
C
D
E
F
G
H
I
J
K
L
M
N
O
P
Q
R
S
T
U
V
W
X
Y
Z

Rules and Considerations: Loading KEYB with no options displays a list of available keyboards.

Important Messages: None

Examples: To set the keyboard to Spanish, type the following command at the System Console:

LOAD KEYB SPANISH

To get a list of available keyboards, type the following command at the System Console:

LOAD KEYB

To change from one language to another, unload the current keyboard type, then load the different keyboard type. To unload a keyboard type, use the following command:

UNLOAD KEYB Option

Notes: None

See Also: LANGUAGE

LANGUAGE

Purpose: Displays or changes the preferred NLM language used to present NLM screens, text, and so on at the server's console.

Syntax: **LANGUAGE** [*language_designation*] [*options*]

Option	Function
language_designation	Replace *language_designation* with the language name or ID number in which you want NLMs and console commands to appear.
options	Replace *options* with one of the following:
LIST	Displays a list of available languages.
REN id new_name	Renames a language specified by its ID number to the name specified by *new_name*.

Rules and Considerations: English is the default language for NetWare NLMs.

Using LANGUAGE with no language or options displays the current language.

NLMs and the operating system look to SYS:SYSTEM\NLS\ Language_ID_Number for their message files.

You can also rename a language by specifying the number of the language to be renamed, and then specifying the new name.

Important Messages: None

Examples: To set the language to Spanish, type the following command at the System Console:

LANGUAGE 14

or

LANGUAGE SPANISH

A
B
C
D
E
F
G
H
I
J
K
L
M
N
O
P
Q
R
S
T
U
V
W
X
Y
Z

A
B
C
D
E
F
G
H
I
J
K
L
M
N
O
P
Q
R
S
T
U
V
W
X
Y
Z

To get a list of available languages, type the following command at the System Console:

LANGUAGE LIST

To check the current language, type the following command at the System Console:

LANGUAGE

To rename the English language to something such as US, type the following at the system prompt:

LANGUAGE REN 4 US

Notes: NetWare 3.12 and 4.10 currently ship with five languages: English, French, German, Spanish, and Italian. Any additional languages you want to support require the installation of a language module that must be purchased separately from Novell. Additional language modules include Canadian French, Chinese, Danish, Dutch, Finnish, Japanese, Korean, Norwegian, Portuguese, Russian, and Swedish.

See Also: KEYB

LIST DEVICES

Purpose: Lists all physical devices recognized by the server. Also displays device information and, in 4.10, registers devices.

Syntax: `LIST DEVICES`

Options: None

Rules and Considerations: The following items are considered devices to a NetWare server: disk drives, tape drives, optical drives, and other miscellaneous storage devices.

Important Messages: None

Examples: To list all the devices recognized by the server, enter the following at the System Console:

`LIST DEVICES`

Notes: None

See Also: SCAN FOR NEW DEVICES

LISTDIR

Purpose: Lists subdirectories and information about their creation date, inherited rights mask, and your effective rights in them.

Syntax: `LISTDIR` `path options`

Option	Function
`path`	Specifies the directory path for which you want more information. The path can include the volume, directory, and subdirectory.
`option`	Specifies one or more of the following options:
`/Rights`	Lists the Inherited Rights Masks of all subdirectories in a specific directory.
`/Effective rights`	Lists the effective rights for all subdirectories of the specified directory.
`/Date or /Time`	Lists the date or time or both that a subdirectory was created.
`/Subdirectories`	Lists a directory's subdirectories.
`/All`	Lists all subdirectories, their Inherited Rights Masks, effective rights, and their creation dates and times.

Important Messages: None

Examples: To list all subdirectories, inherited rights masks, effective rights, and creation dates for everything in the WP51 directory, type the following command:

`LISTDIR TRAINING_SOLUTIONS\SYS:APPS\WP51 /A`

Notes: NetWare 4.10 uses the NDIR command with the /DO option.

See Also: FILER, RIGHTS, TLIST, NDIR

LOAD

Purpose: This command loads (links to the operating system) NetWare Loadable Modules (NLMs) at the file server console.

Syntax: `LOAD` *path* `NLM` *parameter*

Option	Function
path	Represents the full path to the directory that contains the loadable module. The path variable can begin with either a valid DOS drive letter or a valid NetWare volume name. If you do not specify a path and the SYS: volume has not been mounted, the operating system (OS) assumes that the NLM is in the default DOS partition or directory. After the volume SYS: has been mounted, the OS assumes the loadable module is in the SYS:SYSTEM directory.
NLM	Specifies the name of one of the following types of NLMs:

Type of NLM	File Extension
Disk drivers	*.DSK
LAN drivers	*.LAN
Name space	*.NAM
NLM utilities	*.NLM

Consult either Novell, your reseller, or a third-party dealer for other available NLM's.

parameter	Settings are specific to each NLM. Refer to the NLMs documentation for more information.

Rules and Considerations: To load modules automatically each time the server boots, store the appropriate LOAD commands in the

A
B
C
D
E
F
G
H
I
J
K
L
M
N
O
P
Q
R
S
T
U
V
W
X
Y
Z

AUTOEXEC.NCF or STARTUP.NCF file. See AUTOEXEC.NCF and STARTUP.NCF for more information.

All NLMs should be certified by Novell, Inc. If you run any third-party NLMs, check on NETWIRE, on the NSEPRO CD-ROM or with your Novell authorized reseller for a list of Novell approved NLMs. If you load a module that is not approved, your server might ABEND (an ABnormal END) and data can become corrupted. The DOMAIN command can be used to help protect your server from misbehaved NLMs under 4.10 only.

NLMs will not load under any of the following conditions:

♦ The server cannot find the loadable module.

♦ The server does not have enough free memory.

♦ The module is dependent on another module that is not loaded.

♦ You used an invalid parameter.

♦ LOAD is not entered before the module name.

♦ You used an invalid command in the NCF files.

Important Messages: With NetWare 4.10, if the NLM was loaded into the OS_Protected DOMAIN, all supporting NLMs also must be in that domain.

Examples: To load the industry standard disk drive that supports many different hard disk drive controllers, enter the following command:

```
LOAD ISADISK
```

Notes: An NLM links itself into the OS and allocates a portion of server memory for its own use.

Some NLMs will check the system memory for the existence of required NLMs at load time and automatically preload the required NLMs if necessary.

See Also: DOMAIN, INSTALL, MODULES, MONITOR, UNLOAD

LOGIN

Purpose: Accesses the named or default server and invokes your login script on that particular file server.

Syntax: LOGIN [*option*] [*fileserver¦tree/login_name*] [*scriptparameters*]

Option	Description
option	May be one or more of the following:
	/Script /NoAttach /Clearscreen
fileserver	Identifies the file server you want to log in to
tree	Identifies the NetWare Directory Services tree to which you want to log in
login_name	Specifies your user name or login name (account name, for example)
scriptparameters	Specifies the parameters set in your login script

The following are options for 4.10 only.

Option	Description
/NoScript	Does not run a login script, and does not automatically log out of other servers
/No Banner	Prevents the NetWare welcome banner from displaying
/NOSWAP	Specifies LOGIN is not to swap to extended or expanded memory, or to disk
/S path¦object name	(4.10) Specifies a particular login script, its location, and the object name of the object script that should be run

continues

A
B
C
D
E
F
G
H
I
J
K
L
M
N
O
P
Q
R
S
T
U
V
W
X
Y
Z

Option	Description
/Bindery	Specifies to log in under bindery emulation
/PRofile=	Specifies a particular profile script to use during the login process
/SWAP = *path*	Runs external commands from the login script and places them into expanded or extended memory, when path is provided
/TRee	Specifies to log in to a tree
/VER	Displays version information for this utility, and provides a list of the files needed by this utility to run
/?	Help, lists command line syntax

Rules and Considerations: Under NetWare 4.10, MAP also performs the functions of the ATTACH command and NLIST performs the functions of the SLIST command. Users on a 2.x or 3.x server can use the older SLIST and ATTACH commands on a 4.10 server if it has bindery emulation configured.

You can include a LOGIN command in your AUTOEXEC.BAT file. Then when you boot your workstation, it will attach itself to the logically closest file server. This becomes your default server.

If you automatically attach several servers simultaneously, you can synchronize your password on all the servers where you use the same login or user name. If you change the password, LOGIN prompts if you want to synchronize passwords on all servers.

If you enter LOGIN with no parameters, you are prompted for required parameters.

A LOGIN implies a LOGOUT, and thus logs you out of other servers. To access another server and remain logged in to your default server, use the ATTACH command instead.

Important Messages: To make troubleshooting easier, have a copy of LOGIN on a floppy in case the LOGIN directory gets corrupted.

Notes: The work station must connect to a server before running LOGIN.

Use SLIST to get a report of all servers on the network. SLIST also displays the default server. The default server's login directory is the file area you are reading LOGIN from.

If the password notification is set to Yes in 4.10, users are notified when their passwords will expire each time they log in. For older versions of NetWare, use the WRITE command with the variable "PASSWORD_EXPIRES" to notify users each time they login.

See Also: ATTACH, IPX, IPXODI, LOGOUT, NETX, SLIST

A
B
C
D
E
F
G
H
I
J
K
L
M
N
O
P
Q
R
S
T
U
V
W
X
Y
Z

A
B
C
D
E
F
G
H
I
J
K
L
M
N
O
P
Q
R
S
T
U
V
W
X
Y
Z

LOGOUT

Purpose: Logs you out of file servers to which you are attached.

Syntax: LOGOUT *fileserver options*

Options: Replace fileserver with the name of the server from which you want to log out. If you do not specify a file server, you will be logged out of all file servers to which you are attached.

If you want to see version information and a list of files used by the LOGOUT command, use the /VER option.

In 4.10, you can also use the /T option to log out of all servers in the NDS tree, but not log out of any NetWare 2.2 or 3.1x servers.

In 4.10, you can also use /? to view online help.

Rules and Considerations: When you log out of a file server, drive mappings to that server disappear. You must have a search drive mapped to the PUBLIC directory of at least one of the servers you are still attached to, or you cannot execute any NetWare utilities.

When logging out, change to drive F or make note of your current drive letter. The current drive letter will be the only one valid after issuing the LOGOUT command. If you log out from drive X, you must return to drive X to log in again because drive F will be invalid.

Important Messages: None

Example: To see the LOGOUT command's version number and a list of files required to run this utility, enter the following command:

LOGOUT /VER

See Also: ATTACH, CX, LOGIN, NLIST, SLIST

MAGAZINE

Purpose: Verifies that all magazine requests (such as Insert Magazine or Remove Magazine) have or have not been satisfied from the NetWare server.

Syntax: `MAGAZINE` *option*

Options: Replace *option* with one of the following:

Option	Function
INSERTED	Confirms that the requested magazine was inserted in response to an "Insert Magazine" console message
NOT INSERTED	Confirms that the requested magazine was not inserted in response to an "Insert Magazine" console message
REMOVED	Confirms that the requested magazine was removed in response to a "Remove Magazine" console message
NOT REMOVED	Confirms that the requested magazine was not removed in response to a "Remove Magazine" console message

Rules and Considerations: This command is designed for use with removable media when it is installed in the server for shared access. This would include CD-ROMs, read/write optical drives, and so on.

Important Messages: None

Examples: To inform NetWare that the requested magazine had been removed, type the following command at the System Console:

`MAGAZINE REMOVED`

To inform NetWare that the requested magazine had been inserted, type the following command at the System Console:

`MAGAZINE INSERTED`

Notes: None

See Also: CDROM, MEDIA

MAKEUSER

Purpose: This utility creates and deletes user accounts on a regular basis. MAKEUSER is commonly used to set up user accounts for new students each semester, to create accounts for temporary employees, or to batch add many users at once. Workgroup managers often use MAKEUSER to create their users.

MAKEUSER was incorporated into the NETADMIN utility for NetWare 4.10. See NETADMIN in the Essential Menu Utilities section.

Syntax: MAKEUSER

Options: None

Rules and Considerations: To create and delete users with the MAKEUSER command, you first must create a USR script file. This file contains the keywords necessary to create the user(s), assign rights, assign trustee restrictions, assign a home directory to new users, or delete existing users from the system.

To create or modify a USR script file, you must be in the directory where that file is located. You can use any ASCII text editor with USR files, but the file must be saved in ASCII format and have a USR extension.

You must process the USR file with MAKEUSER before the accounts are created or deleted.

The keywords used in a USR file to create and delete users in MAKEUSER are as follows:

#ACCOUNT EXPIRATION month, day, year

#ACCOUNTING balance, lowlimit

#CLEAR or #RESET

#CONNECTIONS number

#CREATE user name [option ...]

#DELETE user name

#GROUPS group

#HOME_DIRECTORY path

#LOGIN_SCRIPT path

#MAX_DISK_SPACE vol, number

#PASSWORD_LENGTH length

#PASSWORD_PERIOD days

#PASSWORD_REQUIRED

#PURGE_USER_DIRECTORY

#REM or REM

#RESTRICTED_TIME day, start, end

#STATIONS network, station

#UNIQUE_PASSWORD

Important Messages: If the USR file contains errors, you might see a message similar to the following:

```
Error  :  Line 001, Undefined keyword
Warning:  Line 002, Group expected
Please fix the error in the file and try it again.
```

Notes: Create a directory for all USR files. When you create a USR file, the MAKEUSER command places the file in the current directory.

See Also: UIMPORT, USERDEF

MAP

Purpose: Lists, creates, or changes logical drive mappings in the NetWare environment.

Rules and Considerations: You can have a maximum of 26 drive mappings, 16 of which can be search mappings. Search maps are created from the end of the alphabet in a descending order. The drive letter assigned to the search map is added to the DOS environment variable PATH.

When issued without parameters, MAP will display the current drive mappings.

When attempting to map a drive to a specified path, the path named in the MAP command must exist.

You must be attached to at least one file server before you can map drives to it.

Syntax: `MAP` `parameters drive:=path`

Options: `parameters` can be one of the following:

Option	Description
INSert	Allows you to change the order maps are searched by inserting a new search map between two existing search mappings
DELete	Deletes a drive mapping
REMove	Deletes a drive mapping
Next	Maps next available drive letter to the specified path
ROOT	Maps the drive as fake root (useful for Windows applications)
drive	The drive letter mapped to the directory you want to work with
path	Directory path you intend to work with

continues

A
B
C
D
E
F
G
H
I
J
K
L
M
N
O
P
Q
R
S
T
U
V
W
X
Y
Z

Option	Description
Change	A toggle that allows you to change a drive mapping from search to a regular map or vice versa
W	Master environment should not be changed
Physical	Maps to physical volume; must be used as the first or second option
No Prompt	MAP will not prompt when overwriting search or local drives; must be placed first or second on the command line
/Ver	Displays version information for this utility, and lists the files it needs in order to run

Important Messages: If a valid DOS drive is used in the MAP command, the user will be asked to verify overwriting the drive assignment. To regain access to the local drive, use MAP DEL driveletter, where driveletter is the local disk's identifier.

Examples: To list all currently active mappings, type the following:

MAP

Your screen display should resemble the following:

```
Drive A:  maps to a local drive
Drive B:  maps to a local drive
Drive C:  maps to a local drive
Drive D:  maps to a local drive
Drive E:  maps to a local drive

Drive F:= TRAINING_SOLUTIONS/SYS:
Drive G:= TRAINING_SOLUTIONS/SYS:USERS/GUEST /
SEARCH1:=Z:. [TRAINING_SOLUTIONS/SYS: /PUBLIC/]
SEARCH2:=Y:. [TRAINING_SOLUTIONS/SYS: /PUBLIC/
IBM_PC/MSDOS/V5.00]
```

To map a fake root for applications (such as Windows applications) that write files to or create directories from the root directory, type the following:

MAP ROOT H:=SYS:WINAPPS

If you then type MAP to view the active drive mappings, you should see the following screen display:

```
Drive A:  maps to a local drive
Drive B:  maps to a local drive
Drive C:  maps to a local drive
Drive D:  maps to a local drive
Drive E:  maps to a local drive

Drive F:= TRAINING_SOLUTIONS/SYS:
Drive G:= TRAINING_SOLUTIONS/SYS:USERS/GUEST
Drive H:= TRAINING_SOLUTIONS/SYS:WINAPPS /
SEARCH1:=Z:. [TRAINING_SOLUTIONS/SYS: /PUBLIC/]
SEARCH2:=Y:. [TRAINING_SOLUTIONS/SYS:/PUBLIC/
IBM_PC/MSDOS/V5.00/]
```

The space between the end of the path and the last slash indicates that this is a fake rooted drive.

To map an additional search drive, type the following:

MAP S16:=SYS:APPS\FOXPRO

By typing **S16:** for the search drive, you automatically assign it to the next available search drive position open.

Notes: Drive mappings are valid only for the active session unless you save them in your login script.

From a fake root, you cannot use the DOS CD (change directory) command to return to the original root directory. To change to the original root, you must remap the drive. Or you can type the CD command and reference the volume level as follows:

CD SYS:

The MAP command accepts either forward slashes (/) or backslashes (\) as part of the path. To maintain consistency with DOS, however, it is suggested you use only backslashes (\) in the path designation.

Under NetWare 4.10, mappings can be created by mapping to an NDS volume object. This allows you to map to servers and volumes not in the current NDS context. If you wanted to map to the directory

A
B
C
D
E
F
G
H
I
J
K
L
M
N
O
P
Q
R
S
T
U
V
W
X
Y
Z

APPS\LOTUS located in the CN=ACCT_SYS.OU=CORP.0=
MASTER_INC context, issue the following:

```
MAP G:=.ACCT SYS.CORP.MATER INC:APPS\LOTUS
```

To change the regular mapping of drive H to a search mapping, issue the
map command with the C option:

```
MAP C H
```

See Also: LOGIN, SESSION, SMODE

MATHLIB

Purpose: Loads a library of support routines, if your server has a math coprocessor (such as a 386 machine with a math coprocessor or a 486DX machine).

Syntax: `LOAD` *path* `MATHLIB`

Option	Function
path	Specifies the path to the directory containing the NLM. It can begin with either a DOS drive letter or a NetWare volume name.

Rules and Considerations: If you do not specify a path, the operating system assumes the NLM is in SYS:SYSTEM.

If you need MATHLIB, the following modules need to be loaded in the exact order listed as follows:

1. STREAMS

2. CLIB

3. MATHLIB

If you type LOAD MATHLIB, these additional modules are automatically loaded.

Important Messages: None

Notes: To make sure that the modules necessary for MATHLIB load automatically when the file server boots, add the following commands to the AUTOEXEC.NCF file.

LOAD STREAMS

LOAD CLIB

LOAD MATHLIB

See Also: CLIB, INSTALL, MATHLIBC, STREAMS

MATHLIBC

Purpose: Loads a library of support routines if your server does not have a math coprocessor (such as a 386 machine without a math coprocessor).

Syntax: `LOAD` *path* `MATHLIBC`

Option	Function
path	Represents the full path to the directory containing the NLM. It can begin with a valid DOS drive letter or NetWare volume name.

Rules and Considerations: You must load STREAMS and CLIB before you load MATHLIBC.

The following modules must be loaded in the exact order listed as follows:

1. STREAMS

2. CLIB

3. MATHLIBC

These modules will be automatically loaded when you issue the LOAD MATHLIBC command if they were not loaded prior to issuing this command.

If you do not specify a path, the operating system assumes that the NLM resides in SYS:SYSTEM. (Use SEARCH to set up additional paths for searching.)

Important Messages: None

Notes: To make certain that the NLMs necessary to support MATHLIB load when the file server boots, add the following commands to the AUTOEXEC.NCF file:

```
LOAD STREAMS
LOAD CLIB
LOAD MATHLIBC
```

See Also: CLIB, INSTALL, MATHLIB, STREAMS

MEDIA

Purpose: Verifies that all media requests (such as Insert Media or Remove Media) have or have not been satisfied from the NetWare server.

Syntax: `MEDIA` *option*

Options: Replace *option* with one of the following:

Option	Function
INSERTED	Confirms that the requested media was inserted in response to an "Insert Media" console message
NOT INSERTED	Confirms that the requested media was not inserted in response to an "Insert Media" console message
REMOVED	Confirms that the requested media was removed in response to a "Remove Media" console message
NOT REMOVED	Confirms that the requested media was not removed in response to a "Remove Media" console message

Rules and Considerations: This command is designed for use with removable media when it is installed in the server for shared access. This includes CD-ROMs, read/write optical drives, and so on.

Important Messages: None

Examples: To inform NetWare that the requested magazine had been removed, enter the following at the System Console:

`MEDIA REMOVED`

To inform NetWare that the requested magazine had been inserted, enter the following at the System Console:

`MEDIA INSERTED`

Notes: None

See Also: CDROM, MAGAZINE

MEMORY

Purpose: Views the total amount of the memory the operating system can address in the file server.

Syntax: MEMORY

Options: None

Rules and Considerations: NetWare 3.x and 4.10 address all memory installed in an EISA computer automatically. If you have either a Micro Channel or ISA computer, the operating system only addresses up to 16 MB of memory. Use the REGISTER MEMORY command to enable the operating system to address the memory above 16 MB.

If you have a PCI bus computer, NetWare 4.10 addresses up to 64 MB.

If you are using 16-bit cards in an EISA machine that need memory buffers in the first 16 MB of ram, you will need to utilize the REGISTER MEMORY command also.

Important Messages: None

Examples: To display all of the memory the operating system can address, type the following:

MEMORY

See Also: REGISTER MEMORY

MEMORY MAP

Purpose: Displays bytes of memory allocated to DOS as well as to the server. In NetWare 4.1 SFT III, also displays bytes of memory allocated to DOS, the IOEngine, and the MSEngine (or unclaimed memory if the MSEngine is not loaded when MEMORY MAP is run).

Syntax: MEMORY MAP

Rules and Considerations: In SFT III servers, MEMORY MAP must be run from the IOEngine. Otherwise, the MEMORY MAP command will be mistaken for the MEMORY command.

In NetWare 4.10, MEMORY MAP displays bytes of memory allocated to DOS and to the server's memory.

Examples: To display the number of bytes of memory used by DOS and the NetWare 4.10 server, type the following at the system console prompt:

MEMORY MAP

Important Messages: None

Notes: None

See Also: MEMORY

MENU

Purpose: Provides access to custom menus created using any ASCII text editor.

Syntax: MENU [*path*] *filename*

Options: Replace *path* with the drive letter and directory structure under which the filename is saved. Replace *filename* with the name of the menu file being called.

Rules and Considerations: If the menu file name has an MNU extension, the file name can be entered without that extension. If the file name ends with any other extension, the extension must be used when issuing the MENU command.

Important Messages: None

Notes: None

See Also: NMENU

MIRROR STATUS

Purpose: Displays status information for all mirrored logical partitions.

Syntax: `MIRROR STATUS` *partition*

Options: Include the partition to also see the partition's physical device number.

Rules and Considerations: None

Important Messages: MIRROR STATUS can return one of five messages about the status of mirroring at the server. Each is listed below:

`Not Mirrored`	The partition is not set up to be mirrored.
`Orphaned State`	The partition appears to have "lost" its mirrored partition. Check the mirroring configuration using the INSTALL utility. The configuration could be invalid or a drive might have failed and needs to be replaced.
`Fully Synchronized`	The mirrored partitions are identical and are functioning correctly.
`Out of Synchronization`	One of the partitions does not have the same data and remirroring has not begun.
`Being Remirrored`	The partitions are being remirrored currently. Percentage completed also will be displayed.

Options: To display the status of mirroring at the server, type the following at the System Console:

`MIRROR STATUS`

Notes: If your server is an SFT III server, you must run MIRROR STATUS from the MSEngine.

See Also: ABORT REMIRROR, INSTALL, REMIRROR PARTITION

A
B
C
D
E
F
G
H
I
J
K
L
M
N
O
P
Q
R
S
T
u
V
W
X
Y
Z

MODEM

Purpose: Interacts with the modem to allow commands to be directed specifically to the modem. This command is used with the LOAD RS232 command.

Syntax: MODEM *options*

Option	Function
@ *name*	Enables you to issue commands to the modem from within a file, instead of manually issuing the commands.
speed	Enables you to specify the baud rate of your modem.

Important Messages: None

See Also: RS232

MODULES

Purpose: Displays information about the modules currently loaded at the file server. You see the short name of the module, the long name of the module, and version information about your LAN and disk driver modules.

Syntax: `MODULES`

Options: None

Important Messages: None

See Also: LOAD, MONITOR

A
B
C
D
E
F
G
H
I
J
K
L
M
N
O
P
Q
R
S
T
U
V
W
X
Y
Z

MONITOR

Purpose: Tracks and displays the activities of all workstations that are logged in or attached to the file server. Also displays the activities of VAPs and enables you to see which files each station is using and possibly locking. MONITOR also displays the file server's utilization.

Syntax: `MONITOR station_number`

Option: Replace *number* with the station you want to monitor; six stations are displayed at one time. If you omit *number*, stations 1 through 6 are displayed by default. To see stations 7 through 12, enter any number in that range.

Rules and Considerations: Include a station number if you want to monitor the activities of one specific workstation. This information can be obtained using the FCONSOLE command.

The MONITOR command screen displays information on six stations at once.

MONITOR also displays the operating system version and the percentage of file server utilization.

When a workstation requests a transaction, MONITOR displays up to five files and a file status message. A file server running NetWare in dedicated mode also can display two status letters. File status also can have an identifier, and the request area often will display a message.

Important Messages: None

Examples: `MONITOR`

Notes: Execute MONITOR if you suspect an application has crashed at a particular workstation. The display might show W for 20 minutes on a small file, indicating a Write operation has locked the workstation.

Every file shown has an accompanying DOS task number to the left of the status field.

The request area to the right of each station number indicates the most recent file server request the workstation made. The following is a list of valid requests that NetWare might display:

```
Alloc Resource Record
Begin Trans File
Clear File
Clear File Set
Clear Record Set
Close File
Clr Phy Rec
Clr Phy Rec Set
Copy File
Create File
Dir Search
End of Job
End Trans
Erase File
Floppy Config
Get File Size
Lock File
Lock Phy Rec Set
Lock Record
Log Out
Log Pers File
Log Phy Rec
Log Record
Open File
Pass File
Read File
Rel Phy Rec
Rel Phy Rec Set
Rel Record Set
Rel Resource
Release File
Release File Set
Release Record
Rename File
Search Next
```

A
B
C
D
E
F
G
H
I
J
K
L
M
N
O
P
Q
R
S
T
U
V
W
X
Y
Z

A
B
C
D
E
F
G
H
I
J
K
L
M
N
O
P
Q
R
S
T
U
V
W
X
Y
Z

Semaphore
Set File Atts
Start Search
Sys Log
Unlock Record
Win Format
Win Read
Win Write
Write File

See Also: CLEAR STATION, FCONSOLE, OFF

MOUNT

Purpose: Places a volume in service. By mounting the volume, users have access to the information about that volume. The MOUNT command is used while the file server is running.

Syntax: `MOUNT` *volume_identifier* or *ALL*

Option	Function
volume_identifier	In NetWare 2.2, supply the volume number to be mounted. NetWare 3.x and 4.10 require you to supply the volume's name to be mounted.
ALL	Enables you to mount all volumes without specifying the names of each volume.

Rules and Considerations: If you have volumes that are not used often, it is wise to leave them dismounted until you need them. When you mount a volume, it uses file server memory; this lessens the amount of memory you have available for file caching. When a volume mounts, NetWare checks both copies of the FAT table to see if they match. NetWare also loads the FAT table into memory and then caches and indexes it.

Important Messages:

```
Volume  volume_name could NOT be mounted.
Some or all volume segments cannot be located.
```

This message is displayed if the volume you specified does not exist or has a problem.

```
Mirrored copies of the FAT don't match
Volume not mounted.
```

This message is displayed if there is an error encountered when comparing the two FAT tables. If you get this error, you should run VREPAIR.

A
B
C
D
E
F
G
H
I
J
K
L
M
N
O
P
Q
R
S
T
u
V
W
X
Y
Z

A
B
C
D
E
F
G
H
I
J
K
L
M
N
O
P
Q
R
S
T
U
V
W
X
Y
Z

Notes: Volume SYS must be mounted before any workstations can attach to or log in to the server. When volume SYS is mounted (using bindery emulation) on a 2.2, 3.1x, or 4.10 server, the binderies are opened. If the volume to be mounted is on CD-ROM, use the CD command, not the MOUNT command.

See Also: CD, DISPLAY VOLUMES, DISMOUNT, VREPAIR

MSERVER

Purpose: Loads the IOEngine on a NetWare 4.1 SFT III server.

Syntax: MSERVER *option*

Options	Functions
-ns	Loads the IOEngine without using the IOSTART.NCF file so that commands in the IOSTART.NCF file can be changed.
-na	Loads the IOEngine without using the IOAUTO.NCF file to let you change the modules loaded by the IOAUTO.NCF file.
-ns -na	Loads the IOEngine without using either the IOSTART.NCF or IOAUTO.NCF files.

Rules and Considerations: This command is run from the file server's DOS prompt. If no IOSTART.NCF file exists, and the -NS parameter is not used, you are prompted for an IOEngine name and IPX internal network number.

All parameters must be typed in lowercase.

Examples: To load the NetWare 4.1 SFT III IOEngine without running the IOSTART.NCF file, type the following at the file server DOS prompt:

MSERVER -ns

Important Messages: None.

Notes: None

A
B
C
D
E
F
G
H
I
J
K
L
M
N
O
P
Q
R
S
T
U
V
W
X
Y
Z

NAME

Purpose: Displays the name of the file server.

Syntax: NAME

Options: None

Rules and Considerations: When you invoke the NAME command, you see the name of the file server in a format similar to the following:

This is server TRAINING_SOLUTIONS

Important Messages: None

See Also: CONFIG, DISPLAY SERVERS, FCONSOLE, MONITOR, SLIST

NCOPY

Purpose: Copies one or more files from one location to another.

The NCOPY command works much like the DOS COPY command. The big difference between the two is that NCOPY performs the copy at the file server. The DOS COPY command reads data from the file server and then writes the data back to the file server over the network. The NCOPY command is much faster and does not slow down the network as much as the DOS COPY command would.

The NCOPY command is placed in the PUBLIC directory during installation.

Syntax: NCOPY *path* **FILENAME** *to path* **FILENAME** *option*

Leave a space between the source file name and the destination directory path. The NCOPY command supports wild-card characters and up to 25 directory levels. When the copied file lands in the destination directory, it retains the original's date and time.

Option	Function
/A	Copies only files that have the archive bit set. Will not reset the archive bit.
/C	Copies files without preserving the attributes or name space information.
/E	Copies empty subdirectories when you copy an entire directory with the /S option.
/F	Forces the operating system to write sparse files.
/I	Notifies you when attributes or name space information cannot be copied.
/M	Copies only files that have the archive bit set, and will reset the archive bit after copying.
/P	Preserves the current file attributes in version 2.2. If NCOPY is used without the /P, then attributes on the copied files are set to Non-Shareable, Read/Write.

Option	Function
/S	Copies all subdirectories and files in them.
/V	Verifies that the original file and the copy are identical.
/R	(4.10 only) Keeps compressed files compressed.
/RU	(4.10 only) Keeps compressed files compressed even when copying files to a storage medium that does not support compression.
/?	Displays usage guide.
/VER	Provides version information for this utility, and a list of files needed by this utility in order to run.

Rules and Considerations: You can use wild cards to copy more than one file at a time. The NCOPY command automatically preserves a file's attributes. The NCOPY command can copy to or from a local drive as well.

Important Messages: None

Examples: To copy all the dbf files from drive G: to drive H:, type the following:

```
NCOPY G:*.dbf H:
```

To copy all of the DAT files from the REPORTS directory to the ARCHIVE\JULY directory, type the following:

```
NCOPY SYS:DATA\REPORTS\*.DAT SYS:ARCHIVE\JULY
```

You then see the source and destination of the file as well as the names of the files being copied; it should resemble the following:

```
From        TRAINING_SOLUTIONS/SYS:DATA/REPORTS
To          TRAINING_SOLUTIONS/SYS:ARCHIVE/JULY
            MASTER.DAT to  MASTER.DAT
            MAILING.DAT to  MAILING.DAT
2 files copied.
```

See Also: FILER

A
B
C
D
E
F
G
H
I
J
K
L
M
N
O
P
Q
R
S
T
U
V
W
X
Y
Z

NCUPDATE

Purpose: Automatically updates workstation NET.CFG files with a new context when a container has been moved or renamed in the NetWare Directory Services tree.

Syntax: `NCUPDATE` *options*

Options	Functions
/?	Displays online help.
/VER	Provides information about the version number for this utility, and a list of files required by this utility in order for it to run.
/NP	Prevents the prompt to update the name context in the NET.CFG file from being displayed.

Rules and Considerations: Can be run from the command line, but is generally run from a container login script.

Use NetWare Administrator or NETADMIN to place the command to run this utility in the login script of the container.

Examples: To make certain all users who log in to a container have the NCUPDATE command run for them, place the following in the login script for the container:

```
IF LOGIN_ALIAS_CONTEXT = "Y" THEN BEGIN
        MAP INS S1:=fileserver/SYS:PUBLIC
        #NCUPDATE /NP
        MAP DEL S1:
END
```

In the preceding example, replace *fileserver* with the name of the file server whose SYS:PUBLIC path is being addressed.

Important Messages: None

Notes: None

See Also: NETADMIN

NDIR

Purpose: Lists detailed file and subdirectory information, including NetWare specific information, and can view information about files such as dates, size, owner, attributes, and archive information. The NDIR command can perform the following functions:

- ♦ List files and subdirectories

- ♦ Search a volume for a file

- ♦ List specific files

- ♦ Use wild cards to list related files

- ♦ Use an option to list or sort files

- ♦ Use several options to list or sort files

- ♦ List Macintosh files

- ♦ View information on directories such as owner, creation date, Inherited Rights Filter, and effective rights

Syntax: `NDIR` *path option*

Option	Function
path	Identifies the directory path leading to and including the directory and file you want to list. You can include a file chain of up to 16 file names.
option	Can be one of the following:
	Display options
	Attribute options
	Format options
	Restriction options
	Sort options

A list of the options follows. Use a space between multiple options.

/Files Only	Sorts and displays only files.
/SUB	Sorts and displays all subdirectories from your current path.
/Directories Only	Sorts and displays only directories.
/Continuous	Scrolls display continuously.
/?	Displays help.

The following display options are for 4.10 NetWare only.

/FInd	Displays the location of a file while using your current search drives as the search path.
/VOLume	Displays volume information.
/Volume SPAce	Displays space limitations that were placed on a volume.
/VERsion	Displays version information and provides a list of files required by this utility to run.

The attribute options are as follows.

RO	Lists files that have the read only attribute set.
SH	Lists files that have the shareable attribute set.
A	Lists files that have their archive attribute set. Files are displayed in the backup format, which lists the last modified and last archived dates. The archive flag is set whenever a file is modified.
X	Lists files that are flagged as execute only.
H	Lists files or directories that have the hidden attribute set.
SY	Lists files or directories that have the system attribute set.
T	Lists files that have been flagged as transactional.

The following attribute options work with version 3.1x and 4.10.

P	Lists files or directories that have the purge attribute set.

CI   Lists files flagged as copy inhibited. Restricts copy rights of users logged in from Macintosh workstation. Only valid for files.

DI   Lists files or directories flagged as delete inhibited. Prevents users from erasing directories or files even if they have the erase right.

RI   Lists files and directories flagged as rename inhibited. Prevents users from renaming directories and files even if they have the Modify right.

The following options work under 4.10 only.

DC   Lists files that are not compressed regardless of the volume default.

DM   Lists files that are not migrated to a secondary storage medium regardless of volume default.

IC   Lists files that are compressed immediately.

RW   Lists files that are read-write.

The following attribute will modify any of the preceding attributes regardless of version.

[NOT]   Can be used with all the previous attribute options to look for files that don't have the specified qualities.

The following are format options.

/R   Lists inherited and effective rights on files and subdirectories, lists rights filters, compression and migration status, and file attributes.

/D   Lists date and time information for files and directories.

The following options are for version 3.1x and 4.10 only.

/MAC   Lists Macintosh subdirectories or files in a search area. When you list only Macintosh files or subdirectories, they appear with their full Macintosh names.

/LONG   Lists all Macintosh, OS/2, and NFS long file names for the file under all loaded name spaces in a given search area.

A
B
C
D
E
F
G
H
I
J
K
L
M
N
O
P
Q
R
S
T
U
V
W
X
Y
Z

The following options are version 4.10 specific.

/COMP	Lists file and compression sizes.
/DE	Lists specific name space information.
/DA	Lists when files were last accessed, updated, archived, created, and copied.

This list of restriction options enables you to view files according to owner, date, or size. All options can use the [NOT] to list files that do not qualify.

/OW[NOT] EQ *user*	Lists files not created by a specific user.
/SI[NOT] GR ¦ EQ ¦ LE number	Lists file sizes that are not greater than, equal to, or less than a certain number.
/UP[NOT] BEF ¦ EQ ¦ AFT *mm-dd-yy*	Lists files not last updated on, before, or after the date specified.
/CR[NOT] BEF ¦ EQ ¦ AFT *mm-dd-yy*	Lists files not created on, before, or after the date specified.
/AC[NOT] BEF ¦ EQ ¦ AFT *mm-dd-yy*	Lists files not last accessed on, before, or after the specified date.
/AR[NOT] BEF ¦ EQ ¦ AFT *mm-dd-yy*	Lists files not archived on, before, or after the specified date.

The following list includes available sort options.

/SORT SI	Sorts display by file size from least to greatest.
/SORT CR	Sorts display by creation date for earliest to latest.
/SORT OW	Sorts display alphabetically by owner names.
/SORT AC	Sorts display by last accessed date from earliest to latest.
/SORT AR	Sorts display by last archive date from earliest to latest.
/SORT UP	Sorts display by last update from earliest to latest.

`/SORT UN`	Stops all sorting.
`[REV]`	Can be used by all proceeding sort options to reverse the sort order.

Rules and Considerations: Use a forward slash (/) before the first element of the option list and backslashes (\) in path names. Each NDIR command can include up to 16 file names.

Important Messages: None

Examples: To list only files in all subdirectories on the NetWare volume SYS, type the following:

`NDIR SYS:*.* /SUB FO`

The FO option excludes the listing of any subdirectory names found during the directory search.

To view all files in the current path by creation date from the latest to the earliest (reverse order), type the following:

`NDIR *.* /REV SORT CR`

Notes: You can combine several restriction options in a single NDIR command line. For a full listing of all options and logical operators supported, use NDIR /HELP or refer to the documentation included with NetWare.

See Also: FILER, FLAG, GRANT

A
B
C
D
E
F
G
H
I
J
K
L
M
N
O
P
Q
R
S
T
U
V
W
X
Y
Z

NETBIOS

Purpose: Enables workstations to run applications that support IBM's NETBIOS networking calls. You also can view NetWare NETBIOS version information, determine whether NETBIOS has been loaded, determine which interrupt it is using, or unload NETBIOS.

Syntax: NETBIOS *options*

Option	Function
I	Views version information, whether NETBIOS has been loaded, and which interrupt it is using. Using this switch will not reload NETBIOS.
U	Unloads NETBIOS from memory.

Important Messages: This is not the true IBM NETBIOS protocol; it is an emulator that runs on top of IPX.

Examples:

NETBIOS

Notes: The functioning of the NETBIOS emulator can be modified with options in the NET.CFG ASCII configuration file.

See Also: IPX, IPXODI, NETX

NETX

Purpose: NETX is the DOS shell that provides an interface between the application and DOS. NETX intercepts all interrupt 21h DOS requests and inspects each one. After inspection, the shell either passes the request to the DOS interrupt routine or keeps it and converts the request into the appropriate NCP request, and sends it to IPX/SPX for transmission to the file server.

Older versions of the shell included NETx.COM. The X in NETX.COM is replaced with the version of DOS you are using at the workstation—NET3.COM for DOS 3.x, NET4.COM for DOS 4.x, and NET5.COM for DOS 5.x. There is a generic version of NETx.COM called NETX.COM. The newest version of NETX 3.26 has an EXE extension.

Syntax: `NETX option`

Option	Function
/I	Displays information about the shell type and the revision level of the NETx file.
/U	Unloads the NETx shell from the workstation's memory. NETx must be the last terminate-and-stay-resident (TSR) program loaded.
PS=*servername*	Specifies your preferred server. The shell attempts to attach you to the server you specify rather than the first available.

Rules and Considerations: NETX must be loaded after IPX.COM has been loaded.

Important Messages:

`Not running on top of DOS 3.x.`

This message means you tried to load the wrong version of NETX. Use the VER command to find the version of DOS you are using and execute the proper NETX command. If you are running DOS version 5 or 6 and get this message, you need to upgrade to a newer NETX or switch to VLMs.

See Also: EMSNETX, IPX, IPXODI, XMSNETX

A
B
C
D
E
F
G
H
I
J
K
L
M
N
O
P
Q
R
S
T
U
V
W
X
Y
Z

A
B
C
D
E
F
G
H
I
J
K
L
M
N
O
P
Q
R
S
T
U
V
W
X
Y
Z
.

NLIST

Purpose: Enables users to view information about NDS objects such as users, groups, servers, and so on. Also enables users to search on objects and/or their properties.

Syntax: NLIST [*classtype*] [=*objectname*] [WHERE [*property*] [*operator*] [*value*]] [/*options*]

Options: Replace classtype with the object's NDS type (or class) such as AFP SERVER, ALIAS, COMPUTER, COUNTRY, DIRECTORY MAP, GROUP, NETWARE SERVER, ORGANIZATION, ORGANIZATIONAL ROLE, ORGANIZATIONAL UNIT, PRINT SERVER, PRINTER, PROFILE, QUEUE, USER, or VOLUME. The * character may also be used to indicate all object classes.

Replace =objectname with the name of the object for which you are searching or about which you want to view information. The * character also may be used to indicate all objects in this class.

WHERE can be used to narrow a search, but must be used with property, operator, and value to do so. The property will vary based on the NDS object being queried. The operator keyword can be replaced by EQ (equals), LT (less than), GT (greater than), NE (not equal), LE (less than or equal to), or GE (greater than or equal to). The value needs to be appropriate for the property being queried (for example, Password Length requires a numeric value) and can be a single value or a range of values.

PROPERTY displays the value of a specific property. The property will vary based on the NDS object being queried.

NLIST supports the following **Options:**

/CO= (Context)	Determines in what context the search will be conducted or begin.
/A (Active)	When used with the classtype USER, displays users who are currently logged in.
/D (Details)	Displays all the object's properties.
/N (Name)	Displays the object's names.

/SHOW (property)	Displays an object's specified property.
/TREE	Displays all tree names that are visible for this login.
/S (Subcontainers)	Broadens the search to include subcontainers.
/B=servername (Bindery)	Used to perform queries and actions on a bindery-based server (NetWare 2.x- or 3.1x-based). Replace servername with the file server's name.
/C (Continuous)	Does not pause after displaying a screen full of information.
/? (Help)	Displays online help for NLIST.
/VER (Version)	Provides version information and displays a list of all files needed by this utility in order to run.

Rules and Considerations: The NLIST command can be used without being logged in. All you need is an attachment to the NDS system.

NLIST can only be used to query NDS information on workstations running the NetWare DOS Requester (VLM.EXE). It can query only bindery information on workstations running the NetWare shell (NETX.EXE).

On a bindery-based system NLIST can only search for GROUP, QUEUE, SERVER, USER, and VOLUME.

Use quotation marks around properties that contain a space (for example, "Network Address").

Examples: To list all servers throughout the entire NDS structure running NetWare 4.10, type:

NLIST SERVER WHERE VERSION = 4.10 /CO=[ROOT] /S

To list all active users throughout the entire NDS structure, type the following:

NLIST USER /A /CO=[ROOT] /S

To list all active users in the current context, type the following:

NLIST USER /A

To list all the properties of user JACOB (who is in the current context), type the following:

```
NLIST USER=JACOB /D
```

To list all alias objects throughout the entire NDS structure, type the following:

```
NLIST ALIAS /CO=[ROOT] /S
```

Notes: NLIST is syntax particular. If you have problems getting a search to occur correctly, try viewing the online help through the NLIST /? option to make sure you have the command syntax correct.

See Also: CX, FCONSOLE, FILER, NETX, SLIST, USERLIST

NMAGENT.NLM

Purpose: Manages LAN drivers by collecting and storing information about them as they are loaded. The following three resources are tracked:

Network Management Triggers

Network Management Managers

Network Management Objects

Syntax: `LOAD` *path* `NMAGENT`

The path should be specified only if the NMAGENT.NLM file is not in the SYS:SYSTEM directory.

Options: None

Rules and Considerations: The NMAGENT (Network Management Agent) command must be loaded prior to any LAN drivers being loaded to enable it to register and track LAN drivers. If NMAGENT has not been loaded, NetWare will attempt to load NMAGENT before it honors a request to load a LAN driver.

Examples: To load NMAGENT from the SYS:LOGIN directory, type the following:

`LOAD SYS:LOGIN/NMAGENT`

To load NMAGENT from the SYS:SYSTEM directory of file server FS1, type the following:

`LOAD NMAGENT`

Notes: To see the resources tracked by NMAGENT use the Resource Utilization option of MONITOR.

See Also: LOAD

A
B
C
D
E
F
G
H
I
J
K
L
M
N
O
P
Q
R
S
T
U
V
W
X
Y
Z

NMENU

Purpose: Runs customized menus from a user's workstation.

Syntax: `NMENU menuname`

Options	Functions
menuname	Replace this option with the name of the menu to be run. The menu must have a DAT extension.
/?	Used without a menu name. It displays online help.

Rules and Considerations: The menu (with a .DAT extension) must already exist and be accessible to the user (user must have Read and File Scan rights to the directory containing the menu) from the workstation.

Examples: To run a menu file called USER.DAT, with a search drive already set to the container where this menu can be found, the user types the following:

`NMENU USER`

Important Messages: None

Notes: None

See Also: EXIT, MENU

NPAMS

Purpose: Loads the NPAMS (*NetWare Peripheral Architecture Mirrored Server*) module on a NetWare SFT III server. This module must be loaded to mount a CD-ROM as a NetWare volume.

Syntax: LOAD NPAMS

Rules and Considerations: Used only when mounting a CD-ROM volume on a NetWare SFT III server. It must be loaded in the MSEngine after loading the CD-ROM driver, and the NPAIO.DSK disk driver NLM in the IOEngine.

Examples: Type **LOAD NPAMS** to load this NLM on a NetWare SFT III server.

Important Messages: None

Notes: None

A
B
C
D
E
F
G
H
I
J
K
L
M
N
O
P
Q
R
S
T
U
V
W
X
Y
Z

NPATH

Purpose: Allows a user to view the search path currently set for NetWare drives.

Syntax: **NPATH** *uname fname /option*

Options	Functions
uname	Replace with a utility name.
fname	Replace with either the message or a Unicode file name when you see a message indicating that a message file is missing. Message files end with .MSG, .HEP, .IDX, or .XLT.
/option	Replace with any of the following options:
A (All)	Displays the path for all occurrences of the specified file.
D (Details)	Provides language, version, date, and time information for the specified file.
UNI	Lists paths to Unicode files.
UNI D	Displays code page and country code for the workstation, list of Unicode files needed to run the utility, and path to the files.
?	Displays online help.
VER	Displays the utility's version number and a list of files it requires in order to run.

Rules and Considerations: You can search for multiple files by including all of the file names (separate each one with a comma).

If a Unicode file is specified and no extension is given, the utility defaults to the country code set for this workstation.

This utility can be run without Unicode files.

Examples: To see all occurrences of SEND.MSG, type the following at the workstation prompt:

`NPATH SEND.MSG /A`

To also see the version number and other information for the SEND utility, type the following at the workstation prompt:

`NPATH SEND.MSG /A /D`

Important Messages: None

Notes: None

A
B
C
D
E
F
G
H
I
J
K
L
M
N
O
P
Q
R
S
T
U
V
W
X
Y
Z

NPRINT

Purpose: Spools a DOS text file from disk to a NetWare print queue. The NPRINT command is the NetWare substitute for the DOS PRINT command.

Syntax: NPRINT *filespec options*

Option	Function
Banner=*banner name*	Determines whether a banner (a word or phrase up to 12 characters) is printed. Spaces are entered by using the underscore character (above the minus on most keyboards). The default is the name of the file you are printing.
Copies=n	Specifies the number of copies to print from 1 to 999 4.10 allows up to 65,000.
Delete	Deletes a file immediately after it is printed. 4.10 uses DEL instead of D.
Form=name	Specifies the name or number of a previously defined form. The default is the form specified in your default print job configuration if it has been defined. 4.10 default is job 0.
FormFeed	Sends a form feed to the printer after the job has printed. The default is enabled. 4.10 uses FF instead of F.
Job=jobname	Specifies which print job configuration to use. Print job configurations can be created using PRINTCON. A single print job configuration can define the settings for all of the options for NPRINT with a single option.
NAMe=username	Specifies the name that appears on the top part of the banner page. The default is the user's login name.
NoBanner	Prints without the banner page. The default is for the banner page to print.

Option	Function
/? or /H	Displays initial online help screen.
/ALL	Displays all help screens when uses with the /? or /H option.
Details	Displays a job's printing parameters.
HOLD	(4.10) Holds the sent print job in the queue until released using PCONSOLE or NetWare administrator.
NoFormFeed	Does not send a form feed to the printer after the job has printed. The default is to send a form feed to the printer after a job has printed.
NoNOTIfy	Prevents the operating system from notifying you when a print job has finished printing. (This option is only necessary if NOTIfy is enabled in your print job configuration and you want to ignore it.)
NoTabs	Stops NetWare from altering your tabs before they are sent to the printer. Also called "byte stream." NT is the default.
NOTIfy	Notifies you when the print job has been sent to the printer. Notify is the default in 4.10.
Queue=*queuename*	Identifies which queue the job is sent to. Queues can be defined with PCONSOLE.
Server=*servername*	Specifies which server the print job should be sent to for printing. The default is the current server.
Tabs=*n*	Indicates the number of spaces between tabs, ranging from 0 to 18. The default is 8 spaces.
Verbose	(4.10) Displays more information about printers, print queues, and job configuration than the show option.
J=name	(4.10) Specifies a different print job to use other than the default.
Printer	(4.10) Indicates to which printer object the print job is redirected.
/VER	Displays version information, and provides a list of files required by this utility in order to run.

A
B
C
D
E
F
G
H
I
J
K
L
M
N
O
P
Q
R
S
T
U
V
W
X
Y
Z

A
B
C
D
E
F
G
H
I
J
K
L
M
N
O
P
Q
R
S
T
U
V
W
X
Y
Z

Rules and Considerations: To use the NPRINT command, NetWare printing must be configured and working. To configure NetWare printing, refer to the PCONSOLE, PRINTCON, PRINTDEF, and NetWare Administrator utilities.

If you execute NPRINT with the filespec to print and no options, the file will be sent to the print queue specified in the default print job configuration. If no default print job configuration has been set, the print job will be sent to the name of your default queue; see the SPOOL command.

Print job configurations are created with the PRINTCON menu utility program.

Forms should be defined prior to their specification in a print job. The PRINTDEF menu utility is used to create custom forms.

Important Messages:

`Access to the server FS1 denied.`

This error occurs if you attempt to use NPRINT to print to server FS1 using the FS1 option, and you were denied access to the server. The GUEST account usually is used to attach to another server for printing purposes. If the GUEST account has a password assigned, you will get this error message.

To correct the error, attach to the server you are trying to print from and supply your correct user name and password for that server, or get the supervisor to remove the password requirements for the GUEST user.

`Illegal banner specification. (length 1 - 12)`

This error occurs if you attempt to use the `banner=` option without entering a banner name, or if you enter a banner longer than 12 characters.

To print a print job without a banner, use the NB option instead of trying `banner=`(nothing).

Examples: To send 10 copies of the OLDMEMO.TXT file in the root directory of drive A: to the printer serviced by the print queue HPLASER, type the following:

`NPRINT A:\OLDMEMO.TXT Q=HPLASER C=10 NB NOTIFY`

The print job prints without a banner, and the user is notified when the print job has been completely sent to the printer.

To send one copy of the MYMEMO.TXT file in the current directory to the printer serviced by PRINTQ_1, type the following:

```
NPRINT MYMEMO.TXT Q=PRINTQ_1
```

The print job prints with a banner showing the user's name on the upper half and MYMEMO.TXT on the lower half. The user will not be notified when the print job is completed.

To send the file 123DATA.PRN to print using predefined settings from a print job configuration called TOSHIBA, type the following:

```
NPRINT 123DATA.PRN J=TOSHIBA
```

This print job configuration contains settings for tabs, notification, form feeds, banners, copies, and so on. Print job configurations are created with the PRINTCON utility.

Notes: Use the NT (No Tabs) option when sending anything other than straight ASCII text. By using NT you tell NetWare not to translate the print job. This is sometimes referred to as sending a byte stream file.

Be careful when using the Delete option while printing a file you cannot reproduce. In the case of a paper jam, or even in some instances when a printer is turned off, when you send something to its print queues, you could be left without your printout and without the file necessary to re-create the printout.

Use the NB (NoBanner) option when sending EPS (Encapsulated PostScript) files to a PostScript printer to be certain that the banner information does not interfere with the printing of the postscript information. The NT option should be used as well.

Use the NFF option when the file you are printing contains a form feed as the last character. If so, an extra blank page is printed after your print file. If this is the case, print the file with the NFF option. Otherwise, do not use this option as most printers require some type of form feed command at the end of a job in order to print out the last page when it does not contain a full page of text or graphics.

Use PCONSOLE to cancel erroneous print jobs that you have started printing using NPRINT.

See Also: CAPTURE, ENDCAP, PCONSOLE, PRINTCON, PRINTDEF, SPOOL

A
B
C
D
E
F
G
H
I
J
K
L
M
N
O
P
Q
R
S
T
U
V
W
X
Y
Z

NVER

Purpose: Reports the versions of NetBIOS, IPX/SPX, LAN driver, workstation shell, workstation DOS, and file server operating system for your file server and workstation. When run on an OS/2 workstation NVER will display information about the OS/2 requester.

Syntax: NVER

Option	Function
/?	Displays NVER help
/VER	Provides version information and a list of files needed by this utility for it to run
/c	Continuous, disables pausing at the end of each screen of information

Examples:

NVER

The NVER displays the following sample output when run from a workstation using the DOS shell NETX:

```
NETWARE VERSION UTILITY, VERSION 3.12
IPX Version: 3.02
SPX Version: 3.02

LAN Driver: NetWare Ethernet NE2000 V1.03EC (891227) V1.00
            IRQ = 2, I/O Base = 340h, no DMA or RAM

Shell:    V3.10 Rev. A
DOS:      MSDOS V5.00 on IBM_PC

FileServer: FS1
Novell Dedicated NetWare V2.2(100) Rev. A (02/11/91)
```

When run on a workstation using the DOS requester VLM, the NVER
utility displays information similar to the following:

```
DOS:    V5.00
Link Support Layer:  Version 2.01
Lan Drivers:
Board 1:             Intel EtherExpress 16 Ethernet Adapter
Version:             2.30
Frame type:          ETHERNET_802.2
Maximum frame size:  1514 bytes
Line speed:          10 Mbps
Interrupt number:    5
Port number:         0320-032f
Node address:        [AA001B1561]
Protocol Stack:
Description:         IPX Internetwork Packet Exchange
Version:             2.11
Network address:     [04311100]
Binding Information: Board 1 Protocol ID = 0
IPX API version:     3.30
SPX API version:     3.30
VLM: Version 1.02 Revision A using Extended Memory
Attached file servers:
Server name: NW40FS01
Novell NetWare v4.10 (July 12, 1993)
```

Notes: Use DOS redirection (>) to redirect NVER output to a file or
printer. You will find the version information handy when trying to
diagnose software problems or find differences between two workstations.

See Also: FCONSOLE, IPX, MONITOR, NETX, SYSCON

A
B
C
D
E
F
G
H
I
J
K
L
M
N
O
P
Q
R
S
T
U
V
W
X
Y
Z

NWUNPACK

Purpose: Used to decompress an individual file from the installation disks or CD-ROM.

Syntax: **NWUNPACK** *source_path:filename destination_path:filename*

Option	Function
source_path	Specify the full path indicating where the file to be unpacked is currently located
destination_path	Specify the full path to the target directory where you want the file being unpacked placed
filename	The first reference is to the name of the file to be unpacked, and the second reference is the name the file is to use once it is unpacked

Examples:

NWUNPACK a:VNETWARE.386 C:\windows\VNETWARE.386

The preceding example will unpack the VNETWARE.386 file from a disk in drive A. The file will be placed in the windows directory of drive C.

Important Messages: None

See Also: NWXTRACT

NWXTRACT

Purpose: Expands and copies files from the installation CD-ROM or disks to a network or local disk.

Syntax: `NWXTRACT` *path filename* ¦ *groupname* *[destination]* *[/option]*

Option	Description
path	Must supply the DOS path to the master data file (FILES.DAT).
filename	Replace *filename* with the name of the file you want to extract.
groupname	Extract or replace *groupname* with the group of files you want to extract. A list of valid group names can be obtained from the electronic text online help system.
destination	Replace destination with the DOS path to where you want the extracted files placed.
option	Replace *option* with one or more of the following:
	S (Server) — Copies the files to their normal location (SYS:SYSTEM, SYS:PUBLIC, and so on) on the specified server.
	T (Type) — Specifies the type of file to be extracted such as DOS, MAC, OS2, SER (server), Unix, and WIN (windows).
	VER — Provides information about the version and displays a list of files needed by this utility to run.
	? (Help) — Provides online help information.

A
B
C
D
E
F
G
H
I
J
K
L
M
N
O
P
Q
R
S
T
U
V
W
X
Y
Z

Examples: To extract NETADMIN.EXE from the CD-ROM drive installed as DOS drive G: and place it in its normal place on the server, type the following:

```
NWXTRACT G:NETADMIN.EXE /S=NW40FS01
```

To view online help, type:

```
NWXTRACT /?
```

See Also: NWUNPACK

OFF

Purpose: Clears the file server console screen.

Syntax: OFF

Options: None

Examples:

OFF

Important Messages: None

Notes: Using OFF to clear an active NetWare console screen adds to the life of your video display and increases performance slightly.

See Also: CLS, MONITOR

PAUDIT

Purpose: Displays the system's accounting records including login time, logout time, service charges, and intruder detection information.

Syntax: `PAUDIT`

Options: None

Rules and Considerations: To use PAUDIT, the accounting services first must be installed on your file server using SYSCON.

Examples: To display systems information, type the following:

`PAUDIT`

The screen returns information such as the following:

```
12/15/92 21:34:37  File server FS1
      NOTE: about User DKLADIS during File Server services.
      Login from address 99000001:00001B0ACD9C.
12/15/92 22:40:07  File Server FS1
      NOTE: about User DKLADIS during File Server services.
      Logout from address 99000001:00001B0ACD9C.
12/16/92 7:49:12  File Server FS1
      NOTE: about User SUPERVISOR during File Server services.
      Login from address 99000001:0080C820A5FB.
12/16/92 9:23:56  File Server FS1
      NOTE: about User SUPERVISOR during File Server services.
      Logout from address 99000001:0080C820A5FB.
12/16/92 9:24:36  File Server FS1
      NOTE: about User LBUCK during File Server services.
      Login from address 99000001:00001B0ACD9C.
```

Important Messages: None

Notes: PAUDIT.EXE is located in SYS:SYSTEM. Make sure you change to SYS:SYSTEM before you try to run PAUDIT.

Press Pause on newer 101-key keyboards to stop the scrolling, or press Ctrl+S on older keyboards.

A
B
C
D
E
F
G
H
I
J
K
L
M
N
O
P
Q
R
S
T
U
V
W
X
Y
Z

You can redirect output from PAUDIT to a file with the DOS redirection operator (>), such as **PAUDIT > TODAY.AUD**.

You can reset the accounting detail by erasing the NET$ACCT.DAT file in the SYS:SYSTEM directory.

See Also: ATOTAL

PAUSE

Purpose: Suspends execution of an NCF file until a key is pressed.

Syntax: `PAUSE`

Rules and Considerations: Typically used in NCF files when you want to suspend further execution until a key is pressed.

Examples: The following is an example of using the PAUSE command in an NCF file:

```
LOAD MONITOR
RESET ROUTER
PAUSE
DISPLAY NETWORKS
PAUSE
CLS
```

Notes: Functionally equivalent to the PAUSE command used in batch files under DOS.

See Also: ECHO OFF, ECHO ON, REM

PING

Purpose: Load a module to send an ICMP echo request packet to an IP node, in order to determine if a specific IP node can be reached on your internetwork.

Syntax: `LOAD PING`

Rules and Considerations: When prompted, provide the host name or IP address in the "Host Name" field. You also can specify the number of seconds between transmissions, and the size of the packets to be sent. Specify packet size in bytes. Pressing the Escape key then starts the sending of packets.

Examples: To load this module, type the following at the file server console:

`LOAD PING`

Important Messages: None

Notes: To stop the sending of packets, you must press the Escape key a second time and exit the PING module.

PRINTER

Purpose: The PRINTER console command is used to configure printers and print queues. It also can be used to control them. The PRINTER console command is only used if Core Printing was installed on the server. See INSTALL version 2.2 for more information on Core Printing.

Syntax:

PRINTER options

or

P options

Options: The PRINTER command has many options, as shown in the following list. Be sure to substitute a valid printer number for the variable *n*. Valid printer numbers range from 0 to 4.

Option	*Function*
PRINTER	Lists information about printers attached to the file server, including online status, mounted forms, form number mounted, and the number of queues that are being serviced.
PRINTER HELP	Lists printer commands available from the file server console.
PRINTER *n* ADD QUEUE	Adds an existing queue to *queuename* [AT PRIORITY] printer *n*.
PRINTER *n* CONFIG	Shows the configuration for printer *n*.
PRINTER *n* CREATE *port*	Creates a NetWare printer process for a particular port. Valid port options are COM1, COM2, LPT1, LPT2, and so on.
PRINTER *n* CREATE	Changes configuration of a serial COMx options printer *n* attached to the file server's serial printer port x.

The options that are not specified remain unchanged. These options include the following:

Baud is the baud rate in bits per second

Wordsize is the number of data bits

Parity is the type of parity

XonXoff is handshaking

Stopbits is the number of stop bits

Poll is the polling period

Option	Function
PRINTER *n* DELETE QUEUE *queuename*	Stops a printer from servicing a particular queue temporarily. The queue may be added again with PRINTER *n* ADD QUEUE *queuename*.
PRINTER *n* FORM FEED	Sends a form feed to printer *n*.
PRINTER *n* FORM MARK	Prints a line of asterisks (*) marking the current top of form for printer *n*.
PRINTER *n* MOUNT FORM *frm*	Changes the type of form mounted in printer *n* to form number *frm*. Use PRINTDEF to define forms.
PRINTER *n* POLL period	Sets the polling period (amount of time the printer process waits to check printer queues for print jobs). The polling period default is 15 seconds and may be set from 1 to 60 seconds.
PRINTER *n* QUEUE	Displays a list of printer queues and priority levels.
PRINTER *n* REWIND *p* PAGES	Restarts the current print job on printer *n*, first rewinding the print job *p* number of pages. If the print job does not contain form feeds, or you attempt to rewind more than nine pages, the print job will restart at the beginning.

Option	Function
PRINTER *n* START	Restarts a printer that has been stopped with PRINTER *n* STOP.
PRINTER *n* STOP	Stops printer *n*. The printer can be restarted with PRINTER n START.

Rules and Considerations: Valid printer numbers range from 0 to 4.

Important Messages: None

Examples: To use the PRINTER console command to set up NetWare core printing for a laser printer attached to LPT1: as printer 0 on the file server and assign it to an existing print queue named HPLASER, type the following:

PRINTER 0 CREATE LPT1
PRINTER 0 ADD HPLASER

To print a line of asterisks at the top of the page to check form alignment on a matrix printer attached to the file server as printer 2, type the following:

PRINTER 2 FORM MARK

To restart a printout a couple of pages back after a printer jam on a printer attached to the file server as printer 1, type the following:

PRINTER 1 REWIND 2 PAGES

Notes: The PRINTER command controls and creates print jobs that also are controlled through several NetWare menu utilities. See PCONSOLE, PRINTDEF, PRINTCON, and SYSCON for more information on creating and controlling printer processes and print jobs.

See Also: PCONSOLE, PSC, PSERVER (DOS executable), PSERVER (loadable module), PSTAT

A
B
C
D
E
F
G
H
I
J
K
L
M
N
O
P
Q
R
S
T
U
V
W
X
Y
Z

PROTOCOL

Purpose: Enables you to view registered protocols on the server, or register additional protocols or frame types.

Syntax: PROTOCOL [REGISTER *protocol* frame id#]

Option	Definition
REGISTER	Used to register an additional protocol.
protocol	Replace with the protocol name.
frame	Replace with the name of the frame type used by this protocol.
id#	Replace with the Protocol Identification Number. This is a unique hexadecimal number that tells the NetWare operating system how to recognize data coming from a network board using this designated communication protocol.

Examples: To display a list of protocols supported at your file server, type the following:

PROTOCOL

Notes: Using PROTOCOL REGISTER is only necessary for a few unusual cases, such as using a newer medium.

Consult your Novell Authorized Reseller for approved protocol NLMs.

See Also: CONFIG

PSC

Purpose: The PSC command offers many of the same features as the NetWare PCONSOLE menu utility regarding printer status checking and print server control. If you use PSC, these status checking and print server control features are available from the DOS command line.

Syntax: NetWare 3.1x uses the following syntax:

PSC PS=*printservername* P=*printernumber* options

NetWare 4.10 versions use the following syntax:

PSC PS=*printservername* P=*printernumber* [S=*Netware_Server*] options

Replace *printservername* with the name of the print server you want to check or manage.

Replace *printernumber* with the number of the printer you want to check or manage.

Replace *Netware_Server* with the name of the server containing a print server you wish to control. This option was added to allow you to control print servers located on other file servers.

See the following table for a list of valid options.

Option	Description
AB (ABort)	Cancels the current print job and continues with the next print job in the queue.
CD (CancelDown)	Use this option to reverse the effects of the "Going down after current jobs" selection in PCONSOLE.
STAT (STATus)	Displays the status of the printer.
PAU (PAUse)	Pauses printing temporarily.
STO (STOp)	Stops the printer. Use STOP [Keep] to resubmit the current job. Without Keep, the current job is deleted.

continues

Option	Description
STAR (STARt)	Starts the printer after it has been paused or stopped.
MA *Character* (MArk)	Prints a line of characters on the current line.
FF (Form Feed)	Advances the printer to the top of the next page. The printer first must be paused or stopped.
MOF=*n* (MOunt Form)	Replaces *n* with the number of a form that has been defined in PRINTDEF.
PRI (PRIvate)	Changes a remote printer to a local printer so that network users cannot access it.
SH (SHared)	Changes a private printer back to shared status.

Rules and Considerations: Print server operators can use any of the PSC features; regular NetWare users can use only the status checking features. The PSC command can be used in batch files to automate control of the printing environment.

You can include PS= or P= or both with the PSC command.

Printer numbers are defined first using the PCONSOLE menu utility when the print server is set up. They then can be used with PSC from the DOS command line.

Important Messages: You must specify the print server name.

In the preceding message, PSC requires that you specify a print server name. If you want to set a default print server, use the SET PSC command. The following message appears if a syntax error appears in the PSC command:

The specified action is not supported.

To correct this problem, retype the PSC command line carefully and check spelling and syntax.

To stop an unwanted printing of the current job on print server ACCTNG, type the following:

PSC PS=ACCTNG P=1 STOP

To notify NetWare that you have changed the type of paper loaded in printer 2 on print server ADMIN to a paper type of 35, type the following:

`PSC PS=ADMIN P=2 MOF=35`

Notes: Many of these functions can be performed with PCONSOLE if a menu-driven utility is preferred. PSC is particularly helpful in batch files.

See Also: PCONSOLE, PRINTER

A
B
C
D
E
F
G
H
I
J
K
L
M
N
O
P
Q
R
S
T
U
V
W
X
Y
Z

PSERVER.EXE

Purpose: Use PSERVER to configure a workstation as a dedicated print server.

Syntax: `PSERVER` *fileservername printservername*

Option	Description
fileservername	The *fileservername* parameter is used to specify the file server on which printservername is defined
printservername	A valid print server name is required for the *printservername* parameter

Rules and Considerations: Before you can run PSERVER, you first must use the NetWare PCONSOLE command to configure the print server.

Print servers running on a dedicated workstation use the PSERVER.EXE command. They can support up to 16 printers, and can service queues for up to eight file servers.

To run PSERVER, you must have access to IBM$RUN.OVL, SYS$ERR.DAT, SYS$HELP.DAT, and SYS$MSG.DAT. These files are in the public directory or with PSERVER if you have moved it.

Important Messages: If you have a print server named LASERS and the following message appears, you already started a print server named LASERS.

There is already a print server named LASERS running.

If you want to load a second print server with the same configuration as LASERS, create another print server and give it a different name.

If the following message appears when you try to print from your workstation on the network, your workstation does not have enough SPX connections:

`There are not enough SPX connections to run the print server.`

To create more SPX connections, add the following line to the NET.CFG or SHELL.CFG file on the workstation:

`SPX CONNECTIONS=60`

Examples: To load a print server named ACCTNG on the ADMIN file server, type the following line:

`PSERVER ADMIN ACCTNG`

Notes: Use the PCONSOLE command from any workstation to shut down a print server that was started with the PSERVER.EXE command.

See Also: PCONSOLE, PSC, PSERVER.NLM, RPRINTER

A
B
C
D
E
F
G
H
I
J
K
L
M
N
O
P
Q
R
S
T
U
V
W
X
Y
Z

PSERVER.NLM

Purpose: Loads the print server engine as a process on a NetWare file server. PSERVER.NLM is a loadable module.

Syntax: `LOAD` *path* `PSERVER` *printservername*

The path should be specified only if the PSERVER.NLM file is not in the SYS:SYSTEM directory.

Rules and Considerations: Before you can load PSERVER, you must use the PCONSOLE NetWare menu utility to set up print queues, print servers, and printers.

The *printservername* under NetWare 4.10 should be a complete NDS name to ensure correct loading. If the complete name is not used, the server will try to find the print server object in the bindery context (if activated).

NetWare 4.10's PSERVER.NLM can support a maximum of 256 printers, including as many as 5 local printers depending on the number of parallel and serial ports physically installed in the file server. The NetWare 4.10 PSERVER.NLM also can support up to 256 remote printers through the NPRINTER command.

Each printer supported by PSERVER requires 256 KB of server memory. To support all 256 printers under 4.10 requires approximately 5 MB of additional file server memory.

The NetWare 3.1x PSERVER.NLM command can support a total of 16 printers, including as many as 5 local printers depending on the number of parallel and serial ports on the server.

NetWare 3.1x's PSERVER.NLM command can support up to 16 remote printers using the RPRINTER command.

PSERVER.NLM cannot service queues on other servers. See PSERVER.EXE for this capability.

Important Messages: None

Examples: To start a print server called MAIN that has already been configured with the PCONSOLE menu utility, switch to the 3.x file server console and type the following command:

```
LOAD PSERVER MAIN
```

To start a print server in NetWare 4.10 called MAIN that has already been set up in the TRAINING organizational unit under the SOLUTIONS organization, switch to the file server console and enter the following command:

```
LOAD PSERVER CN=MAIN.OU=TRAINING.O=SOLUTIONS
```

Notes: It usually is desirable to load PSERVER automatically each time you boot the file server. To do so, use the INSTALL command to include a LOAD PSERVER printservername command in the server's AUTOEXEC.NCF file. Replace printservername with the name of the print server you want to load.

See Also: INSTALL, NPRINTER, PCONSOLE, PSC, PSERVER.EXE, RPRINTER

A
B
C
D
E
F
G
H
I
J
K
L
M
N
O
P
Q
R
S
T
U
V
W
X
Y
Z

PSTAT

Purpose: Displays printer status information.

Syntax: **PSTAT** S=*servername* P=*printer*

Option	Function
S=*servername*	Designates the name of a valid file server
P=*printer*	Designates printer as either a valid printer name or printer number

Rules and Considerations: Before you can use the PSTAT command to check printers on a server, you first must attach or log in to the server.

You do not need to supply the name of the server (S= option) if it is the default server.

Important Messages: None

Notes: An offline printer will be listed as on-line until you attempt to print to it.

Use the PCONSOLE NetWare menu utility to obtain individual print job status.

See Also: PRINTER, PSC

PURGE

Purpose: Prevents previously erased files from being salvaged. Immediately frees disk space taken by deleted files.

Syntax: `PURGE` [*path/filename*] [`/ALL`]

Option	Description
path	An optional parameter that specifies the path to the deleted files.
filename	An optional parameter that specifies the file name to purge. Also accepts wild-card characters.
/ALL	Deletes all recoverable files in the current directory and in all subdirectories.

Rules and Considerations: If you type PURGE with no options, all of the recoverable files in the current directory will be removed. The PURGE command used with no options has the same effect as entering a file path with the *.* wild cards.

Important Messages: None

Examples: To permanently remove all recoverable erased files on a file server volume, log in as SUPERVISOR and type the following command at the volume root directory:

`PURGE /ALL`

To purge only your DOC files in the SHAREDOC directory on file server FS2 on volume DATA, type the command:

`PURGE FS2/DATA:SHAREDOC\*.DOC`

Notes: When a directory is removed or deleted, all salvageable files are moved to a hidden directory called DELETED.SAV. The DELETED.SAV directory is located off the root of every volume.

Performing a PURGE ALL on large volumes reduces server overhead required to track salvageable files.

See Also: SALVAGE

A
B
C
D
E
F
G
H
I
J
K
L
M
N
O
P
Q
R
S
T
U
V
W
X
Y
Z

QUEUE

Purpose: Creates and maintains NetWare print queues. Displays a list of print queues, including information about the number of jobs in each print queue, print queue name, and the number of printers servicing each queue.

Syntax:

QUEUE *options*

or

Q *options*

Option	Function
HELP	Displays a list of valid options.
queuename CHANGE JOB *jobnumber* TO PRIORITY *prioritylevel*	The *queuename* variable is the name of a valid print queue. The *jobnumber* variable is replaced by a particular print job whose priority you want to change. The *prioritylevel* variable is the new priority level for the print job that you want to change. A priority level of 1 will move the print job to the top of the queue; a priority level of 1 plus the number of jobs in the queue will move the job to the end of the queue.
QUEUE *queuename* CREATE	Use the *queuename* variable for the name for the new print queue. Used in lieu of PCONSOLE to create print queues from the console instead of a workstation.

continues

A
B
C
D
E
F
G
H
I
J
K
L
M
N
O
P
Q
R
S
T
U
V
W
X
Y
Z

Option	Function
QUEUE *queuename* DELETE JOB *jobnumber*	In the *queuename* location, specify the print queue that contains the print job(s) you want to cancel. The *jobnumber* is the actual number of the particular print job. If you type an asterisk for the job number, all print jobs in the queue will be deleted.
QUEUE *queuename* DESTROY	Completely destroys the print queue *queuename* and all of its print jobs.
QUEUE *queuename* JOBS	Displays a list of print jobs for the *queuename* print queue.

Rules and Considerations: Do not use the QUEUE command on a network running the NetWare Name Service.

Important Messages: If the message Queue already exists appears after you enter the QUEUE command, you are attempting to create a queue with the same name as an existing queue. Change the name and reenter the command.

The message The specified Queue does not exist appears if you enter the name of a queue that does not exist on this server. Correct the name and reenter the command.

The message Unknown Queue Command appears if you enter the QUEUE command incorrectly. Retype the command and then check the syntax.

Examples: To create a print queue for dot-matrix printers, type the following at the console:

QUEUE MATRIX CREATE

To create a print queue specifically for the sales staff, type the following at the console:

QUEUE SALES CREATE

To list all the print jobs in a print queue named HPLASER, type the following command at the console:

QUEUE HPLASER JOBS

To display a list of queues and their current status at the console, type the command:

QUEUE

Notes: You can use the PCONSOLE utility instead of the QUEUE command to manage print queues. PCONSOLE must be used on NetWare Name Service (NNS) networks.

See Also: PCONSOLE, PRINTER, PSC

A
B
C
D
E
F
G
H
I
J
K
L
M
N
O
P
Q
R
S
T
u
V
W
X
Y
Z

REGISTER MEMORY

Purpose: Enables NetWare to recognize more than 16 MB of system memory. When NetWare's auto register memory feature does not work or must be turned off, 4.10 can register up to 3.25 gigabytes of memory.

Syntax: `REGISTER MEMORY` *memstart memlen*

Options: Replace *memstart* with 1000000 (in most cases). This indicates that the memory being registered starts at the 16 MB boundary.

Replace *memlen* with the hexadecimal length of the memory block.

Rules and Considerations: When using a Microchannel or an EISA-based 32-bit machine you must reserve memory buffers for 16-bit cards before registering memory.

The memory length, memlen, must end on an even paragraph boundary divisible by 0×10. This must also be specified as a hexadecimal number.

To have the memory registered automatically at file server boot time, include the command in the server's AUTOEXEC.NCF file right after the file server name and internal IPX lines. This command must be issued before the SYS: or other volumes are mounted.

If your server has a 16-bit ISA host adapter driver that must be loaded in memory below 16 MB, use the SET AUTO REGISTER MEMORY ABOVE 16 MEGABYTES=OFF command in the STARTUP.NCF file, followed by the LOAD disk_driver and REGISTER MEMORY commands.

Important Messages: None

Examples: To make the file server recognize 16 MB of additional memory starting at the 16 MB boundary, type the following command at the console:

`REGISTER MEMORY 1000000 1000000`

See Also: LOAD, MEMORY, REGISTER MEMORY

A
B
C
D
E
F
G
H
I
J
K
L
M
N
O
P
Q
R
S
T
U
V
W
X
Y
Z

REINITIALIZE SYSTEM

Purpose: Entered at the file server console, REINITIALIZE SYSTEM enables any configuration changes that have been made since the NETINFO.CFG file was run.

Syntax: `REINITIALIZE SYSTEM`

Rules and Considerations: This command compares the version of the NETINFO.CFG file last run, with the current version of the file. If there are any new commands in the current version, it runs those commands. It also notifies *Simple Network Management Protocol* (SNMP) NLMs that it is being run so that these NLMs are made aware of the NETINFO.CFG changes.

Examples: To run changes in the NETINFO.CFG file made after the last time this file was accessed, type the following at the system console:

`REINITIALIZE SYSTEM`

Important Messages: None

Notes: Any NLMs affected by the changes in the NETINFO.CFG file are first unloaded, then reloaded. If the NLM cannot be unloaded, the changes are not made.

If you have any doubts as to whether or not the changes will become effective by running REINITIALIZE SYSTEM, it is best to down the server and reload it, or manually unload the affected NLMs, then run REINITIALIZE SYSTEM.

See Also: INETCFG

REM

Purpose: Defines a comment line in an NCF file.

Syntax: `REM` `comment`

Options: Replace `comment` with whatever note or message you want to include in the NCF file.

Rules and Considerations: Typically used in NCF files when you want to include notes or other information for an internal reference that you do not want executed.

The remark statement or character should be the first thing on the command line.

The following are considered remark or comment lines:

```
REM
;
#
```

Examples: The following is an example of using the remark commands in an NCF file:

```
ECHO OFF
REM Load the BTRIEVE NLM for access to the company database.
LOAD BTRIEVE
# Let's load MONITOR to enable its screen saver feature.
LOAD MONITOR
; Load the Remote Management NLMs last!
LOAD REMOTE
LOAD RSPX
CLS
```

Notes: Functionally equivalent to the REM command used in batch files under DOS.

See Also: ECHO OFF, ECHO ON, PAUSE

A
B
C
D
E
F
G
H
I
J
K
L
M
N
O
P
Q
R
S
T
U
V
W
X
Y
Z

REMIRROR

Purpose: Restores a duplexed or mirrored drive pair when one drive has been replaced.

Syntax: REMIRROR *drivenumber*

Options: None

Rules and Considerations: In the *drivenumber*, specify the drive that needs to be updated. The REMIRROR command updates the hard disk drive to contain the same information as the mirrored drive.

Important Messages:

```
Mirror drive will be auto remirrored.
```

If the preceding message appears after the system boots, the file server noticed during the boot that the mirror drive had been replaced or previously had failed. The file server automatically attempts to REMIRROR the drive if the drive previously failed or was replaced; you do not have to enter REMIRROR manually in this situation.

The following error message indicates that mirroring has failed on the file server CSOS drive 01, which affects the SYS volume:

```
Mirroring turned off on CSOS. Drive 01 failed. Mirroring turned off
on SYS.
```

To correct this problem, type REMIRROR 01. If the REMIRROR fails, you should attempt to repair the drive using VREPAIR.

Examples: To update partition 01 so that it matches drive 00 in a mirrored pair, type the following command:

```
REMIRROR PARTITION 01
```

Notes: Remirroring hard disk drives is often a slow process. During the remirror operation, file server response is slow because one drive's information is being copied in the background.

If you do not shut down the file server after a mirrored drive pair has failed, REMIRROR will need to copy only the information that has changed since the mirror process failed. If you shut down the server, REMIRROR must copy the entire contents of one drive to the other drive, which is a lengthy process.

See Also: ABORT REMIRROR, REMIRROR PARTITION, VREPAIR

A
B
C
D
E
F
G
H
I
J
K
L
M
N
O
P
Q
R
S
T
U
V
W
X
Y
Z

REMIRROR PARTITION

Purpose: Begins remirroring of a duplexed or mirrored partition pair when one partition has been replaced or returned to service.

Syntax: `REMIRROR PARTITION` *partitionnumber*

Options: Replace *partitionnumber* with the number of the logical partition you want to remirror.

Rules and Considerations: The REMIRROR PARTITION command updates the out-of-sync partition to contain the same information as the active mirrored drive.

Ordinarily the server remirrors partitions automatically. The REMIRROR PARTITION command would be used if partition remirroring had stopped due to an ABORT REMIRROR command or general partition remirror error.

Important Messages:

```
Mirror drive will be auto remirrored.
```

If the preceding message appears after the system boots, the file server noticed during the boot that the mirror partition had been replaced or previously had failed. The file server automatically attempts to REMIRROR the partition if it previously failed or was replaced; you do not have to enter REMIRROR manually in this situation.

The following error message indicates that mirroring has failed on the file server Training_Solutions drive 01, which affects the SYS volume:

```
Mirroring turned off on Training_Solutions. Drive 01 failed.
Mirroring turned off on SYS.
```

To correct this problem, type the following:

`REMIRROR PARTITION 0`

Examples: To update drive 01 so that it matches drive 00 in a mirrored pair, type the command:

`REMIRROR PARTITION 0`

Notes: Remirroring partitions is a slow process. During the remirror operation, file server response is slow because one drive's information is being copied in the background.

If you do not shut down the file server after a mirrored partition pair has failed, REMIRROR will need to copy only the information that has changed since the mirror process failed. If you shut down the server, REMIRROR must copy the entire contents of one partition to the other drive, which is a lengthy process.

A tape backup of the affected volume should not be attempted during a drive remirror.

See Also: ABORT REMIRROR, REMIRROR, VREPAIR

A
B
C
D
E
F
G
H
I
J
K
L
M
N
O
P
Q
R
S
U
V
W
X
Y
Z

REMOTE

Purpose: Enables you to use the ACONSOLE or the RCONSOLE utility to run the file server console from a remote PC.

Syntax: **LOAD** *path* **REMOTE** -E *remotepassword*

Option	Description
remotepassword	Replace this variable with the password that you want all remote administrators to use.
-E	(4.1) Use only if requiring the password to be encrypted. This also requires you to first load REMOTE with a password that is not encrypted. Then, run REMOTE ENCRYPT to determine the password's encrypted value.

Rules and Considerations: The path need only be specified if REMOTE.NLM is not found in the SYS:SYSTEM directory.

In NetWare 3.11, the *remotepassword* variable defaults to the SUPERVISOR password if no password is specified.

You must load RSPX after REMOTE is loaded so that you can access the file server from a network workstation using the RCONSOLE utility.

You must load RS232 after REMOTE is loaded so that you can access the file server from a remote computer (not connected to the network) through a modem using the ACONSOLE utility.

Load either RSPX or RS232, not both.

Important Messages: None

Examples: To load remote file server console support using the password SECRET, type the following command at the console:

```
LOAD REMOTE SECRET
LOAD RSPX
```

In 3.11, to load remote file server console support using the SUPERVISOR password, type the following at the console:

```
LOAD REMOTE
LOAD RSPX
```

To load remote file server console support from a remote PC using a modem with the password set to ABCDEFG, type the following at the console:

```
LOAD REMOTE ABCDEFG
LOAD RS232 1 2400
```

Notes: You can access the remote console even when the file server console is in use, and both can display different information.

In 4.10, you cannot use the supervisor's (ADMIN's) password unless it has been specifically set as the password for REMOTE.

See Also: ACONSOLE, RS232, RSPX

A
B
C
D
E
F
G
H
I
J
K
L
M
N
O
P
Q
R
S
T
U
V
W
X
Y
Z

REMOVE

Purpose: Deletes users and groups from file and directory trustee lists.

Syntax:

REMOVE USER *username* FROM *path option*

or

REMOVE GROUP *groupname* FROM *path option*

The *username* and *groupname* variables indicate either a user or a group that is to be removed from a directory or file trustee list. Indicate the path to the directory or file in the *path* variable.

Option	Function
/S	Removes the user or group from all subdirectories in the specified path
/F	Removes the user or group from files in the specified path

Rules and Considerations: The USER and GROUP specifiers are necessary only when users and groups have the same name; otherwise, the REMOVE command automatically distinguishes between users and groups.

If you enter REMOVE with only a user or group name, the user or group is removed from the trustee list of the current directory.

Important Messages:

User or group "HORST" not found.

In the preceding example, the message indicates that no user or group named HORST exists on this server. Reenter the command with the correct name.

CSOS/APPS:ALLDOCS
User "FRED" no longer a trustee to the specified directory.

```
Trustee "FRED" removed from 1 directories.
```

The preceding example message confirms that the user FRED was successfully removed as a trustee from the directory ALLDOCS on disk volume APPS of file server CSOS.

```
CSOS/APPS:DATENTRY
Group "TEMPS" no longer a trustee to the specified directory.
```

```
Trustee "TEMPS" removed from 1 directories.
```

The preceding example message confirms that the group TEMPS was successfully removed as a trustee from the directory DATENTRY on disk volume APPS of file server CSOS.

```
CSOS/SYS:JUNK
No trustee for the specified Directory.
```

The previous sample error message displays when a user or group exists but it is not a trustee of the specified directory or file.

Examples: To remove the group TEMPS as a trustee from the DATENTRY subdirectory on volume APPS of server CSOS, type the following command:

REMOVE GROUP TEMPS FROM CSOS\APPS:DATENTRY

To remove the user FRED from the trustee list of the ALLDOCS subdirectory on volume APPS of file server CSOS, type the following command:

REMOVE FRED FROM CSOS/APPS:ALLDOCS

To remove the user FRED from the trustee list of all the subdirectories of the ALLDOCS directory on volume APPS of file server CSOS, type the following command:

REMOVE FRED FROM CSOS/APPS:ALLDOCS /S

Notes: Refer to the NetWare documentation on SYSCON and FILER NetWare menu utilities for related information.

The /S option only removes the user or group from the trustee lists of every subdirectory of the specified directory path; the /S option does not affect the trustee rights to the specified directory.

See Also: GRANT, MAKEUSER, REVOKE, RIGHTS, TLIST

REMOVE DOS

Purpose: Removes DOS completely from the file server's memory, eliminating access to DOS.

Syntax: `REMOVE DOS`

Options: None

Rules and Considerations: After you remove DOS from the file server, the system will perform a warm boot when you issue the EXIT or RE-START Server command at the file server console; the system does not return to DOS.

If you remove DOS from the file server, Network Loadable Modules (NLMs) cannot be loaded from floppy disk drive partitions or the servers DOS hard drive partitions.

After using REMOVE DOS, you cannot access any DOS floppies or DOS hard disk partitions.

Important Messages:

`DOS access has been removed from file server.`

The previous message displays after DOS is successfully removed from memory. To reload DOS access, shut down the file server and reboot.

Examples: To remove DOS access from the file server, type the following command:

`REMOVE DOS`

Using this command ensures that unauthorized NLMs cannot be loaded at the file server console.

Notes: If you use the REMOVE DOS command to disable DOS access on the file server, you still can copy NLMs into the SYS:SYSTEM subdirectory from a workstation.

See Also: EXIT, SECURE CONSOLE

RENDIR

Purpose: Renames a file server subdirectory without affecting the trustee rights to that directory.

Syntax: RENDIR *dirpath newname*

Rules and Considerations: If you do not have the modify right to a directory, you cannot change its name.

The RENDIR command renames a directory, but it does not affect the directory's trustee or user rights.

(4.10) /? can be used to view online help.

(4.10) /VER can be used to see the command's related version information and a list of files required by this command in order to run.

Important Messages:

```
Directory renamed to DEPTDOCS.
```

The preceding message confirms that you successfully renamed a sample directory to DEPTDOCS.

```
The path specification (directory name) was incorrect.
```

The preceding message appears if you try to rename a subdirectory that does not exist or one that does not exist on the specified directory path. Correct the original directory path and name and retry the command.

Examples: To rename the MYDOCS subdirectory to DEPTDOCS on the DOCS volume of file server FS3, type the following command:

```
RENDIR FS3/DOCS:MYDOCS DEPTDOCS
```

If you want to give the current directory a new name, you can use a period (.) to specify the current directory path. To duplicate the previous example, use the Change Directory command (CD) to make the FS3/DOCS:MYDOCS subdirectory current, and then type:

```
RENDIR . DEPTDOCS
```

A
B
C
D
E
F
G
H
I
J
K
L
M
N
O
P
Q
R
S
T
U
V
W
X
Y
Z

Notes: Changing directory names with RENDIR does not update MAP commands in DOS batch files or NetWare login scripts. If you do use RENDIR to rename a directory that you previously accessed using MAP commands, rewrite any affected MAP commands in the login scripts and batch files.

See Also: FILER, NWADMIN, SYSCON

RESET ROUTER

Purpose: Updates inaccurate or corrupted router tables that result from file server or network bridge failure.

Syntax: `RESET ROUTER`

Rules and Considerations: The RESET ROUTER command is used only when inaccurate or corrupted router tables must be rebuilt.

Important Messages:

`Router has been reset.`

According to the preceding message, the router table for this server has been rebuilt.

Examples: To rebuild the router on a NetWare file server, go to the file server console and type the following command:

`RESET ROUTER`

Notes: The router tables are automatically updated every two minutes. Use the RESET ROUTER command on every network file server to update the router table sooner than the automatic two-minute time period.

See Also: DISPLAY NETWORKS, DISPLAY SERVERS, TRACK OFF, TRACK ON

RESTART

Purpose: Reloads the NetWare 4.1 SFT III IOEngine on one server, leaving the other server running. Can also be used to force the server to switch from the primary to the secondary server.

Syntax: RESTART

Rules and Considerations: This command can only be used on mirrored SFT III servers.

Example: To restart the server, type the following at the appropriate IOEngine for SFT III:

RESTART

Important Messages: If you receive an "unknown command" message, it indicates that you attempted to execute RESTART from an MSEngine, instead of from an IOEngine.

The following error message is displayed if the servers were not mirrored before running RESTART:

WARNING!!! Not every disk is remirrored. Answering yes may cause some volumes to dismount and open files to be lost. Are you sure you wish to halt then restart the primary server?

Notes: None

RESTART SERVER

Purpose: Restarts the server after downing without first exiting to DOS.

Syntax: `RESTART SERVER [option]`

Options: Replace *option* with one or more of the items listed here.

Option	Description
-ns	Do not execute the server's STARTUP.NCF file
-na	Do not execute the server's AUTOEXEC.NCF file

Rules and Considerations: Before issuing this command, the DOWN command must have been executed.

Important Messages: If you try to restart the server before issuing the DOWN command, a message similar to the following appears at the console:

```
The server is not DOWN. To restart the server you must first
issue the DOWN command.
```

Examples: To restart a downed NetWare 4.10 server, type the following at the System Console:

`RESTART SERVER`

To restart a downed NetWare 4.10 server and not execute the STARTUP.NCF file, type the following at the System Console:

`RESTART SERVER -NS`

To restart a downed NetWare 4.10 server and not execute the AUTOEXEC.NCF file, type the following at the System Console:

`RESTART SERVER -NA`

A
B
C
D
E
F
G
H
I
J
K
L
M
N
O
P
Q
R
S
T
U
V
W
X
Y
Z

A
B
C
D
E
F
G
H
I
J
K
L
M
N
O
P
Q
R
S
T
U
V
W
X
Y
Z

To restart a downed NetWare 4.10 server and not execute either the STARTUP.NCF or AUTOEXEC.NCF file, type the following at the System Console:

`RESTART SERVER -NS -NA`

See Also: DOWN, EXIT

REVOKE

Purpose: Enables you to revoke individual trustee rights for files or directories from users and groups.

Syntax:

REVOKE *rightslist path* **FROM** USER *username* /SUB or /FILE

REVOKE *rightslist path* **FROM** GROUP *groupname* /SUB or /FILE

Option	Description
rightslist	The rightslist can consist of one or several of the following rights attributes. Each attribute must be separated by a space.

	Right	Description	NetWare 2.2 or 3.1x
	ALL	All	BOTH
	A	Access Control	BOTH
	C	Create	BOTH
	E	Erase	BOTH
	F	File Scan	BOTH
	M	Modify	BOTH
	R	Read	BOTH
	S	Supervisor	3.1x
	W	Write	BOTH

Option	Description
path	Optional variable that defaults to the current directory if no path is specified.
username	Specifies a single existing user who will have her rights revoked.

continues

Option	Description
groupname	Specifies a single existing group that is to have its rights revoked.
/SUB	Includes files and subdirectories of the selected directory.
/FILE	Includes files and subdirectories of the selected directory.

Rules and Considerations: The *rightslist* variable can consist of one or several rights separated by spaces.

If the path is omitted, REVOKE will default to the current directory.

The /FILE and /SUB flags cannot be used in the same command.

The /SUB (subdirectory) flag used with REVOKE affects only subdirectories of the selected directory; the directory is not affected.

You must include the USER or GROUP identifiers only if the user or group you want to modify has the same name as another user or group.

Important Messages:

No trustee for the specified directory.

The preceding message appears if the specified directory does not exist. Check the spelling and retry the command.

User or group ACCNTG not found.

In the preceding example, no user or group was found with the name ACCNTG. Check the user or group name and retry the command.

CSOS/DOCS:SPECDOCS
Trustees access rights set to [RWC MFA]

Rights for 1 directories were changed for DEDE.

The preceding example confirms the E (Erase) trustee right was successfully revoked from user DEDE in the SYS:SPECDOCS directory.

Examples: To block the user DEDE from erasing files in the SPECDOCS subdirectory on volume DOCS of the default file server, type the following command:

```
REVOKE E DOCS:SPECDOCS FROM USER DEDE
```

To remove the user STEPHEN completely from the subdirectory
SHAREDOC on the VOL1 volume on file server SP1, type the following
command:

```
REVOKE ALL SP1/VOL1:SHAREDOC FROM USER STEPHEN
```

Continuing with the last example, to revoke the erase right for all the files
in the SHAREDOC subdirectory for group ADMIN, type the command:

```
REVOKE E SP1/VOL1:SHARDOC FROM GROUP ADMIN /FILE
```

Notes: When you revoke rights, make sure you do not alter the rights for
the EVERYONE group in the LOGIN, MAIL, and PUBLIC system directories. If these rights are changed, the system will not work as expected.

See Also: GRANT, REMOVE, RIGHTS, TLIST

A
B
C
D
E
F
G
H
I
J
K
L
M
N
O
P
Q
R
S
T
U
V
W
X
Y
Z

RIGHTS

Purpose: NetWare version 2.2 and 3.1x displays your effective rights to a file or subdirectory. NetWare 4.10 also allows you to modify user or group rights.

Syntax: NetWare 2.2 and 3.1x has the following syntax:

RIGHTS *path*

NetWare 4.10 has incorporated the older GRANT, REVOKE, TLIST commands into RIGHTS. RIGHTS has the following syntax:

RIGHTS *path* [[+/-]*rightslist*] [/*option*]

Option	Function
path	Specifies a valid NetWare volume, a directory, subdirectory, or file path. The path can be listed, for example, as FS1/SYS:SYSTEM.

The following are for NetWare version 4.10 only.

Option	Description
rightslist	Replace *rightslist* with a list of rights to grant or revoke. The list of rights is preceded by a + (plus grants the rights) or a - (minus revokes the rights).

The following table lists valid rights that can be granted or revoked:

Right	Function
S (Supervisory)	Gives all privileges to the file, directory, or volume.
R (Read)	Gives open and read privileges to the file, directory, or volume.
W (Write)	Gives open and write privileges to the file, directory, or volume. Allows modification of a file's content.

Option	Description
C (Create)	Gives create privileges in the directory or volume. Allows creation of files and directories that do not yet exist.
E (Erase)	Gives erase (or delete) privileges to the file, directory, or volume.
M (Modify)	Gives modify privileges to the file, directory, or volume. Allows modification of the name or attributes of a file, directory, or volume. Does not allow modification of a file's content.
F (File Scan)	Gives file scan privileges to the file, directory, or volume. Allows the file, directory, or volume to display during a DOS DIR or NetWare NDIR scan.
A (Access Control)	Gives access control privileges to the file, directory, or volume. Allows other users and groups to control access to a file, directory, or volume.
N (None)	Revokes all privileges from the file, directory, or volume.
ALL (ALL rights)	Grants or revokes all rights except SUPERVISORY.

Replace option with one or more of the following.

Option	Description
/F	Displays or modifies the Inherited Rights Filter for a file, directory, or volume.
GROUP=groupname	Modifies the trustee assignment of the specified groupname.
/Inherited	Displays the user and group trustee assignments that created the current inherited rights set. Also shows from where the inherited rights originated.
/Sub	Includes subdirectories below the current level. 4.10 uses S.
/Trustee	Displays user and group trustee assignments. 4.10 uses T.

continues

Option	Description
NAME=*username*	Modifies the trustee assignment of the specified user name.
/C	Displays output continuously to the screen instead of pausing after each full screen.
/?	Displays on-line help screen.
REM (Remove)	(4.10) Removes user or group as a trustee.
/VER	Displays version information and a list of files needed by this command in order for it to run.

Important Messages:

```
Specified path not locatable.
Usage:  RIGHTS [path]
Rights = All ¦ Read ¦ Write ¦ Create ¦ Erase ¦ Modify
                    ¦ Filescan ¦ Access Control
```

If the previous message appears, you specified a directory path that does not exist. Correct the directory path and try again.

Example: The following sample output lists a user with all rights to the MISCDOCS directory of volume PROGS on 2.2 file server CSOS:

```
CSOS\PROGS:MISCDOCS
Your Effective Rights for this directory are [RWCEMFA]
            May Read from File.  (R)
            May Write to File.  (W)
            May Create Subdirectories and Files.  (C)
            May Erase Subdirectories and Files.  (E)
            May Modify File Status Flags.  (M)
            May Scan for Files.  (F)
            May Change Access Control.  (A)

            You have ALL RIGHTS to this directory area.
```

The following example output lists a user with limited rights to the PUBLIC directory of volume SYS on file server CSOS:

```
CSOS\SYS:PUBLIC
```
Your Effective Rights for this directory are [R   F]

```
              May Read from File.  (R)
              May Scan for Files.  (F)
```

Notes: See the NetWare menu utilities SYSCON and FILER for menu driven access to directory and file rights.

See Also: GRANT, REMOVE, REVOKE, TLIST

A
B
C
D
E
F
G
H
I
J
K
L
M
N
O
P
Q
R
S
T
U
V
W
X
Y
Z

ROUTE

Purpose: Allows NetWare servers to support IBM Source Routing.

Syntax:

LOAD [path] ROUTE [option]

Replace path with the valid NetWare path to the NLM. By default the server will look for the NLM in SYS:SYSTEM.

Option	Function
BOARD=number	Specifies the logical board number for which you want to change parameters or load ROUTE. Replace number with the network board's logical board number.
NAME=boardname	Specifies the board name you assigned as an alternative to using a board number.
CLEAR	Clears the Source Routing Table (roughly equivalent to RESET ROUTER for IPX).
DEF	Prevents frames that have an unknown (for instance, default) destination address from being sent across IBM Single Route bridges.
GBR	Specifies that all General Broadcast Frames are to be sent as All Routes Broadcast frames.
MBR	Specifies that all Multicast Broadcast Frames are to be sent as All Routes Broadcast frames.
REMOVE=number	Removes a specified node address from the server's Source Routing Table. Replace number with a 12 digit hex number.
RSP=rvalue	Specifies how the server should respond to a broadcast request.

Option	Function
UNLOAD	Specifies the board from which you want to remove source routing support. Can use BOARD=number with this command to specify which board to unload.
TIME=*seconds*	Specifies how often the Source Routing Table should be updated.
XTX=*number*	Specifies how many times to transmit using timeout. Default is 02 times. Range is between 00 and 255 seconds.

Rules and Considerations: The ROUTE NLM typically is only used when a NetWare server is installed into an IBM Source Routing environment. If one or more bridges or routers on a network support Source Routing, it might be necessary to use the ROUTE NLM to correctly communicate with them.

Route can be loaded re-entrantly.

Examples: To load the ROUTE NLM and support Source Routing on a NetWare server's logical board number 1, go to the System Console screen and type:

LOAD ROUTE BOARD=1

See Also: INETCFG, LOAD

A
B
C
D
E
F
G
H
I
J
K
L
M
N
O
P
Q
R
S
T
U
V
W
X
Y
Z

·A
B
C
D
E
F
G
H
I
J
K
L
M
N
O
P
Q
R
S
T
U
V
W
X
Y
Z

RPL

Purpose: To enable IBM PC diskless workstations to boot directly to the network.

Syntax: `LOAD` *path* `RPL`

Options: Replace *path* with the full path to this NLM. By default, NetWare will look in SYS:SYSTEM.

Rules and Considerations: This NLM typically is required by network boards with boot PROMs, which are not IPX specific. Most notably among these are IBM PC and PS/2 diskless workstations using IBM network boards.

If you are running non-IBM diskless workstations and encountering problems connecting to a server, check the documentation to see if this NLM is required for your type of boot PROM(s).

Examples: To load RPL.NLM, go to the System Console and type the command:

`LOAD RPL`

Notes: Using the TRACK ON console command might help you determine if this NLM is warranted. An IPX specific boot PROM will issue a "Get Nearest Server" request, which will display in the TRACK ON screen. If your boot PROMs are not generating this message in the TRACK ON screen, check their documentation to see if this NLM is required for your type of boot PROM(s).

See Also: DOSGEN, IPX, LOAD, TRACK OFF, TRACK ON

RPRINTER

Purpose: Connects a workstation printer to the network as a remote printer. RPRINTER also is used to disconnect workstation printers from the network.

Syntax: **RPRINTER** *printservername printer flag*

Option	Description
printservername	Specify the print server that includes the printer you want to connect to the network.
printer	Specify the printer number for the remote printer. This number represents the printer configuration that was defined using the PCONSOLE command.

The following are valid flag options:

Flag Option	Function
-R	Disconnects the remote printer
-S	Displays the status of the remote printer

If neither of the flag options are specified, the remote printer is connected.

Rules and Considerations: RPRINTER runs as a TSR (terminate-and-stay-resident) program on the user's workstation. For this reason, the RPRINTER utility requires workstation memory.

If a user's local printer is connected to the network as a remote printer, the user must print to a captured network printer port using the CAPTURE command, rather than directly to the local printer port.

If more than one remote printer is attached to a workstation, the RPRINTER TSR must be loaded for each printer.

A
B
C
D
E
F
G
H
I
J
K
L
M
N
O
P
Q
R
S
T
U
V
W
X
Y
Z

A
B
C
D
E
F
G
H
I
J
K
L
M
N
O
P
Q
R
S
T
U
V
W
X
Y
Z

The NetWare shells must be loaded on the workstation before the RPRINTER TSR is loaded.

To run RPRINTER, the workstation must have access to the following files:

IBM$RUN.OVL

RPRINT$$.EXE

RPRINTER.HLP

SYS$ERR.DAT

SYS$HELP.DAT

SYS$MSG.DAT

Important Messages:

No print servers are operating.

If the preceding message appears, no printer servers are running. Start a printer server and try to connect the remote printer. These files should be in Public or to wherever RPRINTER was copied.

RPRINT$$.EXE not found.

If the preceding message appears, the RPRINTER utility was not installed with the capability to access all the necessary files. Reinstall RPRINTER so that all the files listed in the "Rules and Considerations" section are available when you run RPRINTER.

Examples: To load RPRINTER on a workstation that has been set up properly for remote printer 2 on print server ADMIN, type the following command:

RPRINTER ADMIN 2

To remove the remote printer defined in the previous example, type the following command:

RPRINTER ADMIN 2 -R

To check the status of remote printer number 2 on print server ADMIN, type the following command:

RPRINTER ADMIN 2 -S

Notes: To support a remote printer, the workstation must not be rebooted. If a workstation supporting remote printers is rebooted, the

RPRINTER TSR must be reloaded for each remote printer connected to the workstation.

The commands for connecting remote printers can be loaded by the AUTOEXEC.BAT file of the workstation if the NetWare shells are loaded before the RPRINTER utility is run.

For example, include the following commands in AUTOEXEC.BAT:

```
CD\NET
IPX
NETX
RPRINTER ADMIN 2
CD \
```

The preceding example assumes that IPX, NETX, RPRINTER, and all required files are located in C:\NET.

See Also: CAPTURE, PCONSOLE, PSERVER

A
B
C
D
E
F
G
H
I
J
K
L
M
N
O
P
Q
R
S
T
U
V
W
X
Y
Z

A
B
C
D
.E
F
G
H
I
J
K
L
M
N
O
P
Q
R
S
T
U
V
W
X
Y
Z

RS232

Purpose: Enables you to access the file server console over asynchronous communications ports or a modem. The RS232 command is used with the REMOTE.NLM.

Syntax: `LOAD RS232 comport speed options`

Option	Description
`comport`	Valid options for this variable are 1 for COM1 or 2 for COM2
`speed`	Valid options for this variable are 2400, 4800, or 9600 for the data transfer rate of the modem
`options`	(4.10) Replace options with N to specify a null modem cable, C to use enable callback functions, or both.

If you do not enter the comport or speed variables when RS232 is loaded, you will be prompted to do so.

Once RS232 is loaded, you can use several commands, including RS232 to view the driver settings; MODEM to interact with the modem; MODEM @ *name* to give the mode commands from a named file; or MODEM command to direct a specific command to the modem.

Examples: To load remote support for a 9600 bps modem attached to COM2 on the file server, type the following command:

`LOAD RS232 2 9600`

Notes: REMOTE.NLM must be loaded before RS232 so that you can use ACONSOLE to connect as a remote console.

See Also: ACONSOLE, LOAD, RCONSOLE, REMOTE, RSPX

RSPX

Purpose: Used with the REMOTE.NLM, RSPX enables you to access the file server console from a workstation using the RCONSOLE utility program.

Syntax: `LOAD RSPX`

Options: None (3.1x), SIGNATURES OFF/ON (4.10)

Rules and Considerations: To run a remote console, you first must load REMOTE and then RSPX.

You can specify the path for loading RSPX in 4.10. You also can allow RSPX remote console packets to be turned off, which is necessary if using a NetWare 3.11 RCONSOLE utility when accessing a NetWare 4.10 server.

Examples: To load RSPX.NLM after REMOTE.NLM is loaded, type the following command:

`LOAD RSPX`

To see online help for RSPX, type the following command:

`RSPX HELP`

Notes: Use the RCONSOLE menu utility to access the remote console that has loaded REMOTE.NLM and RSPX.NLM. RCONSOLE can be used at any workstation on the LAN.

See Also: ACONSOLE, LOAD, RCONSOLE, REMOTE, RS232

A
B
C
D
E
F
G
H
I
J
K
L
M
N
O
P
Q
R
S
T
U
V
W
X
Y
Z

RTDM

Purpose: Real Time Data Migrator is part of the NetWare High Capacity Storage System (HCSS). It enables the capability to mount slower secondary media (such as tape or read/write optical) and migrate data from the server's higher speed primary media (magnetic hard disk) to the slower secondary media.

Syntax: LOAD *path* RTDM

Options: Replace *path* with the full NetWare path to the NLM. NetWare will look in SYS:SYSTEM by default.

Examples:

LOAD RTDM

Notes: Reference the documentation supplied with the data migration products purchased for more information.

See Also: LOAD

SCAN FOR NEW DEVICES

Purpose: Checks the disk channels for new disk hardware that has been added since the last time the server was booted.

This command can be used to register devices added after the server was booted, causing them to be displayed when the LIST DEVICES command is issued.

Syntax: SCAN FOR NEW DEVICES

Examples: To scan the disk channels for a newly installed SCSI hard disk, type the following at the system console:

SCAN FOR NEW DEVICES

Notes: This command does not show any output.

See Also: CD-ROM, LOAD, MODULES

SCHDELAY

Purpose: Helps prioritize the various server processes to use less of the server's CPU when the server is very busy.

Syntax: `LOAD SCHDELAY` *processnames* `=` *number*

Options:

Replace *processnames* with the process or processes for which you want to schedule delays.

Replace *number* with the scheduling delay number you want the process to use.

Rules and Considerations: If you load SCHDELAY with no parameters, a list of processes and their current SCHDELAY values will be displayed.

You can undo all SCHDELAY values that have been set by replacing processnames with ALL PROCESSES and replacing number with 0. This forces the server to give all processes the same priority.

Examples: To have NetWare reduce the amount of CPU time allotted to the disk remirroring process, type the following at the system console:

`LOAD SCHDELAY REMIRROR PROCESS = 2`

To list the current SCHDELAY values, type the following at the system console:

`LOAD SCHDELAY`

To run all processes without delay, type the following at the system prompt:

`LOAD SCHDELAY ALL PROCESSES = 0`

Notes: Scheduling values also can be viewed in MONITOR under the "Scheduling Information" option.

See Also: LOAD, MONITOR

SEARCH

Purpose: Sets a path at the file server to search for NLMs and network configuration (NCF) files.

Syntax: SEARCH *option*

Options: If the SEARCH command is entered by itself with no option, the current search paths appear.

Option	Function
ADD *number searchpath*	Adds an additional path to the current search path. The *number* variable is optional and refers to the desired position for inserting the new search path. The *searchpath* variable refers to the new search path.
DEL *number*	Deletes an existing search path. The number variable refers to an existing search path and must be included.

Rules and Considerations: Unless SEARCH is used, NetWare examines only the SYS:SYSTEM directory when looking for NLM and NCF files. If volume SYS: has not been mounted NetWare looks on the default DOS directory where SERVER.EXE was executed from.

If you use the SEARCH ADD command without specifying a number, the new search path is appended to the end of the search paths. Placing this command in the AUTOEXEC.NCF file causes it to be automatically run when the server is booted.

Important Messages: None

Examples: To search the SYS:NLM and SYS:SYSTEM directories for NLM and NCF files, type the following command:

SEARCH ADD SYS:NLM

To list the current search paths, type the following command:

SEARCH

A
B
C
D
E
F
G
H
I
J
K
L
M
N
O
P
Q
R
S
T
U
V
W
X
Y
Z

To delete the search path in the second position, type the following command:

SEARCH DEL 2

Notes: Use SEARCH if you keep NLMs in directories other than the SYS:SYSTEM directory. If you use SEARCH, you do not need to specify the path for the LOAD command every time you load these NLMs.

Using SECURE CONSOLE disables SEARCH.

See Also: LOAD, MOUNT, REMOVE DOS, SEARCH, SECURE CONSOLE

SECURE CONSOLE

Purpose: Enhances the security of the server's console by performing four major functions:

♦ Limits NLM loading to the SYS:SYSTEM directory. Anything not in SYS:SYSTEM will not be loaded.

♦ Prevents keyboard entry into the OS debugger.

♦ Restricts system date and time change to only console operators.

♦ Removes DOS from the file server. In 4.10, DOS is sent to disk cache.

Syntax: SECURE CONSOLE

Examples: To secure the server's console on a NetWare 4.10 server, type the following command at the System Console:

SECURE CONSOLE

Notes: The server must be rebooted to reverse the effects of SECURE CONSOLE. This command disables the SEARCH command.

See Also: REMOVE DOS, SEARCH

A
B
C
D
E
F
G
H
I
J
K
L
M
N
O
P
Q
R
S
T
U
V
W
X
Y
Z

SECURITY

Purpose: Displays a list of possible security problems. This list can include users, passwords, login scripts, and access privileges.

Syntax: SECURITY /C

Option	Description
/C	Optional switch that continuously lists potential security violations without pausing at the end of every screen page.

Rules and Considerations: To use the SECURITY program, you must log in as the supervisor or as a supervisor equivalent. The SECURITY program is run from the SYS:SYSTEM directory.

Important Messages:

```
Usage: security [/Continuous]
```

If the preceding message appears after you enter the SECURITY command, you ran the SECURITY program with incorrect syntax. Reenter the command again with the correct syntax.

The following sample output of the SECURITY program shows the types of violations you might encounter:

```
SECURITY EVALUATION UTILITY, Version 2.23

User BRANDON
  Has password expiration interval greater than 60 days
  Has no password assigned
  No Full Name specified

Group ACCT
  No Full Name specified

User DANNY (Full Name: Danny R. Kusnierz)
  Is security equivalent to user SUPERVISOR
  Has password expiration interval greater than 60 days
  Has no password assigned
```

```
User DEDE (Full Name: Dede Kusnierz )
  Is security equivalent to user SUPERVISOR
  Has password expiration interval greater than 60 days

User GUEST
  Has no login script
  Has no LOGIN_CONTROL property
  No Full Name specified

Group EVERYONE
  No Full Name specified

User SUPERVISOR (Full Name: System Supervisor)
Does not require a password
```

Examples: To print a list of potential security violations on a printer at the LPT1 port, type the following command:

SECURITY > LPT1:

Notes: Run SECURITY every time you modify the rights of a user or a group to ensure that you did not mistakenly introduce any security breaches into the system.

See Also: GRANT, NETADMIN (4.10), REVOKE, RIGHTS, SETPASS, TLIST

A
B
C
D
E
F
G
H
I
J
K
L
M
N
O
P
Q
R
S
T
U
V
W
X
Y
Z

SEND

Purpose: Enables you to send short messages from your workstation to any of the following: logged-in users or groups, the file server console, a particular workstation, or a set of workstations.

Syntax: **SEND** *messagetext* TO *destination*

Option	Function
messagetext	Specifies the message, which can be a maximum of 44 characters minus the length of the sending user's name.
destination	Specifies the user or group that will receive the message. Using any of the following formats, this variable can designate users, groups, the file server console, specific workstations, or all workstations.

The following are valid options for destination:

Option	Function
USER *userlist*	Enables you to send messages to one or several users. The USER specifier is optional. The *userlist* variable is an optional file server name followed by the name of a user. Multiple users are separated by commas.
GROUP *grouplist*	Enables you to send messages to one or several groups. The GROUP specifier is optional. The *grouplist* variable consists of an optional file server name followed by the name of a group. Separate multiple groups with commas.
servername /CONSOLE	Enables you to send messages to the file server console. The optional *servername* variable specifies a file server; CONSOLE specifies the file server console.
servername /EVERYBODY	Enables you to send messages to all workstations. The optional *servername* variable specifies a file server; EVERYBODY specifies all workstations.

Option	Function
STATION servername /stationlist	Enables you to send messages to specific workstations. The STATION specifier is optional. The following variables are optional: `servername` defaults to the current server; `stationlist` consists of a station number. Additional station numbers are separated by commas.

Rules and Considerations: A message sent with the SEND command can be a maximum of 44 characters in length. Because the user name of the person sending the message is included in the message line, the actual message length will be less than 44 characters. When the supervisor sends a message to another user, the maximum text length sent is 34 characters because the user name supervisor is 10 characters long.

If no file server name is specified, the default file server is used.

Users must be logged in to receive messages.

The workstation and login name of the sending user are displayed with the message text.

To send messages to users or groups on another server, you must be attached to that server.

Important Messages:

```
User/Group FS1/ALL does not exist.
```

If the preceding message appears, the user or group you specified does not exist. Reenter the message with a valid user or group name.

```
Message sent to CSOS/SUPERVISOR (station 1).
```

In the preceding example, the message was sent successfully to user SUPERVISOR logged in on station 1.

```
Message not sent to CSOS/HEATHER (station 2)
```

According to the preceding example, your message was not sent to the user HEATHER. Either HEATHER used the CASTOFF utility so that her workstation cannot receive messages or her workstation's incoming message buffer is full. To undo the effects of CASTOFF, HEATHER must use the CASTON utility to reenable message receipt. If the cause is a full message buffer, HEATHER must read enough messages to make room in the buffer.

Examples: To send a note to all members of the group STAFF about the 4:00 staff meeting, type either of the two following commands:

`SEND Remember - Staff mtg at 4:00 TO GROUP STAFF`

`SEND Remember - Staff mtg at 4:00 TO STAFF`

To send a note to the file server console to request that the console operator mount form 2 into printer 3 on the file server, type the command:

`SEND Pls mount form 2 in printer 3 TO CONSOLE`

To send a personal note to user JESSICA, type the command:

`SEND How about dinner tonight @ 8:00 TO JESSICA`

Notes: If you send a message to a user who is not currently logged in, the message will not be saved. To send messages that are longer than the maximum size allowed for your ID, you must purchase an E-mail package. E-mail packages enable you to send messages to users who are not currently logged in.

Receiving a message stops all processing under DOS. For this reason, do not send messages to unattended workstations, unless you are ready to explain why you stopped the user's computer from completing its task while the user was away from their desk.

See Also: BROADCAST, CASTOFF, CASTON

SEND

Purpose: Enables you to send short messages from the file server console to specific users, all users, or to workstations.

Syntax:

SEND *messagetext*

or

SEND *messagetext* TO *userlist*

or

SEND *messagetext* TO *stationlist*

Option	Description
messagetext	Specifies a message that can be up to 55 characters in length.
userlist	Specifies the user(s) who is to receive the message. Multiple users are separated by commas.
stationlist	Consists of a station number. Additional station numbers are followed by commas.

Rules and Considerations: A user must be logged in to receive a message from the console with the SEND command.

If a user list or station list is not specified, the message is sent to all workstations.

Examples: To remind all logged in users that the system will be shut down for maintenance this afternoon at 5:00, type the following command:

SEND Dont forget! Server shutdown today at 5:00

To send a message from the console to the user MICHAEL, type the following command:

A
B
C
D
E
F
G
H
I
J
K
L
M
N
O
P
Q
R
S
T
U
V
W
X
Y
Z

`SEND Stop sending junk messages to the console! TO MICHAEL`

To send a message from the console to workstations 14 and 17, type the following command:

`SEND Please LOGOUT now!!!! TO 14,17`

Notes: NetWare 2.2 uses the BROADCAST command instead of the SEND command.

Workstations receiving messages halt all processing under DOS. Do not send messages to unattended workstations unless you are willing to explain why you interrupted the user's computer as it processed tasks while the user was away from her desk.

See Also: BROADCAST, CASTOFF, CASTON

SEND

Purpose: Allows users to send short messages from their workstation to any of the following: logged in users, a predefined group of logged in users, the file server console, a particular workstation, a set of workstations, or some combination of the above. Also controls how incoming messages are handled by a workstation.

Syntax:

For NDS objects (NetWare 4.10):

```
SEND [ "messagetext" [ TO ] [ username ¦ groupname ¦ servername ]
[ /A= [ A ¦ N ¦ C ¦ P ] ] [ /P ] [ /S ] [ /? ]
```

For bindery objects (NetWare 2.x, 3.1x, or 4.0 bindery emulation objects):

```
SEND [ "messagetext" [ TO ] [ servername/ [ username ¦ groupname
¦ station number ] ] [ servername/ [ CONSOLE ¦ EVERYONE ] ] [ /B ]
```

Options: Replace messagetext with the message (up to 44 characters) you want sent.

Replace *username, groupname,* or *servername* with the intended recipient of the message.

Replace *station number* with the connection ID assigned by the server to the attached workstation.

Option	Description
/A= (Accept)	Determines what messages the workstation will accept. Four parameters control what and how messages are accepted.
A	Accepts all messages.
N	Accepts no messages.
C	Accepts messages only from the server's system console.

continues

Option	Description
P	Accepts messages, but in polled mode. The last message sent is stored at the server until the workstation polls the server for messages (see /P).
/P (Poll)	Polls the server to retrieve the last message sent.
/S (Show)	Displays the current mode of operation (for instance, A, C, N, or P).
/? (Help)	Displays online help.
/B (Bindery)	Indicates SEND is to operate in bindery mode.
CONSOLE	In Bindery mode, message should be sent to the server's console.
EVERYBODY	In bindery mode, message should be sent to the server's group EVERYONE.
/VER	Displays version information, and a list of files needed to run this command.

Rules and Considerations: The message can be a maximum of 44 characters in length.

In NDS mode, user objects must either be in the current context or be specified with a complete or partial name.

In Bindery mode, if no file server name is specified the default file server is used.

Users must be logged in to receive messages.

The workstation and login name of the sending user are displayed with the message text.

Important Messages: The following message would occur if SEND was unable to transmit the message:

```
Message not sent to CN=JACOB.OU=TRAINING_SOLUTIONS.O=GENDREAU_ENT
(station 2)
```

Either JACOB used the /A=N option so that his workstation cannot receive messages or his workstation's incoming message buffer is full. To undo the effects of /A=N, JACOB must use the /A=A option to reenable message receipt from other workstations. If the cause is a full message buffer,

JACOB must read and acknowledge messages quickly enough to make room in the message buffer.

Examples: To send a message to all members of the group STAFF reminding them about the 4:00 p.m. staff meeting, type the following command at the workstation:

```
SEND "Remember - Staff mtg at 4:00" TO STAFF
```

To send a message to the server's console to request that the server operator clear a workstation's connection with the server, type the following command at the workstation:

```
SEND "Please clear station 2's connection" TO TRAINING_SOLUTIONS
```

To send a message to an individual user with the common name JANE, type the following command at the workstation:

```
SEND "How about lunch @ 12:00?" TO CN=JANE
```

or

```
SEND "How about lunch @ 12:00?" TO JANE
```

Notes: The message will be displayed on the very first line of the workstation's display. If the *username* specified is not in your current context, you must include the full NDS name.

Receiving a message stops all processing at the workstation (except in MS Windows in 386 Enhanced mode) until the user acknowledges receipt of the message. For this reason, you should not send messages to unattended workstations, unless you are ready to explain why you stopped the user's computer from completing its task while the user was away from his or her desk. It is also a good idea to include the SEND /A=N command in the login script or AUTOEXEC.BAT file of workstations that are dedicated to specific processes, such as mainframe gateways, communication servers, print servers, and so on.

See Also: BROADCAST, SEND

SERVER

Purpose: Installs or boots a NetWare 3.1x or 4.10 file server.

Syntax: SERVER *parameter*

Options: Replace *parameter* with one of the following:

Option	Description
-S [*path*]*filename*	Specifies a file other than STARTUP.NCF to read during boot. Replace *filename* with the alternate file's name. If you do not specify a *path* SERVER.EXE will look for the alternate file in the current directory.
-NA	Prevents SERVER.EXE from executing the AUTOEXEC.NCF file.
-NS	Prevents the execution of STARTUP.NCF and AUTOEXEC.NCF by SERVER.EXE.
-C *buffersize*	Replace *buffersize* with the block size for the cache buffers. Do not use a buffer size larger than the physical block allocation size. Support values are 4 KB, 8 KB, 16 KB and the default is 4 KB.

Rules and Considerations: After NetWare executes SERVER.EXE, it attempts to run the commands in STARTUP.NCF and AUTOEXEC.NCF if these files have been created.

Important Messages:

```
*** This machine does not have an 80386 microprocessor ***
    NetWare 4.10 CANNOT BE RUN ON THIS MACHINE!!!
```

The preceding message informs you that NetWare must be run on a system with an 80386 or higher processor. Install NetWare on a file server with an 80386 or higher processor. Early 386 processors will fail this test due to an error with floating point processing.

```
Insufficient memory to run NetWare 3.11
  (requires at least 1 megabyte of extended memory)
```

The preceding message informs you that NetWare requires 1 MB of extended RAM (usually reported as 1640 KB) or 2 MB of RAM on most systems to load. If you have an extended memory manager loaded, you will get this message, too.

Examples: To begin the installation process on a new file server that has an 80386 or higher CPU, the required amount of extended RAM, and the network card or cards already installed, type the following command:

SERVER

To start the file server process on a NetWare file server that has NetWare installed, type the following command at the DOS prompt:

SERVER

Notes: SERVER.EXE will load much faster from a DOS partition on the hard drive than from floppy.

SERVER.EXE is the file that contains the serial number and concurrent user count.

See Also: DOWN, LOAD, REMOVE DOS, SECURE CONSOLE

A
B
C
D
E
F
G
H
I
J
K
L
M
N
O
P
Q
R
S
T
U
V
W
X
Y
Z

SET

Purpose: Enables you to display or change the values that tune the performance of the NetWare operating system.

Syntax: SET *variable = value*

Options: The SET command entered without a variable displays the list of available categories to choose from. Version 3.x has 9 options, 4.x has 12.

Option	Function
variable	Specifies a variable to change its setting.
value	Specifies a value to be assigned to the variable. Consult the *System Administration* manual for a list of variables and their allowed values.

Examples: To display the list of parameter categories, type the following command:

SET

To change a file server that encrypts passwords to allow passwords from workstations that are not encrypting, type the following:

SET ALLOW UNENCRYPTED PASSWORDS=ON

Notes: See FCONSOLE, SET TIME, and TIMESYNC for more information on setting the server's date and time.

See Also: MONITOR, SERVMAN

SET TIME

Purpose: Enables you to set the time or date or both from the console on a NetWare file server.

Syntax: `SET TIME` *mo/dy/yr hh:mm:ss*

Options: SET TIME entered without any parameters displays the current system time.

Rules and Considerations: You can set the date and time independently or together.

To set the time, substitute the hour in 24-hour format for `hh`, the minutes for `mm`, and the seconds for `ss`.

Times entered greater than 24 hours will be changed to 24 hours. For example, 25:15:00 becomes 01:15:00.

Important Messages: None

Examples: To set the date and time to 1 minute before midnight on New Years Eve, 1999, type the following:

`SET TIME 12/31/99 23:59:00`

To set the time to 3:15 in the afternoon, type the following:

`SET TIME 15:15:00`

To change the date to February 10, 1994, type the following:

`SET TIME 2/10/94`

Notes: Workstation dates and times will not correspond to the corrected file server date and time until the workstation shells are reloaded or they use the SYSTIME command.

Time also can be entered in 12-hour format if it is followed by AM or PM.

You can change the date to a date up to but not including the year 2080.

See Also: SET, SYSTIME, TIME

A
B
C
D
E
F
G
H
I
J
K
L
M
N
O
P
Q
R
S
T
U
V
W
X
Y
Z

SET TIME ZONE

Purpose: Displays or sets the file server's time zone. This information is used by CLIB in 3.1x NetWare, also to keep the server and NDS in sync with other servers on the network in NetWare 4.10.

Syntax: SET TIME ZONE = *timezone* [*hour* [*daylighttime*]]

Options:

Replace *timezone* with the server's time zone.

Replace *hour* with the number of hours west of Greenwich mean time (GMT).

Replace *daylighttime* with a three-letter abbreviation for the daylight saving time code.

Rules and Considerations: For NetWare versions 3.1x this command is used by CLIB to supply time zone information to other NLMs. It will not update your server's time automatically, use the SET TIME command.

In NetWare 4.10 this command is used by the TIMESYNC.NLM to keep all the NDS servers in the network in correct time synchronization.

This command will automatically be added to the AUTOEXEC.NCF file during a NetWare 4.10 installation or upgrade. Ordinarily there is no reason to change it unless the server is physically relocated to another time zone.

Examples: The following line should appear in a server's AUTOEXEC.NCF file if it is located in Phoenix, Arizona:

SET TIME ZONE = MST7

(Arizona does not support daylight saving time.)

The following line should appear in a server's AUTOEXEC.NCF file if it is located in Waterloo, Iowa:

SET TIME ZONE = CST7CDT

See Also: CLIB, SET TIME, TIMESYNC

SETPASS

Purpose: Enables users to change their passwords if they have the rights to do so.

Syntax: **SETPASS** `servername options`

Option	Description
`servername`	Optional variable that is set to the name of the file server that stores the password you want to change
`username`	Name of user whose password you want to set, if not your own
`options`	Replace with /? to view online help, or /VER to display version and related-files information

Important Messages:

`You are not connected to file server ABRACADABRA.`

In the preceding example, you typed **SETPASS ABRACADABRA** and thought that your current password would be changed to ABRACA-DABRA. To change your password correctly, type **SETPASS** without any parameters and follow the prompts.

`Access denied to NRP1/BRANDON, password not changed.`

The preceding example message shows the current password for user BRANDON was entered incorrectly at the SETPASS prompt. Retry the command by entering your current password.

Examples: In the following example, BRANDON changes his password using the SETPASS prompts. The passwords he types are not displayed on screen when they are entered. BRANDON presses Enter after responding to the prompts.

`F:\USERS\BRANDON>SETPASS`

`Enter old password for NRP/BRANDON:NCC1701`

```
Enter new password for NRP/BRANDON:NCC1701A

Retype new password for NRP/BRANDON:NCC1701A

The password for NRP/BRANDON has been changed.
```

Notes: NetWare security relies largely on users who must keep their passwords secret. Use SETPASS often to change your password, which helps to maintain a high level of security. You also can increase the security of your passwords by not using words associated with family, hobbies, friends, and so on. The best passwords are arbitrary combinations of letters and numbers.

When you change your password, if you are attached to multiple servers as the same users and the passwords are the same, SETPASS will ask if you would like to synchronize your passwords. Answering Yes will update all of the attached servers with your new password.

See Also: ATTACH, LOGIN, MAP

SETTTS

Purpose: Allows users to set and view logical and physical record locks for the Transaction Tracking System.

Syntax: SETTTS [*logical level* [*physical level*] [N ¦ D]] [/?]

Options: Replace *logical level* or *physical level* with the numeric value to which you want TTS set for this workstation. The levels indicate how many record locks TTS will ignore before tracking the transaction. Valid numeric values are 0 to 254.

SETTTS supports the following options:

Option	Function
N (None)	Sets both logical and physical record locks to 0 (none)
D (Disable)	Disables the logical and physical settings
/? (Help)	(4.10) Displays on-line help for SETTTS
/C	Provides continuous scrolling of output
/VER (Version)	Provides version information and a list of related files needed for this command to run

Rules and Considerations: When you log out or power off the workstation, the settings are reset to 0.

A value of 255 also disables a setting.

Examples: To view the current TTS settings for a workstation, type:

SETTTS

To reset both logical and physical settings for a workstation to the default (0), type the following:

SETTTS N

A
B
C
D
E
F
G
H
I
J
K
L
M
N
O
P
Q
R
S
T
U
V
W
X
Y
Z

To disable the logical level and set the physical level to 6, type the following:

SETTTS D 6

To view the online help, type the following:

SETTTS /?

See Also: DISABLE TTS

SLIST

Purpose: Lists file servers that are available for your workstation.

Syntax: **SLIST** *servername* /C

Option	Function
servername	Specifies a file server. If you enter SLIST with a file server name, the file server displays if it is available.
/C	Specifies that SLIST continuously scroll the screens instead of pause at the end of every screen page.

Rules and Considerations: If you enter SLIST without a file server name, a list appears of every available file server.

Important Messages:

```
Server CSOS2 not found.
```

The preceding message shows the requested file server, CSOS2, is not available. In this case, the preceding command was SLIST CSOS2.

Examples: The following is example output from the SLIST command:

```
Known NetWare File Servers   Network     Node Address        Status
-- -- -- -- --
CSOS                         [19910001] [ 2608C0B39CA]       Default
TRAINING-311                   [ 1 ]    [ 1B23785B3 ]
Total of 2 file servers found
```

In the preceding example server CSOS which has Default after the network and node addresses is the server of your default DOS drive if you are logged in. If you run SLIST prior to the login command the Default server is the server whose login directory you are in.

See Also: LOGIN, MAP, NLIST

SMODE

Purpose: Enables you to set or view the method a program uses to search for data files and overlays.

Syntax: **SMODE** *filepath searchmode* /**SUB**

Option	Description
filepath	Consists of an optional path and a file specification (wild cards are allowed).
searchmode	Specifies the type of search method you want to use. Valid search modes include the following:

	0	The shell default. Program follows instructions in SHELL.CFG.
	1	If the program specifies a directory path, it will search only that path. If no path is specified, the search extends through all search drives.
	2	If the program specifies a directory path, it searches only that path. If no path is specified, only the default directory is searched.
	3	Similar to the preceding search mode. If, however, the search is Read Only, the search is extended to directories in the search drives.
	4	(reserved, do not use)
	5	If the program specifies a directory path, it searches that path followed by the search drives. If no path is specified, the default directory is searched, followed by the search drives.
	6	(reserved, do not use)
	7	If the program specifies a directory path, that path is searched first. Then, if the open request is Read Only, the program searches the search drives.

Option	Description
	If no directory path is given, the program searches the default directory. Then, if the open request is Read Only, the program searches the search drives.
	If *searchmode* is not specified, the current search modes of the selected files appear.
/SUB	Extends the effect of the commands to all subdirectories of the requested directory. A file path must be used if /SUB is included.

Rules and Considerations: SMODE operates on executable files and ignores nonexecutable files.

Important Messages:

`No EXECUTABLE files could be found with pattern *.*`

The preceding sample message displays when SMODE is executed in a directory that has no executable files. Change to a directory that contains executable files or specify the path to the desired files.

`Mode 4 is reserved.`

The preceding sample message displays when you attempt to set a reserved search mode. To correct this problem, assign a valid search mode.

Examples: To set the program 123.EXE so that it does not search for data files on search drives, type the following command:

SMODE 123.EXE 2

Notes: The default for most executable files is search mode 0 (shell default). You can set the default shell variable SEARCH MODE = *searchmode* in the NET.CFG file which should be located in the directory from which you load your DOS workstation shells.

See Also: MAP, FLAG

A
B
C
D
E
F
G
H
I
J
K
L
M
N
O
P
Q
R
S
T
U
V
W
X
Y
Z

SPEED

Purpose: Displays a number that represents the relative speed of a NetWare file server.

Syntax: SPEED

Options: None

Important Messages: None

Examples: To display the relative speed of a NetWare file server, type the following command:

SPEED

Notes: The reported speed of a NetWare file server is relative. A speed of 300 compared to a speed of 150, for example, shows that the first file server is twice as fast as the second. For an accurate comparison of two file servers, both servers must run the same version of NetWare. An 80386SX CPU running at 16 MHz should get a rating of approximately 95. An 80386DX CPU running at 16 MHz should get a rating of approximately 120. An 80486DX/33 EISA based machine should get a rating of approximately 915. And a Pentium-based EISA server will get speed ratings of 3000 or above.

SPOOL

Purpose: Creates, maintains, and lists spooler mappings to print queues. These mappings are required to setup default print queues for CAPTURE and NPRINT. It also supports applications written to printer numbers instead of print queues.

Syntax:

`SPOOL`

or

`SPOOL` *printernumber* `TO QUEUE` *queuename*

Rules and Considerations: If you enter SPOOL without a printer number or a queue name, the current spooler mappings display.

Valid options for the *printernumber* variable range from 0 to 4.

Valid *queuename* options include any existing print queue name.

Important Messages:

```
Spooler 0 is directed into printer HPLASER
Spooler 1 is directed into printer MATRIX1
```

A SPOOL status message similar to this appears when the SPOOL command is entered with no options.

Examples: To spool printer 1 to a print queue named HPLASER3, type the following command:

`SPOOL 1 TO QUEUE HPLASER3`

To display a list of current spool mappings, type the following:

`SPOOL`

Notes: You can include SPOOL commands in the AUTOEXEC.SYS file for NetWare 2.2 or AUTOEXEC.NCF file for 3.1x and 4.10. By placing the SPOOL command in one of these files it automatically loads when the file server is started.

See Also: CAPTURE, NPRINT, PRINTER, QUEUE

A
B
C
D
E
F
G
H
I
J
K
L
M
N
O
P
Q
R
S
T
U
V
W
X
Y
Z

SPXCONFG

Purpose: Configures NetWare SPX parameters.

Syntax: `LOAD SPXCONFG` *option...option*

Option	Function
A=	Sets SPX watchdog abort time-out in ticks (A tick is 1/18 of a second)
V=	Sets SPX watchdog verify time-out (in ticks)
W=	Sets SPX Ack wait time-out (in ticks)
R=	Sets SPX default retry count
S=	Maximum concurrent SPX sessions
Q=1	Quiet mode: suppresses display of the settings
H	Displays a help screen
I	IPX maximum socket table size

Rules and Considerations: You must specify a path if SPXCONFIG.NLM is not installed in the SYS:SYSTEM directory.

Important Messages: None

Examples: To load SPXCONFG, type the following command:

`LOAD SPXCONFG`

and an SPXCONFG menu appears.

See Also: INETCFG, IPX

SPXS

Purpose: Used with NLMs that support the STREAMS-based IPX protocol services.

Syntax:

LOAD SPXS (3.1x, 4.10)

or

LOAD SPXS LDLFILE=*name* (4.10)

Options: Replace *name* with the name of a data file containing SPX timer defaults and physical packet size tables.

Rules and Considerations: To properly load STREAMS-based IPX/SPX protocol services for an NLM that requires these services, load these NLMs in the following order:

1. STREAMS.NLM (autoloaded in 4.10)

2. CLIB.NLM

3. TLI.NLM

4. IPXS.NLM

5. SPXS.NLM

Important Messages: None

Examples: To load SPXS, type the following command:

LOAD SPXS

See Also: CLIB, IPXS, STREAMS, TLI

A
B
C
D
E
F
G
H
I
J
K
L
M
N
O
P
Q
R
S
T
U
V
W
X
Y
Z

STREAMS

Purpose: Provides an interface among NetWare and other transport protocols. STREAMS is loaded before CLIB or STREAMS-based protocol services.

Syntax: `LOAD STREAMS` *msgsize=N*

Options: (4.10) Replace *msgsize =N* with a maximum message size, specified in bytes. Default is 8.192. Range is between 4,096 and 65,535.

Rules and Considerations: STREAMS must be loaded before CLIB is loaded. It is usually autoloaded by any module that needs it.

To properly load STREAMS-based IPX/SPX protocol services for an NLM that requires it, load these NLMs in the following order:

1. STREAMS.NLM

2. CLIB.NLM

3. TLI.NLM

4. IPXS.NLM

5. SPXS.NLM

Important Messages: None

Examples: To load STREAMS, type the following command:

`LOAD STREAMS`

See Also: CLIB, IPXS, SPXS, TLI

SYSTIME

Purpose: Enables you to view and change the date and time on your workstation to that of a file server.

Syntax:

`SYSTIME`

or

`SYSTIME` *fileserver*

Option	Function
fileserver	Specifies a file server that is to be used to set the date and time of a user's workstation
/VER	Displays version information and a list of files required by this utility in order to run
/?	Displays online help

Rules and Considerations: If a file server is not specified, SYSTIME configures your workstations date and time to that of the default file server.

Important Messages:

`Current System Time:   Monday  November  11, 1992  3:06 pm`

The preceding example appears when the SYSTIME command is used without any parameters.

`You are not attached to server HELP.`

The preceding example displays when a nonattached file server is specified. Attach to the requested file server or reenter the command with a valid file server name.

A
B
C
D
E
F
G
H
I
J
K
L
M
N
O
P
Q
R
S
T
U
V
W
X
Y
Z

Examples: To set the workstation date and time to that of the default file server, type the following command:

`SYSTIME`

Notes: If you change the time on the file server with the SET TIME console command, you can synchronize the workstation clock with the file server clock by using SYSTIME.

See Also: SET TIME, TIME

TIME

Purpose: Displays the date and time at the file server console.

Syntax: `TIME`

Options: None

Rules and Considerations: TIME displays only the system date and time. You must use SET TIME to change the date or time.

Important Messages: None

Examples: To display the current system date and time at the file server console, type the following:

```
TIME
```

Notes: See FCONSOLE, SET TIME, and TIMESYNC for more information on setting the server's date and time.

See Also: SET TIME, SYSTIME

A
B
C
D
E
F
G
H
I
J
K
L
M
N
O
P
Q
R
S
T
U
V
W
X
Y
Z

TIMESYNC

Purpose: Synchronizes the server's time with other 4.10 servers across the network and allows monitoring of a server's internal time.

Syntax: LOAD [*path*]**TIMESYNC** [*parameter*]

Option	Description
path	Replace path with the full path to the TIMESYNC.NLM file if it is not in the search path for NLMs. By default, the server searches the SYS:SYSTEM directory.
parameter	Replace parameter with an option from the following table.
ADD Time Source = *servername*	The maximum length of servername is 48 characters; it is used to add a server to the time source list. The time source list specifies servers to check time with.
Configuration File = *path*	The settings for all of these parameters can be set in the TIMESYNC.CFG file. The TIMESYNC.CFG file is read when TIMESYNC loads. Replace path with the full path to the configuration file, including its name.
Configured Sources = *value*	If value is equal to ON, then the TIMESYNC NLM only checks with servers set through the ADD Time Source option. If set to OFF, TIMESYNC checks with any server that advertises itself as a time source. OFF is the default.

Option	Description
`Directory Tree Mode = value`	Set value to OFF to look for time source servers on the entire network. Set to ON to look only in this server's Directory Tree. Default is ON.
`Hardware Clock = value`	The default for value is ON. Setting it to off tells the server not to read the machine hardware clock because a time signal is being received from an external source (such as an atomic clock). All servers in the Directory tree must be set the same.
`Polling Count = #`	Replace # with the number of packets to exchange with other servers when polling for time. Larger numbers increase network traffic. The default value of # is 3.

Rules and Considerations: The TIMESYNC NLM is loaded by the server at startup automatically; rarely will you need to load it manually.

Examples: To load the TIMESYNC NLM and specify a configuration file, type the following at the server console:

```
LOAD TIMESYNC CONFIGURATION FILE = SYS:SYSTEM\TIMESYNC.CFG
```

Notes: See the SET command section of the Utilities Reference manual for more information on TIMESYNC parameters.

Also See: SERVMAN

A
B
C
D
E
F
G
H
I
J
K
L
M
N
O
P
Q
R
S
T
U
V
W
X
Y
Z

TLI

Purpose: Supports STREAMS and CLIB and enables them to use transport protocols such as SPXS and IPXS. TLP is an NLM that stands for Transport Layer Protocol.

Syntax: `LOAD TLI`

Options: You can specify the path from which to load TLI if it is other than the default for NLMS.

Rules and Considerations: Both STREAMS and CLIB must be loaded before loading TLI because TLI supports STREAMS and CLIB.

One of the STREAMS protocol modules, such as SPXS or IPXS or both, must be loaded after TLI is loaded.

Important Messages: None

Examples: To completely load STREAMS support with IPXS and SPXS at the file server console, enter these modules in the following order:

1. STREAMS.NLM

2. CLIB.NLM

3. TLI.NLM (will autoload STREAMS and CLIB if needed)

4. IPXS.NLM

5. SPXS.NLM

See Also: CLIB, IPXS, SPXS, STREAMS

TLIST

Purpose: Displays a list of trustees for the specified file or directory.

Syntax:

TLIST *dirpath option*

or

TLIST *filepath option*

Option	Function
dirpath	Specifies a NetWare directory on the currently logged file server.
filepath	Specifies a NetWare file path on the currently logged file server.
option	Lists group or user trustees or both, depending on the specified option. Leave *option* blank to list both group and user trustees. Specify GROUPS to list group trustees, or specify USERS to list to user trustees.

Rules and Considerations: Wild cards are supported for directory and file specifications. You must be logged in as Supervisor or be a supervisor equivalent to use TLIST.

If you do not specify USERS or GROUPS in the *option* parameter, both will be displayed.

Important Messages:

```
NRP\PROGS:UTILITY
No trustees found.
```

The preceding example shows that the specified directory has no group or user trustees. Use GRANT or SYSCON to assign trustees.

```
Path does not exist.
```

A
B
C
D
E
F
G
H
I
J
K
L
M
N
O
P
Q
R
S
T
U
V
W
X
Y
Z

A
B
C
D
E
F
G
H
I
J
K
L
M
N
O
P
Q
R
S
T
U
V
W
X
Y
Z

The preceding message displays when a directory or file specification is entered that does not exist. Enter the correct directory or file specification.

Examples: To display the trustees of the SHAREDOC directory on volume DATA of file server NRP if you are currently logged into this file server, type the following command:

`TLIST NRP/DATA:SHAREDOC`

The previous command displays the following output:

```
NRP\DATA:SHAREDOC
User trustees:
  DEDE [RWCEMFA] Dede Kusnierz
  FRED [RWCEMFA] Fred Flintstone
  —

Group trustees:
  SECS [    ]
```

To list the user trustees of the PUBLIC directory on the default file server, type the following command:

`TLIST SYS:PUBLIC USERS`

To list the group trustees of the PUBLIC directory on the default file server, type the following command:

`TLIST SYS:PUBLIC GROUPS`

Notes: To specify the current directory or the parent directory quickly, use the period (.) and double period (..) DOS specifications instead of typing the entire directory name.

See Also: GRANT, REMOVE, REVOKE, RIGHTS

TOKENRPL

Purpose: Loads file server support enabling stations without floppy disk drives but with Token Ring network adapters to boot from the file server.

Syntax: `LOAD TOKENRPL`

Options: None

Rules and Considerations: TOKENRPL supports remote program loading only on Token Ring network adapters.

The network adapters in the workstations that do not have floppy disk drives must also support RPL (Remote Program Load).

Important Messages: None

Examples: To enable Token Ring workstations that do not have floppy disk drives to attach to a NetWare 3.11 file server when they first boot, enter the following command at the file server console:

`LOAD TOKENRPL`

Notes: Working with workstations that do not have floppy disk drives requires much planning. See the NetWare Administration manual for a complete explanation of TOKENRPL.

See Also: DOSGEN

A
B
C
D
E
F
G
H
I
J
K
L
M
N
O
P
Q
R
S
T
u
V
W
X
Y
Z

TRACK OFF

Purpose: Turns off the display of router traffic from the file server console.

Syntax: TRACK OFF

Options: None

Rules and Considerations: The TRACK OFF command is needed to turn off the display of router activity only after it has been turned on with TRACK ON.

Important Messages: None

Examples: To disable the display of router activity from the file server console, type the following:

TRACK OFF

See Also: TRACK ON

TRACK ON

Purpose: Displays information used to build router tracking tables. Two types of information are displayed, RIP (Router Information Protocol) and SAP (Service Advertising Protocol). RIPs contain router table updates that are sent between routers. RIPs also are used by workstations seeking a server to attach to. SAPs are used to alert the router tables of the location of services such as: file servers, print servers, fax server to name a few.

Syntax: `TRACK ON`

Options: None

Rules and Considerations: The TRACK ON command can be entered at the file server console or at the console prompt of a router running ROUTER.EXE.

TRACK ON displays connection, network, and server requests.

IN requests are those the file server or router is receiving. OUT requests are those the file server or router is sending.

Important Messages: None

Examples: To enable display of the routing activity of the file server at the file server console, type the following:

`TRACK ON`

See Also: TRACK OFF

A
B
C
D
E
F
G
H
I
J
K
L
M
N
O
P
Q
R
S
T
U
V
W
X
Y
Z

UIMPORT

Purpose: To import an existing non-NDS (NetWare Directory Services) database for use in an NDS tree.

Syntax: **UIMPORT** `control_file data_file options`

Options	Functions
`control_file`	Provides the name of the file with information regarding how the user data should be loaded into the directory.
`data_file`	Provides the name of the ASCII text file that contains all of the attribute values.
`options`	Replace *options* with any of the following:
	/? Displays online help.
	/VER Displays version information and a list of files needed by this utility in order to run.
	/C Provides continuous scrolling of resulting output.

Rules and Considerations: The data file must be a delimited ASCII text file. The most common delimiter is a comma.

The control file defines how records in the data file are to be imported into NDS, and which fields (NDS properties) the data is to be placed into.

Examples: To see version information for the UIMPORT utility, type the following at the prompt:

UIMPORT /VER

Important Messages: None

Notes: None

A
B
C
D
E
F
G
H
I
J
K
L
M
N
O
P
Q
R
S
T
u·
V
W
X
Y
Z

UNBIND

Purpose: Removes a communications protocol from a LAN driver for a network adapter card that was added to the LAN driver with BIND.

Syntax: UNBIND *protocol* **FROM** *landriver*

Option	Description
protocol	The previously bound communications protocol, usually IPX
landriver	The name of the LAN driver from which to remove the communications protocol

Rules and Considerations: A protocol must have been added to a LAN driver with the BIND command in order for you to unbind it.

Currently supplied NetWare LAN drivers include NE1000, NE2, NE2000, NE232, RXNET, and TOKEN, although any vendor-supplied LAN driver can be specified.

Important Messages: None

Examples: To remove the IPX protocol from the NE232 LAN driver at the file server console, type the following:

UNBIND IPX FROM NE232

Notes: When you unbind a protocol from a LAN driver, the LAN that was supported by that driver and all the workstations supported by that protocol can no longer communicate through the file server.

You can also specify board parameters, which must be specified the same way they were when you used the related BIND command.

See Also: BIND

UNLOAD

Purpose: Removes a NetWare Loadable Module (NLM) from file server memory.

Syntax: **UNLOAD** *nlmname*

Option	Description
nlmname	The name of the NLM to unload from memory

Important Messages: None

Examples: UNLOAD NE232

Notes: Use UNLOAD to remove unnecessary maintenance modules such as INSTALL that have been loaded for temporary use. After the NLM is unloaded, the memory it previously occupied returns to caching, which usually increases system performance.

Do not use UNLOAD to remove any NLMs necessary to the operation of your file server. This appears obvious, but the always "up" nature of a 386 file server might make you forget when you unload the particular NLM that some maintenance tasks require that you inform the users that the LAN will be unavailable, or that a particular feature they expect to use will be unavailable.

If an NLM you want to unload is required by another NLM, it will not unload unless the other NLM is first unloaded.

See Also: LOAD, VREPAIR

A
B
C
D
E
F
G
H
I
J
K
L
M
N
O
P
Q
R
S
T
u
V
W
X
Y
Z

UNMIRROR

Purpose: Manually shuts down mirroring on a dedicated file server.

Syntax: UNMIRROR *drivenumber*

Option	Description
drivenumber	Substitute the drive number of one drive of a mirror pair

Rules and Considerations: After mirroring has been shut down on a particular drive, that drive no longer is updated with disk drive activity.

Hot fix remains in effect for the other drive in the mirror pair.

Important Messages:

`Invalid physical drive specified.`

The preceding message indicates that you did not specify a drive number when entering the UNMIRROR command. Retry the command with the correct drive number specified.

`Physical drive and its mirror do not exist or are totally shut down.`

This message indicates that you have specified a drive number that does not exist, or is not available. Retry UNMIRROR with the correct drive number specified.

Examples: To turn off mirroring on drive 01, which you intend to replace with a new drive after you shut down the server, type the following:

`UNMIRROR 01`

Notes: The UNMIRROR command generally is useful only if: the mirroring feature is not working correctly; one of the drives in a drive pair keeps failing enough to slow performance but not enough for the operating system to disable mirroring; or if you intend to remove the specified drive after shutting down the file server.

Disabling mirroring leaves you with only hot-fix protection on the remaining drive.

If you accidentally unmirror a drive, be careful to specify the correct drive number when you invoke REMIRROR, or the newer information will be overwritten with the older information of the unmirrored drive.

See Also: DISK, REMIRROR

A
B
C
D
E
F
G
H
I
J
K
L
M
N
O
P
Q
R
S
T
u
V
W
X
Y
Z

UPLOAD

Purpose: Lets you run the installation utilities from an existing network or from a hard disk instead of from disk.

Syntax: UPLOAD

Rules and Considerations: After entering this command, you are prompted to provide the letter of the source drive (where the installation disk will be read) and then the destination drive (where the files are to be copied).

Important Messages: None

See Also: INSTALL

UPS

Purpose: Loads hardware support for an uninterruptible power supply on a file server.

Syntax: **LOAD UPS** *type port, discharge recharge wait*

Option	Description
TYPE=*name*	Replace *name* with one of the following: DCB, EDCB, MOUSE, STANDALONE, KEYCARD, other.
PORT=*ioadd*	Replace *ioadd* with the hexadecimal port address of the card specified by TYPE. No PORT address required if TYPE = mouse.
DISCHARGE=*rate*	*rate* is the number of minutes the UPS can power the server. Check the UPS manual and play it safe. Default is 60. Range is 1 to 3976821 minutes.
RECHARGE=*rate*	Replace *rate* with the number of minutes it takes to recharge the battery after normal power is restored. Default is 60 Range is 1 to 3976821 minutes.
WAIT=*number*	In 4.10 only, replace *number* with the amount of time in seconds to delay UPS activation after a power fault is detected. Range is 1 to 300 seconds.

Rules and Considerations: If the UPS command is entered without parameters, you will be prompted to supply parameters.

The UPS must be one supported by the UPS.NLM, or you will have to use the NLM supplied with the UPS.

UPS.NLM must be loaded before UPS support is enabled.

Important Messages:

```
WARNING: UPS hardware configuration error was detected. Check for
errors in your UPS hardware configuration settings.
```

If you receive the preceding message, the UPS NLM was not loaded

A
B
C
D
E
F
G
H
I
J
K
L
M
N
O
P
Q
R
S
T
u
V
W
X
Y
Z

because of a configuration error. LOAD the UPS.NLM again, correcting the settings for the online and low battery configuration.

```
UPS is shutting down server GROUP1. Commercial power has failed and
the battery is too low.
```

This message indicates that file server GROUP1 has been automatically shut down by the UPS software because it recognized a power failure and the battery was too low or ran down because commercial power was out too long. To correct this, wait until commercial power is restored and then restart the file server process.

Examples: To install UPS hardware support and be prompted for the parameters, type the following:

LOAD UPS

Notes: Use INSTALL.NLM to put the LOAD UPS parameters line into your AUTOEXEC.NCF to make sure that UPS support is loaded when the file server is booted.

See Also: UPS STATUS, UPS TIME

UPS

Purpose: Displays the status of an uninterruptible power supply.

Syntax: UPS

Options: None

Important Messages:

UPS Monitoring Disabled

You receive the preceding message if no UPS is attached to your system, or if there is no SERVER.CFG file enabling the UPS.

UPS enabled on NPR3

The preceding message displays at file server boot time to indicate that the SERVER.CFG contained proper information and UPS monitoring has been enabled.

Examples: To check the current status of a UPS attached to the file server at the file server console, type the following:

UPS

To enable the UPS on a NetWare 2.x file server to include the appropriate command lines in the SERVER.CFG file, type the command:

UPS TYPE=*n*

Replace *n* with one of the following numbers:

   1 for stand-alone monitor boards

   2 for host bus adapter (e.g. DCB)

   3 for SS keycard

   4 for PS/2 mouse ports

To specify 10 minutes as the amount of time that users have to log out after a loss of commercial power, type the following command:

UPS DOWN=10

A
B
C
D
E
F
G
H
I
J
K
L
M
N
O
P
Q
R
S
T
u
V
W
X
Y
Z

To specify 30 seconds as the amount of time in seconds that passes before users are notified that commercial power has been restored, enter the following command:

```
UPS WAIT=30
```

Notes: Refer to the manuals supplied with the UPS to find out the valid setting for the UPS DOWN= setting in the SERVER.CFG file. If the time you set for the server to shut down is longer than the battery will last, users will not be given ample notice to complete their work and the file server will be shut off by the UPS before the operating system has had a chance to down the file server.

See Also: DOWN

UPS STATUS

Purpose: Checks the status of the UPS attached to the file server.

Syntax: UPS STATUS

Options: None

Rules and Considerations: UPS must be loaded before UPS STATUS is a valid command.

Important Messages:

??? Unknown Command

The preceding message informs you that you have not loaded the UPS.NLM file for UPS support. You must LOAD UPS before UPS STATUS is available.

Examples: To check the current status of the uninterruptible power supply attached to the file server, type the following:

UPS STATUS

Notes: When you invoke the UPS STATUS command, the times displayed are usually based on those entered with the UPS TIME command and are therefore not guaranteed. If UPS recognizes less power than was expected from one of the more intelligent UPS devices, or if battery power fails, the file server will be terminated regardless of the displayed status.

See Also: UPS, UPS TIME

A
B
C
D
E
F
G
H
I
J
K
L
M
N
O
P
Q
R
S
T
u
V
W
X
Y
Z

UPS TIME

Purpose: Sets or changes the estimates for UPS battery discharge and recharge times.

Syntax:

`UPS TIME discharge recharge wait`

Options:

Option	Description
DISCHARGE=rate	rate is the number of minutes the UPS can power the server. Check the UPS manual and play it safe. (4.10) Default is 20. Range is 1 to 3976821 minutes.
RECHARGE=rate	Replace rate with the number of minutes it takes to recharge the battery after normal power is restored. Default is 60. Range is 1 to 3976821 minutes.
WAIT=number	In 4.10 only, replace number with the amount of time in seconds to delay UPS activation after a power fault is detected. Default is 15. Range is 1 to 300 seconds.

Rules and Considerations: The UPS loadable module must be loaded before UPS TIME is a valid command.

Examples: To set the UPS battery backup time to 15 minutes and the recharge time to 30 minutes, type the following:

`UPS TIME 15 30`

Notes: Do not enter times that do not conform to the ratings for your UPS. Under certain conditions, your equipment can be severely damaged if a battery backup was run down to a complete loss of power before the file server and UPS were shut down.

Enter valid times for the discharge, as this will guarantee that the file server is not prematurely switched off by the UPS before the software shuts down the file server process.

See Also: UPS, UPS STATUS

USERLIST

4.11
Nlist User

Purpose: Displays a list of logged-in users and some status information for those users.

Syntax: USERLIST *userspec /C /option*

Option	Description
userspec	An optional file server specification followed by a user name for which you are requesting status. The wild-card character * may be used.
/A	Displays network address information with the user list display.
/O	Displays object type information with the user list display.
/C	Displays a continuous list without pausing at the end of each screen page for long lists.

Important Messages:

```
User Information for Server CSOS
Connection  User Name      Login Time
— — — — —   — —  — —       — —  — —
No users named FS2.
```

The preceding message shows that the requested user named with the USERLIST command was not found. In this case it appears as if the slash was not typed after the file server name. Type the slash after the file server name and try again.

```
You are not attached to server FS2.
```

The preceding message shows that you tried to check the user list on file server FS2, but that you are not attached to it. Log in to it or attach to it, and then retry the USERLIST command.

Examples: If you type **USERLIST /A**, you receive output as follows:

```
User Information for Server NORTH386
Connection  User Name       Network  Node Address  Login Time
----------  ----------      -------  ------------  ----------
    1       * SUPERVISOR    [CDC]    [ 1B1EFDDB]   9-14-1992 9:10 am
    2       *SU1            [  5]    [ 1B191D38]   9-14-1992 9:30 am
```

If you type **USERLIST /O**, you receive output as follows:

```
User Information for Server NORTH 386
Connection  User Name       Login Time          Object Type
----------  ----------      ----------          -----------
    1       * SUPERVISOR    9-14-1992  9:10 am      User
    2       *SU1            9-14-1992 10:28 am      User
```

Notes: The asterisk in the user listing shows which entry displays the information for your workstation. Thus, if you are logged in on more than one workstation, you can determine which connection you are at without having to use the WHOAMI command.

See Also: NLIST (4.10), SLIST, TLIST, WHOAMI

VAP

Purpose: Displays a list of loaded value-added processes on a NetWare 2.x file server.

Syntax: VAP

Rules and Considerations: The VAP command displays not only a list of all loaded VAPs, but also the console commands the VAP will accept.

VAPs are loaded by copying them to the SYS:SYSTEM directory of the file server. The VAPs are loaded after the file server is booted.

Because VAPs also can be loaded on routers, the VAP command also works at the (:) prompt on routers.

Important Messages:

```
No Value Added Processes loaded.
```

This message is displayed if you have not loaded any VAPs. To load VAPs, they must be copied into the SYS:SYSTEM directory. They are enabled after the server is booted.

Examples: To view a list of all loaded VAPs and the command available to them, type the following:

VAP

See Also: OFF

A
B
C
D
E
F
G
H
I
J
K
L
M
N
O
P
Q
R
S
T
U
V
W
X
Y
Z

A
B
C
D
E
F
G
H
I
J
K
L
M
N
O
P
Q
R
S
T
U
V
W
X
Y
Z

VER

Purpose: Checks the file server's NetWare operating system version, release, and user count information from the file server console.

Syntax: VER

Options: None

Important Messages:

```
Dedicated Netware V2.2(100) Rev. A 2/11/91
```

This sample message displays operating system version, user count, revision, and release date.

Examples: To check the version information, type the following:

VER

See Also: CONFIG, FCONSOLE, MONITOR, NVER, VERSION

VERSION

Purpose: Displays version information for NetWare EXE files containing version information.

Syntax: VERSION *filespec*

Option	Function
filespec	Specifies the location of the file to check on the file server including the file server and directory name as well as the file name

Rules and Considerations: Wild cards are supported.

If you invoke VERSION against a file without version information, the file's checksum is calculated.

Important Messages:

```
NET$OS.EXE:
  Version Dedicated NetWare V2.2
  (C) Copyright 1983-1991 Novell Inc.
  Checksum is 61FD.
```

The preceding message displays example output from the VERSION command.

Examples: To display the previous output, type the following:

VERSION SYS:SYSTEM/NET$OS.EXE

See Also: NVER, VER

VERSION

Purpose: Displays the NetWare operating system version and copyright information at the file server console.

Syntax: VERSION

Options: None

Important Messages: None

Examples: To display the operating system version number and copyright information at the file server, type the following:

VERSION

See Also: NVER, VER

VOLUMES

Purpose: Displays a list of available drive volumes from the file server console.

Syntax: VOLUMES

Options: None

Rules and Considerations: The VOLUMES command lists only volumes that currently are mounted.

Examples: For a list of mounted volumes, type the following at the file server console:

VOLUMES

Notes: Flags are also displayed in 4.10 and are the following:

Cp   File compression enabled
Sa   Block suballocation enabled
Mg   Migration enabled

See Also: DISMOUNT, MOUNT

A
B
C
D
E
F
G
H
I
J
K
L
M
N
O
P
Q
R
S
T
U
V
W
X
Y
Z

A
B
C
D
E
F
G
H
I
J
K
L
M
N
O
P
Q
R
S
T
U
V
W
X
Y
Z

VREPAIR

Purpose: VREPAIR is used to repair Netware volumes with data errors on them. In version 2.2, the VREPAIR utility is run from a DOS prompt of a downed server. For version 3.1x and 4.10, VREPAIR is an NLM that can run while the server is online, although it cannot be run on a volume that is mounted.

Syntax:

VREPAIR (2.2)

or

LOAD VREPAIR (3.1x)

or

LOAD VREPAIR *logname* (4.10)

Rules and Considerations: Other volumes can be accessed while a defective volume is being repaired by VREPAIR, unless that volume being repaired is SYS.

The VREPAIR command should be invoked whenever file allocation table (FAT) errors, disk read errors, mirroring errors at boot time, or power failures have corrupted a volume.

Rerun VREPAIR until it completes with no errors; this could take three or more passes.

In 4.10, you can include a path and file name for a log into which VREPAIR information can be stored.

Important Messages:

```
Error reading in volume directory.
```

or

```
Invalid available entry.
```

or

```
Invalid deleted file block.
```

or

```
Invalid directory number code.
```

or

```
Invalid user restriction node...too many trustees.
```

or

```
Invalid Maximum Space defined in Subdirectory.
```

or

```
Invalid volume header / root directory entry.
```

The preceding messages indicate that NetWare had trouble mounting a volume. Invoke VREPAIR to repair.

Examples: To invoke the VREPAIR command on a damaged NetWare volume, type the following:

LOAD VREPAIR

Notes: The VREPAIR command sometimes causes loss or damage to files. You should have a good backup and be prepared to replace some data after executing VREPAIR, although the command usually does not cause data loss.

Because VREPAIR cannot be run on a volume that is currently mounted, copy VREPAIR.NLM and the name space support module to the file server's boot partition. Then run VREPAIR from the file server's boot partition.

See Also: DISMOUNT, LOAD, MOUNT

A
B
C
D
E
F
G
H
I
J
K
L
M
N
O
P
Q
R
S
T
U
V
W
X
Y
Z

WATCHDOG

Purpose: Monitors file server connections.

Syntax: `WATCHDOG START=startsecs INTERVAL=intervalsecs COUNT=intervalcount`

Option	Description
startsecs	Specify in seconds how long you want the file server to check a new connection. The time can be between 15 and 1,200 seconds with 300 seconds as the default.
intervalsecs	Specify how long the interval between checks should be, in seconds. The intervalsecs variable ranges from 1 to 600, with a default of 60 seconds.
intervalcount	The number of intervals that must go by before clearing an active connection, ranging from 5 to 100 with a default of 10.

Important Messages: None

Examples: To enable WATCHDOG with the defaults, type the following:

`WATCHDOG`

To enable WATCHDOG with your own settings, type the following:

`WATCHDOG START=10 INTERVAL=5 COUNT=20`

Notes: Place the WATCHDOG command in the AUTOEXEC.SYS to load it automatically when the file server is booted.

See Also: MONITOR

A
B
C
D
E
F
G
H
I
J
K
L
M
N
O
P
Q
R
S
T
U
V
W
X
Y
Z

WHOAMI

Purpose: Displays connection, identification, and security information for the current user.

Syntax: WHOAMI [*servername*] *option*

Options: If you type WHOAMI and do not include parameters, you receive the user name, server name, workstation connection, NetWare version, and login time.

Option	Description
servername	Unless a file server is specified, information is provided for all attached servers
/C	Provides continuous scrolling of the output
/ALL	Displays group membership and security equivalence along with the basic WHOAMI information
/G	Displays group information along with the basic WHOAMI information
/O	Displays object supervisor information along with the basic WHOAMI information
/R	Displays effective rights for each attached volume along with the basic WHOAMI information
/S	Displays security equivalencies along with the basic WHOAMI information
/SY	Displays general system information along with the basic WHOAMI information
/W	Displays workgroup manager information along with the basic WHOAMI information
/?	(4.10) Displays online help
/VER	(4.10) Displays version information and a list of files required for this command to run

Rules and Considerations: You must be logged in to a file server to run WHOAMI.

If you type **WHOAMI** without any parameters, the user name, server name, workstation connection, NetWare version, and login time appear.

Only one option at a time can be entered with WHOAMI.

Important Messages:

```
You are not attached to server DANNY.
```

This message indicates what happens if you enter **WHOAMI** followed by some text—in this case, **WHOAMI DANNY**. To correct this, type **WHOAMI** without any options, or try one listed in the examples that follow.

Examples: If you type **WHOAMI**, you receive information similar to the following:

```
You are user DENISE attached to server NRP2, connection 7.
Server NRP2 is running Dedicated NetWare V2.2(100) Rev. A.
Login time: Tuesday  November  12, 1991  4:14 pm
```

If you type **WHOAMI /ALL**, you receive information similar to the following:

```
You are user BOB attached to server FINI, connection 1.
Server FINI is running Dedicated NetWare V2.2(50) Rev. B.
You are a workgroup manager.
Login Time: Thursday  November  14, 1991  7:14 am
You are security equivalent to the following:
    EVERYONE (Group)
You are a member of the following groups:
    ACCOUNTING
    EVERYONE
    SHIPPING
[RWCEMFA]  SYS:
[RWCEMFA]  VOL1:
Server CSOS is not in a Domain.
```

See Also: NLIST, USERLIST

A B C D E F G H I J K L M N O P Q R S T U V **W** X Y Z

WSGEN

Purpose: An installation utility that creates an IPX.EXE file specific to a particular workstation's configuration.

Syntax: `WSGEN`

Options: None

Rules and Considerations: The WSGEN command requires, at a minimum, a LAN driver disk for the network adapter card to complete execution.

WSGEN requires DOS 3.0 or higher to run.

Important Messages: None

Notes: Use IPX I after generating an IPX.EXE file with WSGEN to check its version, supported LAN adapter, and configuration option.

See Also: DCONFIG, IPX, NETX, VLM

WSUPDATE

Purpose: Updates workstation files with newer versions held on the server.

Syntax:

WSUPDATE *source dest*

or

WSUPDATE /**F**=*scriptfile*

Option	Description
source	Location and name of source file
dest	Location and name of file to be replaced with newer version
scriptfile	*scriptfile* is a file created to contain a list of source destination pairs for automatic executions
/?	Provide online help
/VER	Displays version information and list of files required for this command to run

Rules and Considerations: WSUPDATE replaces files with newer versions only.

Important Messages: None

Examples: To update the workstation shells easily, copy the updated shells into one of the search drives on the network and type the following on an MS-DOS 5 workstation using the regular memory workstation shell:

WSUPDATE F:\PUBLIC\NET5.COM A:\NET5.COM

To update the workstation shells (or any DOS files) at login time, create a WSUPDATE configuration file for each user's workstation and execute the WSUPDATE program from the user's login script. If the user's

WSUPDATE script file was named WSUPDRK.CFG, you would type the following into the login script:

`IF_DAY_OF_WEEK = Tuesday, RUN #WSUPDATE /F=WSUPDRK.CFG`

Notes: A sample WSUPDATE script might resemble the following:

```
F:XMSNET5.COM A:XMSNET5.COM
F:IPX.COM  A:IPX.COM
```

Do not accidentally replace the IPX.COM file on a workstation with an IPX.COM generation intended for another workstation. Although the NETx flavors are generic, the IPX.COM file must be generated for a particular workstation adapter card.

WSUPDATE can be run from a batch file. Several options are then available.

Option	Function
/ALL	Will search all mapped drives.
/C	Copy new over old file without creating a backup.
/CON	Scroll output.
/E	Erase any existing log file. Also use /L option.
/L=*pathfile*	Create a logfile. Specify the path.
/F=*pathfile*	Specify the path (location) and name of a file containing workstation update commands.
/LOCAL	Search any local drives.
/N	Create specified directory.
/P	Require a prompt before proceeding.
/O	Update even the Read Only files.
/R	Save old file with a .OLD extension.
/S	Search for outdated files.
/V	Update CONFIG.SYS and rename old one to CONFIG.VLM.

See Also: EMSNETX, IPX, NETX, XMSNETX

WSUPGRD

Purpose: Lets you upgrade the IPX LAN driver on a workstation to the corresponding ODI driver.

Syntax: **WSUPGRD** *path options*

Options	Functions
path	Specify the path and file name of the current IPX driver.
options	Replace with any of the following options:
/C	Exits with error level 1 if upgrade is not performed, instead of exiting with no error code, so that other batch file commands can be run if this command is being run from a batch file.
/N	Does not delete the old LAN driver. If old LAN driver has the same name as the new LAN driver, however, it will be overwritten.
/E#	Use 0, 1, or 2 in place of #. Using 0 does not update the AUTOEXEC.BAT file. Using 1 does update the AUTOEXEC.BAT file. Using 2 (the default) deletes the line that loads the driver file from the AUTOEXEC.BAT file, and calls a new batch file (STARTNET.BAT) from which the driver and related files are then loaded.
/S	Suppresses NET.CFG file generation.

Rules and Considerations: To have the hardware ID in the master configuration table of the ODI driver printed, use the /I option, but do not use it with any other option.

You can use the /? option to view online help information for this utility. You can also use /VER to see the version number and a list of files required by this utility.

Examples: To upgrade the current workstation file and keep the older IPX driver, assuming it has a different file name, type the following at the prompt, or include the line in a batch file:

```
WSUPGRD C:/NWCLIENT/NE3200 /N
```

Important Messages: None

Notes: IPX.COM is the default driver name.

A
B
C
D
E
F
G
H
I
J
K
L
M
N
O
P
Q
R
S
T
U
V
W
X
Y
Z

XMSNETX.COM or XMSNETX.EXE

Purpose: The XMSNET*x* command loads the NetWare shell driver and moves most of the commands in NET*x*.COM from DOS memory to extended memory above 1 MB. This arrangement frees approximately 34 KB of the DOS 640 KB base memory. About 6 KB must remain in base memory to handle various interrupts and some data.

Syntax: `XMSNETX`

Option	Function
-I	Enables you to see which version of the shell driver you are using, without actually loading it into memory
-U	Unloads the shell driver from memory, but must be the last TSR program loaded for this to function properly

Rules and Considerations: IPX.COM must be loaded before you attempt to load XMSNETX.EXE.

Older versions used the x to represent the version of DOS you were running at the workstation. MS-DOS 5, for example, requires you to issue the command as **XMSNET5**.

All NETX.COM parameters in the shell configuration files SHELL.CFG and NET.CFG work with the extended memory shell.

Important Messages: Novell is discontinuing support of DOS shells (NETX, EMSNETX, XMSNETX); you should switch to the DOS requester (VLM).

Examples: Issue the following form of the command to load the shell driver into expanded memory:

`XMSNETX`

Notes: For ease of use, copy the XMSNETX.EXE (or COM) file to the workstation's boot disk and include the file name (XMSNETX) in the AUTOEXEC.BAT file. This automatically loads the shell driver when you boot your workstation.

A
B
C
D
E
F
G
H
I
J
K
L
M
N
O
P
Q
R
S
T
U
V
W
X
Y
Z

A
B
C
D
E
F
G
H
I
J
K
L
M
N
O
P
Q
R
S
T
U
V
W
X
Y
Z

The extended memory shell works with all NetWare versions and operates under the same conditions as the regular NetWare DOS shell v3.01 and above.

The extended memory shell replaces the current NETX.COM shell option and is intended for use by users who have extended memory.

See Also: EMSNETX, NETX

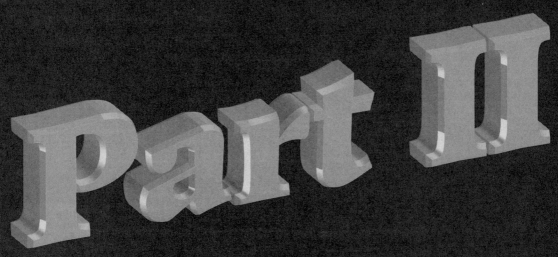

Part II

Menu Reference

Introduction

Menu Utility Reference Introduction

The following menus are those most often used by system administrators and consultants when working on NetWare systems. As with the command line utilities, you can summon the utilities from the following:

- ◆ Functioning console
- ◆ Downed console
- ◆ Logged in, or connected, workstation
- ◆ Non-logged in, or non-connected, workstation

An icon following the menu name indicates from where the utility was summoned. The versions of NetWare in which the utility works also are denoted by icons.

ACONSOLE

NetWare's ACONSOLE utility lets you send screen and keyboard information to and from a remote file server using a modem. ACONSOLE provides an asynchronous connection that does not guarantee packet delivery and can result in a message such as No Response from Server.

You can run ACONSOLE from a workstation connected to the network, or from a standalone PC. To use ACONSOLE from a network workstation, log in to the network as user SUPERVISOR, then type **ACONSOLE** and press Enter. From the main menu, choose Connect to Remote Location, and choose the file server from the resulting phone list. Enter either the SUPERVISOR user password, or the password assigned to the remote file server.

 You can only use the SUPERVISOR password if volume SYS: is mounted at the remote file server.

When access has been granted, you will see the active file server screen or the remote system console screen. If, however, a keyboard lock password exists for this file server, you will first be prompted for that password before the active file server or remote system console screen is presented.

ATCON

The ATCON (*AppleTalk CONsole*) utility is new to NetWare 4 and is used at the file server console to monitor, configure, and diagnose operational problems with AppleTalk routers and network segments. It also is used to verify that AppleTalk routers are connected to the internetwork and to monitor *AppleTalk Update-based Routing Protocol* (AURP) status. ATCON uses *Simple Network Management Protocol* (SNMP) to access information about the various components of the AppleTalk network to access statistical and diagnostic information from the local network system.

To use ATCON, type **LOAD ATCON** at the file server console and press Enter. The ATCON Available Actions menu opens. From this menu you can choose to view a variety of items of information (see fig. 1).

```
Available Actions

AURP information
Interfaces
Log files
Lookup network entities
Packet statistics
Protocol configuration
Routing Table
Zones list
```

Figure 1
ATCON Available
Actions menu.

You can view the following information using ATCON:

♦ IP Tunnel Status

♦ Interface Address Information

♦ AppleTalk Message Logging Levels

♦ NetWare Log Files

♦ AppleTalk Router Packet Statistics

♦ AppleTalk Protocol Stack Configuration

♦ AppleTalk Routing Table Maintenance Protocol (RTMP)

♦ AppleTalk Router Zones

Viewing IP Tunnel Status

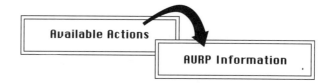

Selecting AURP Information from the ATCON Available Actions menu lets you view AURP-related information. AURP parameters configure the router to use AURP for tunneling AppleTalk through Internetwork Protocol (IP). You enable or disable AURP using the INETCFG utility. Using the FILTCFG utility, you can configure filters for AppleTalk as well as for other protocols.

Interfaces

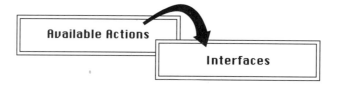

Selecting Interfaces from the ATCON Available Actions menu lets you view information about addresses of interfaces connected to the AppleTalk router.

Log Files

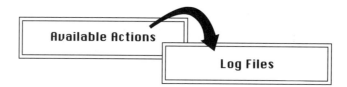

Selecting Log Files from the ATCON Available Actions menu lets you set
the logging levels for AppleTalk messages, as well as view two NetWare
log files: system and volume.

Lookup Network Entities

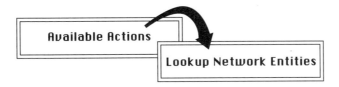

Selecting Lookup network entities from the ATCON Available Actions
menu lets you perform a query to see what services are available on the
AppleTalk network.

Packet Statistics

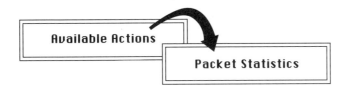

Selecting Packet statistics from the ATCON Available Actions menu
lets you view statistics being tracked by the AppleTalk router.

Protocol Configuration

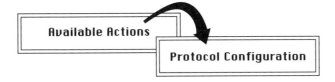

Selecting Protocol configuration from the ATCON Available Actions menu enables you to see information about the AppleTalk protocol stack. The AppleTalk stack is a suite of AppleTalk Phase 2 protocols introduced to provide support for the following:

♦ Several AppleTalk zones on a single network

♦ Token ring networks

♦ Thousands of nodes on a network

♦ More efficient routing techniques to improve multiprotocol-environment performance

Routing Table

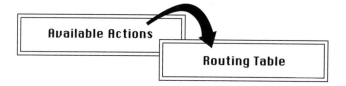

Selecting Routing Table from the ATCON Available Actions menu lets you view information about the database of routing information maintained by AppleTalk for NetWare's RTMP routing protocol.

Zones List

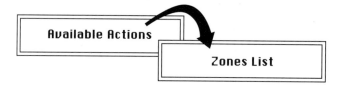

Selecting Zones list from the ATCON Available Actions menu lets you view a list of up to 255 zones—groups of physically-connected devices located on one or more networks.

AUDITCON

The AUDITCON utility is a NetWare 4 utility run from a workstation attached to the network. AUDITCON is provided to help network administrators ensure the accuracy and confidentiality of network transactions and information. It provides access by a third-party (an independent individual) to information about network transactions, allowing for independent auditing of the network.

To load the AUDITCON utility, type **AUDITCON** at a network workstation and press Enter. The Available Audit Options menu opens.

> *The network administrator must activate auditing before an auditor can audit any NDS or file system activity. In addition, the network administrator must create a directory into which the auditor can save audit reports. The network administrator must also create the auditor as a user object, assigning the Browse object right to the container objects the auditor will be responsible for auditing. The auditor must also be given either the Supervisor trustee right or all rights except the Supervisor right to the directory where the audit reports will be stored. As with other users, the auditor needs a drive mapped to the directory where the audit reports will be saved, if a search drive mapping to SYS:PUBLIC does not exist in the system login script. As a minimum, the auditor needs the Browse object right and the File Scan directory trustee right to SYS:PUBLIC so that access to AUDITCON and the Unicode files will be possible.*
>
> *Selecting Enable Container Auditing lets the network administrator enable network auditing for an Organization or an Organizational Unit container object.*

Although auditors can monitor what network users do on the network, auditors have no rights to open, view, or modify any files other than the audit data and history files, with one exception. If the network administrator grants rights to the auditor to containers or other non-auditing files, the auditor will have rights to those files. Those rights, however, must be specifically granted and are not part of network auditing.

Auditors can audit both file system activity at the volume level, and NetWare Directory Services (NDS) events at a volume's file system or at a server. After the network administrator enables auditing, establishes an auditor user object, and makes access to files possible for the auditor, the network auditor can then use the AUDITCON utility to accomplish a variety of tasks. The tasks the auditor can perform using the AUDITCON utility are as follows:

- ♦ Audit the directory tree

- ♦ Change from one context to another

- ♦ Log in to the current volume as the auditor

- ♦ Change the server you are currently accessing

- ♦ Change the volume you are currently accessing

- ♦ View information about auditing status, file size, file size threshold, maximum file size, and the size of the current volume's history file

Auditing the Directory Tree

Before you can record or view auditing information, you must set up the audit environment, then choose which items are to be audited. You use AUDITCON to accomplish both tasks.

Set up the Audit Environment

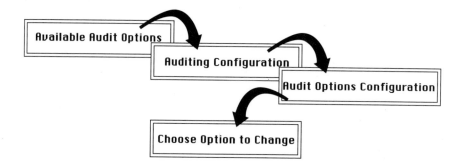

Selecting the setup option you want to specify and then entering the settings you prefer for your work environment lets you define the auditing environment most appropriate for you. You can define setup options for the following:

♦ **Audit File Maximum Size.** The maximum size the audit file should be allowed to become. Specify this file size in bytes.

♦ **Audit File Threshold Size.** The size the audit file must become before warning messages are issued. Specify this file size in bytes, setting it to approximately 90 percent of the Audit File Maximum Size.

♦ **Automatic Audit File Archiving.** Specifies automatic backup of the audit file. You must also specify Days Between Audit Archives, Hour of Day to Archive, and Number of Old Audit Files to Keep if you set this option.

♦ **Days Between Audit Archives.** Number of days between automatic backup of the audit file.

♦ **Hour of Day to Archive.** Time the audit file backup should occur.

♦ **Number of Old Audit Files to Keep.** How many old backup file copies of the audit file should be kept, after which the oldest of the audit file backup copies will be deleted.

♦ **Allow Concurrent Auditor Logins.** When set to Yes, more than one auditor (using the same password) can be simultaneously logged in to a specific container or volume.

♦ **Broadcast Error Messages to All Users.** When set to Yes, all users see any audit-related error messages, rather than having them broadcast only to the file server console.

♦ **Force Dual-Level Audit Passwords.** When set to Yes, a second password is needed whenever an audit setting is changed.

♦ **Archive Audit File.** This is the first of three options (Dismount Volume and Disable Audited Events are the other two options) of actions that occur when the audit data file is full. This option automatically closes the audit data file when it reaches its maximum file size, then archives the file, and starts a new data audit file. This option does not affect users on the network.

♦ **Dismount Volume.** When set to Yes, the volume being audited will be dismounted if the audit data file reaches its maximum size, or if an unrecoverable write error occurs, requiring the network administrator's password to remount the volume.

♦ **Disable Audited Events.** When set to Yes, users can no longer perform the task being audited after the audit data file reaches its set maximum size.

♦ **Disable Event Recording.** When set to disable, no audit events are recorded once the audit data file reaches its set maximum size.

♦ **Minutes Between Warning Messages.** Sets number of minutes between each warning broadcast.

Choose Items to be Audited

To create audit reports, you must have first collected information about network transactions. Because not all types of transactions need to be audited, you have a choice over what is audited. To exercise that choice, you must select which items will be audited.

Selecting Auditing Configuration from the Available Auditing Options menu makes it possible for you to select which options you want to set to be audited. You can select from options to audit volumes, as well as from options to audit NDS.

If you select to audit volumes, you can select from the following options:

♦ **Audit by Event.** This option lets you select which types of events should be audited. You have four events from which you can choose: File Events, QMS Events, Server Events, and User Events.

♦ **Audit by File/Directory.** This option lets you select files and directories to be audited. It provides a list of files and directories from which to choose.

♦ **Audit by User.** This option lets you select one or more users whose transactions you want to audit.

♦ **Audit Options Configuration.** This option lets you make choices for setting up your work environment.

♦ **Change Audit Password.** This option lets you change the auditor's password for this volume.

♦ **Disable Volume Auditing.** This option lets you disable volume auditing, but requires the supervisor to enable auditing if you choose to do so at a later date.

♦ **Display Audit Status.** This option lets you see information about Audit Data and History Data for this volume.

If you select to audit NDS, you can select from the following options:

♦ **Audit by DS Event.** This option lets you choose NDS events to be audited from a list.

♦ **Audit by User.** This option lets you choose a specific user to be audited.

♦ **Audit Options Configuration.** This option lets you configure audit file parameters to customize your work environment.

♦ **Change Audit Password.** This option lets you change the auditor's password associated with this container.

♦ **Change Audit Password Two.** This option lets you change the second auditor's password when Force dual-level password has been set to Yes.

♦ **Disable Container Auditing.** This option lets you disable auditing for this container.

♦ **Display Audit Status.** This option lets you see information about this container's Audit Data file.

Changing Context

If you are not currently in the correct context, you can change context from inside the AUDITCON utility. After you have selected Change Session Context, enter the context to which you want to change.

Logging in as the Auditor

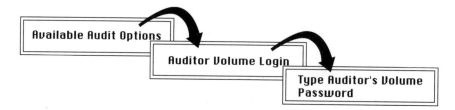

Selecting Auditor Volume Login from the Available Audit Options menu, then providing the auditor's password for the current volume when prompted, lets you log in to a volume as the auditor. If the current context is not the same as the server and volume displayed at the top of the AUDITCON Available Audit Options screen, you can change your current server or volume as discussed in the two following sections.

Changing Servers

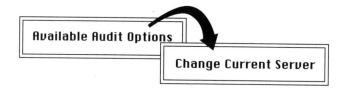

Selecting Change Current Server from the Available Audit Options menu, then selecting the required server, lets you change your context from one server to another.

Changing Volumes

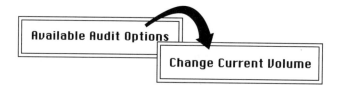

Selecting Change Current Volume from the Available Audit Options menu, then selecting the required volume, lets you change your context from one server to another.

Viewing Audit Information

After auditing is set up and audit information has been collected and saved, you can create and view reports, as well as see records in the Audit Data file. To customize the information you view, you create report filters. Report filters let you select specific information from the Audit Data file to be included in a report. Creating several different report filters gives you the option of generating different reports containing a variety of information.

Report Filters

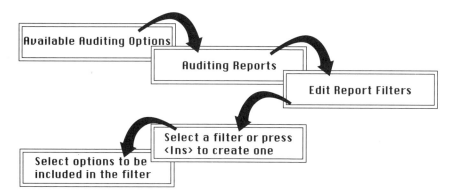

Selecting Edit Report Filters from Auditing Reports lets you select an existing filter to apply to the contents of the Audit Data file, or create a new filter. When creating a new filter, the options from which you can choose are as follows:

◆ **Report by Date/Time.** This option lets you choose a time period within which all events recorded in the Audit Data file will be included in the report.

◆ **Report by Event.** This option lets you choose which types of events— file, QMS, server, or user—are to be chosen from the Audit Data file to be included in the report.

♦ **Report Exclude Paths/Files.** This option lets you choose not to include specific files or directories in the report.

♦ **Report Exclude Users.** This option lets you choose not to include specific users in the report.

♦ **Report Include Paths/Files.** This option lets you choose a specific directory path or file to be included in the report.

♦ **Report Include Users.** This option lets you choose specific users to include in the report.

Whenever a filter contains Include and Exclude options which conflict with each other, the selected Exclude options are given priority over the selected Include options.

Reports

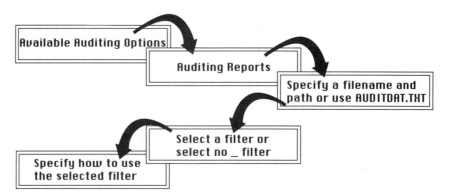

After you select what can be included in or excluded from a report, you can send the report to a file, or view it on the screen.

Selecting where to send the report file as well as which filter to use when creating the report, and then saving the filter or using it without saving it creates the report and stores it to a file.

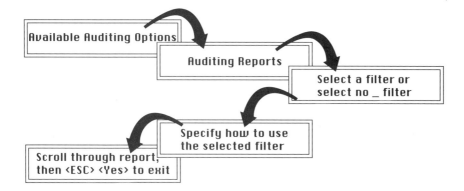

Selecting a filter to apply to the audit report you are viewing lets you see
the report on the screen, instead of sending it to a separate file.

BRGCON

BRGCON is a *NetWare Loadable Module* (NLM) used to manage objects on a NetWare for an OS/2 bridge. With BRGCON you can manage remote or local bridges, view basic configuration information, view spanning tree protocol and transparent bridging information, view bridge port information, and view information about supported network interfaces. Each of these tasks can be performed by selecting the related option from the BRGCON Available Options menu.

To see the BRGCON Available Options menu as shown in figure 1, type **LOAD BRGCON** at the file server console and press Enter.

```
           Available Options
┌──────────────────────────────────────┐
│ SNMP Access Configuration            │
│ View Configuration                   │
│ Spanning Tree Information             │
│ Transparent Bridging Information      │
│ Ports                                │
│ Interfaces                           │
└──────────────────────────────────────┘
```

Figure 1
The BRGCON
Available Options
menu.

From the BRGCON Available Options menu, you can select any of the following options:

♦ SNMP Access Configuration

♦ View Configuration

♦ Spanning Tree Information

♦ Transparent Bridging Information

♦ Ports

♦ Interfaces

SNMP Access Configuration

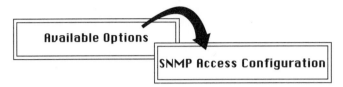

Simple Network Management Protocol (SNMP) is an industry standard that specifies the format to use when collecting network management information. Selecting the SNMP Access Configuration option from the BRGCON Available Options menu lets you do the following:

♦ Choose a bridge to be monitored

♦ Choose the local network (default) or a remote network (using IPX or TCP/IP) to be monitored

♦ Set how frequently information is retrieved (polled) through SNMP

View Configuration

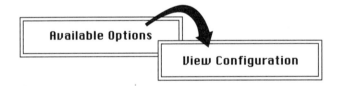

Select the View Configuration option from the Available Options menu to see basic configuration information about a bridge.

Spanning Tree Information

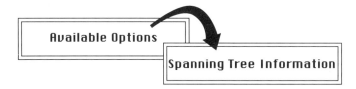

Select Spanning Tree Information from the Available Options menu to view protocol-related spanning tree information. Through SNMP you can set the label and priority of the spanning tree. In addition, if the spanning tree is the root bridge, you can also set the following spanning tree items:

♦ The spanning tree's maximum age

♦ The spanning tree's hello time

♦ The spanning tree's forward delay

Transparent Bridging Information

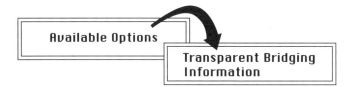

Selecting Transparent Bridging Information from the Available Options menu lets you see information related to transparent bridging, and lets you see the Filtering/Forwarding table for the bridge. In addition, and because of SNMP, you can set the aging time for the transparent bridge.

Ports

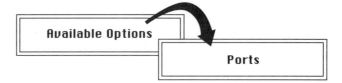

Selecting Ports from the Available Options menu lets you accomplish the following:

♦ See a list of this bridge's active ports

♦ Choose an active port and view information about the port

♦ See source route information for each port

♦ See transparent bridging information for each port

♦ See spanning tree information for each port

Interfaces

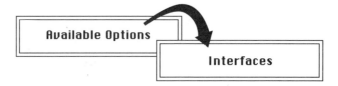

Selecting Interfaces from the Available Options menu lets you see those network interfaces that currently are supported. For each interface, you can see more information by selecting that interface.

COLORPAL

The COLORPAL utility is virtually the same in 2.2 and 3.x; however, it has changed significantly in NetWare 4.

COLORPAL is used with all NetWare utilities to define the color schema that is presented to users when they are using the menu-driven utilities, such as SYSCON, FCONSOLE, and FILER. The default color palettes (palettes 0–4) are used to define the color arrangements of the NetWare utilities. Additional color palettes (starting at palette 5) are used to define the color assignments for the menus that are created with the menu utility.

NetWare menu-driven utilities use color palettes 0 through 4 only. User menus created with the MENU utility can use the default palettes 0 through 4 as well as custom palettes. If the palette option is not specified when creating a custom menu, it will use color palette 0.

NetWare's default color palettes are set to blue, yellow, and white. Anytime these default palettes are changed, the change is reflected in all the menu utilities; it is not possible to change the colors of a specific menu utility. And because COLORPAL saves its main color table in a file (IBM$RUN.OVL) in the PUBLIC directory, all changes made while running COLORPAL from the PUBLIC directory will affect all color monitors on the network. COLORPAL changes do not usually affect the visual clarity of the menus when started from an IBM-type monochrome monitor. However, there are several types of monitors—AT&T monitors, RGB monitors, composite monitors, and so on—for which visual clarity can be adversely affected by any changes made to the default color palettes. The default colors provide the best clarity for the widest variety of hardware, and it is best not to change them.

It is possible, however, to change the color of the menu utilities for a specific user or station. To change the color palettes for an individual, start COLORPAL from a location other than SYS:PUBLIC, such as the user's HOME directory. When you access COLORPAL from another directory, the IBM$RUN.OVL will automatically be copied to that location. When that station logs in to the server, it will use the altered version of IBM$RUN.OVL.

Because the system looks for the IBM$RUN.OVL file in your first search drive, to make the color changes take effect, you must start the menu from the directory where the altered IBM$RUN.OVL file is located, or you can use the MAP command to assign the first search drive to the alternate location, where the new file exists.

NetWare's utilities use the available color palettes in the following way:

♦ Palette 0 defines the colors of lists, menus, and normal text

♦ Palette 1 defines the colors of the main headers and screen backgrounds

♦ Palette 2 defines the colors of the help screens

♦ Palette 3 defines the colors of the error messages

♦ Palette 4 defines the colors of the exit and alert portals

To start COLORPAL, type **COLORPAL** from a workstation and the COLORPAL main menu appears (see fig. 1).

Figure 1
COLORPAL's main menu.

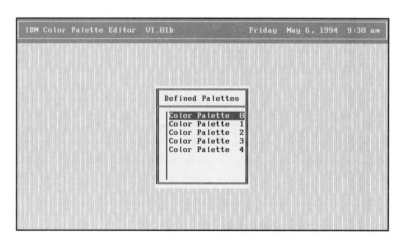

Changing Colors

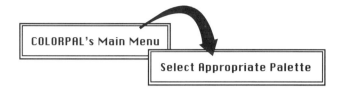

COLORPAL's Main Menu

Select Appropriate Palette

To change a color palette, move the highlight bar with the arrow keys until it is covering the palette that you want to change. Pressing Enter will bring up the Edit Attribute and Current Palette menu boxes.

The Edit Attribute window displays the attributes you can change. The color attributes as they appear in the menus are as follows:

- ♦ Background Normal is used for the field on which the menu titles and text are displayed

- ♦ Foreground Normal is used for normal test and border displays

- ♦ Foreground Intense is used to highlight the test and borders for menu options currently active

- ♦ Background Reverse is used for the highlight bar

Select the color palette you want to change by highlighting the appropriate location and pressing Enter. Use the arrow keys to move through the available options. When the highlight bar covers the appropriate option, select that option by pressing Enter. Then you will be provided with a list of available colors.

At COLORPAL's main menu, press Ins. A new color palette (color palette 5) will be created and will automatically be made available as an option. To create a custom menu scheme, move the highlight bar to color palette 5 and press Enter. The Edit Attribute, as well as the Current Palette menu options, will appear. You then can use these menus to create a custom menu scheme.

Start COLORPAL from a location other than SYS:PUBLIC. Make sure that this location is specified as your first search drive. You also can use a short machine type other than IBM in the SHELL.CFG file to force a workstation or group of workstations to use a different set of color palettes. In this situation only those stations booting with a SHELL.CFG file will be affected. The short machine type option determines which OVL file will be loaded. To use this method, add the following command to the workstation's SHELL.CFG file:

```
SHORT MACHINE TYPE = (optional OVL file name)
```

Monochrome Monitors and COLORPAL

The CMPQ$RUN.OVL file is often used for monochrome monitors that are affected by the intensity contrast of the normal color palette offerings. Monochrome monitors rarely are affected by the COLORPAL settings, but to force a workstation with a monochrome monitor to use CMPQ$RUN.OVL, change the short machine type to Compaq by adding the following line to the SHELL.CFG file:

```
SHORT MACHINE TYPE = CMPQ
```

When you are done using COLORPAL, press Esc to back out of your selection. You then will be given the option to save your changes. After selecting YES or NO, press Esc again to leave COLORPAL's menus.

COLORPAL in NetWare 4

COLORPAL enables you to change or set NMENU colors (NMENU is NetWare 4's new menu utility). In NetWare 4, however, the COLORPAL utility has had some significant changes made to it. You no longer have to work with palettes (color palettes 0–9). As shown in figure 2, simply highlight the type of text or part of the menu where you want to change the color, then press Enter to display a color palette that you navigate by using the arrow keys. A white highlight box will indicate your current location in the color palette. In NetWare 4, foreground colors are designated by an asterisk placed on a background color. A red asterisk on a blue background, for instance, represents a color combination of red text on a blue background. Make a selection by pressing Enter. This simplified method makes it easier to change colors.

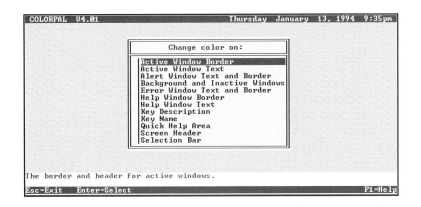

Figure 2
NetWare 4
COLORPAL's main
menu.

COLORPAL will check the overlay file for 10 monochrome and 10 color palettes. If the number of palettes is more or less than 10, COLORPAL will fail. By default, prior versions of COLORPAL had only one monochrome palette, but the number of palettes could be extended to 10 (more than 10 could be created, but only 10 were used). If you try to use your color palettes from older versions of NetWare and have more than 10 palettes defined, you receive an error message indicating that you are attempting to use an incorrect COLORPAL file. To avoid this problem, re-create your color palettes using NetWare 4's COLORPAL utility.

DSPACE

The DSPACE utility enables you to limit a user's disk space on a NetWare 2.2 and NetWare 3.1x server. In NetWare 4.10, DSPACE functions are performed with NWADMIN or NETADMIN.

On a 286 server, disk space is limited on a server-by-server basis. On a NetWare 3.1x server, disk space is limited by volume. Regardless of the version, you can limit subdirectory structures as well as change file servers, set user restrictions, and set directory restrictions.

DSPACE's main menu has three main options (see fig. 1):

♦ Change File Server

♦ User Restrictions

♦ Directory Restrictions

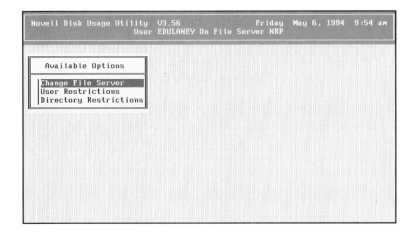

Figure 1
The DSPACE main menu.

Change File Server

The Change File Server option provides a list of available servers. To look for a server that is not listed, press Ins. Otherwise, highlight the correct server and press Enter.

User Restrictions

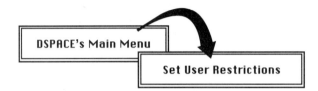

To limit a particular user's disk space, select the User Restrictions option from DSPACE's main menu, and then select the user whose disk space you want to limit. After selecting the user, a list of available volumes appears. Select the correct volume and press Enter. The screen in figure 2 appears.

Figure 2
DSPACE's User Disk
Space Limitation
Information screen.

```
          User Disk Space Limitation Information

User:   GUEST
Volume: SYS
Limit Space:      Yes
Available:      1024 Kilobytes
In Use:            0 Kilobytes
```

The only user-definable fields in this screen are the Limit Space field and the Available field. To set the amount of disk space that is available to a user, first switch the Limit Space field to Yes, and then type the amount of disk space that you want to make available.

Setting Directory Restrictions

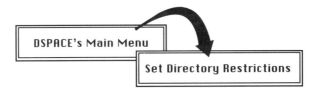

Selecting the Directory Restrictions option from the main menu brings up a directory path window in which you can specify the directory with which you want to work. You can either manually type the directory designation or press Ins to get a listing of the available directories. Press Enter after selecting the correct directory, and the screen in figure 3 appears.

Figure 3
The Directory Disk Space Limitation Information screen.

The Limit Space field and the Directory Space Limit field are the only user-definable fields. You must enter Yes in the Limit Space field before space restrictions can be set in the Directory Space Limit field. After indicating that you want to limit directory space, you can type the specific limitation.

If you restrict volume SYS and run out of space, you will not be able to print because volume SYS is where print jobs are temporarily stored.

See Also

CHKVOL

NETADMIN

NWADMIN

SYSCON

FCONSOLE

In versions prior to NetWare 3, FCONSOLE was one of NetWare's most useful management utilities. In NetWare 3, however, most of the vital information that was gathered in FCONSOLE was moved to the MONITOR utility. And in NetWare 4, all remaining FCONSOLE statistics and functions were moved to different utilities, primarily the MONITOR utility.

In NetWare 3.x you can perform the following management functions with FCONSOLE:

- ◆ Broadcast messages
- ◆ Change current server
- ◆ View detailed current user connection information
- ◆ Shut down the file server from a remote location
- ◆ View and alter the status of the file server
- ◆ View the version of NetWare currently running on the server

NetWare 2.2 enables you to perform the following additional functions:

- ◆ Check file lock activity
- ◆ Obtain LAN driver information
- ◆ Purge all salvageable files
- ◆ See file server statistics

Users also can use FCONSOLE to obtain limited information about the network (such as files in use and the version of NetWare). The Supervisor also can delegate some of the network management tasks by creating a console operator. A *console operator* is a user, or group of users, to whom the Supervisor of a NetWare 3.x network grants console operator rights so that they can operate FCONSOLE. (In NetWare 4, the MONITOR utility is used; you can access MONITOR through the RCONSOLE utility.) Figure 1 shows FCONSOLE's main menu.

Figure 1

FCONSOLE's main menu.

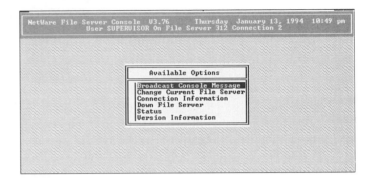

Broadcast Console Message

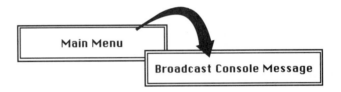

One of the more useful features of FCONSOLE is its capability to send messages to users on the network. Messages can be up to 55 characters in length and often are used by the Supervisor.

Users can avoid getting a message that is sent from the command line by using the CASTOFF command. When the Supervisor sends a message with FCONSOLE, however, the CASTOFF command is ignored, thus ensuring that all users receive the broadcast message. The CASTOFF command with the /ALL option, however, will block a broadcast message. In addition, a broadcast message can be sent from the server's console through the BROADCAST command.

When you select Broadcast Console Message from FCONSOLE's main menu, a box appears in which you can enter a message of up to 55 characters. This message will be received by all of those logged in or attached to that particular server. To send a message, type the message and press Enter.

The Broadcast Message function is backward compatible to 2.0a and forward compatible through NetWare 4. That is, if you send a message from FCONSOLE in NetWare 3, even users employing NetWare 2 and NetWare 4 can receive the broadcast message (if they are attached to the server).

Change Current Server

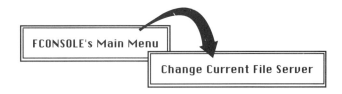

Select Change Current Server from FCONSOLE's main menu and a screen appears listing the file servers to which you currently are connected. To attach to a server that is not in the list, press Ins. A list of all available servers appears. Select the server that you want to establish a connection to and press Enter. You then are prompted to type your user name and, if needed, your password. The new server then appears in the list of available servers.

To change to a new server, select the server from the list and press Enter. Confirmation of your new connection is displayed in the header, which states the new connection information.

To log out of a file server, highlight the server and press Del. To change the user name that you are logged in under, press the F3 key.

Connection Information

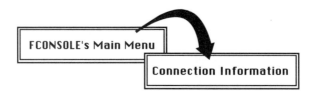

Select Connection Information from FCONSOLE's main menu by high-lighting it and pressing Enter. A Current Connection screen appears that lists all the logical connections for a given server. The connection information is updated every 2 seconds, by default.

To broadcast a message to a specific user, select the user from the Current Connection screen and press Enter. Then select Broadcast Console Message from the Connection Information menu. A blank message box appears in which you can enter a message of up to 55 characters. Pressing Enter sends the message and returns you to the Connection Information screen. Press Esc to cascade back to the main menu.

Other Information

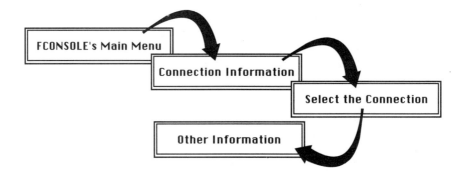

The Other Information option on the Connection Information menu provides network Administrators with additional user connection information. It provides the name of the user, the time a user logged in to the network, and the network address of a user's workstation.

Clear Connection

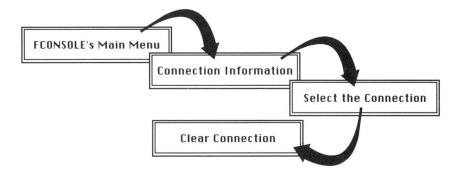

This option applies to NetWare version 2.2 only.

To clear a user's connection, highlight it on the Current Connections menu, and then select Clear Connection from the Connection Information menu. This menu choice is only available if you have supervisory rights.

Logical Record Locks

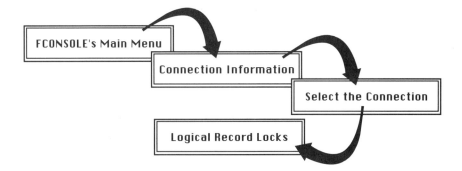

This option applies to NetWare version 2.2 only.

To check all the logical record locks that are active for an individual user, choose that user from the Current Connections menu, and then select Logical Record Locks from the Connection Information list of choices.

Open Files/Physical Records

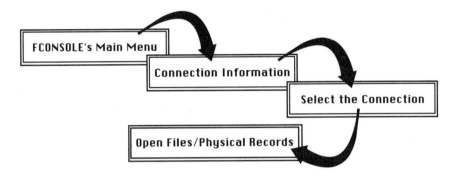

This option applies to NetWare version 2.2 only.

Selecting Open Files/Physical Records from the Connection Information menu shows the actual locks on records that are physically in place for a specified user. These locks prevent another user/station from accessing or changing a range of bytes within that file. A list appears showing all the files the user has open. Highlighting one of these files enables you to choose File Status and see the types of tasks that are transpiring on the file, as well as the available options.

Semaphores

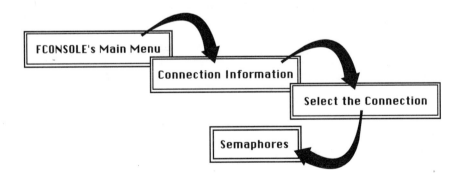

This option applies to NetWare version 2.2 only.

The semaphore information on a particular user is available as a menu choice from the Connection Information menu after the user has been chosen from the Current Connections menu. This information reports the current status of *semaphores*—limits on how many tasks can access a resource simultaneously.

Task Information

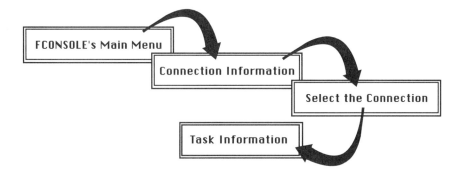

This option applies to NetWare version 2.2 only.

Task information for a user shows both the connection status and the active tasks. Connection Status merely reports whether the connection is waiting for a semaphore or lock; Active Tasks shows in which tasks the user/connection is currently involved.

Usage Statistics

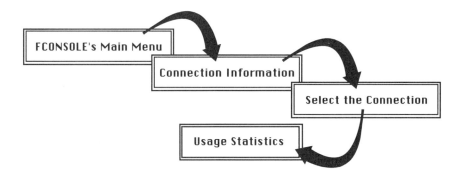

This option applies to NetWare version 2.2 only.

The Usage Statistics option, which is available from the Connection Information menu after you select a user from Current Connections, shows the following:

♦ Connection time in hours and minutes

♦ Number of requests that have been received in that time

♦ Number of disk bytes read

♦ Number of disk bytes written

Down File Server

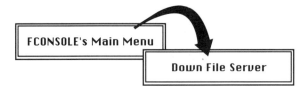

Selecting the Down File Server option from FCONSOLE's main menu enables the network supervisor to shut down a file server remotely. After selecting the Down File Server option, a verification box appears. Choose Yes to complete the task, or No to back out of the task. If the server has open files or connected users, selecting Yes brings up another verification screen. This screen is your last warning. If you select Yes from this screen, the file server is forced down and all user connections are lost.

File/Lock Activity

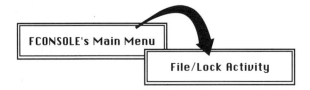

This option applies to NetWare version 2.2 only.

The information available in the File/Lock Activity menu is similar to that of the Connection Information menu. The difference is that the Connection Information menu offers the information on an individual user/connection, whereas the File/Lock Activity menu offers the information for the server.

Current Transactions

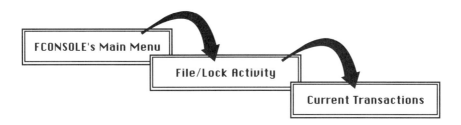

This option applies to NetWare version 2.2 only.

To see the current transactions that are transpiring on the server, select Current Transactions from the File/Lock Activity choice on FCONSOLE's main menu.

File/Physical Records Information

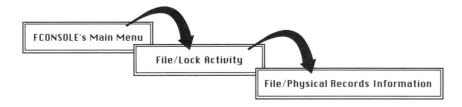

This option applies to NetWare version 2.2 only.

Selecting the File/Physical Records Information option prompts you to enter a directory path and then a file name. Next select File Status to see information about the current usage of the file, including how the file is being used and by which user. This information includes statistics for the following:

♦ Use count

♦ Open count

♦ Open for read

♦ Open for write

♦ Deny read

♦ Deny write

♦ Status

Logical Lock Information

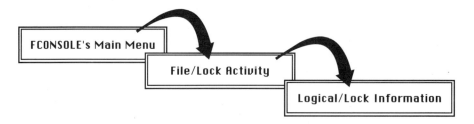

This option applies to NetWare version 2.2 only.

Selecting the Logical Lock Information option prompts you to enter a logical record name and then reports information on use count, share count, and status. Logical locks are used by applications to limit the number of users who can simultaneously open data.

Semaphore Information

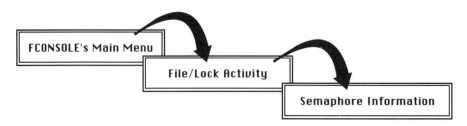

This option applies to NetWare version 2.2 only.

The Semaphore Information option on the File/Lock Activity menu prompts you for the name of a specified semaphore. After you enter the name of a semaphore, Semaphore Information shows the open count and value of that semaphore, as well as the connection task.

LAN Driver Information

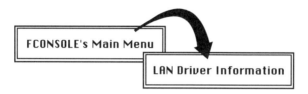

This option applies to NetWare version 2.2 only.

The LAN driver information available from this selection shows the configuration of the server. Information presented includes the following:

♦ Network address

♦ Node address

♦ LAN board type

♦ Configuration

♦ Hardware option

Purge All Salvageable Files

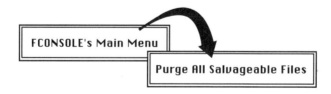

This option applies to NetWare version 2.2 only.

Selecting the Purge All Salvageable Files option from FCONSOLE's main menu offers two choices: Yes and No. Choosing No returns you to the main menu without further action. Choosing Yes removes all deleted files from the server and makes the space they had been occupying available for use by new files.

File Server Statistics

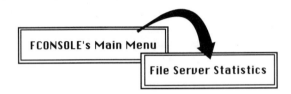

This option applies to NetWare version 2.2 only.

File Server Statistics contains information about transactions transpiring on the file server. In versions of NetWare 3.11 and later, this information was moved to the MONITOR utility. After this menu choice has been selected, the following additional options appear:

♦ Cache Statistics

♦ Channel Statistics

♦ Disk Mapping Information

♦ Disk Statistics

♦ File System Statistics

♦ LAN I/O Statistics

♦ Summary of Activity

♦ Transaction Tracking Statistics

♦ Volume Information

Status

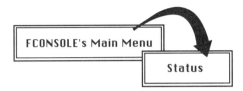

Selecting the Status option from the main menu provides you with the following information:

- ♦ Server date
- ♦ Server time
- ♦ Login restriction status
- ♦ Transaction tracking status

To change any of these parameters, use the arrow keys to highlight the desired location and press Enter. Type the new information and press Esc to save the changes.

Highlight the Allow users to login status line and press N to lock out new users from the server; press Y to reenable login. To disable Transaction Tracking, toggle this option back. Press E to enable Transaction Tracking and D to disable it.

Version Information

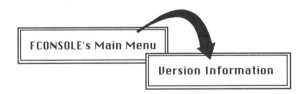

Select Version Information from the FCONSOLE's main menu and a version information dialog box appears. This dialog box provides you with the following information:

- Version of NetWare
- Version date
- Number of available users
- NetWare's copyright information

See Also

FILER

NETADMIN

NWADMIN

SESSION

SYSCON

VOLINFO

FILER

FILER is a workstation utility that enables you to control volume, directory, and file information. With FILER, users can list files, delete files, rename files, and copy files. FILER can be used as a Supervisor utility to create directories and assign security to those directories. It also gives Supervisors the ability to change file attributes and view other useful information about a server's directories and files.

 FILER has changed significantly between NetWare 3 and NetWare 4 (see FILER 4).

Five selections are available in FILER's main menu, as shown in figure 1.

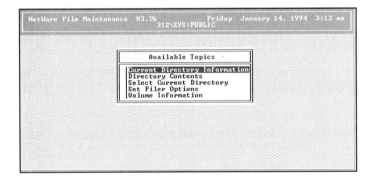

Figure 1
FILER's main menu.

Filer's main menu options provide the following functions:

♦ **Current Directory Information.** This option shows information about the directory, including creation date, owner, current effective rights, inherited rights mask, directory attributes, trustees, and current effective rights.

♦ **Directory Contents.** This option shows the files and subdirectories of the current directory. (When a directory is selected, pressing Enter enables you to make that directory your current directory.) The rights you currently have determine which options you see. (To see all the options, log in as Supervisor or a Supervisor equivalent.) When a file or a directory is selected, it can be copied, moved, or viewed. Users can also view or set file and directory information such as copy inhibit, delete inhibit, and so on.

♦ **Select Current Directory.** This option enables you to move around within the directory structure.

♦ **Set FILER Options.** This option enables you to change the default settings of the FILER utility.

♦ **Volume Information.** This option enables you to view information about the volume on which the current directory is located. You can see the volume's total size, the free space that is left on the volume, the maximum number of directory entries, and how many directory entries the volume has remaining.

Current Directory Information

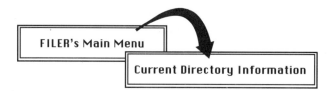

Selecting Current Directory Information from FILER's main menu displays a screen similar to the one shown in figure 2. This screen is called the Directory Information for PUBLIC screen (where PUBLIC is the directory currently selected), and it shows the information that can be viewed or changed for the current directory.

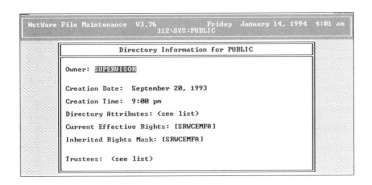

Figure 2
The Directory Information screen for the PUBLIC directory.

To change any of the information, highlight the appropriate field and press Enter. Pressing Enter on some of the fields—for example, the Directory Attributes fields—brings up a list of available selections. If the list is empty (contains no options), press Ins. You will then be provided with a list of the available options. Mark a specific option by highlighting it and pressing Enter, or mark several options with the F5 key. After marking the options that you want to add to the list, press Enter.

If you highlight a field and press Enter, and the list that appears does contain options, you can add more options by following the preceding steps, or you can remove an option by highlighting the option and pressing Del. If, however, the field that you select does not bring up a list of available options, you will have to type the new value. Selecting the Creation Time field, for instance, brings up a list of available new times. After selecting the Creation Time field, type the new value.

Change Directory Owner

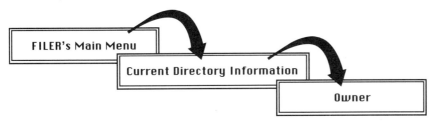

To change the owner of a directory, select Current Directory Information from FILER's main menu, highlight the Owner field in the Directory Information screen, and press Enter. A Known Users dialog box will appear. Move the cursor to the desired user and press Enter. You then will be presented with the options box shown in figure 3.

Figure 3
FILER's Change
Ownership Option
box.

Change Subdirectory Owner

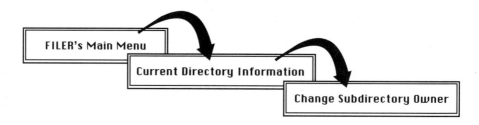

From the Change Ownership Option box, you can choose Change Owner-ship for Entire Subdirectory Structure, which includes all the files in the current directory as well as all the files and subdirectories from this point in the tree down. Or you can select Change Ownership for this Subdirectory, to change ownership of the current subdirectory. Make your selection by highlighting the appropriate choice and pressing Enter. You then will be taken back to the Directory Information screen, in which the owner status line will reflect the new change.

Creation Date

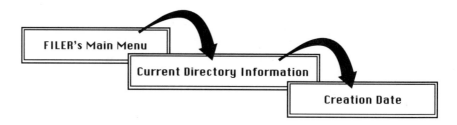

To change the creation date of a directory, highlight the Creation Date field in the Directory Information screen and type the new creation date.

The date displayed is the date on which the selected directory was created, and is displayed in the form September 20, 1993. When changing the date, you must press Enter on the Creation Date field and then press the Backspace key to delete the current date. You then can enter the new date using the above form, or by using the form MM-DD-YYYY. If you enter the date as 09-20-1993, NetWare will change it to September 20, 1993.

Creation Time

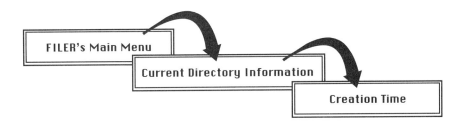

To change the creation time of a directory, highlight the Creation Time field in the Directory Information screen, and delete the current creation time by pressing the Backspace key. You then can type the new creation time. The creation time of the directory is displayed in a 12-hour format, (HH:MM am\pm); however, you can enter the time in either a 12-hour or a 24-hour format.

Directory Attributes

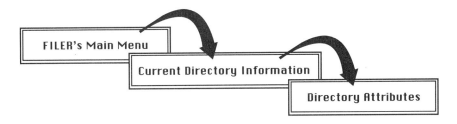

To change directory attributes, highlight the Directory Attributes option in the Directory Information screen and press Enter. The Current Attributes screen will appear, which will be blank unless the attributes list has been previously modified. To add an attribute, press Ins and choose one of the following five attribute options:

♦ **Delete Inhibit.** This attribute prevents any user from deleting the file.

♦ **Hidden Directory.** Adding this attribute to a directory prevents a common DOS DIR scan from seeing it.

♦ **Purge Directory.** This attribute informs NetWare that a file is to be purged automatically when the file is deleted.

♦ **Rename Inhibit.** This attribute makes it so that no user can give the file a new name.

♦ **System Directory.** Specifies that a directory in a system directory will hide the directory from a DIR scan. Just like a system file, it prevents a directory from being removed (deleted). To remove an attribute from the Current Attributes list, highlight the particular attribute and press Del.

Inherited Rights

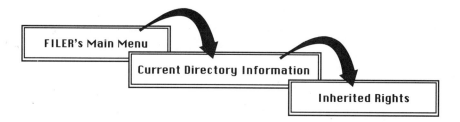

To change or modify inherited rights attributes, highlight the Inherited Rights Mask option in the Directory Information screen and press Enter. A window will appear that lists the current inherited rights. To change these rights, press Ins and select the rights from the list of available rights that appears just right of the current inherited rights box. Multiple rights can be marked using the F5 key; this list then can be added by pressing Enter. The opposite also is true. Multiple rights can be revoked by marking them with F5 and pressing Del.

> **Note** *In 2.2, inherited rights are represented as Maximum Rights Mask.*

Trustees

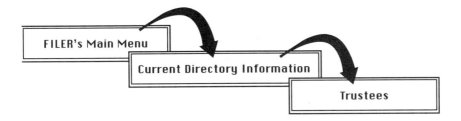

A Supervisor or other user who has access control rights in the current directory or its parent directory can add, delete, and modify user or group trustees. After choosing Current Directory Information from FILER's main menu, choose Trustees in the Directory Information screen to see a list of current directory's trustees and trustee rights. Press Ins to view a list of other users and groups defined on your file server. To add a user or group trustee, highlight the user or group and press Enter. You also can add several users or groups by marking them with the F5 key. To add the marked list to the list, press Enter. To revoke a user or group as a directory trustee, highlight the user or group (or use the F5 key to mark several users or groups) and press Del.

After adding a directory trustee, you can modify the trustee's rights by highlighting the user or group and pressing Enter. The Other Rights window appears (see fig. 4), indicating the available user's or group's current rights. To add rights, highlight or mark the rights and add them to the user's or group's current rights by pressing Enter.

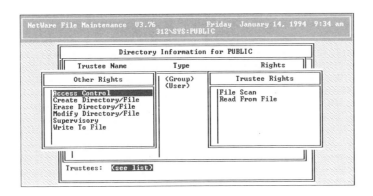

Figure 4
NetWare's available trustee rights.

Directory Contents

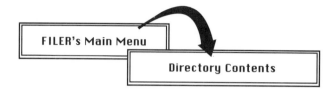

Selecting the Directory Contents option enables you to manage your NetWare server's file structure. In fact, the functions that can be performed from the Directory Contents section of FILER are some of the most powerful and most often used options in FILER. Included in this section of FILER is the capability to delete or move an entire subdirectory, which includes the subdirectory's structure and all the files below the current directory. After selecting Directory Contents from the main menu, a display listing the current directory's files and subdirectories appears.

Multiple files and subdirectories can be moved or deleted, but directories and files have to be deleted separately.

Highlighting a directory and pressing Enter brings up the options list shown in figure 5.

Figure 5
A list of available options after selecting a subdirectory with FILER.

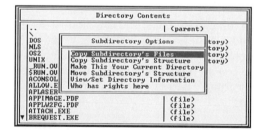

To use FILER to manage files, select Directory Contents from FILER's main menu. Locate the correct subdirectory and use the arrow keys to locate the desired file. After the file or files have been found, mark them with the F5 key, or in the case of a single file, press Enter. The File Options screen appears (see fig. 6).

Figure 6
Options available for managing files from within FILER.

If you highlight one of the first two options (Copy File or Move File) and press Enter, a Destination dialog box appears. You then can type the destination to which you want the file to be copied or moved and press Enter. Or, you can press Ins and select the desired location from the Available Network Directories screen.

The Copy File option copies the file to the new location and leaves the original file, while the Move File option copies the file to the new location and then deletes the moved file from its original location.

The View File option enables you to view the contents of a file; however, only ASCII (text) files can be properly viewed with the View File option. To view a text file, highlight the file and select the View File option from the File Options list.

Selecting View/Set File Information brings up the following information on a file:

♦ Attributes

♦ Owner

♦ Inherited Rights Mask

♦ Trustees

♦ Creation Date

♦ Last Accessed Date

♦ Last Archived Date

♦ Last Modified Date

The file information can be changed by moving to the field and pressing Enter. Pressing Enter enables you to either type the new information, or select the new information from a provided list. For instance, pressing Enter on the Inherited Rights Mask field brings up a list of the current inherited rights for the selected file. To add a new right, press Ins, select the right that you want to add by highlighting it in the Other Rights screen, and then press Enter. To remove or revoke an inherited right, highlight the right and press Del. In both cases, multiple rights can be marked with the F5 key.

To change the information in some of the fields, such as the Creation Date field, highlight the field and press Enter. Use the Backspace key to remove the existing value and then type the new desired value in its place.

The following information also is displayed in the File Information screen, but these fields cannot be edited from this location.

- ♦ Owning Name Space
- ♦ File Size
- ♦ EA Size
- ♦ Short Name

The Owning Name Space field represents the file structure type (for example, DOS, MAC, or NFS). The File Size field, as its name implies, indicates the size of the currently selected file. The EA size field is the Extended Attributes size, and is used to show the size of files, such as MAC or OS/2 files that use the extended attribute feature. The Short Name field displays the name of the file as if it were a DOS file with an eight-character name and a three-digit extension. Figure 7 is an example of a File Information screen.

Figure 7
FILER's File
Information screen.

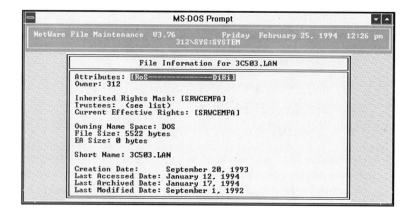

Selecting the Who has rights here option brings up a screen similar to the one seen in figure 8. This screen contains a list of the trustees who have been given rights to the directory structure at a higher lever. Trustees that have been given rights to the directory at a higher level also will have rights to the selected file. This screen also lists each type and trustees' security equivalencies.

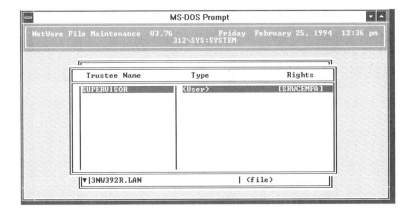

Figure 8
The Who has rights here file information screen.

No additions, deletions, or modifications can be made from this location.

Select Current Directory

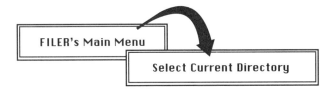

To change your location or to cascade through the directory, choose Select Current Directory from FILER's main menu. This displays the Current Directory Path window, which acts much like a DOS command line. Type the desired location and press Enter, or press Ins. Pressing Ins presents you with a list of available network directories. You can choose the directory by highlighting the directory and pressing Enter. Your selection will be reflected in the Current Directory Path window; to have this become your current location, press Enter. The header will indicate your new location.

Set FILER's Options

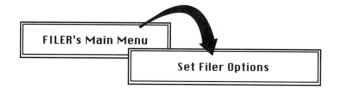

The settings established here determine how FILER acts when operations are carried out. The following table lists and describes the default settings, all of which can be changed at this screen.

Option	Default	Setting Explanation
Confirm Deletions	No	Each file deletion does not have to be confirmed.
Confirm File Copies	No	Each file copied does not need to be verified.
Confirm File Overwrites	Yes	If a file exists in the target directory, verification will take place before the file being copied will overwrite the one already in that location.
Notify Extended Attributes/Long Name Lost	No	You are not notified when the attributes and long file names are not preserved.
Exclude Directory Patterns	Blank list	A list can be created by pressing Ins and entering a desired pattern.
F5		To remove a pattern, press Del. To remove multiple patterns, use the F5 key to mark a list of patterns andthen press Del.

Option	Default	Setting Explanation
Include Directory Patterns		An asterisk represents all possible subdirectories, which is the default setting.
Exclude File Patterns	Blank list	A list can be created by pressing Ins and entering a desired pattern.
Include File Patterns		An asterisk is used to display all files.
File Search Attributes	Blank list	To add an attribute to the list, press Ins. To remove an attribute, highlight it and press Del. To remove multiple attributes, use the F5 key to mark them and then press Del.
Directory Search Attributes	Blank list	To add an attribute to the list, press Ins. To remove an attribute, highlight it and press Del. To remove multiple attributes, use the F5 key to mark them and then press Del.

 Exclude patterns override Include patterns.

Volume Information

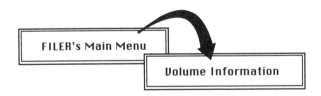

Choosing Volume Information in the main menu brings up the following information about your current volume (see fig. 9).

Figure 9
Volume information
that can be viewed
from FILER.

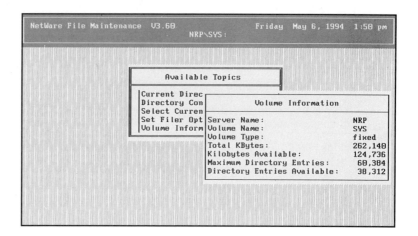

See Also

FILER 4

NWADMIN

NWUSER

SESSION

SYSCON

VOLINFO

FILER 4

NetWare 4's FILER utility has undergone some significant changes, but the main premise of the utility remains the same: It is a text-based utility that enables the network Administrator to manage files and directories. The graphical equivalent would be NWADMIN. Filer, however, is a convenient method of managing NetWare's file system, especially if your workstation is not capable of running Windows or OS/2. (You also can use individual command-line utilities to perform most of the same functions) FILER's main menu (see fig. 1) provides the following options:

- ◆ Manage files and directories
- ◆ Manage according to search pattern
- ◆ Select current directory
- ◆ View volume information
- ◆ Salvage deleted files
- ◆ Purge deleted files
- ◆ Set default filer options

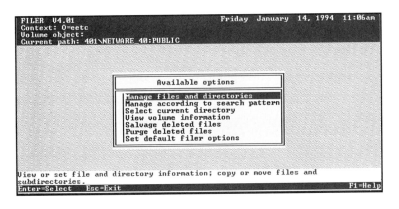

Figure 1
FILER's main menu in NetWare 4.

Manage Files and Directories

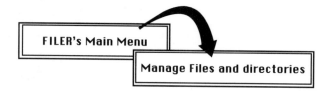

Selecting the Manage files and directories option brings up a directory context box. This box lists all the files and subdirectories in the current context. To move down a level in the directory structure, highlight the subdirectory and press Enter. To move up a level, highlight the parent directory and press Enter. To create a new subdirectory in this current location, press the Ins key. To remove a subdirectory, highlight the appropriate directory and press Del. To manage or view a file's or directory's contents, highlight the appropriate file or directory and press F10.

If you select a directory, the Subdirectory option menu appears, providing the following choices:

♦ Copy subdirectory's files

♦ Copy subdirectory's structure

♦ Move subdirectory's structure

♦ Make this your current directory

♦ View/set directory information

♦ Rights list

Copy Subdirectory's Files

The Copy subdirectory's files option enables you to copy the files in the subdirectory to a different place in the directory structure.

Copy Subdirectory's Structure

The Copy subdirectory's structure option enables you to copy the entire subdirectory, including the files, to a different place in the directory structure.

Move Subdirectory's Structure

The Move subdirectory's structure option enables you to move the entire subdirectory, including the files, to some other place in the directory structure.

Make This Your Current Directory

Highlighting the Make this your current directory option and pressing Enter makes this directory your current directory, and a screen appears that lists the contents of your subdirectory location.

View/Set Directory Information

The View/set directory information option enables you to view information such as Owner name, Creation time and date, Directory attributes, Trustees, and Rights.

Rights List

Selecting the Rights List option enables you to view the trustees to this subdirectory, as well as their type and rights.

If the current directory is highlighted and F10 is pressed, the only option you are given is the View/set directory information option. If this option is selected, an information screen appears (see fig. 2).

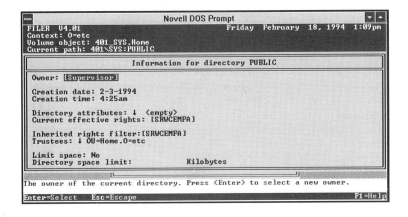

Figure 2
The Information for directory screen.

If you highlight a file and press F10, the File options menu appears, giving you the following choices:

♦ Copy file

♦ View file

♦ Move file

♦ Rights list

♦ View/set file information

Copy File

This option lets you copy a file to another location in the directory structure. When a file is copied to another location in the directory structure, the file is also left in its original location.

View File

This option lets you view the contents of the selected file. However, only text or ASCII files can be properly viewed.

Move File

This option lets you move the file to another location in the directory structure. When a file is moved, the file is relocated, and a copy of the file is not left in the original location.

Rights List

Selecting the Rights List option lets you view a list of the trustees of the selected file, the type of object the trustee is, and the rights this trustee has been given for this file. This location is for viewing purposes only; none of the items can be modified. To add or delete trustees, use the View/set directories information or the View/set file information option.

View/Set File Information

Selecting View/set file information brings up the Information for file screen (see fig. 3).

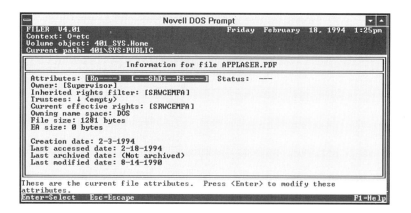

Figure 3

The Information for file screen.

When modifying or adding attributes to a file, pressing Enter and then Ins gives you access to a list of attributes that are not currently in use. You can then use the F5 key to mark attributes or select the attributes one at a time by pressing the Enter key. Either method makes the selected attributes active. You also can highlight an attribute and press Del to remove it from the current list of active attributes for the file.

Attributes include the following:

♦ **Archive Needed.** This attribute specifies that a file needs to be archived. When a backup program is run, it clears this attribute from the file. If the file is modified, the archive attribute is again assigned to the file.

♦ **Copy Inhibit.** When this attribute is given to a file, the file cannot be copied. (This attribute is only valid for Macintosh files.)

♦ **Delete Inhibit.** This attribute prevents users from deleting the file.

♦ **Don't Compress.** As its name implies, the Don't Compress attribute does not allow a file to be compressed. Assigning this attribute "overrules" the compress settings specified at the directory or volume level.

♦ **Hidden File.** Adding this attribute to a file prevents a common DOS DIR scan from seeing it. It also prevents the file from being deleted or copied (from DOS).

♦ **Immediate Compression.** This attribute lets NetWare 4's compression algorithm compress the file without having to wait for the specified compression settings; it compresses as soon as the server has time.

- **Purge.** This attribute purges the file automatically when the file is deleted.

- **Read Only.** When the Read Only attribute is given to a file, that file cannot be written to or changed.

- **Rename Inhibit.** This attribute disallows users from giving the file a new name.

- **Shareable.** With the Shareable attribute specified, the file can be opened by more than one user at a time. The Shareable attribute is usually used in conjunction with the Read Only attribute.

- **System File.** Specifying a file as a system file hides the file from DOS DIR scans and prevents it from being deleted or copied (much like a hidden file).

- **Transactional.** When a file is specified as Transactional, the Transactional Tracking System is activated, helping to prevent data corruption by ensuring that either all changes are made to a file when it is being modified, or that no changes are made.

Manage According to Search Pattern

Selecting Manage according to search pattern enables you to search for a specific file(s) or directory using search patterns and filters. A search pattern represents the capability to find a specific file with the use of wild cards, such as *.* or *.???. You also can also use filters to help narrow the search parameters. You could search for all files, for example, yet filter out every file that has been assigned a certain attribute or is located in a specific directory, and so on. Figure 4 shows the available filtering and search pattern options.

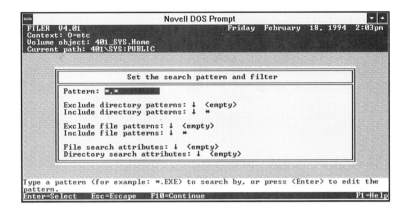

Figure 4
The available filtering
and search pattern
scenarios.

Select Current Directory

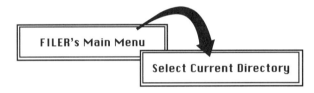

The Select current directory option enables you to view, set, or change
your current context, volume, and new path. When this option is selected,
an option box appears showing the current directory. To change the
directory, type the location or press Ins. This brings up a list of available
directories. You can cascade up the directory structure by highlighting
the ".." (parent directory) and pressing Enter. After you have selected the
correct directory, press Enter, and the current directory path window
reflects the changes. To accept these changes, press Esc, Enter. You are
then returned to the Available Options menu.

View Volume Information

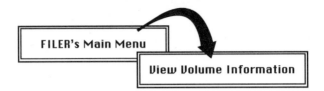

Selecting View volume information option bring up a volume information options menu, which contains the following three options:

- ♦ Statistics
- ♦ Features
- ♦ Dates and times

Statistics

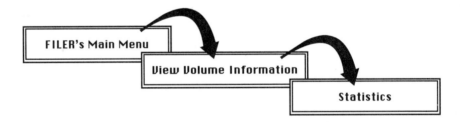

Selecting Statistics brings up the Volume statistics screen (see fig. 5).

Figure 5
The Volume statistics screen.

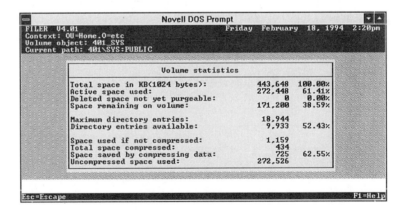

Features

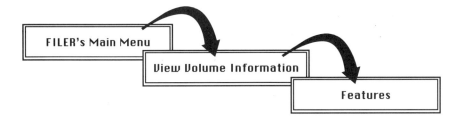

Selecting Features brings up a list of current features, such as Volume
type, Block size, Name space, and Installed features. Figure 6 shows a
sample of a features screen.

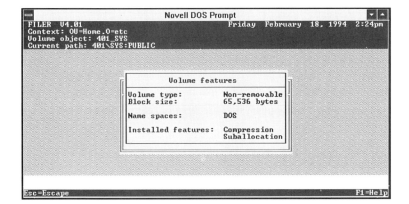

Figure 6
The Volume features
screen.

Dates and Times

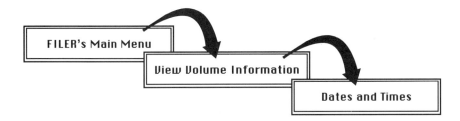

Selecting the Dates and times option provides the following information:

♦ Creation date and time

♦ Owner

♦ Last modified date and time

♦ Last archived date and time

This information is shown in figure 7.

Figure 7
The Volume dates and times screen.

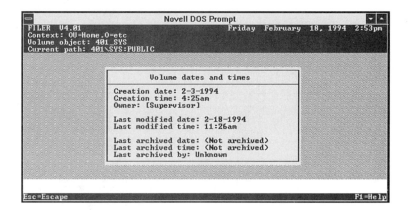

Salvage Deleted Files

The Salvage deleted files option enables you to recover files that were accidentally deleted, as least until the files are purged. After selecting this option, the Salvage menu appears (see fig. 8).

Figure 8
The Salvage menu.

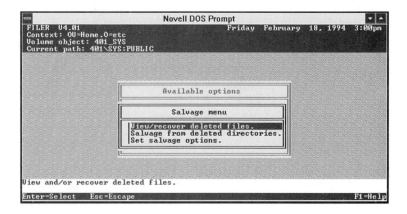

View/Recover Deleted Files

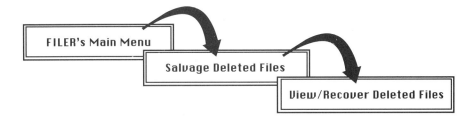

Select the View/recover deleted files option from the Salvage menu, and a dialog box appears asking for the name of the file pattern. Enter the file pattern of your choice (either a complete file name or a file name using the wild cards ? and *). Use the default * to bring up all the files that have been deleted, but not yet purged, then scroll through the files using the arrow keys. After you find the file you want to restore, press Enter. A "Recover this file" option box appears. Choose Yes or No to recover the file. The "Recover this file" option box also provides more specific information on the file that you are about to recover, such as owner, deleted date, modify date, and deletor.

Salvage from Deleted Directories

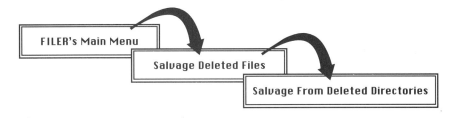

If there is a file in a directory that you want to recover, but that directory also has been deleted, select the Salvage from deleted directories option. You are prompted to enter a search pattern for the deleted directories, and, just like when searching for deleted files, wild cards can be useful. After you enter a search pattern, a list of files that once were contained in that particular directory appears.

SALVAGE functions (of NetWare 3.x) are now included in NetWare 4's FILER utility. These functions enable the user to view a list of deleted files in a directory and even recover files. Information on the files, such as who deleted the file and when it was deleted, helps to you determine if you are about to recover the correct file. Deleted files are saved until the user of Supervisor deliberately purges them or until the NetWare server volume runs out of disk allocation blocks. If the server begins to get low on disk space, NetWare automatically purges files on a first deleted, first purged basis.

It also is possible to use NetWare's SET commands to disable the saving of salvageable files. Turning on this feature increases the performance of your NetWare file server, but it also removes the capability of recovering deleted files. Besides using the SET parameters to turn off salvage options, you can set the purge file system attribute. When a file is flagged with this attribute, the file is purged automatically when it is deleted. When a directory is flagged with the purge attribute, any file that is in that directory is purged when deleted.

If a volume on your NetWare server crashes, and it is mirrored, FILER's salvage option is a great way to make sure that no important files get lost. First use INSTALL to unmirror the hard disks, then use FILER to retrieve any lost files that you might need. After this process, deactivate the server and run REPAIR on the volume. Remount the volume, choose the drive that is most stable, then use INSTALL to remirror the drives.

Set SALVAGE Options

Selecting Set salvage options brings up the Salvage sort options screen shown in figure 9.

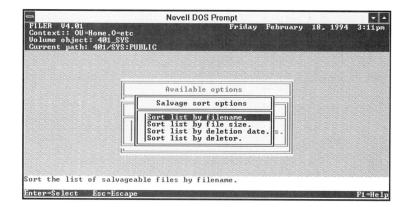

Figure 9
The Salvage sort
options screen.

Purge Deleted Files

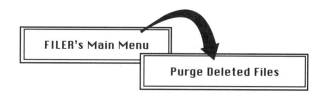

If you select Purge deleted files, a Files pattern box appears. After
entering a pattern or using the default (*), a Purge options menu appears,
providing you with two options: Purge the current directory's files or
Purge the entire subdirectory structure. After selecting one of these
options, a Purge files screen appears, and you seen a directory tree scroll
by. After the process is complete, a message at the bottom of the screen
indicates how many files were purged; pressing Esc returns you to the
Available Options menu.

*Purging old, deleted files is a good habit. Leaving unpurged files
on the drive causes NetWare to "look" for free space each time a
file needs to be written to disk. You also might want to purge files
for security or other reasons.*

Set Default Filer Options

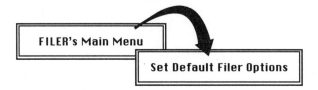

FILER's Main Menu

Set Default Filer Options

Selecting Set default filer options brings up the setting shown in figure 10. To change these options, highlight the appropriate fields and switch between Yes and No by pressing the Y and N keys.

Figure 10
The Filer settings screen.

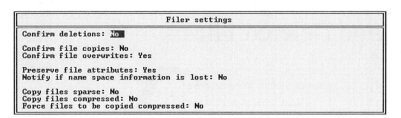

```
                                Filer settings
Confirm deletions: No

Confirm file copies: No
Confirm file overwrites: Yes

Preserve file attributes: Yes
Notify if name space information is lost: No

Copy files sparse: No
Copy files compressed: No
Force files to be copied compressed: No
```

See Also

FILER 3

NWADMIN

NWUSER

FILTCFG

Packets flowing through your network can be controlled using the NetWare 4.10 FILTCFG NLM. FILTCFG is used to help configure and manage network file servers. Using FILTCFG, IPX, TCP/IP, and AppleTalk, packets can be filtered to limit network traffic in general, or to limit it on only a specific section of your network. Filtering packets also is used as a method of increasing network security.

Packets being accepted by a server, as well as those being advertised by a server, can be filtered using information contained within the packets. You can, for example, filter packets to prevent them from being forwarded across the network based on the source or destination addresses and socket numbers they contain, as well as by the type of packet.

The following three types of filters are provided by FILTCFG:

♦ **Packet forwarding.** Both IPX and TCP/IP protocols can take advantage of packet forwarding filters. This type of filter provides the highest level of security a packet filter can provide, but it will not prevent Service Advertising Packets (SAP) from being sent. Even with packet forwarding filters, users will be able to see SAPs for various network services, even though they might not be able to access all of them.

Router packets (packets which are sent from or to routers) cannot have packet forwarding filters applied. Packet forwarding filters are only applied to IPX and TCP/IP packets forwarded to an internal network.

♦ **Service information.** Outgoing IPX packets, incoming SAP packets, and AppleTalk packets can be filtered using service information filters. This type of filter increases network security by reducing the viability of certain network services. Because service information filters are applied only to service information packets, service information filters provide a lower level of security than do packet forwarding filters.

♦ **Routing information.** Outgoing (advertisement) and incoming (acceptance) routing information filters are used for IPX, AppleTalk, and TCP/IP protocols to restrict the visibility of specific networks. Routing information filters function by limiting which routes are added to a specific router's table of available network routers. As routing information filters are applied only to routing information packets, the level of security they provide is quite low. When enabled on a specific router, for example, an outgoing routing information filter can be used to hide some routes from certain routers or from certain areas of the network.

To use FILTCFG, you first must enable filtering for the protocol you want to configure. If you want to filter packets using the TCP/IP protocol, for example, you must first run the Internetworking Configuration (INETCFG) utility to enable filtering for TCP/IP packets. You can then set up or change filtering using the FILTCFG utility.

To use the FILTCFG utility, type **LOAD FILTCFG** at the file server console and press Enter. The Protocol Filters menu opens (see fig. 1).

Figure 1
The FILTCFG Protocol
Filters menu.

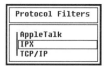

General Parameters

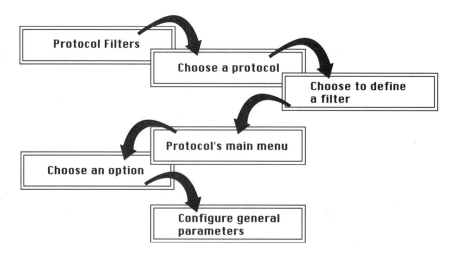

Using the FILTCFG utility, you can set up and modify filtering for each of the supported protocols—AppleTalk, IPX, and TCP/IP.

Selecting the option you want from the main menu of the protocol you selected from the Protocol Filters menu lets you configure one or more parameters. The general parameters you can configure are as follows:

♦ **Status.** If set to Enabled, this will cause the filter category to function. If set to Disabled, no filtering based on this filter category will occur.

♦ **Action.** Set this parameter to switch on (to permit) or off (to deny) an action on the filter list options. If the action is set to be denied, packets matching the specified entry are discarded.

♦ **Exceptions.** Configure this parameter to display a list of filters that are not affected by the status set in Action, press Enter on the Exceptions parameter. Press Ins, Enter, or Del to add a new filter, choose a filter from the existing list of exceptions, or delete a filter from the existing list of exceptions to the Action.

♦ **Filters.** Configure this parameter to display a list of filters. By pressing Ins, you can add a new filter, or you can choose a filter from the list, then modify (press Enter) or delete (press Delete) that filter.

AppleTalk Filtering

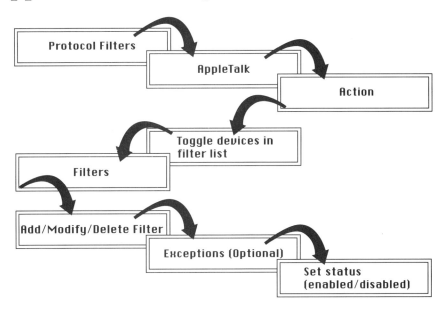

You can filter AppleTalk devices using either the AppleTalk Device Hiding Filters or the AppleTalk Routing Information Filters. These filters prevent service advertising packets from being accessed by users. When filtered areas of the network request AppleTalk services, the filters cause the server or router to drop the AppleTalk Name Binding Protocol (NBP) reply to request for services. The result is that the services are hidden from that part of the network.

IPX Filtering

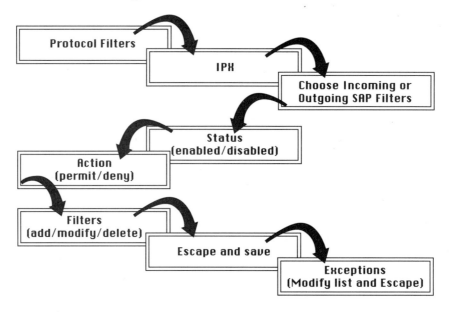

You can create, modify, or delete the following three types of IPX filters:

♦ SAP

♦ RIP

♦ NetBIOS and Packet Forwarding

You can set incoming or outgoing SAP filters to let the server discard SAP information or to restrict SAP information the server sees. When configuring SAP filters, disabling them before configuring helps to prevent temporary service loss.

You can set incoming or outgoing RIP filters, which are used to restrict RIP packets received by a server or router, to provide limited security, and to reduce the update bandwidth and routing table memory requirements. As with SAP filters, disabling RIP filters before configuring them helps to prevent temporary service loss.

You can set or modify IP Routing Information and IP Packet Forwarding filters. IP Routing Information filters limit the incoming routes, and IP Packet Forwarding filters limit the outgoing routes. Routers can use RIP, OSPF, or EGP for exchanging routing information between routers. The IP Routing Information filters can be applied to RIP, EGP, and OSPF routes, but not to directly connected networks. The IP Packet Forwarding filters can be applied to ICMP, TCP, or UDP protocol types.

INSTALL 2.2

Before installing a NetWare 2.2 file server, carefully install all networking hardware and record all hardware settings. Determine which VAPs will have to be installed (Macintosh, printing, and so on). Decide how many bindery objects, TTS transactions, and so on, you will set, and to what level you will set them. After you have carefully planned and recorded all aspects of your NetWare 2.2 network, then you can install the NetWare 2.2 operating system software.

To install NetWare 2.2, insert the SYSTEM-1 disk into the disk drive, type **INSTALL**, and press Enter. Complete each of the four installation modules:

♦ Operating system generation module

♦ Linking and configuring module

♦ Track Zero Test (ZTEST) module

♦ File server definition module

Choosing Advanced Installation from the installation menu opens an introductory welcome screen. Press Enter, and the Operating System Generation screen.

Operating System Generation

When the Operating System Generation screen opens, provide the operating system mode, the nondedicated network address (if appropriate), the number of communication buffers, whether this machine will be the server, whether core printing services should be included, and information about the network boards and disk channels. When all information is complete, press F10 to continue.

Linking and Configuring

When the information is entered and is correct, the INSTALL program links the NetWare operating system. It also creates the following four utilities:

- ZTEST
- INSTOVL
- COMPSURF
- VREPAIR

Track Zero Test

Run ZTEST to verify the hard disk and eliminate any data on that hard disk. The other utilities are used at other times, but the ZTEST utility is run next if you are installing NetWare 2.2 on the file server.

File Server Definition

After preparing all hard disks for use by NetWare, the File Server Definition screen opens. On this screen you provide information about the file server name, maximum number of open files, maximum open index files, name of the volume to be used for TTS backout, maximum number of allowed TTS transactions, whether a user's disk space is to be limited, the maximum number of bindery objects to be allowed, and whether the Macintosh VAP should be installed.

The File Server Definition screen also provides information about the hard disk, the NetWare partition, and NetWare volumes.

When all installation information is complete, the NetWare 2.2 file server installation is complete.

INSTALL 3

The INSTALL utility is used for much more than the initial installation of a NetWare file server. It is used to manage disk drives and to perform such tasks as formatting, partitioning, mirroring, and surface testing hard drives. In addition, you can use INSTALL to get information on your NetWare volumes, such as volume name, block size, and disk size. INSTALL can even be used to determine if a particular volume is mounted. INSTALL also is the easiest place in NetWare 3.1x to create, edit, and save startup files (AUTOEXEC.NCF and STARTUP.NCF), which store crucial file server startup commands.

Figure 1 shows INSTALL's main menu in NetWare 3.1x. The available options are as follows:

- ♦ Disk Options
- ♦ Volume Options
- ♦ System Options
- ♦ Product Options
- ♦ Exit

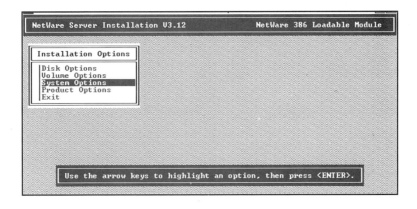

Figure 1
INSTALL's main menu.

Disk Options

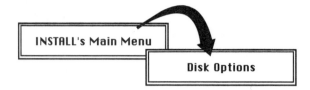

If you select Disk Options from INSTALL's main menu, the Available Disk Options menu appears. The available disk options menu provides the following options:

- ♦ Format
- ♦ Partition Tables
- ♦ Mirroring
- ♦ Surface Test
- ♦ Return to Main Menu

 The disk driver must be loaded before these options are available.

Most of these options are used in the initial NetWare installation phase; however, some vital NetWare functions, such as mirroring drives, can be performed after the initial installation.

Format

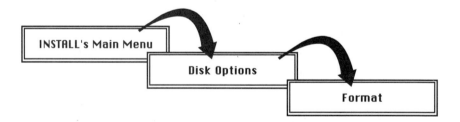

Selecting the Format option from the Available Disk Options menu enables you to format a disk drive or view the status of a disk drive that currently is being formatted. Using INSTALL to format a disk drive is not recommended, however, especially for disk drives that use advanced translation, such as IDE or SCSI drives. For these drives, it is better to leave the "factory" low-level format information on the drive. If your drive does need to be formatted, use the utilities that come with your controller or from the drive manufacturer. If your drives can be formatted, INSTALL enables you to format multiple disk drives at the same time.

Selecting Format brings up a Format Information window as well as a Format Options window. The Format Information window contains a Format Status field. This field displays one of the following values:

♦ **None.** Indicates that you have not tried to format the disk drive.

♦ **Formatting.** Indicates that the disk drive is currently undergoing the formatting process.

♦ **Completed.** Indicates that the formatting process has been completed successfully.

♦ **Failed.** Indicates that the disk drive, controller, or disk driver has a problem, and that the formatting process cannot be completed with the current disk drive, driver, controller combination.

♦ **Not Supported.** Indicates that the disk driver does not support the NetWare format command. Not Supported is often the message that is displayed when a drive uses advanced translation.

Partition Tables

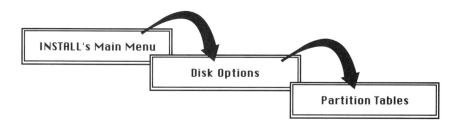

The file server's hard disk drive is divided into logical sections called partitions. One of the file server's hard disk drives can contain both a NetWare partition and an active DOS partition. This method of partitioning enables the machine to boot to DOS first and then load NetWare, thus eliminating the necessity of loading NetWare files from floppy drives.

A NetWare partition consists of a data area, which should be the largest portion of the drive, and a hot fix redirect area, which by default consists of two percent of the available partition area. The Partition Tables menu offers the following options:

♦ Change Hot Fix

♦ Create NetWare Partition

♦ Delete Partition

♦ Return to Previous Menu

After selecting Partition Tables, a Partition Options menu appears. If your drive does not contain any partitions, the Partition Type area of the box indicates that the drive has free space, or contains no partitions. If your drive is partitioned, the Partition Type indicator specifies the type of partitions that are installed on the drive. A drive that has a 35 MB DOS partition and a 600 MB NetWare partition, for example, has a partition table that looks similar to Figure 2.

Figure 2
INSTALL's Partition
Options screen.

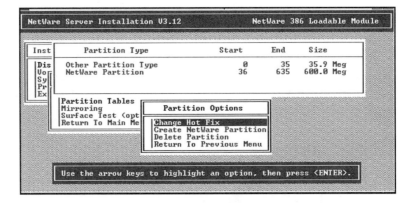

Change Hot Fix

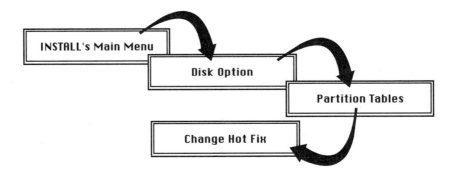

Hot fix enables a hard disk drive to maintain the same data integrity that it had when it was first tested and installed. It does this by redirecting faulty data blocks from the main data storage area to a partition of the drive set aside at installation (the default is 2 percent of the total drive space). This reserved area is called the *hot fix area*.

During normal usage, NetWare performs a read-after-write verification. When a block of data is written to the drive, NetWare immediately reads the data off the drive's surface and checks it against the data (the same data) still in memory. If the two blocks of data are the same (verified), NetWare assumes that the physical location on the disk's surface is good, considers the write operation a success, and releases the data it has in memory.

If the data is not the same, NetWare (after making appropriate retries) places the data onto a different portion of the disk. The bad block on the disk's surface is marked as bad, and NetWare does not attempt to use it again. A single block, however, is not lost because NetWare redirects all inquires for the data assumed to be stored on that section of the drive to the hot fix area where it now is stored.

To change the redirect, or hot fix area, select the Change Hot Fix option from the Partitions Options menu. A window appears that enables you to arrow through the changeable options (data area and redirection area). To change the size of either of these areas, make the change by indicating the appropriate block increase or decrease.

 Changing the hot fix area is only possible when no NetWare volume information is on the drive.

To change the size of the hot fix area, move to the hot fix redirect area and enter the appropriate size in data blocks. After entering the desired size for the data and redirect area press Esc.

To change the size of the hot fix area, select the Change Hot Fix option of the Partition Tables menu, move to the hot fix redirect area, and enter the appropriate size in data blocks.

Create NetWare Partition

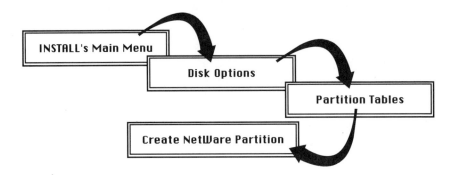

You can only have one NetWare partition on a drive. To partition a server's drive, select the Create NetWare Partition option from the Partition Options menu. After indicating a partition size for NetWare, press Enter. A Partition Verification screen appears, indicating the partition type (for example, NetWare 386), the partition size (600 MB), and the redirect area information. To decrease the size of the partition, move to the partition size field and enter a smaller block number.

Delete Partition

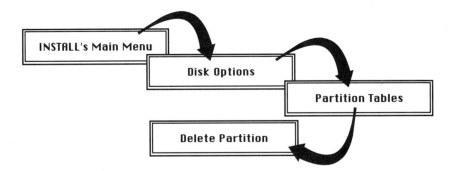

To delete a partition, select the Delete Partition option from the Partition Options menu. A window appears that lists the available partitions. Highlight the correct partition and press Enter. You then are asked to verify that you want to delete the specified partition.

Deleting a partition also deletes all the data that is stored on the partition. Therefore, you cannot delete a partition if it contains a NetWare volume and if that volume is mounted. If you attempt to delete a partition containing a mounted NetWare volume, INSTALL prompts you with a message indicating that you first must dismount the volume, then delete the volume, and then you can remove the partition.

Mirroring

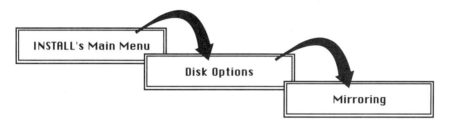

Mirroring drives is the process of duplicating data from one hard partition drive to another. If each hard disk drive has its own controller, however, the process is known as disk duplexing and not as mirroring. Disk duplexing not only protects against disk drive failures, but also against single hard disk controller failures. Disk duplexing also can provide a server with the capability to perform split seeks and simultaneous reads, enhancing performance by as much as 50 percent in some cases.

To mirror a drive or a partition, select the Mirroring option from the available disk options menu. Mirroring a partition means that all of the partitions in that set will be treated as one logical partition. After selecting the Mirroring option, you see a display of the logical NetWare partitions with a status field indicating the partitions' current mirroring status. The status field will contain one of the following status values:

♦ **Mirrored.** Indicates that drives or partitions are mirrored and in sync. To obtain a list of the physical devices that make up a mirrored partition, highlight the partition and press Enter. A list of physical devices appears. To delete a partition from a mirrored set, highlight the appropriate partition and press Del.

♦ **Not mirrored.** Indicates that the mirroring has not yet been set up on the drive or partition. To mirror a partition, select the appropriate partition from the list. You then see a list of devices. To add a partition to a mirrored set, press Ins. This brings up a list of devices. Select the partition to add to the mirrored partition and press Enter (partitions must be approximately the same physical size).

♦ **Out of sync.** If a mirrored set is out of sync, NetWare will not recognize the drives (it will not assume which volume contains the correct data). Changing an out-of-sync partition to a "not mirrored" status will enable you to access the disk (or partition) and the data residing on it. To change the status of a mirror set, select the mirrored set and press Enter. You then can delete a drive or partition (remove it from the mirrored set) by highlighting it and pressing Del. To add a drive to a mirrored set, press Ins. To modify an out-of-sync partition, press F3. Be sure, however, to remirror the good partition, not the one missing data.

Surface Test

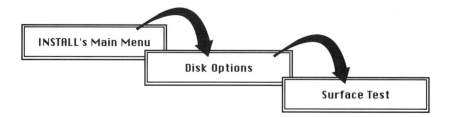

Surface testing a NetWare partition enables NetWare to find all the physical bad blocks of a drive before attempting to place data on them. Two types of surface tests can be run on a drive: destructive and non-destructive. A destructive surface test deletes all data that currently is stored on the drive. A non-destructive surface test leaves the data intact. Another difference between the two types of surface tests is the time it takes to complete them. Because a destructive test is not concerned with the data on the drive, it is faster than a non-destructive test. A non-destructive test can be run while a drive is in production, although it is not recommended. New drives now come from the factory with the bad blocks marked.

With the advent of new NetWare-ready drives, performing a surface test is optional and unnecessary, as well as dangerous, because performing a destructive surface test will scramble your data. Performing a non-destructive surface test introduces the possibility of erasing or incorrectly modifying the factory set bad block list. However, to perform a surface test, select the Surface Test option from the available disk options menu and choose Begin Surface test. You then are given the option of performing a destructive or non-destructive surface analysis.

Volume Options

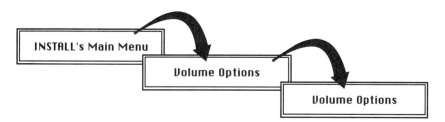

Selecting Volume Options enables you to create, delete, rename, or expand a volume. If your server currently has volumes created, selecting the Volume Options option provides you with a list of volumes. To view the configuration, or to modify a volume, highlight the volume and press Enter. To create a volume, press the Ins key and the Volume Information screen appears (see fig. 3). Enter the desired block and volume sizes and press Esc. You then will be asked if you want to save the changes.

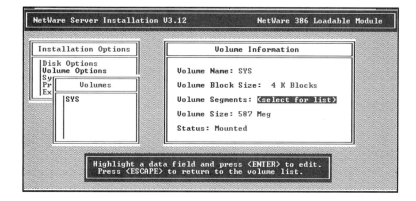

Figure 3
INSTALL's Volume Information screen.

Before creating a NetWare volume, you first must define a NetWare partition. When the first volume is created, the name box is filled in automatically; the new volume is named SYS (the first volume on a server has to be named SYS). Unlike other volume names, you cannot change the name of the SYS volume, but you can change the block size and volume size.

In the Volume Information screen, you have the option of changing the block size of the volume. The smaller the block size, the more memory your server needs, because the smaller the block size, the more memory it takes for the server to track the FAT and directory tables. With a small block size, the hard disk space is used more efficiently, however. The larger the block size, the more sequential the storage and the better the data retrieval time (recommended for large files). The drive holds less data, however (for example, a 2 KB file consumes an entire 64 KB block).

A single volume can span multiple partitions.

System Options

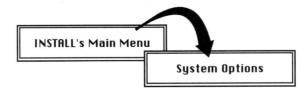

Selecting System Options enables you to set or change the configuration of the file server. During initial installation of a NetWare file server, you should first define a partition, create a volume, and then select System Options. System Options should be the last item selected during the initial installation of a NetWare 386 server. Also, the SYS volume must be mounted before the operations in this menu selection can be used. Selecting System Options gives you access to the following options:

♦ Copy System and Public Files

♦ Create AUTOEXEC.NCF File

♦ Create STARTUP.NCF File

♦ Edit AUTOEXEC.NCF File

♦ Edit STARTUP.NCF File

All LAN and other device drivers need to be loaded for their settings to be included in the STARTUP.NCF and AUTOEXEC.NCF files when they are created.

Copy System and Public Files

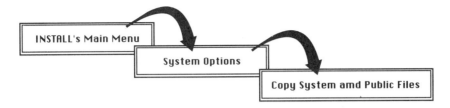

Select the Copy System and Public Files option to install NetWare's operating system files and utilities. You then are given the option of inserting floppy NetWare disks, or pressing F6 to change the location of the source drive. (In NetWare 3.11, you must load INSTALL with a /J parameter to change the location of the source drive.) After selecting the source drive and pressing Enter, you are prompted to put the correct disks in the source drive (if you elected to install from floppies).

Create AUTOEXEC.NCF File

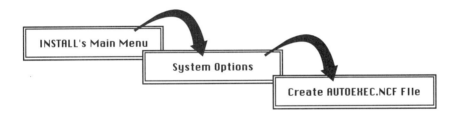

The AUTOEXEC.NCF file is a NetWare server file—much like the DOS AUTOEXEC.BAT file—that is located on the root directory of a DOS drive. The AUTOEXEC.NCF file is used to load modules and set the NetWare operating system's configuration. It stores items such as the server's name, internal IPX number, and other configuration options.

After choosing the Create AUTOEXEC.NCF File option, you are presented with an editor screen, which displays the commands currently in the AUTOEXEC.NCF file. Type the commands that you want in the AUTOEXEC.NCF file and press Esc to save the changes.

An NCF file is to NetWare what a BAT file is to DOS. If you have a list of commands that you load on a regular basis, but do not want to include them in your AUTOEXEC.NCF file, you can create an NCF file using any text editor. Simply name the file and attach the NCF extension. Place the file in the System directory. Whenever you want to load the list of commands, simply type the name of the NCF file.

Create STARTUP.NCF File

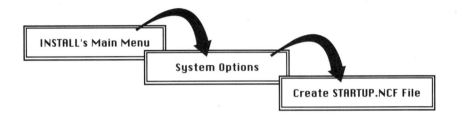

Commands and device drivers loaded by the STARTUP.NCF are the first options loaded by the NetWare operating system. The STARTUP.NCF file contains such items as disk drivers, name space option, and various SET parameters. Because these options have to be loaded before a volume is mounted, the STARTUP.NCF file is located on your boot device.

After choosing the Create STARTUP.NCF File option, you are presented with an editor screen, which displays the commands that were loaded to bring up the server, but before the volumes were mounted. If the commands listed are sufficient, press Esc and answer Yes to the Save Changes dialog box that appears. If the commands need editing, make the necessary changes, and then press Esc.

Changes made to the STARTUP.NCF do not take effect until the server is shut down and brought back up.

Edit AUTOEXEC.NCF File

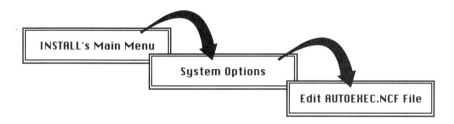

Select the Edit AUTOEXEC.NCF File option and an editing screen appears
with your current AUTOEXEC.NCF file loaded. Make the appropriate
changes, press Esc, and choose Yes in the Save Changes dialog box that
appears.

*The AUTOEXEC.NCF is in the SYS:SYSTEM directory and is
an ASCII text file, which can be edited with any ASCII text
editor.*

Edit STARTUP.NCF File

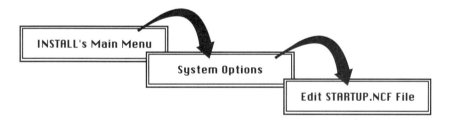

Select the Edit STARTUP.NCF File option and an editing screen appears
with your current STARTUP.NCF file loaded. Make the appropriate
changes, press Esc, and choose Yes in the Save Changes dialog box that
appears.

See Also

SYSCON

INSTALL 4

Installation of today's software usually consists of putting the first disk in drive A and typing **INSTALL**. NetWare 4, however, is a very sophisticated operating system that requires an installer to understand NetWare Directory Services (NDS). The flexibility of NetWare 4's NDS also means it is important to plan your directory structure. With this in mind, take time to familiarize yourself with NetWare 4's NDS.

To start INSTALL, from the server's console, type **LOAD INSTALL** (INSTALL is located in the SYSTEM directory on the SYS volume; by default it is also copied to the NETWARE.40 directory on the DOS boot partition). After loading INSTALL, the following INSTALL main menu appears, as seen in figure 1.

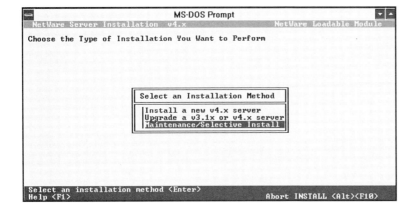

Figure 1
INSTALL's main menu.

The INSTALL utility enables a network administrator to perform the following management functions:

♦ Create, delete, test, and modify NetWare disk partitions

♦ Install NetWare Directory Services

♦ Load and unload disk and LAN drivers

♦ Mirror and unmirror hard disk drives

♦ Create, delete, expand, modify, mount, and dismount volumes

♦ Create and format a DOS partition

♦ Create and modify AUTOEXEC.NCF and STARTUP.NCF files

♦ Copy the public and system files

♦ Perform a surface analysis on a NetWare drive

♦ Install and configure other NLM products on the server

NetWare 4's INSTALL utility has three main options: Install a new v4.10 server, Upgrade a v3.1x or v4.10 server, and Maintenance/Selective Install. This section covers each of these options in some detail.

Install a New NetWare 4.10 Server

Choosing the Install a new v4.10 server option brings up the dialog box shown in figure 2.

Figure 2
NetWare 4's dialog box for installing a new 4.10 server.

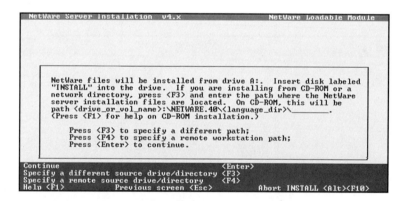

You must complete each of the following steps during an initial installation of a NetWare 4 server.

Enter a Server Name

A server name can be 2 to 47 characters long. You should choose a name that brings meaning to the server. Give the server a name that indicates what its primary function is, or who is using it; this makes it easier for users to remember. Also, use short names—it makes it easier when you have to type the name.

Assign an Internal IPX Number

An internal IPX network number is an internal (1-8) digit hexadecimal number (0-9, A-F) that is used by NetWare to uniquely identify each server on the network. Because the internal IPX number is used as a unique identifier, you should ensure that no two servers have duplicate numbers. In an attempt to avoid an internal IPX number conflict, NetWare randomly generates a number during installation. This is an attempt to help guard against assigning duplicate internal IPX numbers. This creation of a random number does not completely guarantee that duplicate numbers will not be assigned; it merely keeps users who do not know what they are doing from selecting a number such as 1 (or some other number that is easily duplicated).

Most organizations use some type of internal IPX numbering scheme to protect their networks against duplication. If you are installing a new NetWare 4.10 server on a large network and are unsure of your company's policy, check before assigning an IPX number. If you are a small company that is expecting to grow, now would be a good time to devise a numbering scheme. At a minimum, you should realize the importance of keeping this number unique and documenting each number in use.

Select a Disk Driver

Before installing NetWare, you should verify that your controller has a NetWare 4 driver. This driver is absolutely necessary. Without a NetWare 4 driver, the hard disk drive and controller are unable to communicate with NetWare, thus making server installation impossible to complete. You also should verify that you have the latest version of the driver. Using outdated API calls can cause a server to ABEND.

You might have to look at your hard drive controller's documentation to decide which driver you should load. If you have more than one disk controller, you must load the driver multiple times (even if the controllers are the same make and model).

Drivers usually can be purchased from the disk controller manufacturer. Most manufacturers allow you to download drivers from bulletin board systems. Select the appropriate driver from the list supplied and press F10, or insert a floppy disk that contains the driver and press Ins. The screen shown in figure 3 appears.

Figure 3
NetWare 4's Load
Disk Driver screen.

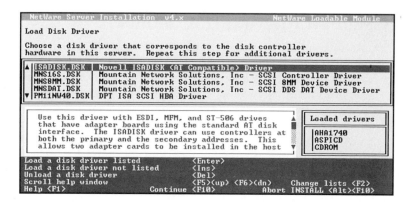

Specify a Server Boot Path

After you install a disk driver, a window appears prompting you to enter a destination path for the server's boot files.

The NetWare disk partitions that are created later in the installation are not accessible without first loading certain files, such as disk drivers. Therefore, you must create a bootable DOS partition for these files. With earlier versions of NetWare, it was common practice to use a floppy drive for a boot disk. This practice is not recommended with NetWare 4, however. Using a floppy drive for a boot disk is slow, and the files required to start the server are becoming so large that they do not fit on a single floppy disk.

Select a LAN Driver

After you load a disk driver, INSTALL prompts you to select and load a LAN driver. Much like disk drivers, LAN drivers are an integral part of the network installation. They enable the server to communicate with other network nodes (workstations and servers). NetWare 4 ships with several LAN drivers, but they are developed by and obtainable from the card manufacturer. You should contact your Ethernet card manufacturer to obtain the most current LAN driver and to verify that it has been tested in a NetWare 4 server.

Previous versions of NetWare enable you to install a server without a LAN driver present. During a NetWare 4 installation, however, the server has to be capable of "looking" at the wire to determine if it is the first server on the network. This procedure requires that a LAN driver be in the server. If a LAN driver is not present, the installation procedure stops when it attempts to "look" at the wire. You then must restart the installation process.

Create Partitions

You can create NetWare partitions automatically or manually. To create them automatically, select the Automatic option, and the INSTALL utility completes the process for you. To create a partition manually, select the Manual option, and walk through the process step by step.

If you do not want to use all remaining space on the drive for a NetWare partition, choose the Manual Partition option. If you plan to mirror or duplex drives, or install NetWare for use on OS/2, choose the Manual option. Otherwise, select the Automatic option.

Create Volumes

Volumes logically segment a drive into areas where data can be stored. A volume can have multiple segments that span multiple hard disks. After a volume is created, it can be expanded by adding a new volume segment. Deleting a segment of a volume destroys all the data on the volume, however. You should consider the following points when creating a volume:

♦ Maximum number of segments in a volume is 32

♦ Maximum number of segments you can create on one hard disk is 8

♦ Maximum number of volumes is 64

♦ One volume must always be named SYS (50 MB minimum)

♦ Mirroring the SYS volume

♦ Creating a single large volume that spans several drives for performance

♦ Creating a volume for each disk, and then mirroring them for fault tolerance

♦ Spanning and duplexing volumes for fault tolerance and performance

♦ Creating a volume for each operating system (Macintosh, Unix, and so on)

♦ More volumes require more memory

Following these recommendations helps ensure that you do not reach or go beyond NetWare's restrictions.

Default Volume Settings

You should be aware that NetWare's default volume settings are as follows:

♦ File compression = ON

♦ Block suballocation = ON

♦ Data migration = OFF

These settings can be changed by highlighting the appropriate location and pressing Y or N to toggle the setting.

File compression provides more disk space by using an algorithm to compress file data. NetWare's compression is done in the background and has little or no effect on performance.

Block suballocation conserves disk space by enabling more than one file to populate a data block. If you set your block size to the maximum setting of 64 KB, for example, every file, even if it is 2 KB, consumes 64 KB. Block suballocation maximizes disk space by storing more than one file in each block.

Data migration enables network managers to decide when a file should be moved off the file server onto a near-line storage device, such as an optical storage device. After a file is migrated off the primary storage, NetWare keeps a record of the file's location. Thus, if a user requests the file, it can be retrieved.

Name the Directory Services Tree

During the initial installation of a server—if it is the first NetWare 4 server on the network—you are asked to name the directory tree. If it is not the first server, you are asked to specify the context in which you want the server to be placed. If it is the first tree, a dialog box, as seen in figure 4, appears. Select Yes <This is the first Directory server>. You then are asked to assign a name to the new directory services tree. In naming a directory tree, you should know that every directory has a root name. The root name is the name of the NetWare Directory Services (NDS) tree. The directory tree name should not be confused with the first level organization container name. The only time you must name the tree is during the installation of the first NetWare 4 server or when you are creating a different tree.

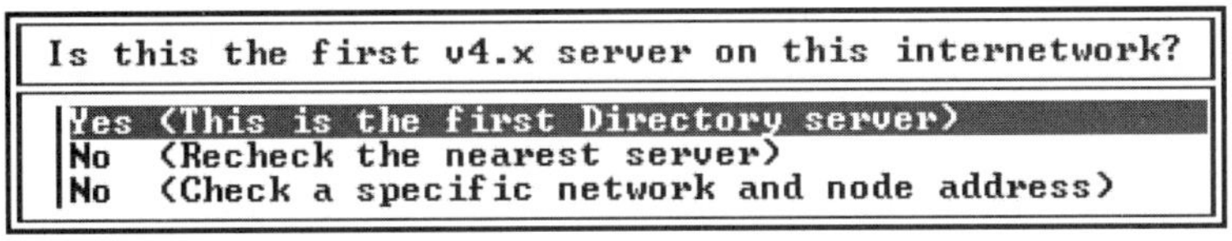

```
Is this the first v4.x server on this internetwork?

Yes (This is the first Directory server)
No  (Recheck the nearest server)
No  (Check a specific network and node address)
```

Figure 4
Prompt verifying
that this is the first
directory service tree
on the network.

Specify a Time Zone

The next step in the initial server installation phase is to specify a server time zone. This time zone is critical for NetWare's Directory Services to decide which changes to the directory are the most recent. A list containing the most popular United States time zone abbreviations will appear. Highlight the time zone in which the server is to be located, and press F10.

Select a Time Server Type

A screen will appear giving you the option to select a server time type. It is critical that NetWare's Directory Services keep track of the most recent changes to the internal database; therefore, it must keep all of the server's times in sync. To do this, NetWare must know which servers have superiority when deciding the correct time. To help determine the "chain of command," assign your server a time type. The following is a description of each of the available time types.

♦ **Single reference server.** This type of time server is the sole source of time on the network. Any time this server's time changes, all other servers on the network synchronize with it.

♦ **Primary server.** This type of time server is a reference time server and provides the correct time to a secondary time server. If multiple primary time servers are on the same network, they "vote" to determine the correct network time.

♦ **Reference server.** This type of time server is most often used when accessing an outside time source, such as Greenwich Mean Time. A reference server does not use or change its internal time clock. A reference server helps primary time servers establish a time through a method known as voting.

♦ **Secondary server.** This type of time server receives time from a single reference, reference, or primary server. Most of the servers on your network should be set up as secondary servers.

The following are guidelines that you should use for setting up your network time servers.

- ◆ Consider the geographical location of each server when selecting its time type

- ◆ Obtain the secondary server's time from a reference server

- ◆ Make sure that each remote site (over a WAN link) has at least one reference server

- ◆ Make sure that each secondary time server has access to more than one reference server

- ◆ Use single reference servers on small networks that do not have a WAN link

- ◆ Do not mix single and primary reference servers.

Specify the Server Context

If this is the first NetWare 4 server on the network, the installation process will suggest the context in which to place the server. For each new server that is installed, NetWare will offer this same context. If the automatically offered context is not the desired context, you can change the context by typing the desired server context. If you want to change the context of the server, enter the correct context and press F10. The Context For This Server screen appears (see fig. 5).

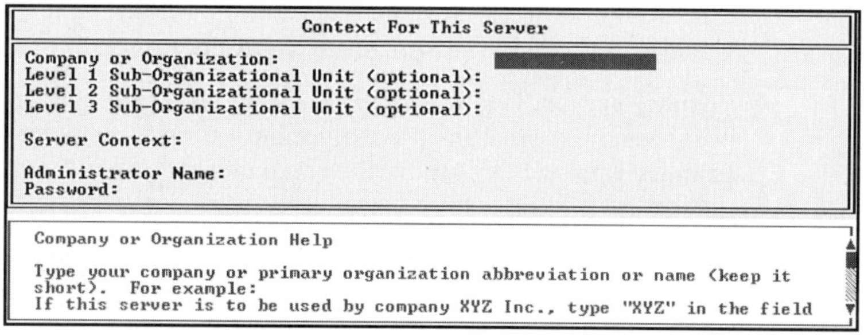

Figure 5
The Context For This
Server screen.

```
┌─────────────────────────────────────────────────────────────────────┐
│                         Context For This Server                       │
│ ┌───────────────────────────────────────────────────────────────────┐ │
│ │ Company or Organization:                                          │ │
│ │ Level 1 Sub-Organizational Unit (optional):      ▬▬▬▬▬▬▬          │ │
│ │ Level 2 Sub-Organizational Unit (optional):                       │ │
│ │ Level 3 Sub-Organizational Unit (optional):                       │ │
│ │                                                                   │ │
│ │ Server Context:                                                   │ │
│ │                                                                   │ │
│ │ Administrator Name:                                               │ │
│ │ Password:                                                         │ │
│ └───────────────────────────────────────────────────────────────────┘ │
│ ┌───────────────────────────────────────────────────────────────────┐ │
│ │ Company or Organization Help                                    ▲ │ │
│ │                                                                   │ │
│ │ Type your company or primary organization abbreviation or name (keep it │ │
│ │ short).  For example:                                             │ │
│ │ If this server is to be used by company XYZ Inc., type "XYZ" in the field ▼ │ │
│ └───────────────────────────────────────────────────────────────────┘ │
└─────────────────────────────────────────────────────────────────────┘
```

Assign a Password

After you set up your directory tree, a screen appears asking you to assign a password for the network administrator, which has the Login ID of ADMIN and is placed in the Organizational container. Type the appropriate password and press F10. After you assign a password, you are informed that directory services has been installed. A screen then appears asking if you want to create or edit the NetWare startup files. The files contain all of the settings that were selected during the install procedure (for example, time server type, time zone, and LAN drivers). Saving them enables your server to boot and load the configuration without intervention. You can edit the startup files from this location, however, to be safe.

Upgrade a NetWare 3.1x or NetWare 4.10 Server

NetWare 4's INSTALL utility enables you to upgrade from any previous version of NetWare. This includes upgrading from NetWare 2 and NetWare 3, as well as from another network operating system.

Two methods are available for upgrading a server: across-the-wire migration and in-place upgrade. In an across-the-wire migration, information from one server is migrated across the network wire to the new server. Data files, bindery information, and print queues are migrated to the working (workstation) hard drive. The information is translated into an appropriate NetWare 4 format and then migrated to the new destination server.

The across-the-wire migration method also consists of two migration options: a standard migration option and a custom migration option. The standard migration option is the simplest of the two choices to use, but is less flexible than the custom migration option. The standard migration option migrates all the information from a NetWare 2 or NetWare 3 server to a NetWare 4 server. The custom migration option is more difficult to use, but offers more flexibility. With the custom option, you can select specific information from the bindery and data files, thus enabling you to upgrade a server, or to combine two servers into one custom NetWare 4 server.

When using the across-the-wire migration method, you must set up an initial NetWare 4 server. You also must have two machines: your old server and the new NetWare 4 server.

The across-the-wire migration method enables you to take advantage of some of NetWare 4's new features, such as block suballocation.

Maintenance/Selective Install

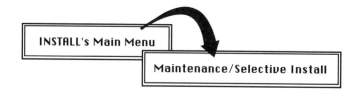

NetWare 4 is the first version of NetWare that has an automatic installation option. If you are familiar with NetWare 3.x, the `Maintenance/Selective install` option should be familiar to you; it just has a few more options. The `Maintenance/Selective install` option enables the network Administrator to install or change portions of a server's configuration, such as disk or LAN drivers, configure and manage disks and volumes, remove directory services, and so on. In addition to making configuration changes, there are several reasons that you should use the `Maintenance/Selective install` option. If for some reason the automatic installation does not finish, or if you are familiar enough with NetWare that you do not want to be "guided" through the installation process, you should use the `Maintenance/Selective install` option.

Selecting the `Maintenance/Selective install` option enables you to do the following:

- ◆ Load additional disk drivers or set disk driver options

- ◆ Install, configure, or unload LAN drivers

- ◆ Manage disk drives (mirroring, partitions, and so on)

- ◆ Install NetWare system files

- ◆ Set up or remove NetWare Directory Services

- ◆ Edit and create NCF files

- ◆ Install or reconfigure NLM products

Disk Driver Options

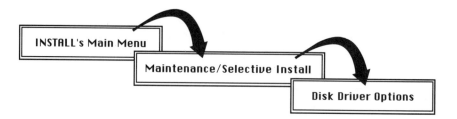

Selecting Disk Driver Options from the Maintenance/Selective Install
menu brings up three windows. The largest of these windows is a
selection window, which is the active window. You can move the highlight bar in the selection window to the desired disk driver. Pressing
Enter brings up a driver parameter option box, which enables you to
specify the address, or in the case of an EISA machine, the slot where the
disk controller is located. Then you are asked if you want to load this
driver. Answer Yes or No.

To remove a disk driver, move the highlight bar to the appropriate driver
and press Del.

*If the driver is not in use (no volumes mounted), it unloads
without any warnings. If the driver is in use, it does not unload,
and you must switch to the System Console screen to determine
why the driver refused to unload.*

*To switch to the System Console screen, press the Alt and Esc
keys simultaneously. If you are in RCONSOLE, press the Alt and
F1 keys. Next, choose the Select a Screen to View option, and then
choose System Console from the list of available options.*

If the disk driver that you want to load is not listed, press Ins. A dialog
box appears in which you press the F3 key and then type the path where
the additional disk driver is located.

The smallest of the three windows, which is located on the lower right
corner of your screen, indicates the drivers currently loaded (see fig. 6).

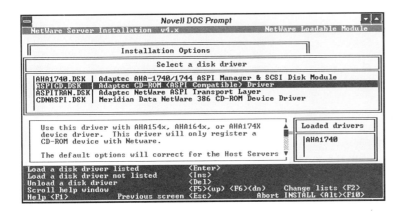

Figure 6
INSTALL's disk driver
screen.

LAN Driver Options

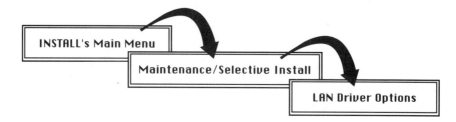

After you select the LAN Driver Options option from the Maintenance/ Selective Install menu, three windows appear. The first and largest of the three windows is a selection window, which is the active window. Highlight the desired disk driver. Press Enter to bring up a LAN driver parameter option box, in which you can specify the LAN driver's I/O address, memory settings, node address, and a frame type. You also can identify the appropriate slot for an EISA machine. After you enter the LAN driver parameters, press F10 to load the driver.

To unload a LAN driver, highlight the appropriate driver and press Del.

You are not offered a second chance when unloading a LAN driver. If you press Del and the driver is currently in use, it is unloaded, and users who are logged in to that particular network receive a message indicating that a network error has occurred, and that their connection has been lost. This could cause users to lose hours of work.

To specify multiple frame types for an individual LAN driver, move the cursor to the Frame Type List option and press Enter. Mark the appropriate frame types by moving the highlight bar to the frame type check box, and then press Enter to select or deselect frame types.

If the LAN driver that you want to load is not listed, press Ins. A dialog box appears in which you press the F3 key and then type the path of the additional LAN driver. The second window is a "help" window that explains driver specifics as you highlight available drivers from the driver list. The smallest of the three windows, which is located on the lower right corner of your screen, indicates the LAN drivers that are currently loaded.

Disk Options

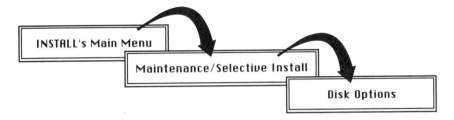

Select Disk Options from the Maintenance/Selective Install menu and the Available Disk Options menu appears. The options available from this menu are as follows:

♦ Modify Disk Partitions

♦ Mirror/Unmirror Disk Partitions

♦ Perform surface test (optional)

♦ Return To Main Menu

Modify Disk Partitions and Hot Fix

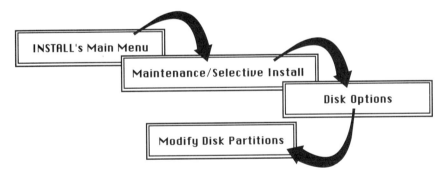

The Modify Disk Partitions and Hot Fix option gives you access to the disk partition option menu in which you can do the following:

♦ Change the hot fix area

♦ Create NetWare disk partitions

♦ Delete any disk partition

When you select Change the Hot Fix Area, you are given the Disk Partition Information screen (see fig. 7).

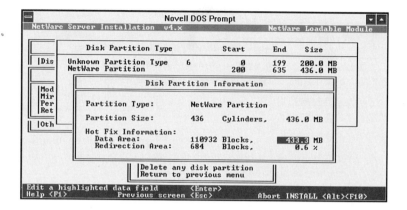

Change Hot Fix Area

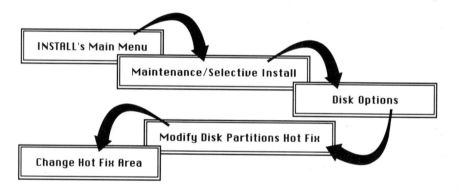

The hot fix area of a NetWare partition enables a server's hard disk to maintain the same data integrity that it had when it was new. It does this by redirecting faulty data blocks from the main data storage area to a partition of the drive set aside at installation (by default this area is 2 percent of available drive space). This reserved area is called the *hot fix area*.

When hot fix gets full, hot fix is shut down and no verification is done.

During normal usage, NetWare performs a read-after-write verification. When a block of data is written to the drive, NetWare immediately reads the data off the drive and checks the data against the same data that it still has in memory. If the two sets of data are the same (verified), NetWare assumes that the physical location on the disk's surface is good, and the write request is considered successful. If, however, the integrity check fails, NetWare (after making the appropriate number of retries) places the data on a different portion of the disk. If any bad blocks are found on the disk's surface, they are marked as "bad," and NetWare avoids trying to use them again. These blocks are then replaced by blocks from the hot fix redirect area.

You can change the (size of the) hot fix area by selecting the Change Hot Fix Area option from the Modify Disk Partitions and Hot Fix menu. Then highlight Reduction Area and enter the percentage of the disk that you want to reserve as the hot fix portion and press Enter. Generally, 2 percent is more than sufficient area to reserve for the hot fix area, and perhaps too much on really big drives that are mapping out bad blocks at the controller anyway, sparing out those bad blocks to other blocks.

The size of the hot fix area can only be changed if no volume information is stored on the drive.

Create NetWare Disk Partition

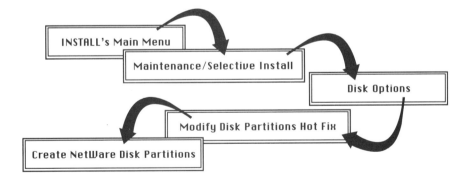

Selecting the Create NetWare disk partition option gives you the following two options:

♦ Automatically

♦ Manually

If you select the Automatically option, INSTALL creates a NetWare partition on the remaining free space on the hard drive. At this time, INSTALL also automatically creates the SYS volume using the entire partition.

 If the automatic option is used, extended DOS partitions will be destroyed (but not the primary DOS partition).

If you select the Manually option, you are given control over defining disk partitions. You can adjust the size of the hot fix area, as well as indicate the size of the partition and volumes.

Deleting Any Disk Partition

To delete a partition of any type, select the Delete Any Disk Partition option. A list of available partitions appears. Highlight the partition that you want to delete and press Enter.

 Deleting a partition also deletes all of the data that is stored on the partition. You cannot delete a partition that contains a mounted NetWare volume. If you attempt to delete a partition and these conditions exist, INSTALL displays a message indicating that you must first dismount the volume, delete the volume, and then remove the partition.

If you select the Delete Any Disk Partition option, highlight the partition (any partition other than the NetWare partition), and press Enter, it will be deleted regardless of whether it contains data.

Mirror/Unmirror Disk Partitions

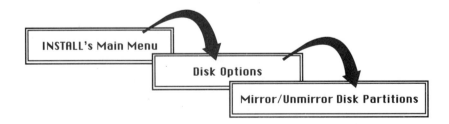

Mirroring is a technique used by NetWare to protect data from hard disk failures by duplicating one hard disk's data on a second disk drive. If two controllers are used, mirroring is referred to as *disk duplexing*. Because it protects against controller failure, duplexing offers enhanced fault tolerance over mirroring.

To mirror or duplex drives, the partitions must be the same size on both drives. If they are not the same size, NetWare adjusts the partitions to make them the same size. You can mirror up to eight disk partitions.

To mirror two partitions, first create the partitions. Next, choose Disk Options from INSTALL's Maintenance/Selective Install menu. Then select the Mirror/Unmirror Disk Partitions option and a Disk Partition Mirroring Status screen appears. Each partition that is created displays one of the following status messages: not mirrored, mirrored, or out of sync. Choose one of the disk devices that shows a "not mirrored" status message. (To unmirror a partition, select the appropriate mirrored device and press Del.)

The first partition becomes the primary partition in the mirrored set. A list of partitions on the selected device appears. Pressing Ins adds that partition to the mirrored set. If the partitions are the same size, the Disk Partition Mirroring Status screen indicates that the two devices are now mirrored.If the partitions are not the same size, NetWare asks if you want to make them the same size.

Perform Surface Test

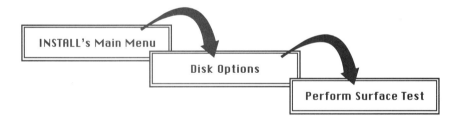

Surface testing a NetWare partition enables NetWare to find all the physical bad blocks of a drive before attempting to place data on them. Two types of surface tests can be run on a drive: destructive and non-destructive. A destructive surface test deletes all data that currently is stored on the drive. A non-destructive surface test leaves the data intact. Another difference between the two types of tests is the amount of time it takes to complete them. Because a destructive test is not concerned with the data on the drive, it is faster than a non-destructive test. A non-destructive test can be run while a drive is in production, although it is not recommended. New drives come from the factory with the bad blocks marked.

With the advent of new NetWare-ready drives, performing a surface test is optional and unnecessary, as well as dangerous. To perform a surface test, however, select the Surface Test Options from the Disk Options menu and choose Begin surface test. You are given the option of performing a destructive or non-destructive surface analysis.

Select the appropriate device and the Disk Surface Test Options and status windows appear (see fig. 8).

Figure 8
The Surface Test Options window.

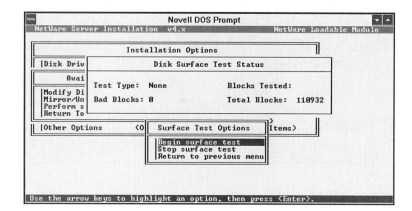

Volume Options

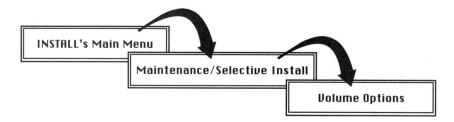

A volume is the highest level of NetWare's file system (much on the same level as DOS's root directory). A volume can be fully contained on a single drive, or can be spanned across several drives. In NetWare 4, a server can support up to 64 volumes. The first volume on a server must always be named SYS and must be at least 50 MB in size. The installation program also creates volume names for all additional disk devices, such as VOL1, VOL2, and so on. Unlike the SYS volume, however, these volume names can be changed to whatever you want. You should use a name that specifies what is on the drive, such as APPS, DATA, and so on. It also is a good idea to keep these names short so that they are easy to type.

If you select Volume Options and no volumes exist on your drive, a blank volume screen appears. To add a volume, press Ins and select a device from the Volume Disk Segment list that appears. You then can type the name of the new volume and change any of the other default options. To view or modify a volume, press the F3 key. To delete a volume, highlight the volume and press Del.

Using the INSTALL utility, volumes can be added (spliced) together or separated.

To mount or dismount a volume, press Enter. At this point, the Volume Information screen appears, which shows the volume name, the volume block size, the volume status, and the file compression, block sub-allocation, and data migration status. To change the volume name (if it is not the SYS volume), press Enter on the Volume Name option and type the new name. You can press Enter on the Status option to dismount a volume. To turn on or off migration, press Enter on the Data migration option. Other status lines cannot be changed from this location.

NetWare's file compression is safe and automatic. File compression is enabled at the volume level. You can use the FLAG command to turn on or off compression for individual files and file types, however. By default, if a file is not used, it is compressed. Options can be set from console to determine how quickly a file is compressed (and other factors) by using SET. File compression can provide 50 to 75 percent more disk storage space.

Block suballocation also saves disk space, but does so by storing files in blocks of 512 KB, even if your volume's data block size is set to a larger size. This lets NetWare store multiple blocks of data within the same physical block.

Data migration is another method of optimizing disk space. It does this by moving files off the server's disks to another offline storage device, such as an optical storage device. Data migration is automatic and user transparent. If a file has been moved to a secondary device and the user requests the file, NetWare 4 still perceives the file as being available and retrieves the file.

License Options

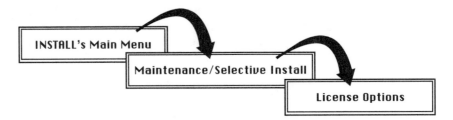

License Options is used to increase your NetWare license satisfaction; for example, from 50 users to 100 users. In NetWare 4, you cannot simply copy a new EXE file to the server to have the server connections increased. To increase your license #, you have to use the license file option.

Select License Options from the Installation Option screen. You then are asked to type the path of the new SERVER.MLS file. Press F3 to specify a different path. Pressing F4 enables you to specify a remote source.

Copy Files Option

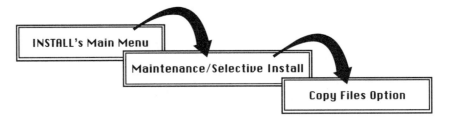

After you have partitioned the drives and created the volumes, you are ready to install the NetWare files. By default, INSTALL creates the directory structure on the SYS volume as shown in figure 10. The files copied from disk or CD-ROM are placed in one of the following directories (see fig. 9).

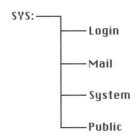

Figure 9
Default directories
created at install.

To start copying files, select the Copy Files option from the Installation
Option window. Then you are asked for the source drive or directory. To
specify a source drive other than drive A, press F3. To specify a remote
location, press F4.

Directory Options

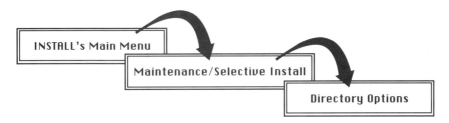

NetWare Directory Services (NDS) is NetWare 4's new directory name
base that effectively stores the names of all the resources available on the
network. These resources include things such as users, printers, servers,
and so on. It is a hierarchical, distributed, and replicated database that
provides a common interface for each network resource. NDS also
enables a user a single point of log in, and the ability to use network
resources without having to know where the resources reside.

After selecting Directory Options, NetWare "looks" out on the network wire to try to find another NDS tree. If no other trees are found, NetWare presents you with a configuration box asking if this is the first NetWare 4 server on the network. If another server containing a directory tree is found, you are asked in which context you want to place the new server. If it is, see the section, "Installing a New NetWare 4.10 Server" at the beginning of this chapter. A server then appears prompting you to specify the correct time zone settings. Move the cursor to the correct time zone and press Enter. Press F10 to save these changes and continue.

Another screen appears in which you specify the type of time server that you want this server to be (see "Installing a New NetWare 4.10 Server" at the beginning of this chapter). Type the Administrator's name and password and press Enter. Finally, another screen appears asking you to enter the name and password that will be used for the network Administrator.

Place the server in the correct server context or create a new context. To save the directory information, press F10.

The INSTALL utility then enables you to view and make changes to the NCF files. NCF files are loaded automatically each time the server is started. To save these files, press F10 and choose Yes.

To install or reinstall mounted volumes into the directory tree, select the Directory Options menu from the Installation Options screen. You then see the Directory Services Options screen (see fig. 10).

Figure 10

The Directory Services Options screen.

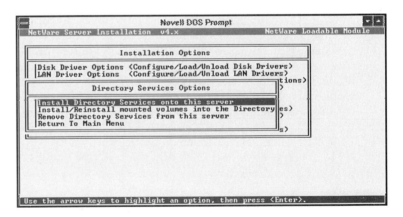

Choose the Install/Reinstall option. This option verifies that a directory volume object exists for the volume. By default, NetWare uses the <server_name>_<volume_name> naming convention for volume objects.

If the volume has not previously been upgraded, trustee IDs on the volume are upgraded from the bindery IDs to directory IDs.

To remove Directory Services (not recommended), select the Remove Directory Services option from the Directory Services Options menu. A screen appears verifying the removal of the tree. Press Enter to continue. You then are asked to authenticate the directory (type a correct administrator name and password). After you authenticate the directory, you are informed of the number of volume objects that have been downgraded (removed from the tree).

NCF Files Options

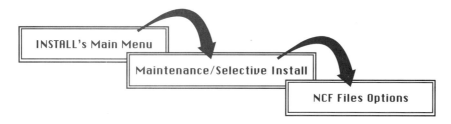

The AUTOEXEC.NCF file is a NetWare server file—much like a batch file—that is located on the SYS volume in the system directory. The AUTOEXEC.NCF file is used to load modules and set the NetWare operation system's configuration. It stores items such as the server's name, internal IPX number, directory information, and other configuration options.

Create AUTOEXEC.NCF File

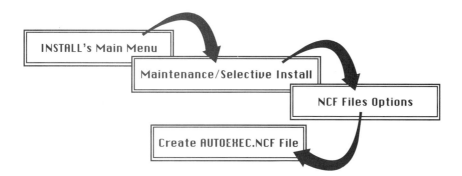

After choosing the Create AUTOEXEC.NCF File option, you are presented with an editor screen. The left side of the editor screen displays the commands currently in the AUTOEXEC.NCF file. The right screen of the editor screen is where you can make changes to the AUTOEXEC.NCF files. Add any necessary commands to the AUTOEXEC.NCF file, and then press the F10 key to save the changes.

An NCF file is to NetWare what a batch file is to DOS. If you have a list of commands that you load on a regular basis, but do not want to include them in your AUTOEXEC.NCF file, you can simply create an NCF file using any text editor. Simply name the file and attach the NCF extension. Place the file in the System directory. Whenever you want to load the list of commands, simply type the name of the NCF file.

Create STARTUP.NCF File

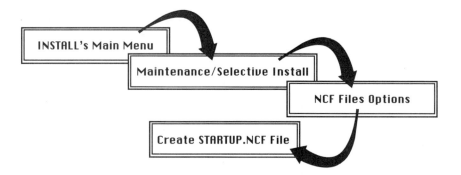

Commands loaded by the STARTUP.NCF are the first commands loaded by the NetWare operating system. The STARTUP.NCF file contains such commands as disk drivers, name space option, and various SET parameters. Because these options have to be loaded before a volume is mounted, the STARTUP.NCF file should be located on your boot device.

After choosing the Create STARTUP.NCF File option, you are presented with a split screen. The left half of the screen displays the commands used to bring up the server; the right half of the screen displays an editing screen. If the commands listed are sufficient, press the F10 key and answer Yes to save the changes. If the commands need editing, make the necessary changes, and then save the file to the appropriate place in the boot drive.

Note *Changes made to the STARTUP.NCF will not take effect until the server is shut down and brought back up.*

Product Options

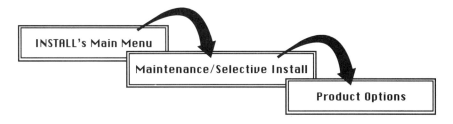

The Product Options option enables you to install and reconfigure NetWare and third-party products. After selecting this option, a screen showing the currently loaded third-party or "other" NetWare products appears (see fig. 11).

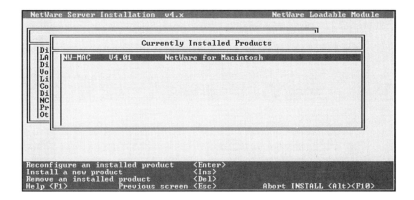

Figure 11
Currently Installed
Products screen.

Other Options

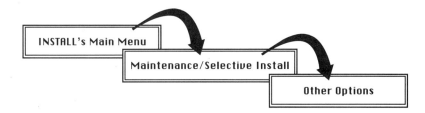

The Other Options selection enables you to do the following:

- ♦ Create a registration disk
- ♦ Upgrade NetWare 3.1x print services
- ♦ Configure communication protocols
- ♦ Copy online documentation
- ♦ Copy computer-based training
- ♦ Create optional disks
- ♦ Install an additional server language

Figure 12 shows the Other Options screen, which appears after you select Other Options (if you are installing from a CD-ROM drive).

Figure 12
NetWare 4 INSTALL's
Other Options screen.

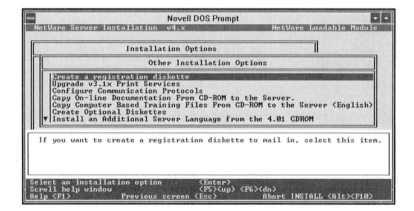

To copy online documentation or computer-based training files, select the appropriate option, and a screen asks you to enter the path from which the files will be installed. Drive A is the default. The most common location is from a CD-ROM drive, however. In this case, the correct path is "D:\NetWare.40\English_____\" (with D being the drive designation, NetWare.40 being the first directory, English being the language, and _____ representing eight underscores).

IPXCON

IPXCON is an NLM used on IPX internetworks to monitor and trouble-shoot IPX routers and network segments. If a network router is a remote router running NetWare Link Services Protocol (NLSP), you can load IPXCON with the /P parameter and view the Link State Packets (LSPs) received by the router.

To load the IPXCON NLM, type **LOAD IPXCON**, and press Enter at the file server console. A screen opens that contains a variety of routing statistics and an Available Options menu from which additional IPXCON features can be utilized (see fig. 1).

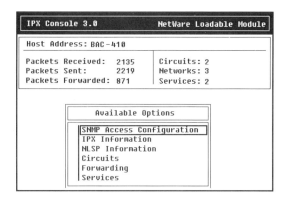

Figure 1
The IPXCON Available Options menu.

The routing statistics information included on the IPXCON screen is as follows:

♦ **Host Address.** This is the router's name.

♦ **Packets Received.** This is the current number of IPX packets received.

♦ **Packets Sent.** This is the current number of IPX packets sent.

♦ **Packets Forwarded.** This is the current number of IPX packets forwarded.

♦ **Circuits.** This is the number of logical network segment attachments the router is using to route packets.

♦ **Networks.** This is the number of networks of which the router is currently aware.

♦ **Services.** This is the number of services to which the router can provide access.

Following are the options included on the Available Options menu:

♦ SNMP Access Configuration

♦ IPX Information

♦ IPX Router Information

♦ NLSP Information

♦ Circuits

♦ Forwarding

♦ Services

IPXCON functions across IPX and TCP/IP networks using SNMP to share information and statistics with remote routers. IPXCON works with the IPXRTRNM.NLM and SNMP.NLM to collect the statistical information it needs.

SNMP Access Configuration

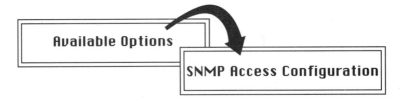

Select SNMP Access Configuration from the Available Options menu to monitor the current system or remote systems and to set the frequency with which information will be polled through SNMP.

IPX Information

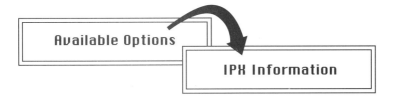

Select IPX Information from the Available Options menu to view IPX packet routing statistics.

IPX Router Information

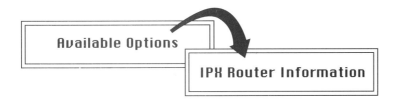

Select IPX Router Information from the Available Options menu to see information about the IPX router.

NLSP Information

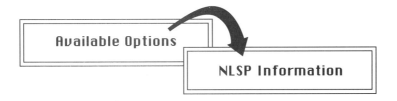

Select NLSP Information from the Available Options menu to see system information, area addresses, neighbors, routers, and LANS. If IPXCON was loaded using the /P option, LSPs are received by the system.

Circuits

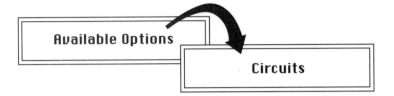

Select Circuits from the Available Options menu to see information about the logical network segment attachments the router is using to route packets (the circuits).

Forwarding

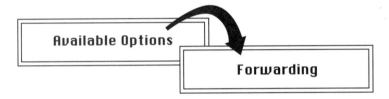

Select Forwarding from the Available Options menu to see the IPX packet forwarding table.

Services

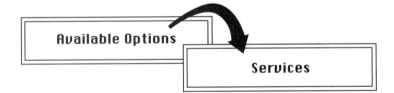

Select Services from the Available Options menu to see information about the services to which the router provides access.

IPXPING

IPXPING is an NLM utility used to check connections to IPX servers and workstations on the internetwork. It checks the connection between the server or workstation and the server sending the IPXPING (the sending node) by sending a series of timed packets (IPXPING request packets) to the IPX target node (server or workstation). The target node sends a response to the sending node (IPXPING reply packet) for each IPXPING request packet it receives. By repeatedly issuing IPXPING request packets and recording response time statistics based on the IPXPING reply packets received, the sending node can collect statistics related to response time.

To use IPXPING, type **LOAD IPXPING** at the file server console and press Enter. The New Target window opens (see fig. 1).

```
┌──────────────────────────────────────────────┐
│                  New Target                    │
│ ────────────────────────────────────────────── │
│  Network: ████████████                         │
│  Node: 000000000002                            │
│  Seconds to pause between pings: 2             │
│                                                │
└──────────────────────────────────────────────┘
```

Figure 1
The New Target window.

Select a target server by entering the network number and node number of the target. Then enter the number of seconds between packet transmissions. Pressing Esc after loading the NLM begins the transmission of IPXPING request packets and the recording of response time statistics.

MONITOR

MONITOR is a utility that grew in importance as versions progressed. MONITOR's operations were limited in 2.2, but they grew in 3.1x as it took on many of the features previously available in FCONSOLE.

The file server information displayed in the MONITOR utility helps the system administrator better understand and manage a NetWare file server. With MONITOR, you can track memory usage, monitor connections, watch file usage, determine which files are locked, and lock the console keyboard. You also can obtain valuable information on other system resources, such as disk information, processor utilization, and LAN/WAN statistics.

With NetWare versions 3.1x and later, MONITOR can be used by the network administrator to determine hardware settings, driver configurations, disk drive status, and volume status, and to lock the console keyboard. You also can obtain valuable information on other system resources, such as disk information, processor utilization, and LAN/WAN statistics. MONITOR simply is one of the best and most useful tools for gathering file server information.

NetWare 2.2's Limited MONITOR Utility

In NetWare 2.2, FCONSOLE serves many of the functions that later became a part of MONITOR. The MONITOR utility brings up a screen that displays information on six workstations. That information tells what those workstations are doing. Some of the options available include the following:

Alloc Resource Record	Begin Trans File
Clear File	Clear File Set
Clear Record Set	Close File

Clr Phy Rec	Clr Phy Rec
SetCopy File	Create File
Dir Search	End of Job
End Trans	Erase File
Floppy Config	Get File Size
Lock File	Lock Phy Rec Set
Lock Record	Log Out
Log Pers File	Log Phy Rec
Log Record	Open Record
Pass File	Read File
Rel Phy Rec	Rel Phy Rec Set
Rel Resource	Release File
Release Record	Rename File
Search Next	Semaphore
Set File Atts	Start Search
Sys Log	Unlock Record
Win Format	Win Read
Win Write	Write File

MONITOR also shows the operating system version, the percentage of file server utilization, and the number of cache buffers that have changed in memory and are awaiting disk write. When a workstation requests a transaction, up to five files and a file status flag are displayed in their screen box. File status can be either of the following:

♦ PERS—showing the file to be logged but not locked

♦ LOCK—meaning the file is locked

Other information that can appear beside each entry includes the following:

♦ H—the transaction is on hold until completion

♦ P (in the first column)—other users are prohibited from reading the file

♦ P (in the third column)—other users cannot write to the file

♦ R—the file is open for reading

♦ T—the file is marked by the TTS system

♦ W—the file is open for writing

Aside from the information presented in this screen, all other functions discussed as available in other versions are accessed through FCONSOLE.

MONITOR in NetWare 3.1x and 4.10

MONITOR's main menu screen is divided into three sections: the header, the upper screen, and the lower screen (see fig. 1). The header shows the operating system version and the date and creation time of that particular operating system version. The upper screen usually displays file server statistics, but it also can change depending upon the menu option you select. The lower screen offers several menu options.

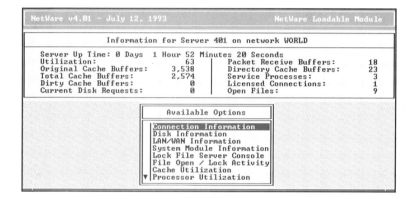

Figure 1
MONITOR's main menu in version 4.

MONITOR's Upper Screen

NetWare 3 and NetWare 4's upper screens are virtually the same. The bottom screen, which lists the Available Options, however, is different. In NetWare 4, you have some options that are not available in NetWare 3. These include Processor Utilization, Memory Utilization, and Scheduling Information.

Starting NetWare 3's MONITOR utility by using the /P option provides you with the Processor Utilization option. This also causes NetWare 3.1x's Available Options list to scroll.

MONITOR's upper screen displays file server statistics (see fig. 2).

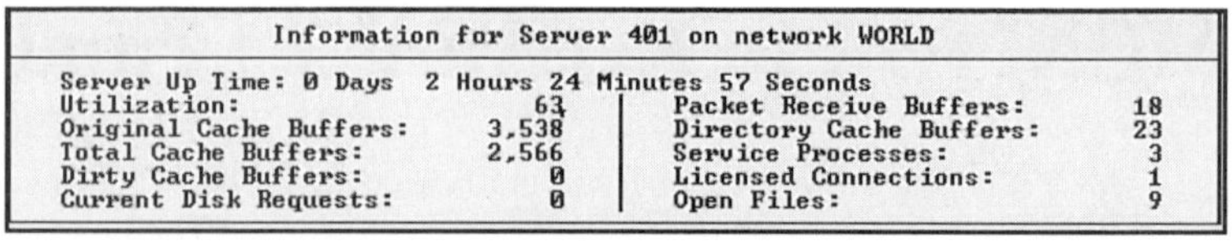

Figure 2
MONITOR's
information screen.

```
┌─────────────────────────────────────────────────────────────────────┐
│              Information for Server 401 on network WORLD              │
├─────────────────────────────────────────────────────────────────────┤
│ Server Up Time: 0 Days  2 Hours 24 Minutes 57 Seconds                │
│ Utilization:                63 │ Packet Receive Buffers:        18    │
│ Original Cache Buffers:   3,538 │ Directory Cache Buffers:       23    │
│ Total Cache Buffers:      2,566 │ Service Processes:              3    │
│ Dirty Cache Buffers:          0 │ Licensed Connections:           1    │
│ Current Disk Requests:        0 │ Open Files:                     9    │
└─────────────────────────────────────────────────────────────────────┘
```

Following is a brief definition of each of the statistics displayed in MONITOR's upper screen.

♦ Server Up Time is the amount of time that has elapsed since the file server was last started.

♦ Utilization is the percentage of processor available cycles that is currently being used. When utilization is low, the file server is "not very" busy. When utilization is high, the file server's CPU is "working hard."

♦ Original Cache Buffers is the original size of the cache buffer pool when the server was brought up (all available memory). When the server's memory is needed for other functions, such as loading an NLM, memory is borrowed from the cache buffer pool. As the cache buffer pool gets lower, access to files on the file server becomes slower.

♦ Total Cache Buffers shows the amount of buffers that currently are available on system for file caching.

♦ Dirty Cache Buffers shows the number of cache buffers that are storing information that has been changed, but not yet written to disk.

♦ Current Disk Requests shows the number of outstanding requests for all the disks in system.

♦ Packet Receive Buffers shows the number of buffers used to hold workstation requests so that service processes can handle them. Packet Receive Buffers are dynamically added to the system as they are needed, until the maximum number is reached. Each packet receive buffer takes up about 1 KB.

♦ Directory Cache Buffers represents the number of buffers available to the file system for directory entry caching. Directory Cache Buffers are dynamically allocated if they are needed.

♦ Service Processes shows the number of processes, "Task Handlers," for the workstation requests. When the workload is too heavy for the current number of service processes to handle, more are dynamically allocated.

♦ Licensed Connections (Connections in Use in NetWare 3.x) shows the number of connections in use that count against the server license in NetWare 4.x. In NetWare 3.x, it shows the number of connections in use, including users attached but not logged in.

♦ Open Files are files on the file server that are currently in use. These files can range from application files to bindery files.

MONITOR's Lower Screen

The lower portion of MONITOR's screen is the Available Options menu (see fig. 3).

Figure 3
MONITOR's
Available Options
menu.

Unlike the MONITOR utility in NetWare 3, the Available Options menu in NetWare 4 scrolls (you cannot see all of the available options without pressing the arrow or PgDn key).

The following is a complete list of the available options in NetWare 4's MONITOR utility:

♦ Connection Information

♦ Disk Information

♦ LAN/WAN Information

♦ System Module Information

♦ Lock File Server Console

♦ File Open/Lock Activity

♦ Cache Utilization

♦ Processor Utilization

♦ Resource Utilization

♦ Memory Utilization

♦ Scheduling Information

♦ Exit

Connection Information

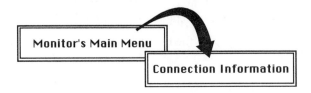

Selecting Connection Information from the Available Options menu displays a list of connections to the file server that currently are in use. When you select a connection from the connection list, its statistics are displayed.

To delete a connection, highlight the connection and press Enter. This terminates the user connection and closes all the files that are in use. You should make sure the user is not actively working, or data might be lost.

Disk Information

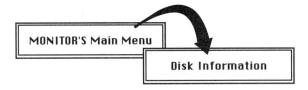

Selecting Disk Information from the Available Options menu displays a list of disk drives that currently are accessible to the file server. To select a drive, highlight it and press Enter. The information in the upper portion of the screen changes and displays the selected drive's statistics. The following is a brief description of these statistics:

♦ Driver is the disk driver used when accessing the disk.

♦ Disk Size is the size of the disk—all partitions included.

♦ Partitions is the number of operation system partitions defined on the disk. A NetWare 386 partition must exist before the Hot Fix statistics will be displayed. NetWare 4 displays partitions as NetWare 386 partitions.

♦ Mirror Status indicates whether the NetWare 386 partition (if one exists) is mirrored.

- `Hot Fix Status` indicates whether a NetWare 386 partition has activated, and if so, its current status.

- `Partition Blocks` is the number of available blocks in the NetWare 386 partition.

- `Data Blocks` is the number of available blocks for files and directories.

- `Redirection Blocks` is the number of available blocks dedicated to Hot Fix redirection.

- `Redirected Blocks` is the number of bad blocks that Hot Fix has found.

- `Reserved Blocks` is the number of redirection blocks reserved for system use.

A screen containing available disk functions appears in the lower portion of the screen. This screen lists operations you might perform on the selected disk. The following options are available:

- Volume Segments on Drive

- Read After Write Verify Status

- Drive Light Status

- Drive Operating Status

- Removable Drive Mount Status

- Removable Drive Lock Status

Volume Segments on Drive

Selecting the `Volume Segments on Drive` option enables you to view the volume segments on a disk. Highlight this field and press Enter.

Read After Write Verify

Selecting `Read After Write Verify` displays the status for the currently selected drive. If the drive does not support the corresponding IOCTL, `Not Supported` is displayed. To change the status, highlight the field and press Enter.

Selecting `Read After Write Verify` provides the following three options:

- Software Level Verify

- Hardware Level Verify

- Disable Verification

If you select Software Level Verify, the device driver is responsible for performing the read-after-write verification of data. If you select Hardware Level Verify, the hardware (DCB or controller) performs the read-after-write verification. If you select Disable Verify, no read-after-write verification is performed.

It is best not to change the verify level parameters because in both NetWare 3 and NetWare 4 the driver reports the level of verification that is being used back to NetWare's MONITOR utility. The level that is in use is often the safest and most efficient combination for the current configuration.

You can elect to disable verification, which improves performance, but decreases fault-tolerance.

Drive Light Status

Selecting Drive Light Status displays the drive light flashing status for the selected drive. If the drive does not support the corresponding IOCTL, Not Supported is displayed. To flash the disk's light, highlight the field and press Enter.

Drive Operating Status

The Drive Operating Status field displays the operating status for the selected drive. Valid values are Active and Inactive. To change the drive status, highlight the field and press Enter. Do not deactivate a drive while the drive is in use because NetWare will be incapable of accessing it.

Removable Drive Mount Status

The Removable Drive Mount Status option is only available for removable drives in NetWare 3's MONITOR utility. It contains the current mount status for the selected drive. To change the status of the drive, highlight the field and press Enter. When you dismount a drive, NetWare cannot access it, so don't dismount a drive that contains any mounted volumes.

Removable Drive Lock Status

Removable Drive Lock Status is only available for removable drives in NetWare 3's MONITOR utility. It contains the drive's current lock status. To change the status, highlight the field and press Enter.

LAN/WAN Information

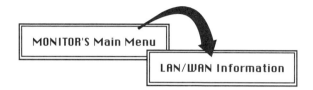

MONITOR'S Main Menu

LAN/WAN Information

Selecting the LAN/WAN Information option provides a list of the LANs or WANs currently in use by the server (network communication cards loaded on the server). When you select a LAN or WAN card from the list, its statistics are displayed. You then can use the arrow keys to move through the statistics. The information contained in this screen can be very valuable in monitoring network traffic, especially if you do not have a network analyzer. The statistics that are available are similar to the following:

♦ **Version.** Displays the version number of the LAN driver.

♦ **Node Address.** Displays the node address of the LAN driver board.

♦ **Protocols.** Displays the protocol stacks to which the LAN driver has been bound.

♦ **Generic Statistics.** The Generic Statistics section displays a list of statistics that are supported by most LAN cards. Use the arrow keys to move up and down in the LAN Statistics section.

♦ **Custom Statistics.** Selecting Custom Statistics displays a list of LAN drivers that has been defined specifically for this LAN driver.

Note   *In NetWare 3, this option is LAN Information.*

System Module Information

Selecting the System Module Information option displays a list of the loadable modules that are part of the system. These modules are loaded and currently running on the server. To see information on a specific module, highlight it and press Enter. The upper part of the screen displays the following information for the currently loaded module:

♦ Module Size is the size of the module's code and data images

♦ Load File Name is the name of the loaded module

A list of resource tags owned by the selected module is displayed in the lower right part of the screen. These resource tags enable you to monitor the amount of system resources used by the selected module. To view additional information about a resource tag, highlight it and press Enter. To return to the system modules list, press Esc.

Lock File Server Console

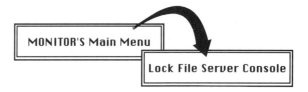

Selecting the Lock File Server Console option disables the capability to use the Alt+Esc method of switching from one console screen to the next (completely locking the keyboard) until a password is entered. Locking the console prevents anyone from having access to the command line functions of a NetWare server.

File Open/Lock Activity

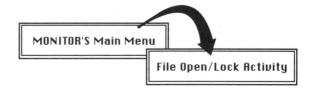

After selecting the File Open/Lock Activity option, select a volume, and then the file whose lock activity you want to view. Use the current list to select volumes and directories on the file server until you find the desired

file. To view the directories on a volume, select the volume. To view the contents of a directory, select the directory. To move back up the tree a level, select "..". When you have located the desired file, highlight it and press Enter.

A screen appears listing the following file lock activity statistics:

♦ Use Count shows the number of connections currently using the selected file (open, locked, logged)

♦ Open Count indicates the number of connections that currently have the file open

♦ Open for Read indicates the number of connections that have opened and read the selected file

♦ Open for Write indicates the number of connections that have opened and written to the selected file

♦ Deny Read indicates the number of connections that have opened the file and denied other stations from reading the selected file

♦ Deny Write indicates the number of connections that have opened the file and denied other stations from opening and writing to the file

♦ Status indicates the current locks placed on the file, including connection number, task number, locked status, and logged status

Cache Utilization

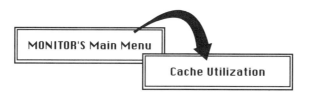

The Cache Utilization option is only available in NetWare 4. Selecting it causes the monitor to split into two sections: an upper screen and a lower screen. The upper screen is MONITOR's original upper screen. The lower screen displays statistics on the server's cache utilization, as seen in figure 4.

Figure 4
MONITOR's Cache
Utilization screen.

Cache Utilization			
Allocate Block Count:	0	Short Term Cache Hits:	100%
Allocated From AVAIL:	2,305	Short Term Cache Dirty Hits:	100%
Allocated from LRU:	0	Long Term Cache Hits:	91%
Allocate Wait:	0	Long Term Cache Dirty Hits:	40%
Allocate Still Waiting:	0	Too Many Dirty Blocks:	0
LRU Sitting Time:	2:12:05.9	Cache ReCheckBlock Count:	0

The options in the Cache Utilization screen are defined as follows:

♦ `Allocate Block Count` is the number of disk cache block requests that have been made since the server was booted.

♦ `Allocated from AVAIL` is the number of disk cache block requests that have been used from the available unused list of disk cache blocks.

♦ `Allocated from LRU` is the number of disk cache block requests that were retrieved from the Least Recently Used (LRU) list of cache blocks.

♦ `Allocate Wait` is the number of times a cache block request had to wait because there were no available cache blocks.

♦ `Allocate Still Waiting` is the number of times a cache block request had to wait behind another request before being fulfilled.

If the Allocate Still Waiting value or the Allocate Wait value are very high (above 25 percent) or incrementing slowly, you have too few cache blocks available and need to add more RAM to your server.

♦ `LRU Sitting Time` is the time since the oldest block in the Least Recently Used (LRU) list was last referenced. If data is being retrieved from cache memory efficiently, the Least Recently Used Sitting Time will be high.

♦ `Long Term Cache Hits` is the percentage of total disk block requests that were already in cache. This particular statistic shows how efficient your server's cache has been since the server was started. For best performance, total cache hits should be above 75 percent.

♦ `Long Term Cache Dirty Hits` is the percentage of disk cache requests that were already in cache, and the block was already dirty.

When a directory request is received by a NetWare server, the request is stored in a segment of server memory known as cache. By storing this request in memory, and not immediately writing the request to disk, NetWare increases its opportunity to enhance

performance. If the request was automatically written to disk, each request would be associated to subsequent changes on the physical disk. But by leaving the request in memory, NetWare can wait to see if a second change to the same entry is coming. If a second, third, or fourth change is made, NetWare increases its physical write ratio to 1:4 instead of 1:1.

When a block of memory is holding data that has not yet been written (physically) to disk, then that memory block is deemed as "dirty."

♦ Short Term Cache Hits is the percentage of disk cache requests read over the last second that were already in cache.

♦ Short Term Dirty Cache Hits is the percentage of disk cache requests read over the last second that were already in cache and that were dirty.

♦ Too Many Dirty Blocks is the number of times a write request was delayed because there were too many dirty blocks.

♦ Cache ReCheckBlock Count is the number of times a disk cache request had to be retried because the target block was being used.

Processor Utilization

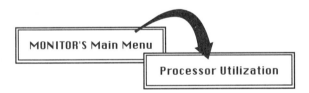

The Processor Utilization option displays processes and interrupts currently being used by the server. Both processes and interrupts can be individually selected to see detailed activity information for the selected item.

By default, the Processor Utilization option is available only in NetWare 4. Loading MONITOR with the /P option in NetWare 3, however, provides you with this option.

Highlight an item and press F3 to show the utilization statistics for the selected item. The active processes (threads) are displayed as well as the available hardware interrupts. Selecting an item displays a processor utilization screen.

Resource Utilization

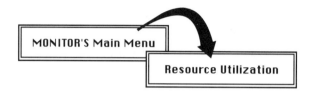

Selecting the Resource Utilization option causes MONITOR's upper and lower screens to change. The upper screen displays the server's memory statistics. Because NetWare 3 and NetWare 4 have different memory pool configurations, the information contained in each is slightly different. Figure 5 is an example of NetWare 4's memory statistics screen (the upper section).

Figure 5
MONITOR's Tracked Resources screen.

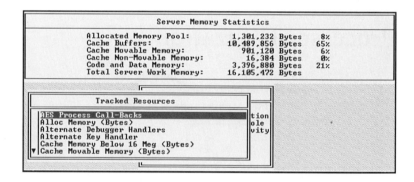

The following is a brief definition of each of these memory pools:

♦ Permanent Memory Pool is the memory used by processes when they don't intend to return it for a while, if ever. When more memory for this pool is needed, cache buffers are transferred to this pool; these cache buffers are never returned to the cache buffer pool. The directory cache buffers, as well as the packet receive buffers, are contained in this pool.

♦ Alloc Memory Pool is the memory used by processes when they don't intend to use it for long periods of time. When more memory for this pool is needed, it is transferred from the Permanent Memory Pool; this memory is never returned to the Permanent Memory Pool. This is the preferred memory pool for loadable modules to use when allocating small pieces of memory.

♦ Cache Buffers is the amount of memory in the cache buffer pool. This memory is currently being used for file caching. The amount of memory in this area should be larger than any of the others.

♦ Cache Movable Memory is memory allocated directly from the cache buffer pool. When it is freed, it is returned to the cache buffer pool. It differs from Cache Non-Movable Memory in that the memory manager can move the location of these memory blocks to optimize memory usage. Volume tables typically use this memory.

♦ Cache Non-Movable Memory is memory allocated directly from the cache buffer pool. When it is freed, it is returned to the cache buffer pool. This memory is used when large pieces of memory are needed.

♦ Total Server Work Memory is the sum of all the memory pools. A list of the resource types defined by the operating system is displayed in the lower portion of the screen. The server tracks resources, such as the Alloc Memory Pool, by forcing procedures to use a resource tag when doing an allocation.

In NetWare 4 and NetWare 3, the lower left part of the screen enables you to view system resources and their associated resource types defined by the operating system. Select a resource tag to display that particular resource tag's statistics.

To view the list of resource tags with a specific resource type, highlight the resource type and press Enter. You then can select a specific resource tag and view more information associated with it.

Memory Utilization

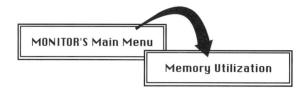

Selecting the Memory Utilization option brings up a screen that displays the allocated memory statistics for all the currently loaded modules. The following is a brief description of each of the displayed statistics (assuming you have installed your volumes with 4 KB blocks).

♦ 4K Cache Pages is the number of cache pages in the memory allocation pool (memory is allocated from the system in 4 KB pages).

♦ Cache Page Blocks consist of one or more 4 KB cache pages, which are requested from the system. After being requested from the system, these blocks are placed in the allocated memory pool.

♦ Percent in Use is the percentage of allocated memory that is currently in use.

♦ Percent Free is the percentage of allocated memory that is not in use by any loaded modules.

♦ Memory Blocks in Use is the number of pieces of memory that have been allocated and that are currently in use by a loaded module.

♦ Memory Bytes in Use is the number of bytes of memory that have been allocated and are currently in use.

♦ Memory Blocks Free is the number, defined as pieces, of current memory that has been released and are currently available for the system to use.

♦ Memory Bytes Free is the amount of memory, in bytes, that is free and available for the system to use.

The lower left section of the screen displays the currently loaded modules. Selecting a module from the list displays memory information for that particular module.

The Memory Utilization option is available only in NetWare 4.

Scheduling Information

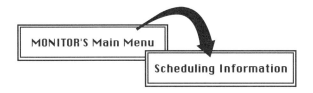

Selecting the Scheduling Information option displays processes currently being run on the server, the load each process takes on the CPU, and the scheduling delay (Sch Delay) value for each process. You also can increase or decrease the Scheduling Delay value for a selected process.

 Selecting this screen generates extra overhead for your server.

Exit

Selecting the Exit option unloads the MONITOR utility from the server's memory and returns you to the server's console.

See Also

NWADMIN

SYSCON

NBACKUP

The NBACKUP utility enables you to back up and restore data on NetWare 2.2 file servers, as well as on local drives. NBACKUP is included with the NetWare 2.2 operating system software and is loaded when the NetWare operating system is installed.

When using NBACKUP to back up or restore data, you must run it from a workstation connected to the network. In addition, you must restore to the same system type from which you backed up.

If you back up a local drive, for example, you must restore to a local drive. You cannot restore a backup of a network directory to a local drive.

NBACKUP's main menu has the following three options:

♦ Change Current Server

♦ Backup Options

♦ Restore Options

Change Current Server

The Change Current Server option provides a list of available file servers from which to choose. After you choose a file server, it becomes your current or default file server. To choose a file server, highlight the file server name and press Enter. After you make a file server choice, you are returned to the main menu.

Backup Options

To perform a backup, you must first choose Backup Options from the main menu, then choose a backup device from the Select the desired Device menu. When backing up a local drive, choose DOS Devices, otherwise, choose the appropriate device name.

After you choose the backup device, the Backup menu appears. From this menu you choose where the session files are to be stored. This is called the *working directory* (a path pointing to a specific location where the backup and error logs are to be stored).

To start the backup, choose Backup By Directory from the Backup menu, and specify the options you want to implement. Press Escape and confirm your choices. When prompted with the Start Backup menu, choose Start Backup Now to begin the backup.

If you prefer, you can choose Start Backup Later. This prompts you for a date and time at which to begin the backup. If you choose this option, your workstation is unavailable for other use until the backup has been run.

Restore Options

After you have performed a backup, you can then restore that backup as needed. To restore a backup, start NBACKUP and choose Restore Options from the main menu. Next, choose Select Working Directory and provide the path to the working directory you specified during the original backup. When the Restore menu opens, choose Restore Session. Choose the session to be restored, and then choose your restore options from the Restore Option screen.

If the backup session you want to restore is not included in the list of sessions to be restored, press Ins, type the exact path pointing to the location of the session files from which to restore, and press Enter. Then choose the appropriate session to be restored.

See Also

SBACKUP

NETADMIN

NetWare 4 is the first version of NetWare to offer this administrative utility. In other versions of NetWare, a combination of utilities, such as SYSCON, SALVAGE, and VOLINFO, are required to perform the same tasks.The NETADMIN (NetWare Administration) utility is the text-based equivalent to the graphical utility NWADMIN, (NetWare Windows Administration). Most of the network administrative tasks are performed with these utilities. Figure 1 shows NETADMIN's main menu.

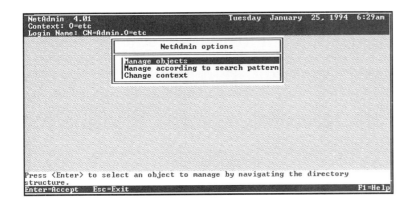

Figure 1
NETADMIN's main menu.

Managing Objects

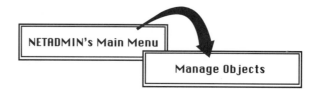

Selecting Manage Objects from NETADMIN's main menu brings up a browse screen. From this screen you can do the following:

♦ View or manage an object

♦ Create an object

♦ Delete an object

♦ Navigate up and down the directory tree

The objects that are listed are of several types. Some objects in NetWare Directory Services (NDS) represent physical entities, while others represent logical entities. Examples of a physical object would be a user object, which represents a person, or a printer object, which represents a printer. A logical entity represents a group of people.

♦ Highlight an object in the object list and press F10 to view or manage the object; if the object is a leaf object you also can highlight the object and press the Enter key.

♦ Press the Ins key to create an object. A list of objects appears. Highlight the type of object that you would like to create and press Enter.

♦ Highlight an object and press Del to delete the object.

♦ Highlight a container object (objects with a + in front of them) and press Enter to navigate down the directory tree.

♦ Highlight the parental periods (..) and press Enter to navigate back up the directory tree.

The Manage Objects section of NETADMIN is where you create, view, manage, or delete an object and its properties; NETADMIN is the test base NDS administration utility.

NDS operates in a logical hierarchical tree structure, starting with an object called the root object. The tree branches out into two other types of objects: the container object and the leaf object. A *container object* is an object that can contain another object. A *server object* can contain user objects, printer objects, print queues objects, and so on. A *leaf object* is an object that cannot contain another object. A *user object* cannot contain a server object (it contains properties).

Because an object represents the location of the data, rather than the physical entity, you can control what functions or rights the physical entity (the person) has by restricting rights to the location of the data. That is, you cannot control the person, but you can control what data the person can access.

In NetWare 4, you can assign rights at the *object* or *property level* (rights to sections of the NDS database). In previous versions of NetWare, you could assign *file system rights* (rights to the files stored on the servers). In NetWare 4, you can assign both file system rights and object rights, as well as rights to specific object properties. Assigning property and object rights separately enables you to control access to sensitive file-based information stored on the server (such as payroll check amounts) and control access to the information or values stored in the properties of an object (such as home phone numbers). The ability to separate these rights can be used not only to restrict access, but also to grant access. You might, for example, want all users to be able to search for all user objects' "work phone" property value. This would enable users to find the extension of a coworker, simply by browsing and searching NDS.

Selecting `Manage objects` brings up a screen with all available objects listed. The following is a list of the available object types, with a brief description of each object type.

♦ **AFP server.** This represents an AppleTalk Filing Protocol server on the network. It provides a logical representation in the directory database to view the actions and characteristics of the AFP server.

♦ **Alias object.** An alias object can be used to provide an object with multiple locations in the directory. Any object in the directory can be aliased. Creating alias objects can be very useful if two or more groups located in different sections of the directory need to access the same object (for example, the server). By creating an alias of the server, both branches of the tree are capable of seeing the server object. When an alias object is created, although both objects appear, actually only one object exists; the alias object simply provides an alternate naming path for locating an object in the directory.

Creating alias objects can provide several other conveniences as well. You can simplify searches of the directory or create alias objects for all objects of a certain type and place them in the same tree context for simplified management or access purposes. An example of this would be to make an alias object of available network modems, creating a modem pool that could be quickly accessed and managed.

♦ **Bindery object.** This represents an object that was upgraded from a bindery-based server, but that cannot be identified. A bindery object cannot have objects below it in the directory tree.

♦ **Computer.** This designates computers that are end-user workstations. A computer object cannot have objects below it in the directory tree.

♦ **Country.** The country object is a container object that can be used to help organize an international Directory tree. A country object can contain an Organization object as well as an alias object.

♦ **Directory map.** A directory map object represents the path of the file system directory. Login scripts can use a directory map object to point to a location. Using the directory object can simplify network management. For instance, if you use a Directory object to point to a common application, such as WordPerfect, login scripts can then point to and call the application by calling that directory map. So if an application is moved, the login scripts do not have to be changed. You can quickly change the directory map object.

♦ **Group.** A group object is a collection of users (user objects) that represent or share a common set of needs.

♦ **Organization.** An organization is a container object used in the hierarchical structuring of the directory tree. An organization object generally is used to designate a division, department, location, or some other logical organizational arrangement. An organization object can contain another organization object, an organizational unit, any leaf object, or an alias object.

♦ **Organizational role.** This is an object created for the purpose of specifying a position that can be filled by people (user objects). This object also enables network administrators to distribute network administration. An organizational role cannot have objects below it in the directory tree.

♦ **Organizational unit.** This is a container object that is similar to the organization object. Like the organization object, it is used to build and simplify the hierarchical structure of the directory. An organizational unit can contain login scripts, another organizational unit object, an alias object, and leaf objects.

♦ **Profile.** A profile object is a login script that can be accessed by users from anywhere in the directory tree. A profile cannot have objects below it in the directory tree.

♦ **Root.** The root object is the base or place holder of the directory tree. It provides the highest point to access different country objects as well as organization objects. If a user has rights to the root object, he has rights to the entire directory tree.

♦ **User.** A user object is a person who has been given rights (of various levels) to use the network and to access the directory tree. A user is a leaf object and cannot have objects below it in the directory tree.

♦ **Volume.** A volume is a physical object that represents a NetWare servers volume. A volume object does not have to have the same name as the actual volume—in fact, it is better if it is not named after the physical volume. A volume object cannot have objects below it in the directory tree. Also, as in prior versions of NetWare, the volume (the physical volume) is the highest level of the file structure.

After selecting a specific object, a server, a volume, a user, a printer, and so on, an actions screen appears. The list of actions that you can perform on an object varies depending on the type of object that is selected. The following are examples of the actions that you can perform on some of the more common objects.

For a volume object, the available actions are as follows:

♦ View or edit properties of this object

♦ Rename

♦ Move

♦ Delete

♦ View or edit the trustees of this object

For a user object, the available actions are as follows:

♦ View or edit properties of this object

♦ Rename

♦ Move

♦ Delete

♦ View or edit rights to files and directories

♦ View or edit the trustees of this object

Most of the other NDS objects will have an action list that resembles one of the preceding actions lists.

After selecting an object from the list of objects, choose View or edit properties of this object to bring up a screen that enables you to edit the object's properties.

Each object contains properties and values, regardless of object type. With a phone list, for example, the properties of the object would be the entries or fields in the phone list, such as first name, last name, phone number, address, and so on. Each of these properties would then have a value (actual data), such as John, Smith, 123-4567, and so on.

Because each object type has a different set of properties the properties screen that appears also will be different.

In NetWare 4.10, two additional options were added to let you manage subtrees (container objects which form part of the directory tree structure). Those two options are Move Subtree and Rename Subtree. Move Subtree lets you move a container object from the root of one NDS partition into a different NDS context. Rename Subtree lets you change a container's current container name to a different container name.

The list of properties offered depends on the type of object that is selected. For instance, when a server object is selected the View or edit NetWare server options screen appears, offering the following options:

♦ Identification

♦ Accounting

- ♦ View Server Information
- ♦ View Server Error Log File
- ♦ Other Properties
- ♦ See also

If a user object is selected, and View or edit properties of this object is chosen, the Actions for User: <selected user name> screen appears. The options available for a user object are as follows:

- ♦ Identification
- ♦ Environment
- ♦ Account restrictions
- ♦ Login script
- ♦ Groups/Security Equals/Profile
- ♦ Change password
- ♦ Postal address
- ♦ See also

For a group, the available options are as follows:

- ♦ Identification
- ♦ Group members
- ♦ See also

As an example, the following section walks you through the View or edit properties of this object option, assuming that a server object was selected.

To manage a server, select the organizational unit in which the server resides, and press Enter. A browse screen appears that displays a list of NetWare servers, volumes, and other objects contained in that context.

When you select a server object, the following menu options appear (see fig. 2):

♦ View or edit properties of this object

♦ Move

♦ Delete

♦ View or edit the trustees of this object

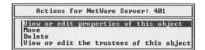

View Edit Properties of This Object

The View or edit NetWare server screen (see fig. 3) appears when you select the View or edit properties of this object option.

Figure 3
NETADMIN's server
management screen.

Identification

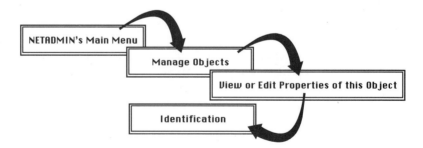

If you select the Identification option, an information list with the following fields appears (each of these fields have a descriptive name that tells you the information contained in them):

- ◆ Server name
- ◆ Server operating system version
- ◆ Status
- ◆ Other names
- ◆ Description
- ◆ Network address
- ◆ Operator
- ◆ User
- ◆ Location
- ◆ Department
- ◆ Organization

Accounting

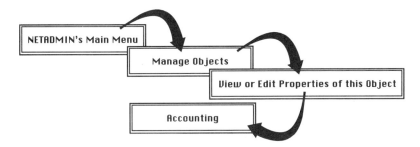

Selecting the Accounting option enables you to charge for certain network services. If accounting has not yet been installed when you select the Accounting option, you are asked if you want to install it; choose Y or N. If accounting previously has been installed, selecting the Accounting option enables you to set or modify the following network service charge rates:

- ◆ Accounting servers
- ◆ Blocks read charge rates
- ◆ Blocks written charge rates
- ◆ Connect time charge rates

♦ Disk storage charge rates

♦ Service requests charge rates

View Server Information

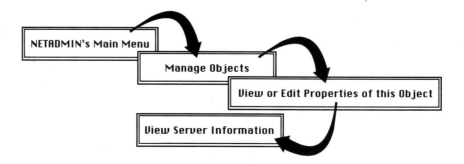

Select the View Server Information option to view the following information:

♦ The server's name

♦ The version of NetWare running on the server

♦ The revision of the server's operating system

♦ The version of system fault tolerance in use

♦ The Transaction Tracking status

♦ The number of connections in use

♦ The number of volumes supported

♦ The server's network address

♦ The server's node address

♦ The serial number of NetWare

♦ The number of the application that is running

View Server Error Log File

To view any errors that have been recorded by the server, select the View Server Error Log File option. A screen appears that shows any errors that have transpired since the last deletion of the error log. If no errors have occurred, no file exists. As you leave the view screen, you will be asked if you want to delete the current log file. If the file is deleted, a new one will be created. If the file is not deleted, any new errors will be appended to the existing file.

Other Properties

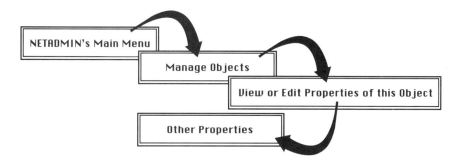

The Other Properties option enables you to create, change, or view a list of other properties—such as printers, print queues, and server volumes—that are managed by the server. Selecting the Other Properties option brings up a screen with the following fields:

♦ Resources, such as volumes, printers, and print queues

♦ Supported services, such as files, print, mail, and NDS

These fields contain a list of the resources and supported services offered by the server. To edit one of the fields, highlight it and press Enter.

To get a list of resources, highlight the Resource field and press Enter. An Available Resources screen appears. To add a resource to this screen, press Ins. You then can type the resource, or press Ins. Pressing Ins again brings up a directory structure. Select a resource from the directory structure and press Enter. The new resource then is added to the list.

This list is for information purposes only. Resources added to this list, such as a print queue, printer, or volume, first must be installed on the server using the proper utility.

To view a list of services, highlight the Services field and press Enter. A screen showing all the available services appears. To add a service to this screen, press Ins. Then you can enter the type of services that this server offers.

See Also

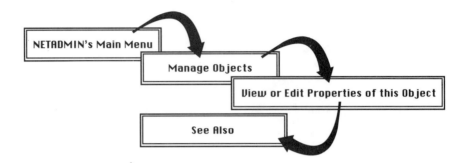

Selecting the See also option enables you to see user-definable information on objects pertaining to a particular object. This option is similar to the "See Also" section of each element in this book. It's a section where you can enter a list of other objects that are located in the NDS tree, and that have relevance to the selected object. For instance, if you select a server object and the selected server has an organizational role object defined to administrate printing, or print queue operator, these objects or the user objects of those assigned as trustees of the organizational role object could be listed. Thus, if users had a problem printing, they could check the See Also menu option to determine who to call.

Move

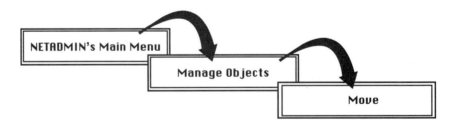

Use the Move option to move the server object to another location within the directory tree. After selecting the Move option, a dialog box with two fields appears: the Old Context field, and the New Context field. Enter the appropriate location and press Enter.

Delete

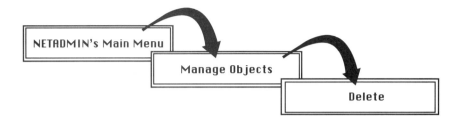

To remove an object from the directory tree, select the object, highlight the Delete option and press Enter. A screen verifying that you want to delete the object appears. To delete object, select Yes.

If you select a server object and then press Enter after selecting the Delete option, a message appears informing you that you cannot delete a server from the directory with this function. To delete or remove a server from the directory tree, the server must be downed. Then you can use the PARTITION MANAGER utility to remove the server.

View or Edit the Trustees of This Object

Viewing and editing trustee objects is similar to assigning trustee rights to a file or directory in NetWare 3. Selecting View or edit the trustees of this object option gives you access to the following access control menu selections, as seen in figure 4.

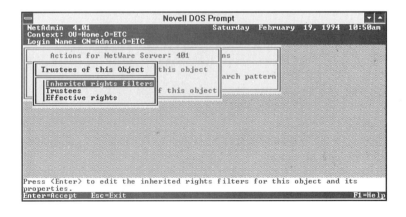

Figure 4
NETADMIN's Trustees of this Object menu.

The three options available from this menu are described here.

♦ **Inherited rights filters.** This option lists the rights that any trustee inherits to the selected object. To be effective, any rights not listed for this object must be explicitly granted.

♦ **Trustees.** This option lists all objects that have property rights explicitly granted for this object.

♦ **Effective rights.** This option enables you to type the name of an object, or browse and select an object, in order to see the object's effective rights.

Selecting any of these options enables you to view, add, or delete entries.

Manage According to Search Pattern

The Manage according to search pattern option, as its name implies, enables you to set a search filter to select a specific object or group of objects that you want to manage. You could, for example, choose to manage all servers, or all users, or you could manage all users whose names begin with the letter T. After choosing the Manage according to search pattern option, the filter screen appears (see fig. 5).

Figure 5
NETADMIN's search patterns screen.

Search patterns	
Enter object name:	*
Object class:	↓ /All classes/
Show alias class (Y/N):	No

The filter screen enables you to search by object name, object class, or a combination of object name and object class. In the name field, you can either type the full name of the object or use wild cards (* and ?). Highlighting the Object class field and pressing Enter brings up a list of object types from which to choose. To add other object classes, press Ins. This brings up a list of object classes that currently are excluded. By default the object class "/All classes/" is included.

You can select a single object class by highlighting it and pressing Enter, or you can mark multiple object classes with the F5 key, and then press Enter. Either way, your search criteria limits the number of objects with which you have to work. Choosing from the list of excluded object classes will automatically remove "/All classes/" as an included entry. The following is a list of available class types:

- Alias
- Computer
- NetWare server
- Organizational role
- Print server
- Printer
- Profile
- Queue
- User
- Volume

Show alias class is the last option in this menu. If the Show alias class option is set to Yes, you can view an alias object rather than the object to which it points. If the Show alias class option is set to No, you can edit the properties of the real object (where the alias is pointing) instead of the alias object.

Changes made in Manage according to search pattern also will affect what is seen when you use Manage objects.

Change Context

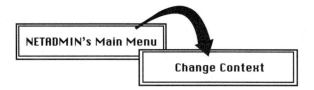

The Change context option enables the network Administrator to manage objects in a different portion of the tree. After selecting the Change context option, a single-line dialog box appears. To change to a different context, either type the name of the context or press Ins to use the browser.

See Also

FILER

NETUSER

NETSYNC3

NETSYNC3 is one of two NETSYNC NLM programs. (NETSYNC4 is the other.) NETSYNC is a management utility that enables you to take advantage of some of NetWare 4's NDS architecture in a *NetSync Cluster* (one or more NetWare 4.10 servers connected to and acting as the host for a maximum of 12 NetWare 3.1x servers). All NetWare 3.1x servers in the NetSync Cluster running NETSYNC3 are synchronized with what Novell calls the super-bindery. The *super-bindery* is a combination of all binderies for all NetWare 3.1x file servers in the NetSync Cluster, the entire combined bindery information of which is then downloaded to all NetWare 3.1x file servers in the NetSync Cluster. All changes to the super-bindery are kept synchronized among NetWare 3.1x servers in the NetSync Cluster.

Managing a NetSync Cluster requires that you load NETSYNC3 on all NetWare 3.1x file servers in the NetSync Cluster. To load NETSYNC3 on a NetWare 3.1x file server, type **LOAD NETSYNC3** at the NetWare 3.1x file server console, and press Enter. You also can autoload NETSYNC3 by adding the appropriate command to the file server's AUTOEXEC.NCF file.

 Before loading NETSYNC3 on any of the NetWare 3.1x file servers in the NetSync Cluster, you first must load NETSYNC4 on the host NetWare 4.10 server in the NetSync Cluster. Then, you must authorize each NetWare 3.1x server attached to the NetWare 4.10 host by completing the Authorized Server Information screen for each NetWare 3.1x file server included in the NetSync Cluster.

Configure the NetSync environment and perform other tasks using the NETSYNC3 Options menu as shown in figure 1.

Figure 1
NETSYNC3 Options
menu.

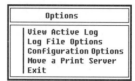

From the Options menu, you can choose any of the following options:

♦ View Active Log

♦ Log File Options

♦ Configuration Options

♦ Move a Print Server

♦ Exit

View Active Log

From a NetWare 3.1x file server, you view the active log display using a text editor. Use it to open the SYS:SYSTEM\NETSYNC\NETSYNC.LOG file. From a NetWare 3.1x file server, you cannot view the active log display using the View Active Log option from the NETSYNC3 Options menu (see NETSYNC4).

Log File Options

To use the log file options from the Options menu and to scroll through the log file history, you must be running NETSYNC4 on a NetWare 4.10 file server (see NETSYNC4).

Configuration Options

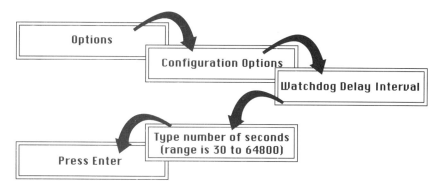

This option enables you to change the interval at which the NetWare 4.10 host is checked. This process of checking the NetWare 4.10 host for proper operation is called *watchdog*. Selecting Watchdog Delay Interval from configuration options enables you to set the frequency at which watchdog operations are performed. By default, the watchdog interval is set to 5 minutes. You can set it anywhere from 30 seconds to 64,800 seconds.

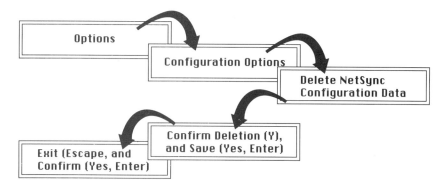

You also can delete configuration data, including the name of the NetWare 4.10 host server, and the NETSYNC3 password.

Move a Print Server

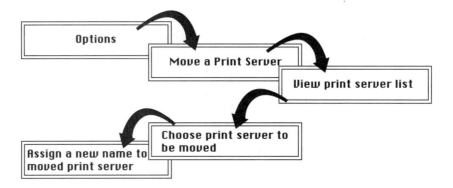

Moving NetWare 3.1x print servers means merging them into one directory on the NetSync 4.10 host server. Merging a print server enables you to manage the print server directory from a single NetWare 4.10 print server. This option is only available if the print server is in the NetSync Cluster.

You can only load PSERVER.NLM once; and PSERVER.EXE does not exist in NetWare 4.10. You must, therefore, merge your NetWare 3.1x print servers when you move them to the host NetWare 4.10 server. When you do, use NPRINTER.EXE in place of both PSERVER.EXE and RPRINTER.EXE.

Exit

This option removes the NETSYNC3 NLM from the file server.

NETSYNC4

NETSYNC4 is the counterpart to NETSYNC3 in a NetSync Cluster. NETSYNC3 runs on NetWare 3.1x NetSync Cluster file servers; NETSYNC4 runs on NetWare 4.10 NetSync Cluster file servers. The NETSYNC4 Options menu is the same as NETSYNC3's, with one exception—the NETSYNC4 Options menu contains an additional option: Edit Server List (see fig. 1).

To use NETSYNC4 on a NetWare 4.10 file server, type **LOAD NETSYNC4** at the NetWare 4.10 file server console, and press Enter. The Options menu opens. This menu contains the following options:

♦ View Active Log

♦ Log File Options

♦ Configuration Options

♦ Edit Server List

♦ Move a Print Server

♦ Exit

View Active Log

NETSYNC4 runs on a NetWare 4.10 file server. Unlike NETSYNC3, which runs on a NetWare 3.1x file server, you can use the View Active Log option to see the active log file as it continuously updates. Because the file is active, it records events as they occur. When you are viewing the active log file, you see events added as they occur.

Log File Options

Selecting Log File Options from the NETSYNC4 Options menu enables you to accomplish the following tasks:

♦ Change the log file size

♦ Toggle the display of events on the log screen

♦ Delete the log file

♦ Disable/enable the log file

Change the Log File Size

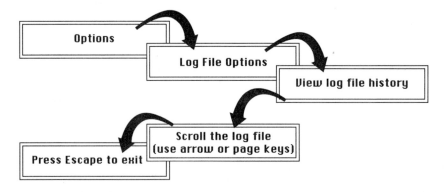

Selecting Maximum Size of Log File from Log File Options enables you to change the default size of the log file from 0.5 MB to any size ranging from 10 KB to 10 MB.

Toggle Events Display

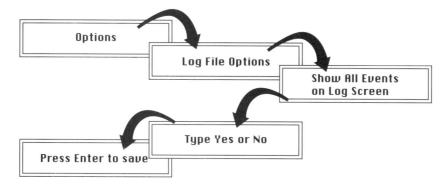

Setting Show All Events on Log Screen to No causes only major events and failed operations to be recorded on the active log screen. Setting it to Yes records even expected failures—those that occur when an anticipated problem arises, such as attempting to add a specific property to an object when that property already exists.

Delete Log File

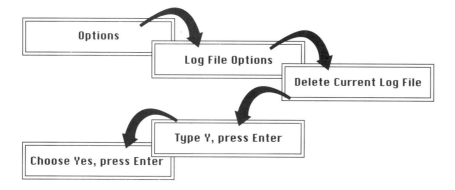

When you want to start over with a clean log file, or you have removed NETSYNC from the file server, you can delete the log file. If you delete the log file without removing NETSYNC, a new log file is automatically created.

Disable/Enable Log File

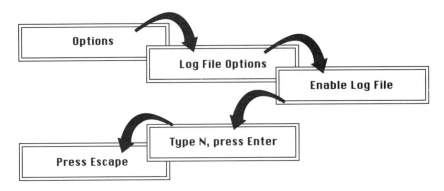

Log files create a certain amount of overhead. You can eliminate this overhead by eliminating the log file. Unless NETSYNC has been running without problems for a while, however, you should consider leaving the log file enabled. To enable the log file, choose Yes. To disable the log file, choose No.

Configuration Options

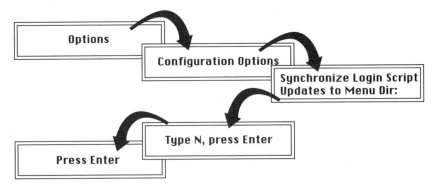

In NETSYNC4, selecting Configuration Options from the Options menu enables you to prevent 3.1x login scripts from being synchronized with 4.10 login scripts. By default, users who log in to the network using NDS bindery services can have their bindery-based login script synchronized to be used in the NDS environment.

You also can delete configuration data, including the names of any authorized NetWare 3.1x servers, their passwords, and the NETSYNC4 password.

Edit Server List

Selecting Edit Server List from the NETSYNC4 Options menu enables you to accomplish the following tasks:

♦ Add or delete authorized servers

♦ Upload a 3.1x file server's bindery

Add or Delete Authorized Servers

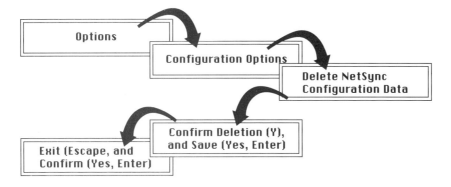

Typing a 3.1x file server name in a blank server name field, and providing the required information, enables you to add a NetWare 3.1x server to the list of authorized servers for this NetSync Cluster.

Selecting Delete NetSync Configuration Data and the name of the NetWare 3.1x server to be deleted enables you to remove a server from the list of currently authorized servers.

Upload a 3.1x Bindery

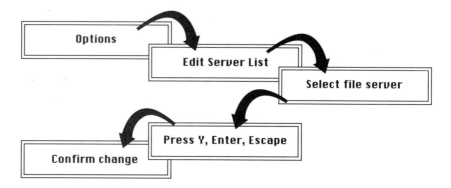

Selecting a file server from the server list, then selecting Copy 3.1x to 4.1 after selecting Edit Server List from the Options menu enables you to copy the NetWare 3.1x file server's bindery to the NetWare 4.1 bindery context. This action corrects out-of-sync binderies.

Move a Print Server

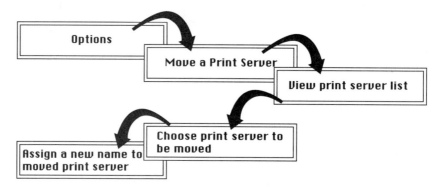

NetWare 3.1x print servers are moved (merged) into one directory on the NetWare 4.1 host file server. To move a print server, follow the process shown in the preceding figure.

Exit

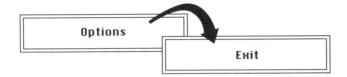

Selecting Exit from the Options menu unloads the NETSYNC4 NLM.

NETUSER

The NETUSER utility is the text equivalent of the NWUSER utility. Both of these utilities enable users to configure their workstation connections to printers, drivers, and servers. In NETUSER, a user also can enable or disable message receiving, and change his context. To start NETUSER, type **NETUSER** from a workstation DOS prompt, and the menu shown in figure 1 appears.

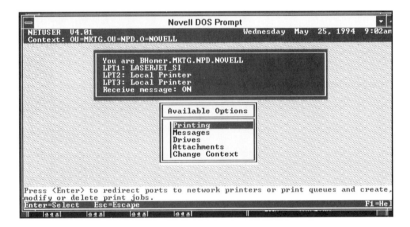

Figure 1
NETUSER's main menu.

When NETUSER is started, in addition to the main menu, a box appears that lists the following information about your current configuration status:

♦ Who you are logged in as

♦ Current capture status for LPT1, LPT2, and LPT3

♦ Receive messages status: on or off

Printing

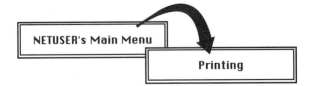

Select Printing to see a list of printer ports that can be captured or redirected to print to a network printer. The Printing option enables you to select a port, change printers, and configure default print jobs. It also can be used to send, modify, pause, or delete print jobs once the port has been captured.

Messages

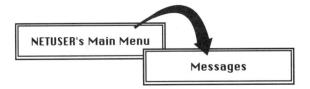

Select Messages to send messages to users or groups, and to set the capability for your workstation to receive messages when on or off.

Drives

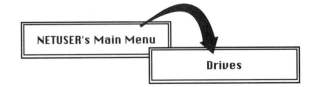

Select Drives to add, modify, or delete standard drive mappings or to search mappings and to view directory effective rights.

Attachments

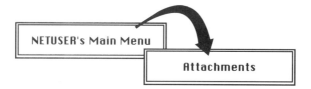

Selecting Attachments enables you to attach or detach network attachments, change your user name, password, and login script, and view information about the file server.

Change Context

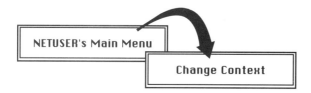

Only available in Directory Services mode, the Change Context option enables you to browse the directory tree and set your current context.

See Also

NPRINT

NWADMIN

NWUSER

PCONSOLE

PRINTCON

NWADMIN

The NWADMIN utility in NetWare 4.10 is a graphical utility that replaces most of the command line utilities used to administrate in earlier Net-Ware versions. With NWADMIN, a network administrator can prepare the network environment for use: creating objects, defining rights, implementing security, and the list goes on. He or she also can use NWADMIN to tune and organize the network, as well as to protect and manage the network resources (NETADMIN is the command line equivalent of NWADMIN). To start NWADMIN, double-click on its icon in Window's Program Manager, or choose File, Run and type the correct file location and file name (for example, F:\SYS:\PUBLIC\NWADMIN).

By default, NWADMIN is not added to a group in your windows desk-top. To create a group and add NWADMIN to the group, follow these procedures:

1. Choose File, New. Then click on the Program Group button in the New Program Object dialog box and select the OK button. A Pro-gram Group Properties dialog box appears.

2. Type a description for the group name and press Enter, or click on the OK button.

   The group icon then is created, and it is active—that is, the window is open.

Now you are ready to create the NWADMIN icon in the newly created group. To do so, follow these steps:

1. If the group to which you want to add the NWADMIN icon is not open, double-click on the group icon.

2. After opening the group icon, choose File, New (the program item should be highlighted) and click on OK or press Enter. A Program Item Properties dialog box appears.

3. Type **NWADMIN** or some other designation in the Description field.

4. Click on the Browse button and use the dialog box to locate the NWADMIN executable file (by default NWADMIN.EXE is located in the Public directory on the SYS volume).

You also might want to define a working directory. If the item is added to a group and a working directory is not specified, the directory where the file resides will be used for the working directory. If this is changed, however, you will need to make sure that all users have rights to the working directory so that they can manage the properties of their own user object.

5. After locating NWADMIN.EXE, highlight the file and click on OK, or double-click on the file name. The file's location and name is then added to the Command Line section in the Program Item Properties screen.

6. Click on OK, and Windows will warn you that the specified location might not be available during later Windows sessions. This simply is informing you that the executable file is located on a network, rather than a local drive. Click on Yes, and you're ready to run NWADMIN.

After starting NWADMIN, a screen showing the NDS tree appears (see fig. 1). To open a section or container of the tree, double-click on that section.

Figure 1
NWADMIN's main screen.

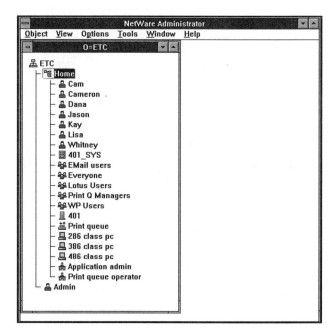

NWADMIN's layout is similar to most Windows utilities, which have a menu across the top of the screen. Click on the menu to view the menu options. The following section describes what you can do from each NWADMIN menu option, as well as each option's particular functions.

Object Menu Options

NWADMIN's Object menu enables you to perform the following administrative tasks:

- ♦ Create objects, such as users, groups, and printers
- ♦ Set the details for objects, such as volumes, printers, and users
- ♦ Define trustee assignments and inherited rights filters
- ♦ Restrict an object's rights to other parts of the tree
- ♦ Salvage files and directories that have been deleted
- ♦ Find the details of an object
- ♦ Move object of files to another location within the tree
- ♦ Copy a file or multiple files
- ♦ Rename a file, directory, or object
- ♦ Delete a file, directory, or object
- ♦ Define a user template
- ♦ Search the directory tree for an item (according to user definable search pattern)
- ♦ Exit NWADMIN

The following is a brief description of NWADMIN's Object menu options.

Create Object

Selecting the Create Object option opens the New Object dialog box that enables you to select which class of object you want to create. Figure 2 shows the list of object classes that you can create.

Figure 2

NWADMIN's New
Object selection
screen.

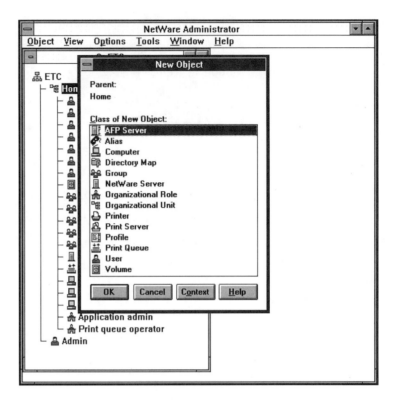

> **Note**
>
> *When you create an object, make sure that you are under the container in which you want the object to be located. If you select a leaf object (an object that cannot contain another object) or do not have the appropriate rights to create an object under the current container, you are not able to select the Create Object option—it is grayed out.*

To create one of the objects shown in Figure 2, complete the following steps:

1. Move to the container in which you want the object to be created.

2. Click on the Object menu.

3. Click on the Create option.

4. Click on the object you want to create.

5. Click on the OK button.

An options box similar to the one in figure 3 appears. Fill in the appropriate information.

 If the object that you want to create is not listed, you cannot create it in the container you selected.

Highlighting a section of the NDS tree and choosing Options, Create brings up a properties dialog screen. (Figure 3 is an example of the dialog box that appears when you choose to create a new user.) Each object created is placed in the NDS tree in your current location.

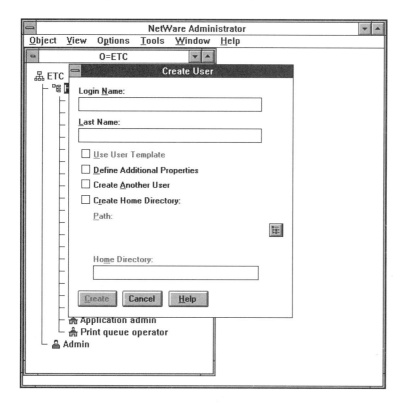

Figure 3
The Create User screen.

After filling in the appropriate values for the objects properties, click on the Create button. (If the Create button is grayed out, all the necessary values have not been filled in.)

After you create an object, it appears in the Browser. To define additional properties for an object, double-click on the object or click on the Define Additional Properties button when you create the object.

If you need to create multiple objects of the same type, select Create Another User. Selecting Create Another User, however, will not enable you to define additional properties. The best way to create multiple users is to create a user template.

In NetWare 4, you can create a user template that contains the default information that you want to apply to each new user object when the new object is created. This is a simple way to give all users the same default property values or to create a series of users with similar properties. A user template is a user object with the name User_Template. If the User_Template object is defined, and you create a user object, you can have the values contained in the User_Template object automatically transferred to the newly created user object by clicking on the Use User Template option in the Create User screen.

The Use User Template option box will be marked by default if the User_Template exists.

After creating an object, the object is displayed in NWADMIN's Browser screen. The Browser screen works similarly to Windows File Manager utility, except you also can manage objects in the NDS tree. To work with an object or to view its corresponding property values, double-click on the object's icon.

To define the object's property values, click on the object's corresponding icon and select the function that you want to perform on the object from NWADMIN's menu. Clicking a specific user icon and then selecting the Details option from the Object menu, for instance, brings up the User Details screen, which is the same screen that appears when you double-click on a leaf object's icon.

The screen, as well as the information contained within, changes depending on which type of object is selected when the Details option is selected. Highlighting a Container object, for instance, enables you to view that container's properties. Highlighting a server object and selecting Details brings up the Server Information screen, which contains information on file rights, print devices, login scripts, intruder detection status, and so on.

Trustees of This Object

Highlighting a new object and clicking on the Trustees of This Object option shows a dialog box that indicates the rights on the selected object. You can click on the Inherited Rights Filter button to define or view the selected object's inherited rights. You also can click on the Effective Rights button to view the rights that another object has to this particular object. And finally, you can click on the Add Trustee button to specify or assign trustees for this object.

The following are step-by-step instructions on performing these administrative tasks.

Inherited Rights

To change the inherited rights filter for certain objects properties only, highlight the object and choose Trustees of This Object from the Object menu. Then click on the Effective Rights button, and choose Selected Properties and the individual property you want to modify. To change the inherited rights filter for all properties of the selected object, select the All Properties button. To remove the inherited rights filter so that all rights can be inherited, select the Clear Filter button.

To define the object rights of the selected object, select the check box next to the object or property that you want to change. If the check box is grayed out, no inherited rights filter exists for the selected object. If the check box is white, that right cannot be inherited by a trustee with a trustee assignment above this point. If the check box is marked (X), that object right can be inherited.

To see another object's effective rights to the selected object, follow these steps:

1. Highlight the appropriate object.

2. Choose the Object menu.

3. Choose the Trustee of This Object option.

4. Choose a trustee from the available trustees list.

5. Choose the Effective Rights button.

To assign a trustee to this object, follow these steps:

1. Highlight the appropriate object (a user, for example).

2. Choose the Object menu.

3. Choose the Trustee of This Object option.

4. Choose the Add a Trustee button.

5. Choose the Trustee object to be added.

6. Choose OK.

To delete a trustee to this object, follow these steps:

1. Highlight the appropriate object.

2. Choose the Object menu.

3. Choose the Trustee of This Object option.

4. Click on the correct Trustee icon.

5. Choose the Delete Trustee button.

6. Choose Yes in the Delete Trustee assignment dialog box.

Rights to Other Objects

Highlighting an object and selecting the Rights to Other Objects option from the Object menu brings up a dialog box similar to the one shown in figure 4. From this dialog box you can view the effective rights of the selected object, and add or delete assignments.

Figure 4
NWADMIN's Rights to Other Objects dialog box.

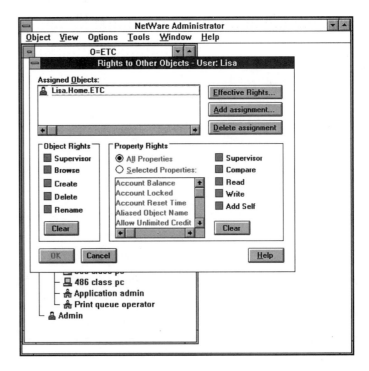

Salvage

The Salvage option of the Object menu is grayed out until you click on a volume or directory object. After you are on an appropriate object, clicking on the Salvage option opens a dialog box that enables you to recover or purge previously deleted files (see fig. 5).

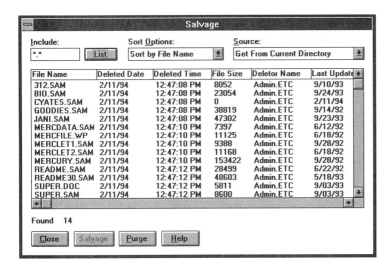

Figure 5
NWADMIN's
Salvage dialog box.

Details

Selecting the Details option from NWADMIN's Object menu opens a dialog box that enables you to view information about the object, file, or directory. The type of information you can view or change varies according to the object you select.

 You can access the detailed information screen by double-clicking on a leaf object.

Move

The Move option of the Object menu enables you to relocate a selected object or file to another location within the directory tree.

To move an object, highlight the object and choose Object, Move. The object that you highlighted will be added to the From section of the screen. Then, in the Destination section of the screen, type the location to which you want to move the object or file and choose OK.

To select multiple leaf objects or files, hold down the Shift key and click on the first object. Next move the cursor to the last object, and while holding down the Shift key, click on the last object. Multiple objects or files are highlighted, and then you can select a destination in the dialog box that appears when the Move option is selected.

Copy

Selecting the Copy option of the Object menu enables you to make a copy of a file. As with the Move option, you can select multiple files.

To copy an object, highlight the object and choose Object, Copy. The object that you highlighted will be added to the From section of the screen. Then, in the Destination section of the screen, type the location to which you want to move the object or file and choose OK.

To make a copy of an object, use the Move option.

Rename

The Rename option of the Object menu enables you to rename any object, file, or directory. If you rename an object, you can save the object's original name in the Other Names property for future reference.

To rename an object, highlight the object and choose Object, Rename. The object that you highlighted will be added to the New Name section of the Rename screen automatically. Type the new name and choose OK.

Delete

Selecting the Delete option from the Object menu enables you to delete the selected object. Highlight the object or file that you want to delete and choose Object, Delete. A dialog box appears asking for deletion confirmation. To delete the file or object, choose OK.

You can delete a container only if it is empty.

User Template

The User Template option enables you to set a default option pattern for each user object that is created under the selected container. Each user object automatically receives the same settings (for example, the login restriction time, password length, disk restrictions, and so on).

Search

The Search option, as its name implies, enables you to search a branch of the directory tree for objects matching a specified pattern.

Exit

Selecting the Exit option from the Object menu closes the NWADMIN utility.

View Menu Options

The View menu options enable you to control how the Browser displays objects. The following is a brief description of the View menu options.

Show Hints

Selecting the Show Hints option displays a description of each menu item at the top of the screen as you scroll through each menu. Selecting Show Hints turns on or off the hints.

Set Context

Selecting the Set Context option from the View menu brings up the Set Current Context dialog box (see fig. 6). This dialog box enables you to change which part of the directory tree you are currently viewing.

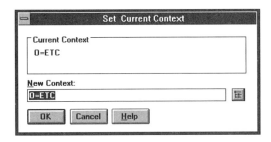

Figure 6
NWADMIN's Set Current Context dialog box.

Include

The Include option opens a dialog box in which you can choose the objects that you want to see in the Browser.

Expand

The Expand option opens the container object that you have selected.

Collapse

The Collapse option closes the container that you have selected.

 A mouse double-click also expands or collapses a container.

Options Menu

NWADMIN's Options menu consists of the following two options: Confirmations and Preferred Name Space.

Confirmations

Selecting the Confirmations option from the Options menu enables you to specify if you want to see a confirmation box each time you delete an object, file, or directory. This option remains set, even after closing NWADMIN.

Preferred Name Space

Selecting the Preferred Name Space option from the Options menu brings up a dialog box in which you can set the name spaces that you want to display for files and directories. If the name space that you select is not available on a volume, DOS (the default name space) is used to display the files and directories on that volume.

Tools Menu

The Tools menu consists of the Partition Manager, Browser, and Remote Console options.

Partition Manager

Selecting the Partition Manager option starts the Partition Manager utility. Partition Manager enables the network administrator to replicate and disperse NetWare 4's distributed database. This means that in a multiserver environment you can have duplicate copies of your database. If one of the partitions (or copies) of the database gets corrupted, deleted, or ruined, a duplicate database can be restored.

Using Partition Manager

Partition Manager enables you to manage your partitions and their replicas. The Partition Manager main window uses colors to show the different types of partitions; containers that are the root of a separate partition are red, and NetWare server objects are blue. The following procedures are possible in Partition Manager.

- ◆ Create a new partition

- ◆ Merge partitions

- ◆ View or modify replicas

- ◆ Repair damaged replicas

- ◆ View partitions on a server

- ◆ Delete a NetWare server object

Figure 7 shows Partition Manager's main screen.

The following is a brief description of Partition Manager's options.

- ◆ **Context.** This option shows your current context in the directory tree.

- ◆ **Partitions.** This option lists the partitions in the current context. It also enables you to view other partitions.

- ◆ **Create as New Partition.** This option creates a new partition out of an existing partition. The selected object becomes the root of the new partition, and a master replica of the new partition is created on the server where the master replica of its parent partition is located.

♦ **Merge Partitions.** This option merges a partition with its parent partition, leaving a single partition. All replicas are merged as well. To choose this option, you must select a partition below the [Root] of the directory tree.

♦ **Replicas.** This option enables you to add, delete, view, or modify the existing replica types.

♦ **Server Partitions.** This option gives you a list of all the replicas stored on a particular NetWare 4 server. This option is not available until you select a NetWare server object.

♦ **Delete Server.** This option deletes a NetWare server object and all its associated information, including its partitions and replicas.

♦ **Close.** This option returns you to the main menu of the NWADMIN utility.

Figure 7
Partition Manager's
main screen.

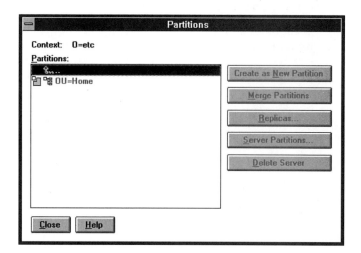

Browser

Selecting the Browser option from the Tools menu opens another Browser window in which the selected object is the first object. If you highlight the object for volume SYS, for example, and then select the Browser option, you bring up a new "browser box" that looks similar to figure 8.

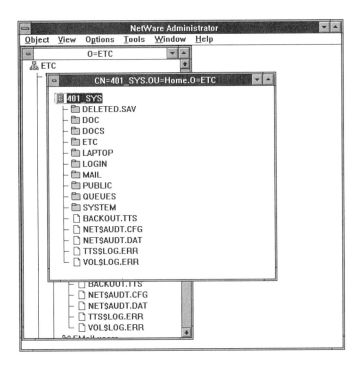

Figure 8
A Browser box
opened on volume
SYS.

Remote Console

Selecting the Remote Console option from the Tools menu activates
NetWare's Remote Console utility (in a Windows DOS Box). Starting
RCONCOLE establishes a remote SPX connection between the work-
station and the server. This enables you to load and unload files and
utilities, and perform other server console commands from the work-
stations (as if you were at the server). Before being able to establish a
Remote Console session between the workstation and server, however,
RSPX and REMOTE must be loaded on the server.

Window Menu

The window menu enables you to change the presentation or the way the
Browse screen appears. The following options are available:

- ♦ **Cascade.** Arranges all Browser windows in overlapping style.

- ♦ **Tile.** Arranges all Browser windows in tile style, in which none of the windows overlap, and each window is smaller.

- ♦ **Close All.** Closes all windows.

 To open a window to view the directory tree again, you must choose the Browser option from the Tools menu.

Help Menu

NWADMIN's Help menu is a standard Windows help menu that lists all topics available, contains a list of glossary terms, and enables you to search for any topic. The Help menu also contains an Error Messages option, which lists all error messages that can appear in the NWADMIN utility.

See Also

CX

NETADMIN

SYSCON

PCONSOLE

Print Console (PCONSOLE) conveys information about your print queues. PCONSOLE enables you to add and delete print jobs from the print queues. From within PCONSOLE, the network supervisor also can add, delete, and rename a print queue and print servers. Users can add, delete, or reorder print jobs as well. When you start PCONSOLE, you will see the following main menu (see fig. 1).

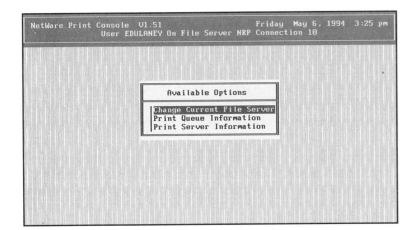

Figure 1
The main PCONSOLE menu in 2.2 and 3.1x.

Select Current File Server

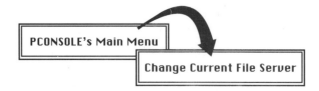

 In 2.2, the selection Change Current File Server is simply Change Current Server.

Selecting Change Current File Server brings up a list of active file servers that are on your network. If you only have one file server, you promptly will be given the Available Options screen. If multiple file servers exist on your network, however, you will have to choose a file server from the list of available servers. To choose a file server, highlight the file server that you want, then press Enter. If the server you want is not listed, press Ins, and NetWare will search for any additional file servers. Again, you will see a list of servers. If the server you want is in the new list, choose it and press Enter. After choosing a server, you are prompted to enter a user name and correct password. Entering a user name and password enables you to establish an attached connection to the selected file server.

PCONSOLE also enables you to change your login name, which often is helpful if you first log in as a user without supervisory privileges and then need to make a change that requires supervisory rights. To log in as a different user without leaving PCONSOLE, select the server you want, and, when the User Name dialog box appears, type the new user name or select a server from the available list and press F3. You then are prompted for a new user name and the appropriate password. PCONSOLE reestablishes a connection under the new user name.

 You cannot change the user name for your PRIMARY or DEFAULT servers. The PRIMARY server is the server you logged in to, and the DEFAULT server owns the drive letter from which you execute PCONSOLE.

Print Queue Information

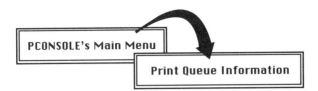

Print Queue Information from PCONSOLE's main menu brings up a list of print queues on the file server that you are currently attached to. From this list, you can examine any queue, or, if you have Supervisor rights, you can add, delete, or rename a queue. To obtain print queue information, select the queue you are interested in and press Enter to display the Print Queue Information screen (see fig. 2).

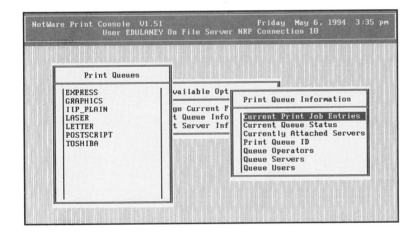

Figure 2
PCONSOLES's Print Queue Information screen.

PCONSOLE offers a different set of options to users, according to their security equivalents and the NetWare version running. From the Print Queue Information screen, all users can do the following:

♦ Determine the print queue's object ID

♦ Obtain a list of the print servers serviced by name

♦ List jobs currently in the queue

♦ See a list of users who can submit jobs to a queue

If, however, you are logged in as a supervisor, authorized queue user, or queue operator, you can do the following:

♦ Allow new jobs to be submitted

♦ Delete existing jobs in a queue

♦ Change information about a job

♦ Obtain the current status of a job

♦ Change print job operator flags

♦ List the print servers currently servicing jobs

The following functions are available only if you are logged in as a supervisor:

♦ List current queue operators

♦ Add queue operators

♦ Delete queue operators

The menu options in PCONSOLE will change according to the rights that you have. This changing set of menu options often can lead to confusion. For the remainder of this PCONSOLE section, it is assumed that PCONSOLE was started by a user with supervisory or equivalent rights.

Current Print Job Entries

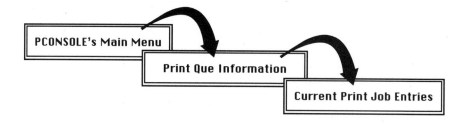

Selecting Current Print Job Entries from PCONSOLE's main menu brings up a list of the current print jobs, as depicted in figure 3. To delete one of these jobs, highlight the job and press Del. A dialog box appears prompting you to verify the deletion.

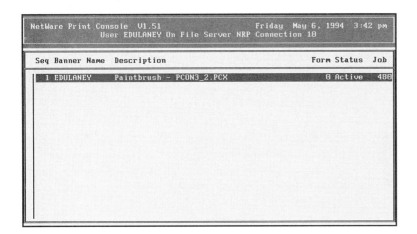

Figure 3
A list of current print jobs, with one job active.

To add a job to the queue, press Ins. A dialog box appears; you can either type the directory in which the file you want to add to the queue is located, or press Ins and select the appropriate directory. In either case, after you enter the correct directory, a list of files will appear. Select the file or mark several files with the F5 key, and press Enter. The Print Job Configuration screen appears (see fig. 4).

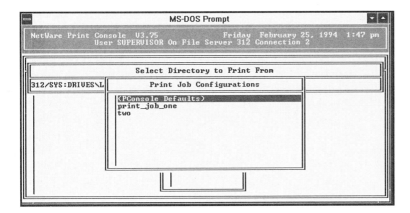

Figure 4
The Print Job Configurations screen.

Select the print job configuration you want to use by highlighting it and pressing Enter. You are then given the New Print Job to be Submitted screen, which contains a list of previously defined option settings. To change the default configuration options, highlight the field you want to change and type the new value. If you want to change the User hold status field from No to Yes, for example, move the cursor to that field and press Enter. Then type the letter **Y**, and the field's value changes.

Some of the option fields will switch, while others will offer a pop-up menu options box, which enables you to choose a selection. After changing options, press Esc and save the changes. The job then is added to the print queue and is printed according to priority.

Print jobs usually are not added from this workstation; most print jobs are added from a workstation that has a printer port captured to a print queue. Many network Administrators, however, find that this location is a handy method to print server error or configuration files.

Current Queue Status

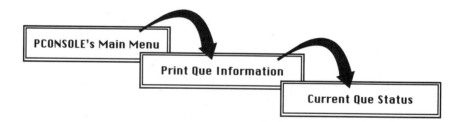

To see the current status of a print queue, highlight the print queue in the print queue list and press Enter. Then choose Current Queue Status from the Print Queue Information options screen. A screen similar to that shown in figure 5 appears.

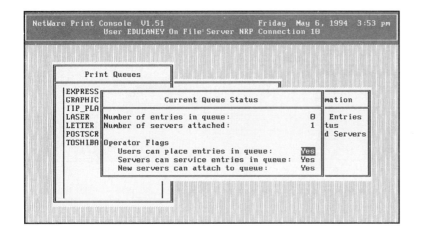

Figure 5
The current queue
status.

The bottom of the status screen contains the following three options:

♦ Users can place entries in a queue

♦ Server can service entries in queue

♦ New server can attach to queue

By default, each of these print queue status line options are set to Yes. To change the status of one of these options, highlight the option and press Enter. You then can turn off the status by typing **N** for No.

Currently Attached Servers

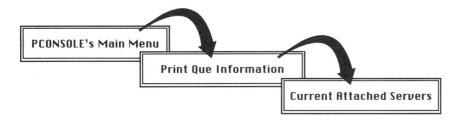

To see the servers to which a queue is currently attached, choose the appropriate queue and then select Currently Attached Servers from the Print Queue Information menu. A box listing the currently attached servers appears. If the print queue is attached to a print server, the print server(s) is listed; if it is not attached, the box is empty.

Print Queue ID

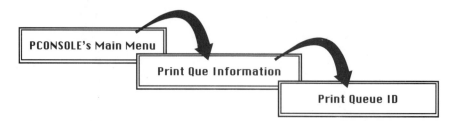

To see the physical object ID number of the queue, as well as the server to which it is attached, select Print Queue ID from the Print Queue Information menu. The object ID number provides the link to a directory that is created with the same object ID number as its name. This directory is usually located in SYS:SYSTEM directory, and this is where the individual files or print jobs get queued or stored until they are completely printed. It is a good idea to make sure that the SYS volume does not run out of disk space, or no new print jobs can be added.

Queue Operators

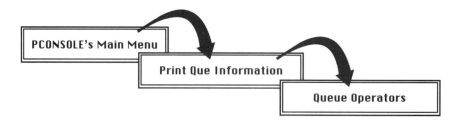

Selecting Queue Operators from the Print Queue Information screen shows the users and groups who can manage the selected print queue. To add an operator to the list, press the Ins key and select the new operator from the Queue Operator Candidates window that appears. You also can mark multiple candidates with the F5 key. After marking the new operators, press Enter, and they will be added to the Queue Operators list. To delete a queue operator, highlight an operator, and answer Yes to the confirmation screen.

Queue Servers

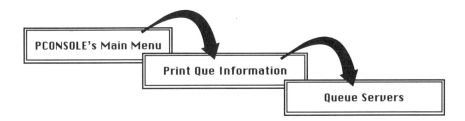

Selecting Queue Servers from the Print Queue Information screen show the servers to which the selected print queue is attached. Every print server has to be serviced by a print queue, or multiple print queues. Being serviced by a queue means that when a print job is sent to a print server, the print server will send that print job to the queue that is servicing the print server.

Queue Users

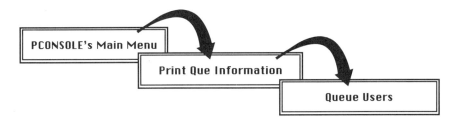

Selecting the Queue Users option brings up a list of the users who are able to use the selected print queue. The group "Everyone" is assigned by default when a print queue is created. To add a user or group of users to this list, press the Ins key. A screen listing all candidate queue users appears. This list contains the users and groups that can be added to the queue users list. To add a user or group, highlight the candidate user and press Enter. To add multiple users or groups, highlight them using the F5 key, then press Enter. To delete a queue user from the list, highlight that user and press Del.

Print Server Information

Selecting Print Server Information brings up a list of current print servers. After selecting a print server from the available list, the Print Server Information screen appears, in which you can do the following (see fig. 6):

♦ Change the password of the printer

♦ Enter, change, or check the full name of the print server

♦ See the print server configuration

♦ Check the print server ID

♦ Enter, see, or delete print server operators

♦ Check the print server status and control

♦ Manage print server users

Figure 6
Options available from the Print Server Information menu.

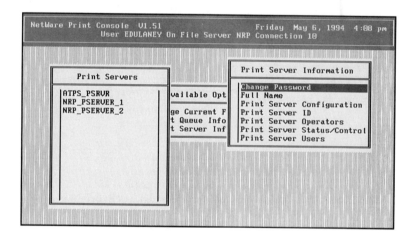

Change Password

Selecting Change Password from the Print Servers Information screen brings up a dialog box. Type the new password for the print server (used when loading and unloading the print server) and press Enter. You are then asked to retype the password to ensure no mistake was made when typing it the first time.

Full Name

Selecting Full Name from the Print Server Information screen brings up a dialog box in which you can type the full name for the print server. This name is meant to be a descriptive name that will help identify the print server. If no full name has been assigned, the dialog box is empty. To add a name, type the name and press Enter. If a name has been given to the print server, the name appears in the box. To change or delete the name, type over the name or use the Backspace key to erase the name entry.

Print Server Configuration

Selecting the Print Server Configuration option brings up the Print Server Configuration menu. This menu contains the following options:

- ◆ File Server To Be Serviced
- ◆ Notify List for Printer
- ◆ Printer Configuration
- ◆ Queues Serviced by Printer

All the options in this menu can be found in other portions of PCONSOLE, except for the Printer Configuration option. Selecting the Printer Configuration option brings up a screen in which you can identify each printer hooked to the print server. After selecting Printer Configuration, a screen appears containing a list of the installed printers. If no printers are installed, each of the lines has a "Not Installed" status. To install a printer, select one of the Not Installed lines by highlighting it and pressing Enter.

Note *Each line also is designated by a number. This number will be used as the printer number.*

After selecting one of the unused printer numbers, the Printer Configuration screen appears. From this screen you can identify the following printer configuration parameters:

- ◆ Name
- ◆ Type
- ◆ Use Interrupts
- ◆ IRQ

♦ Buffer size in K:

♦ Starting Form

♦ Queue service mode

♦ Baud rate

♦ Data bits

♦ Stop bits

♦ Parity

♦ Use X-On/X-Off

After typing the name of the printer, define where the printer is located. Highlight the Type field and press Enter. The Printer Type field appears, which contains a list of available printer location options. To make your selection, highlight the appropriate selection and press Enter.

The "appropriate" selection will differ depending on your printer location: If the printer is directly attached to your print server, you select one of the first seven options; if it is hooked to a workstation that will be running an RPRINTER.EXE (Remote Printer), then you will select one of the remote or last seven options. If the printer has been defined on another file server, select the Defined elsewhere option. You also will need to know which computer port (for example, LPT1, LPT2, COM1, and COM2) the printer is physically attached to.

Select the correct printer type and port location by highlighting the correct option and pressing Enter. You are returned to the Printer Configuration screen where you can continue to set the preceding list of configuration options. Depending on the printer type, however, certain options will not be accessible. If, for instance, you have defined a parallel printer, the options Baud rate, Data bits, Stop bits, Parity, and X-On/X-Off will not be accessible (these options are for serial printers). If you have selected a serial printer, consult your printer manual for the correct settings.

With either a parallel or serial printer, you will need to specify the correct interrupt (common interrupts for printing are COMM1=IRQ3, COMM2=IRQ4, LPT1=IRQ5, LPT2=IRQ7). A PC, whether a server or a workstation, uses interrupts to signal the processor that a temporary interruption in current processing needs to occur. By using an interrupt, personal computers can communicate with attached devices, such as a printer. When specifying the interrupt, you should make sure that the interrupt you are selecting matches the correct settings of the port to which the printer is hooked.

Some computers do not implement interrupts. (This is very common when a remote printer is hooked to a monochrome card that has a parallel port.) If your printer configuration is not working, change the Yes in the Use interrupts field to No. To do this, highlight the Yes indicator and type **N**. This switches the printer to polled mode. The "polled mode" selection will not directly use the computer's interrupt to find the printer, hopefully eliminating your printer problems. Not using an interrupt, however, often causes printing to be significantly slower.

One way to help improve printing performance is to increase the size of the print buffer. The Buffer option controls the flow of data to the print server's internal buffer. The larger the number, the faster the data will be fed to the print server, and thus to the printer. For the best printing performance, match the print buffer parameter to the amount of print buffer memory in your printer—most of the time 3 KB, which is the default setting, is sufficient. This allows the print server to send data to the printer as fast as the printer can accept it. If your printer often starts and stops, however, it is probably waiting for data from the print server, and you should consider increasing the size of the print buffer. Increasing the print buffer's size, however, might retard the file server (more of its time is spent "feeding" data into the more active print buffer).

Print Server ID

Selecting the Print Server ID option provides you with the print server ID, as well as the name of the file server.

Print Server Operators

Selecting the Print Server Operators option brings up a list of all the current operators. You can add names to this list by pressing the Ins key and selecting them from the Candidate Operators screen. To add multiple operators, mark them using the F5 key and press Enter; otherwise, highlight the single operator you want and press Enter.

Print Server Status/Control

Selecting the Print Server Status/Control option brings up the Print Server Status and Control menu, which contains the following options:

♦ File Servers being Serviced, which lists the file servers to which the print server is currently attached.

♦ Notify List for Printer, which brings up a list indicating the users or groups that will be notified if the selected printer has problems. You also can add or delete users and groups from the notification list from this location.

♦ Printer Status, which shows the status of the current printer.

♦ Queues Serviced by Printer, which brings up a list of print queues that are being serviced by the printer.

♦ Server Info, which displays general information, such as print server version, print server type, number of printers attached to the print server, queue service modes, and the status of the current print server.

Print Server Users

Selecting Print Server Users brings up a list of users and groups that currently have the rights to use the print server. By default, the group "Everyone" is added. To add more users to this list, press the Ins key and select the users to be added from the candidate users and groups listed in the Print Server User Candidate screen. To delete a user from the user, highlight the user and press Del.

See Also

CAPTURE

NETADMIN

NETUSER

NPRINT

NWADMIN

NWUSER

PRINTCON

SESSION

SPOOL

SYSCON

PCONSOLE 4

If you are logged in with normal user rights, PCONSOLE enables you to view available print queues, as well as the current print jobs, print servers, and printers (see fig. 1). Users also can manipulate their own print jobs.

If you are logged in as a user assigned as a print queue operator, you can manipulate all print jobs in that print queue. If you are logged in as a user assigned as a print server operator, you can manipulate that print server. If you have sufficient rights in the current context, you can use all of PCONSOLE's functionality on the objects in this context.

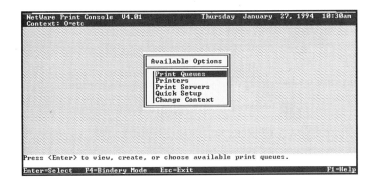

Figure 1
The NetWare 4 PCONSOLE main menu.

Print Queues

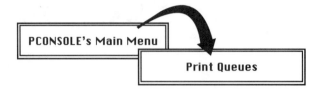

Selecting `Print Queues` enables you to do the following:

♦ Add new print jobs to the print queue

♦ View or delete print jobs already in the print queue

♦ Modify print job specifications for print jobs

Selecting `Print Queues` also brings up a list of current print queues available to you. Now, you can either add, delete, or select a queue. After selecting a queue, you are given many options. These options are only available to authorized print queue users, print queue operators, and network administrators.

Print Jobs

Selecting `Print Jobs` provides a list of the print jobs currently in a specific print queue. This list is updated every five seconds. From within this list, you can add or delete a print job or view and change information about a particular print job.

Use the keys in the following table to manage or view a current print job.

Key	Function
Enter	Shows detailed information about a print job
Delete	Removes selected print jobs from the print queue
Insert	Adds new print jobs to the print queue
F5	Marks multiple print jobs
F7	Unmarks all marked print jobs

Status

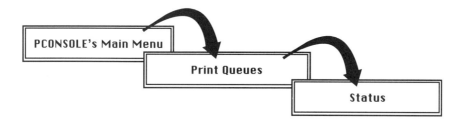

Selecting Status shows the current status of this print queue and enables
a user with appropriate rights to set or change operator flags (see fig. 2).

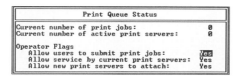

Figure 2
PCONSOLE's Print
Queue Status screen.

Attached Print Servers

Selecting Attached Print Servers brings up a list of print servers that
currently are attached to and servicing the selected print queue.

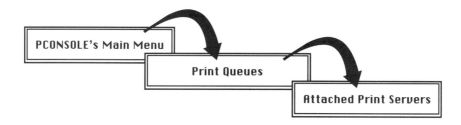

Information

Selecting the Information option shows the Object ID and NetWare server name of the selected print queue. An example of the information that you will be given can be seen in figure 3.

Figure 3
PCONSOLE's Print Queue Information screen.

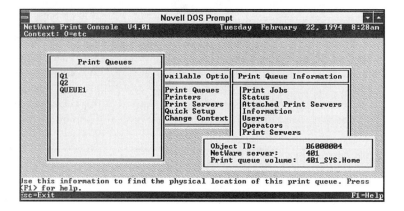

Figure 3
PCONSOLE's Print Queue Information screen.

Users

Selecting Users provides you with a list of the users (for example, Admin), or groups of users (for example, Everyone) that can submit print jobs to this print queue.

Operators

Highlighting Operators and pressing Enter provides a list of the current print queue operators. This also is where a network administrator or a user with supervisory equivalent rights can add or delete print queue operators.

To delete a print queue operator, select Operators; a list of current objects (users, groups, server, and so on) appears. If the user or group of users you want to add or delete as a print queue operator does not appear in the list, you might need to change your directory context. To change your context, highlight the appropriate container (directory location) and press Enter. Highlight the container and press the select key (F10). If the object does appear, highlight the object and press Del to delete the object from the operators list; press Ins to create an object.

Print Servers

Selecting the Print Servers option provides a list of the print servers that can service this particular print queue. Print queue operators can add or delete servers in the list. Press Ins to add a print server to the list or Delete to remove a print server from the list.

Printers

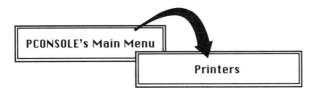

Selecting Printer brings up a list of the currently configured printers. To delete a printer from this list, highlight the printer and press Del. To add a printer to the list, press Ins. After pressing Ins, which will create a new printer, you will be prompted to type the name of the printer (it is best if this name is short, but long enough to adequately describe the printer).

After entering the new printer's name, you will be returned to the list and the new printer that you just added will be highlighted. To define the new printer's configuration, or any other printer's configuration, highlight the printer and press Enter; the Printer Configuration screen appears, as seen in figure 4.

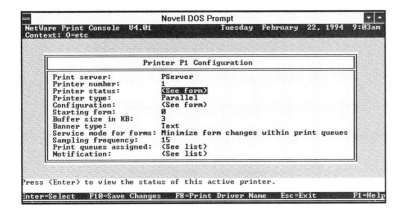

Figure 4
PCONSOLE's Printer Configuration screen.

To set options in the Printer Configuration screen, highlight the correct location and press Enter. (The highlight bar will move only to the locations that are definable.)

The following is a list of the definable printer configuration options:

♦ Printer number (on new printers)

♦ Printer status

♦ Printer type

♦ Configuration

♦ Starting form

♦ Buffer size in KB

♦ Banner type

♦ Service mode for forms

♦ Sampling frequency

♦ Print queues assigned

♦ Notification

Printer Number

Selecting Printer Number (when defining a new printer) enables you to assign a number to the printer. Every printer that is being serviced by the selected print server has to be assigned a number; the number must be unique, and must be in the range of 0 to 254.

If the number you enter is already in use, PCONSOLE reports an error when you try to save the new configuration.

Printer Status

Selecting Printer Status displays a screen that shows the current printer status (see fig. 5).

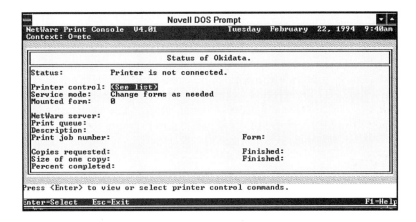

Figure 5
PCONSOLE's Printer Status screen.

The Printer Status screen shows if the printer is connected (in the preceding screen shot the printer was not connected). If the printer is connected and a print job is currently being printed, this screen shows the progress of the print job.

If you are logged in as the user Admin or as a print server operator, you can do the following from this screen:

♦ Change the print queue service mode

♦ Change the currently mounted form

♦ Change the printer service mode

♦ Issue printer service control commands

To change or set any of the options displayed in the window, highlight the option and press Enter. In some cases, highlighting the option and pressing Enter brings up another screen (for example, where the options say See list or See form).

Highlighting Printer Control and pressing Enter brings up a screen that offers the following options:

♦ Pause printer

♦ Stop printer

♦ Start printer

♦ Form feed

♦ Mark top of form

♦ Abort print job

♦ Rewind printer

For the options that do not indicate that a list or additional form (screen) is present, simply highlight the option and press Enter. If there are multiple settings for the selected menu item, pressing Enter brings up a menu list of possible selections from which to choose. You then can select one of the settings by highlighting the option and pressing Enter.

Printer Type

Selecting Printer Type enables you to select the printer type from the following list:

♦ Parallel

♦ Serial

♦ Unix Printer

♦ AppleTalk Printer

♦ Other/Unknown

♦ XNP

♦ AIO

To select the printer type, highlight the correct setting and press Enter.

Configuration

Selecting Configuration displays a screen with all the specific information about this printer's configuration. The information that is listed includes the following fields with their respective options:

Port address (LPT1, LPT2, or LPT3).

Location (Manual Load or Auto Load). NPRINTER.NLM is the only printer driver that can be loaded automatically. If a printer is connected directly to a server or workstation that is not loading PSERVER, you must select Manual Mode. If the printer is connected to the server, and the server is loading PSERVER.NLM, you can use either option

Interrupt (3, 4, 5, 7, 10, 11, None). A PC, whether it's a server or a workstation, uses interrupts to signal the processor that a temporary interruption in current processing needs to occur. By using an interrupt, PCs can communicate with attached devices, such as a printer. When specifying the interrupt, you should make sure that the interrupt you are selecting matches the correct settings of the port to which the printer is hooked.

Some computers do not correctly implement interrupts. (This is very common when a remote printer is hooked to a monochrome card that has a parallel port.) If your printer configuration is not working, switch to polled mode. The polled mode selection will not directly use the interrupt to find the printer. Not using an interrupt, however, often causes significantly slower printing.

Address restriction. This specifies the address or the workstation or server that will be allowed to load the NetWare printer driver. By default, no restrictions are applied.

Network address. If enabled, it will specify the network address of the machine that can load the NetWare printer driver for the currently selected printer. By default, the current station's network address is used.

Node address. If enabled, it will specify the node address of the station that can load the printer driver. If the broadcast address of FFFFFFFFFFFF is used, any workstation that is located on the specified network can load the driver.

The Configuration screen also provides the following fields. These fields, however, are not configurable.

Starting Form

Selecting Starting form identifies the number of the form that is mounted on the printer when the print server is started. Using form numbers is a simple way of making sure that the correct print layout is specified. One situation in which a form would be used is on a printer that is mostly or always used to print on a special form, such as checks. Creating and specifying a form that correctly positions the printed information on the check can simplify network printing. The form that is selected from this location is loaded each time the printer driver is loaded.

Buffer Size in KB

Selecting Buffer Size in KB enables you to specify the size of the print buffer. Each print server has an internal buffer. Increasing the size of the print buffer can increase the printing speed, especially if your printer often stops and starts during a print job. However, increasing the size of remote printer (a printer hooked to a workstation that is not running as a dedicated PSERVER) also increases the amount of RAM that the remote printer configuration will need.

Banner Type

Information on the banner includes the user station that sent the print job, which can be used to indicate the origination of the print job. This can be helpful in a situation where multiple users are printing to the same printer. Selecting `Banner Type` enables you to indicate the type of banner that should be printed. The two options are `Text` and `PostScript`. Specifying the type of banner is important because sending a text banner to a PostScript printer, or vice versa, can hang the printer.

Service Mode for Forms

Selecting `Service mode for forms` enables you to determine how the print server services print jobs. In NetWare, print jobs are serviced according to print queue and printer form. A printer form specifies the length and width of different types of paper used in your printer, such as check or invoice paper. Designation printer forms for print jobs helps prevent print jobs from printing on the wrong paper.

When a print job requests a printer form other than the form currently mounted in the printer, the print job will not be serviced until a new form is mounted. NetWare's service mode option determines how often a print server will require you to change printer forms. The options are as follows:

- **Change Forms as Needed.** You might have to change forms often because the order of print jobs in the print queue and the priority of each print queue is used to decide which print job is to be serviced next.

- **Minimize Form Changes Across Print Queues.** If this mode is turned on, the print server will prioritize print jobs according to the required form. Print jobs requiring the currently mounted form will be serviced first; those requesting a form change will be serviced last. This also means that low-priority jobs that use the mounted form will be serviced before high-priority jobs that need to have a new form loaded.

- **Minimize Form Changes Within Print Queues.** In this mode, the print server requires you to mount a new form for a print job before servicing print jobs with the currently mounted form.

♦ **Service Only Currently Mounted Form.** In this mode, the printer will never request a form change.

♦ **Sampling Frequency.** This indicates how frequently the server will check the print queues for print jobs (in seconds).

♦ **Print Queues Assigned.** Selecting this field displays the list of queues serviced by this printer.

♦ **Notification.** Selecting this field displays the list of users and groups to be notified in case this printer has a problem.

Sampling Frequency

Selecting Sampling frequency enables you to change how often (in seconds) the server will check the print queues for print jobs. The lower the sampling frequency, the faster a submitted print job is processed. Lowering the sampling frequency, however, also takes processing time away from other server functions.

Print Queues Assigned

Selecting Print queues assigned brings up a list of print queues serviced by the selected printer. The screen that appears has three columns: Print Queue, Priority, and State.

From this screen you can add or delete a print queue form the assigned list. To delete a print queue, highlight the print queue and press Del. To add a print queue, press Ins. You then are given the Directory Browse screen that shows the current Directory Objects. To select an object (the desired print queue), highlight the print queue object and press Enter. You can mark and add multiple print queues by using the F5 key.

Selecting Print queues assigned also enables you to change the priority of a print queue in the assigned list. To change the priority of print queue, enter a number form 1 to 10. This number designates which print jobs the print queue will service first; the higher the number, the lower the priority. For instance, priority 1 print jobs are serviced first.

Notification

The screen that appears after selecting Notification is divided into five columns. The first column, Object to be Notified, contains a list of users or groups that will be notified when the printer has a problem.

The second column indicates the object type (user or group). To delete an object from this list, highlight the object and press Del. To add a user to the list, press Ins. You will then be given a Directory Services Browse screen. Select the object that you want to add and press Enter.

After selecting an object, you are given the option to change the third and fourth columns, which are First Notify Interval and Next Notify Interval. These are set in minutes. Enter the amount of time in minutes and press F10 to save the changes.

Notification is sent whenever the printer needs attention (for instance, when it is out of paper or when it is offline). Be sure that the users added to this list need to be notified of the problem. The default object list only contains the print job owner.

Print Servers

Selecting Printer Servers from the menu brings up a list of available print servers (see fig. 6). After selecting the appropriate print server, you are given the following options:

♦ Printers

♦ Information and Status

♦ Users

♦ Operators

♦ Description

♦ Password

♦ Audit

Figure 6
PCONSOLE's Print
Server Information
screen.

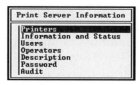

Printers

Selecting Printers displays a list of the printers being serviced by the selected print server. If you have supervisory rights, you can add printers to this list by pressing Insert, and remove them by pressing Delete. Select a printer to view its configuration.

The State column in the window displays the current status of the printer and contains on of the following three settings:

[A]	Indicates that the printer is active
[C]	Indicates that the printer is configured
[AC]	Indicates that the printer is active and configured

Information and Status

If you select the Information and Status option and the print server is active, a screen displaying the following appears:

♦ **Print Server Type.** The type of this print server.

♦ **Print Server Version.** The version of this server.

♦ **Number Of Printers.** The number of printers actively being serviced by this server.

♦ **Current Server Status.** The print server status can be one of the following: Running, Going Down After Current Jobs, or Down.

♦ **Advertising Name.** The name that the print server uses to advertise itself on the network. It can be between 2 and 47 characters long and must be unique. If left to the defaults, it is the same as the print server object.

Users

Selecting Users provides a list of the users and groups who are print server users. To delete a user from the list, highlight the user and press Del. To add a user to the list, press Ins and select the user from the Directory Browse screen.

Operators

Selecting the Operators option displays the users and groups that are operators for the print server. To delete an operator from the list, highlight the user (group) and press Del. To add an operator, press Ins and select the appropriate user from the Directory Browse screen by highlighting it and pressing F10.

Description

The Description option displays a descriptive name for the print server if one has been assigned by the supervisor. The following options are only available to users with Supervisor rights.

Password

The Password option changes the password for the print server. If a password is assigned to a print server, that password must be entered every time the pint server is loaded.

Audit

Selecting Audit brings up the Print Services Auditing screen (see fig. 7). From this location, you can set print services auditing to be enabled or disabled. You also can find the location of the print server audit log file, view the file, and delete the audit log file.

Figure 7
PCONSOLE's Print Services Auditing screen.

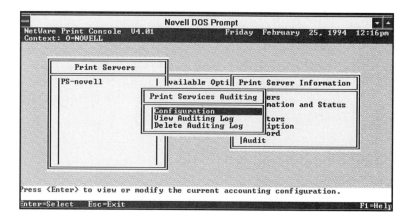

Quick Setup

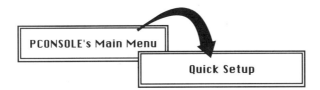

Selecting Quick Setup enables a user with supervisory rights to quickly set up a printer, a print queue, and a print server (see fig. 8). All of the assignments are done automatically (printer to print queue and print server to printer). By default, the new print server is given the name PS-<Current Context Name>, the printer is assigned the name P1 (if it is the first printer), and the print queue is assigned Q1 (if it is the first queue set up with the Quick Setup function).

Figure 8
PCONSOLE's Print Services Quick Setup screen.

Any of the settings in figure 8 can be changed. To change a setting, highlight the setting and press Enter. You then can type the new setting or select the new setting from the options that are provided.

After using Quick Setup, the only other step to setting Network printing functions is to load the print server.

Change Current Context

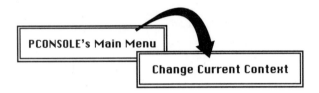

Change current context enables you to select another context in the tree to examine its print queues, print servers, and printers.

See Also

NETADMIN

NETUSER

NWADMIN

PRINTCON

PRINTCON

PRINTCON is a utility in which a NetWare user or supervisor can create special printer set-up configuration files. You could, for example, specify a configuration that prints with a banner or a configuration that automatically makes a second copy. Slight differences exist between versions 2.2 and 3.1x, with the primary difference being that 2.2 does not offer the capability to copy job configurations. PRINTCON's menu is shown in figure 1.

 Even though it's not a menu choice, you can copy print jobs in 2.2 manually. Copy the PRINTCON.DAT file from user's mail directory to another user's mail directory.

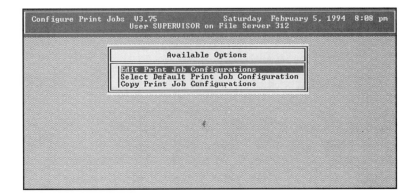

Figure 1
PRINTCON's main menu.

Edit Print Job Configurations

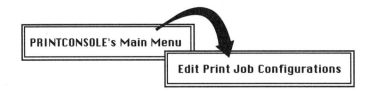

If you select Edit Print Job Configurations, a screen showing the current configurations appears. To define a new print job configuration, press Ins. To delete a print job configuration, highlight the correct job and press Del. To modify or change a configuration, highlight the configuration and press Enter. The Edit Print Job Configuration screen appears (see fig. 2).

Figure 2
The Edit Print Job Configuration screen.

Edit Print Job Configuration "print_job_one"		
Number of copies:	1	Form name: (None defined)
File contents:	Byte stream	Print banner: Yes
Tab size:		Name: SUPERVISOR
Suppress form feed:	No	Banner name:
Notify when done:	No	
Local printer:	1	Enable timeout: No
Auto endcap:	Yes	Timeout count:
File server:	312	
Print queue:	QUEUE-1	
Print server:	(Any)	
Device:	(None)	
Mode:	(None)	

Select Default Print Job Configuration

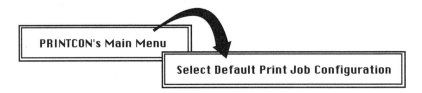

Selecting the Select Default Print Job Configuration option enables you to specify which print job configuration will be used as the default configuration. Select the default configuration by highlighting it and pressing Enter.

Once created, the menu will not let you delete all print job configurations. The last print job configuration used is the default print job configuration and can't be deleted through the menu. To delete the last print job configuration, the file PRINTCON.DAT must be deleted from the user's mail directory.

Copy Print Job Configuration

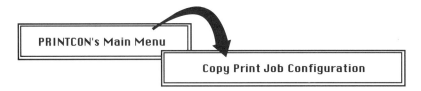

Selecting Copy Print Job Configuration enables the supervisor to distribute a print job to specific users or to let users share a print job configuration with other users. After selecting this option, a box appears asking you to enter the name of the source user. The *source user* is the user whose PRINTCON.DAT file contains the print job that you want to copy. After you enter the correct user name, another box appears asking you to enter the target user. The *target user* is the user to whom you want to give the new print job configuration.

See Also

CAPTURE

PCONSOLE

SYSCON

PRINTCON 4

The PRINTCON utility enables NetWare users to customize and configure print jobs, which greatly simplifies the use of other utilities such as CAPTURE, NETUSER, NPRINT, and PCONSOLE. The PRINTCON utility creates print job configurations called *templates*. Each template determines what the settings of a print job are (printer or print queue, the number of copies, whether you want a banner page, form feed, and so on). Specifying a print job configuration saves the user from specifying the options at the command-line (CAPTURE or NPRINT) or in a menu utility (NETUSER or PCONSOLE).

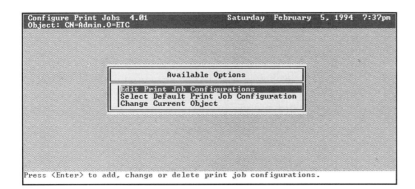

Figure 1
PRINTCON's main menu.

Edit Print Job Configuration

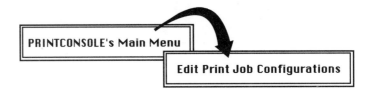

Select the desired print job and the Print Job Configuration screen appears (see fig. 2). You can highlight any of the items and press Enter to edit the field.

Figure 2
PRINTCON's Edit
Print Job
Configuration screen.

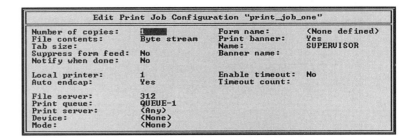

Note

You can change to Bindery mode by pressing F4. When NetWare 4 is operating in Bindery mode, the private database is stored in the PRINTJOB.DAT file in the user's mail directory, whereas the public PRINTJOB.DAT database file is stored in SYS:PUBLIC.

Once in Bindery mode, you can switch back to Directory Services by pressing F4. In NetWare 4's Directory Services, a print job configuration is stored as an attribute of a container or user object. Also, the PRINTCON utility only looks for print job configurations in your current context. If the current object is a user, look for the print job configuration in the container above the user.

Select Default Print Job Configuration

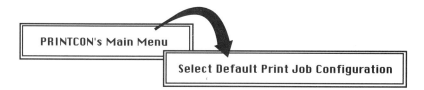

PRINTCON's Main Menu

Select Default Print Job Configuration

The right column of the Select Default Print Job Configuration screen shows the object that contains the print job configuration. To make a print job the default, highlight it and press Enter (default print job is indicated with an asterisk). To remove the default job, highlight the job and press Del. Print job configurations created by a user can only be used by that user. Print job configurations that belong to a server or container object can be used by every user in that context.

If the command line utilities (NPRINT or CAPTURE) are used without specifying a print job configuration, the default print job configuration always is used. If NetWare cannot find a default user configuration, it searches for a print job configuration in the container object.

When NetWare 4 is running in Bindery mode, it searches first for a default print job configuration in the user's private database, and then in the public database.

User objects begin with "CN=username." Container objects begin with "OU=containername" or "O=containername."

Change Current Object

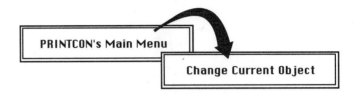

Selecting the Change Current Object option brings up a Change Current Context box, in which you can type the name of the object whose PRINTCON database you want to access. If you are in Bindery Emulation mode, the Change Current Object option changes to Change Current NetWare Server.

See Also

CAPTURE

NETUSER

NPRINT

PCONSOLE

ROUTEGEN

The ROUTEGEN utility is used to generate a NetWare 2.2 *router* (software that enables the exchange of information between network cabling systems). ROUTEGEN is provided as part of the NetWare 2.2 operating system, but is supplied on a separate disk called the ROUTEGEN disk.

To start ROUTEGEN, with the ROUTEGEN disk in a floppy drive, type **ROUTEGEN** and press Enter. An introductory screen appears. After reading it, press Enter to continue. Next, choose the operating system. Your choices are as follows:

♦ Dedicated protected mode

♦ Nondedicated protected mode

♦ Dedicated real mode

 If you chose nondedicated protected mode, supply a network address.

Next, provide a number to specify the number of communication buffers. The default is 150. The range is 40 to 1000.

Choose Driver. From the list of available drivers, choose the appropriate driver. If your driver is not listed, use the appropriate LAN_DRV_XXX, and choose the correct driver.

After choosing the LAN driver configuration option, choose the correct option settings for your LAN board, and then provide the network address. When complete, press F10. The router operating system is then linked and configured, and a ROUTEGEN is complete message is displayed.

SALVAGE

The SALVAGE utility enables you to restore previously deleted but not yet purged files. Recovering a file is possible because NetWare saves deleted files until the user or supervisor purges them, or until the NetWare server volume runs out of disk space. If the server begins to get low on disk space, NetWare automatically purges files on a first-deleted, first-purged basis. If an application deletes a file, it is recoverable with SALVAGE. If the file is overwritten or replaced, however, the old file is not recoverable.

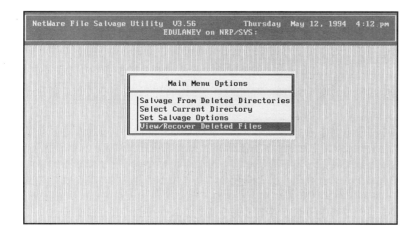

Figure 1
The main menu of SALVAGE.

Files must be deleted with DOS utilities—either DEL or ERASE—for SALVAGE to work. Files removed with PURGE are forever removed from the system.

The SALVAGE utility's main menu offers two or four of the following choices, depending upon which version you use. The first and third choices do not appear in older versions of NetWare.

♦ Salvage from deleted directories

♦ Select current directory

♦ Set SALVAGE options

♦ View/recover deleted files

In NetWare 2.2, SALVAGE also can be started with the name of a directory path following the command, as in the following:

```
SALVAGE F:\APPL\USR\KAREN
```

If you specify a directory or file rather than a volume, however, SALVAGE reduces the path to the volume level and recovers the last files deleted there.

In NetWare 2.2, SALVAGE is limited to the last DELETE or ERASE command given. If you deleted one file by specifying it, then only that file can be restored. On the other hand, if you deleted an entire directory using *.*, then all the files can be recovered because they were deleted with one command.

Salvage from Deleted Directories

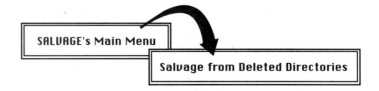

If a file was in a directory and the directory was deleted, you should select the option SALVAGE From Deleted Directories. Choosing this option enables you to look for the deleted file in a directory even if that directory had been previously deleted. After you have found the file that you want to recover, highlight the file and press Enter. Or, if you change into the DELETED.SAV directory before starting SALVAGE, you can pick the View/Recover Deleted Files option. With either option, you are asked if you want to recover the deleted file.

NetWare restores recovered files in a hidden directory called DELETED.SAV, which is a directory off the root of every NetWare volume. To see if the file has been recovered and is in this directory, switch to the hidden directory by typing CD DELETED.SAV from the root directory.

Selecting a Current Directory

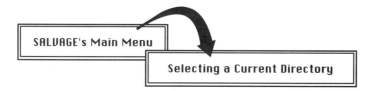

Choosing the Select Current Directory option enables you to change to another directory or volume so that files can be salvaged. After you select this option, a current directory path window will appear. This path window shows the current directory. To change to a different directory, either type the appropriate directory destination or press Ins. Pressing Ins enables you to choose the server and directory that you want to view.

Set SALVAGE Options

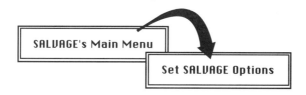

Setting the default salvage options enables you to customize the way the deleted, unpurged files will be listed, which can significantly aid in finding the files that you want to recover. SALVAGE uses one of the following four settings:

- ♦ Sort the list by deletion date
- ♦ Sort list by deletor
- ♦ Sort the list by file size
- ♦ Sort the list by file name

Each of these options is intended to help you locate the appropriate files.

View/Recover Deleted Files

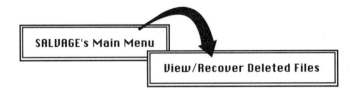

After selecting the View/Recover Deleted Files option, you will be asked to type a file pattern to match. To find all previously deleted files, press Enter. To limit the file search according to entered criteria, type a search pattern (for example *.EXE) and press Enter.

After pressing Enter, you will be given a directory structure that lists all directories and previously deleted files. To move around the directory, highlight the parent directory designators .. or pick the next subdirectory. After you reach the correct location, the file(s) you are looking for should be listed. Highlight the file, or mark the file with the F5 key, and press Enter. Two boxes will appear. One contains some specific information, such as delete date, modify date, deletor, and owner; and the other asks if you want to recover the file. To recover the file, press Y and the file is restored to its original location (if the file was located in a directory that has been deleted, the file is placed in DELETED.SAV directory). The DELETED.SAV is a hidden directory located off of the root directory on the NetWare volume.

To permanently delete a file, also known as purging a file, simply high-light the file and press Del. Two windows will appear; one displays the same information that you get when you recover a file, and the other asks you to verify that you want to permanently purge the file.

Starting SALVAGE from the directory where the files used to be located greatly simplifies the recovery process.

*When attempting to recover a deleted file, you can limit the number of files and directories that you are working with. After you select the Recover option, a box with an * will appear. The * is the default wild-card setting that is all-inclusive. This can be changed to a specific name or to a group of characters. The following procedures will help the recovery process by limiting the number of deleted files that you see.*

- ◆ Type the exact name of the deleted file
- ◆ Use * to match 0 or more of any character
- ◆ Use ? to match exactly one of any character
- ◆ Press F5 to mark multiple files for recovery

Additional NetWare 2.2 Notes

SALVAGE cannot restore files from deleted directories, and recovers them only to the directory/subdirectory from which they were originally deleted. If you accidentally delete a file or group of files, do the following:

- ◆ Remain logged in. After you log out, you cannot recover the file.
- ◆ Issue the SALVAGE command immediately. If you create or delete another file from the same volume, you cannot recover the chosen file.
- ◆ Summon SALVAGE from the same workstation where the deletion took place.

See Also

NETADMIN

NWADMIN

NWUSER

SYSCON

SBACKUP

The SBACKUP utility provided with NetWare 3.1x and 4.x replaces the NBACKUP utility provided with NetWare 2.2. SBACKUP enables you to back up and restore data on NetWare 2.2, 3.1x, and 4.x file servers, as well as on OS/2 network servers, network workstations, and other network services. SBACKUP allows you to select the data you choose to back up, store that data on any supported storage device, and then later retrieve and restore that data.

SBACKUP is provided as a NetWare Loadable Module (NLM) to be run on NetWare file servers as needed. It uses TSA (Target Service Agents) and supports DOS, FTAM, Macintosh, NFS, and OS/2 name spaces.

When using SBACKUP to back up or restore data, you must load the appropriate NLM on each NetWare file server, or the related executable file on each network workstation. When backing up a NetWare file server, the file server to be backed up is referred to as the *target server*. The file server doing the backing up and to which the backup device is attached is called the *host server*.

If, for example, you want to back up a NetWare 3.12 file server (called the target server) from a NetWare 4.1 file server (called the host server), load the TSA for NetWare 3.12 (file TSA312) onto the target server, then load the SBACKUP NLM on the host server. You must load the TSA on the target server. You also must load the SBACKUP NLM on the host server.

 The host server also can be the target server. If this is the case, load both the TSA for the target server and the SBACKUP NLM on the same file server.

If, for example, you have a NetWare 4.10 file server with a backup device attached (host server), and you want to back up that same NetWare 4.10 file server to the backup device, that file server is both the host server and the target server. You must, therefore, load both TSA410.NLM and SBACKUP.NLM on this one server.

The TSAs available for NetWare 2.2, 3.1x, and 4.x file servers are as follows:

- ♦ TSA220.NLM (for NetWare 2.2 file servers)

- ♦ TSA311.NLM (for NetWare 3.11 file servers)

- ♦ TSA312.NLM (for NetWare 3.12 file servers)

- ♦ TSA400.NLM (for NetWare 4.0 file servers)

- ♦ TSA410.NLM (for NetWare 4.1 file servers)

You also can back up a network DOS or OS/2 workstation.

To back up a DOS workstation, load TSADOS.NLM and SBACKUP on the host file server if it is a NetWare 4.1 file server, and TSASMS on the DOS workstation. If it is a NetWare 3.1x file server, load TSA31x.NLM on the host file server, and TSA_DOS on the DOS workstation.

To back up an OS/2 workstation, load TSAPROXY and SBACKUP on the host file server if it is a NetWare 4.1 file server, and load TSAOS2 on the target OS/2 workstation. If it is a NetWare 3.1x file server, load TSA31x.NLM and SBACKUP on the NetWare 3.12 file server, and TSA_OS2 on the OS/2 workstation.

To load a TSA on a target server, type **LOAD** *tsa* and press Enter. Replace *tsa* with one of the TSA NLMs previously listed.

To use SBACKUP to back up or restore NDS databases, load the NDS Target Service Agent (TSANDS) on the host server. Then load SBACKUP.

After the TSA is loaded on the target server, load SBACKUP on the host server. To load SBACKUP on the host server, type **LOAD SBACKUP SIZE=***xxx* **BUFFER=***x*, then press Enter. Replace *xxx* with the available buffer size. Specify the buffer size as 16, 32, 64, 128, or 256 KB, with the default size being 64 KB. Replace *x* with the number of available buffers. The range for available buffers is 2 through 10, with the default being 4.

You can have the TSAs and SBACKUP NLMs loaded for you each time you boot the file server by placing the commands in the file server's STARTUP.NCF file. You also can automatically load the TSA for a network workstation by including the appropriate command in the workstation's NET.CFG or AUTOEXEC.BAT file of a DOS workstation, or the Startup folder of an OS/2 workstation.

When the NetWare 4.10 SBACKUP main menu opens, you will see that it contains the following five options:

♦ Backup

♦ Restore

♦ Log/error File Administration

♦ Storage Device Administration

♦ Change Target to Back Up From or Restore To

Back Up

To perform a backup, you must choose Backup from the Main Menu, then choose a server to be backed up from the List of Servers Available for Backup screen.

Choose a backup device from the Select the desired Device menu. To back up a local drive, choose DOS Devices, otherwise, choose the appropriate device name.

 If there is only one server available from which to choose, you will not see the List of Servers Available for Backup screen.

After you choose the server to be backed up, you also might have to choose from a list of Target Services running on this file server if more than one Target Service has been loaded on this file server. You might, for example, have to choose a DOS workstation, an OS/2 workstation, the NetWare File System, or the NetWare 4.1 directory. When you choose the Target Service (if applicable), enter the Target user name and password if prompted.

 You also have the option of choosing what should be backed up. You can use the Include or Exclude options lists to specify what to back up, or what not to back up.

If the host server has more than one storage device attached, choose the storage device to be used. Otherwise, SBACKUP assumes the single backup device attached to the file server.

Choose the location for session files to be stored. SYS:SYSTEM/TSA/LOG is the default location.

From the Type of Backup screen, choose one of the following:

♦ Full: All Data on Target

♦ Differential: Changes Since Last Full

♦ Incremental: Changes Since Last Backup

♦ Custom: Only Specified Data

Complete the information in the Backup Options screen. Information to provide includes a description of the backup, and whether the current backup session should be appended to a previous backup session. Then press F10 to save your choices.

When the Proceed With the Backup? screen appears, choose one of the following:

♦ No, Return to the Options Form

♦ Start the Backup Now

♦ Start the Backup Later

If you choose to start the backup later, you are prompted for a date and time to start the backup. Otherwise, the backup will begin at midnight that day. If you start the backup now, a Backup Terminated message appears when the backup is complete.

When you have completed a backup, that backup can later be restored as needed.

Restore

To restore a backup, load required files as previously listed, including SBACKUP. Choose Restore from the main menu. Next, choose Select Working Directory and provide the path to the working directory you specified during the original backup. When the Restore Menu opens, choose Restore Session. Choose the session to be restored, then choose your restore options from the Restore Option screen.

If the back up session you want to restore is not included in the list of sessions to be restored, press Insert, type the exact path pointing to the location of the session files from which to restore, and press Enter. Then choose the appropriate session to be restored.

As with the original backup, you can also choose what to restore and what not to restore.

After all files are loaded, and you have chosen Restore from the main menu, choose a NetWare server running the restore Target Services (TSA220, TSA311, and so on). Next, choose a target to which the restore will be made. As with the backup, you can choose to restore to a DOS workstation, a NetWare file system, the NetWare 4.1 Directory, or an OS/2 workstation. Then, when prompted, provide the user name and password.

From the Restore menu, choose Choose a Session to Restore or Restore Without Session Files. Then, specify a path where the session files can be found, if needed, before choosing which session to restore. Choose what should be restored (one file or directory, an entire session, or a custom restore), and provide the needed information (Restore Options) if applicable.

Finally, press F10 to begin the restore, and answer Yes to the Proceed With the Restore prompt.

You might have to provide additional information such as whether to overwrite existing copies of files (called child) or servers, volumes, or directories (called parents), depending on which restoring option you chose.

When the backup is complete, return to the main menu by pressing Enter and then Escape.

NetWare Directory Services (NDS) sessions should only be restored from a backup if all replicas on the network have become corrupted. Otherwise, NDS information should be restored using a non-corrupted replica.

Log/Error File Administration

You can use the Log/error File Administration option to view information about backup and error logs. After choosing this option, choose either View a Log File or View an Error File, then specify where the files are stored (if not the default). Finally, choose the file to be viewed.

Storage Device Administration

By choosing Storage Device Administration from the SBACKUP main menu, you can view media lists, check the status of a device, check the status of the media in a device, access media utilities, rename a storage device, and manage storage media. Choose the media from the list available, then you can perform the various tasks associated with this SBACKUP Storage Device Administration option.

Change Target To Back Up From or Restore To

The Change Target To Back Up From or Restore To option is similar to the Change Current Server option available in NBACKUP. It provides a list of available file servers from which to choose. It displays only those servers that have the appropriate TSA loaded. Choose the file server to be backed up (the Target) from the list provided.

See Also

NBACKUP

SESSION

The SESSION utility is one of NetWare 2 and NetWare 3's best-kept secrets. It is a utility that enables users to map drives, select a file server, create search drives, and so on. It often is difficult for users to remember all of the command line commands that help navigate NetWare on a day-to-day basis. SESSION is a utility that can help users when they forget how to perform a particular function. More specifically, the SESSION utility enables you to do the following:

♦ Perform file server selection and drive mapping related tasks

♦ Change file servers

♦ View groups

♦ Send messages to groups or users

♦ Choose a default drive

♦ Change (temporarily) your drive mappings and search mappings

♦ List user information

 NetWare 4 does not have a SESSION utility. Its features are found in the NETUSER utility.

SESSION is a NetWare user utility, and therefore is run from a DOS prompt at the workstation. To start SESSION, type **SESSION** at the workstation's DOS prompt. SESSION's main menu appears (see fig. 1).

Figure 1
SESSION's
main menu.

```
┌─────────────────────────┐
│     Available Topics     │
├─────────────────────────┤
│Change Current Server    │
│Drive Mappings           │
│Group List               │
│Search Mappings          │
│Select Default Drive     │
│User List                │
└─────────────────────────┘
```

Change Current Server

Selecting Change Current Server provides you with a list of servers to which you currently are attached. To add servers to this list, press Ins and a list of other available file servers appears. Select a file server and press Enter. You then are prompted for a user name and password.

Drive Mappings

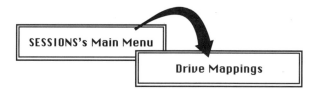

To map a drive, select the Drive Mappings option from SESSION's main menu. A list of your current drive mappings appears. To add an additional mapping to this list, press Ins. A box indicating the next available logical drive mapping appears; either change the drive designation letter, or accept it by pressing Enter. Then, in the box that appears, either type the location of the directory for the drive mapping or press Enter to see a list of available servers (if you have multiple servers). If the correct server is not in the list, press Ins; otherwise, select the server.

After selecting the server, select the correct volume and directory by highlighting the appropriate option and pressing Enter. After choosing the correct path, press Esc; you are returned to the Select Directory option window. To map a drive to the location indicated in this screen, press Enter. A window appears asking if you want this drive mapping to be mapped as a Map Root device. (Map Root enables you to simulate a root directory anywhere in the path, rather than just at the volume level.) Answer Yes or No and the drive mapping is added to your list of current drive mappings.

To delete a drive mapping, select Drive Mappings from SESSION's main menu, then highlight the appropriate drive designation and press Del. To view the effective rights of a drive mapping, select Drive Mappings from SESSION's main menu, then select the drive mapping and press Enter. A box indicating the current effective rights appears.

Changes made from SESSION are temporary; they will be lost when the user logs out. To make the changes permanent, they should be added to the user's login script.

Group List

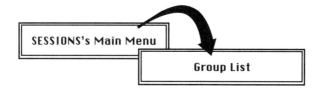

To view a list of groups, select Group List from SESSION's main menu, and a box with a list of groups appears on your screen. To send a message to all of the members contained in one of these groups, select the appropriate group and press Enter. A message dialog box appears in which you can type your message. To send the message, press Enter.

Search Mappings

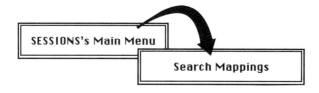

To map a search drive, select the Search Mappings option from the main menu. You then are given a list of your current search drive mappings. To add an additional search mapping to this list, press Ins. A box indicating the next available search drive appears; either change the drive designation number to the number of your choice, or accept it by pressing Enter.

Then a box appears asking you to type the location of the directory for the search drive mapping. You also can press Enter to see a list of available servers (if you have multiple servers). If the correct server is not in the list, press Ins; otherwise, select a server.

After selecting a server, you can designate the volume and directory by highlighting the correct option and pressing Enter. After choosing the correct path, press Esc and you are taken back to the Select Directory option window. To have a search drive mapped to the location indicated in this screen, press Enter.

To delete a search drive mapping, select Search Mapping from SESSION's main menu, then highlight the appropriate search drive designation number and press Del. To view the effective rights of a search drive mapping, select Search Mapping from SESSION's main menu, then select the drive mapping and press Enter. A box appears indicating the current effective rights.

Select Default Drive

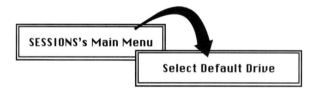

When you choose the Select a Default Drive option from SESSION's main menu, a window appears that contains all the current drive mappings, including the local drives. Highlighting the NetWare drive designations and pressing Enter makes that drive your default drive (when you leave SESSION you will return to this drive).

User List

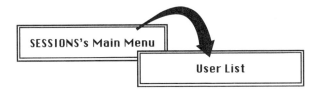

Selecting User List from SESSION's main menu provides you with a list of users who are currently logged in to the file server. If a user is listed more than once, he has logged in to the server from two different workstations.

Selecting a user will give you two options: Display User Information and Send Message. If multiple users are marked with the F5 key, you will not get these options; you will only be allowed to send a message.

To display a user's information, select User List from SESSION's main menu, highlight a user, press Enter, and then choose Display User Information. The following user information is displayed:

♦ Full name

♦ Object type

♦ Login time

♦ Network address

♦ Network node

To send a message to a particular user, select User List from SESSION's main menu and a list of users appears. Select a user, or mark several users with the F5 key, and press Enter. If one user is selected, select Send Message. If multiple users are selected, a message dialog box appears. Enter the message that you want to send and press Enter.

See Also

FILER

NWUSER

SESSION

SYSCON

SYSCON

SYSCON is a menu utility that enables a NetWare supervisor to create users and groups, install and manage accounting, and perform the day-to-day user management routines. These daily routines include creating or changing user and system login scripts, adding or deleting user or directory trustee assignments, and so on. Figure 1 shows SYSCON's main menu.

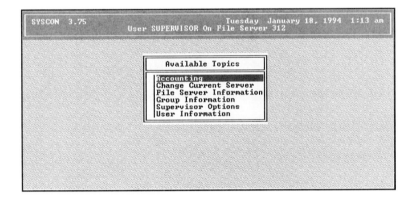

Figure 1
SYSCON's main menu.

 In version 4, SYSCON is replaced by NWADMIN and NETADMIN.

Accounting

Accounting is used to charge users or groups for the use of network resources. With accounting, you can modify the charge for the resources, define which resources are chargeable, and include or exclude a server and its resources as a chargeable commodity.

To install accounting, select Accounting from SYSCON's main menu. Select Yes from the Install Accounting pop-up box. After you install accounting, the following accounting management options appear each time you select Accounting (see fig. 2):

Figure 2
SYSCON's
Accounting screen.

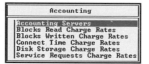

- ◆ Accounting Servers
- ◆ Blocks Read Charge Rates
- ◆ Blocks Written Charge Rates
- ◆ Connect Time Charge Rates
- ◆ Disk Storage Charge Rates
- ◆ Service Requests Charge Rates

Accounting Servers

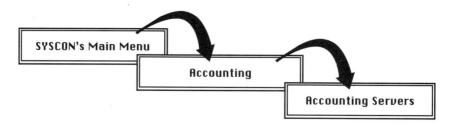

Installing accounting enables the network supervisor to change users for specific use of a server's resource. Selecting Accounting Servers from the Accounting menu provides a list of servers. Servers that have had accounting installed are in the list and users can be charged for the use of the server's resources. Servers not found in the list have not had Accounting installed and cannot charge for resources. Charging for resources is simply a method used by NetWare to keep track of which resources are being used by whom. Reports on network usage then can be printed and used as billing statements, if you plan to charge for the use of network resources.

Charging for resources is an effective method of distributing the costs of a network to different business departments, divisions, or cost centers.

Charge Rates

NetWare's accounting feature enables supervisors to charge for the following network services:

- Blocks read
- Blocks written
- Connect time
- Disk storage
- Service requests

Change Current Server

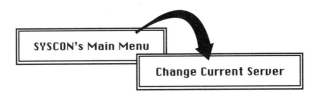

To change to a different server from within SYSCON, choose Change Current Server from the Available Topics menu. A list of servers will appear, displaying all servers to which you currently are attached. If the server that you want is not included in the list, press Ins. A new list of servers showing all currently available servers on the network will appear. To add a server to the currently attached list, select the appropriate server by scrolling through the list and pressing Enter.

File Server Information

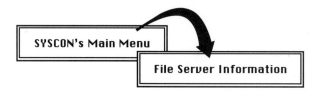

Selecting File Server Information from SYSCON's main menu brings up a list of servers that exit on your network. To get information on a server, select the server from the list and the File Server Information screen appears.

Group Information

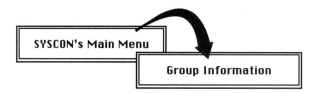

Selecting Group Information from SYSCON's main menu enables a NetWare user to view information regarding a group's status. If you are a supervisor, Group Information enables you to manage the group member list, as well as the group's rights. You also can change trustee directory assignments, create group managers, and manage trustee file assignments.

Information available on the selected group includes the following:

♦ Full name

♦ Managed users and groups

♦ Managers

♦ Member list

♦ Other information

♦ Trustee directory assignments

♦ Trustee file assignments

Supervisor Options

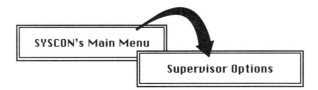

Selecting Supervisor Options enables the network Supervisor to perform the following:

♦ **Set default account balance restrictions.** The default account balance restrictions (see fig. 3) include: setting a password expiration date, limiting the number of concurrent user connections that are permissible, setting the minimum password length, determining how much time is allowed before a password must be changed, determining the number of grace logins allowed, stipulating that a password must be unique, setting an account balance, and setting an account's limits.

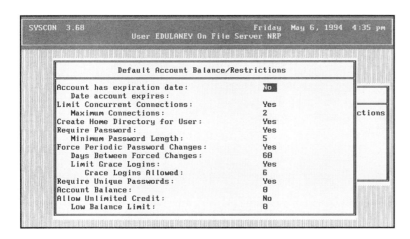

Figure 3
The Default Account Balance/Restrictions options.

♦ **Set default time restrictions.** This option (see fig. 4) determines when a user can log in to a file server. It often is used to keep users from logging in to a server after hours (for backup, security, or other reasons). The default, which is represented by asterisks, allows a user to be logged in at all times. Removing the asterisks prevents the user from logging in during that time period.

Figure 4
The Default Time
Restrictions screen.

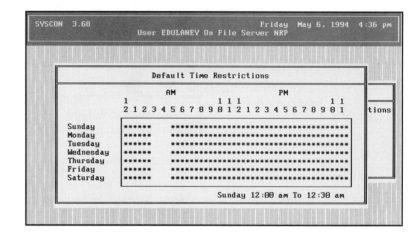

♦ **Edit system AUTOEXEC.NCF file.** This option contains the list of modules loaded during file server startup (see fig. 5).

Figure 5
A sample
AUTOEXEC.NCF in
the NetWare editor.

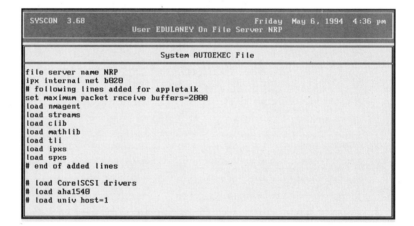

♦ **Create a list of file server console operations.** This option defines users who can control the server via FCONSOLE.

♦ **Enable or disable file intruder detection.** This option lets you specify how many attempts you have and if you are allowed to log in to a server without the correct password. When intruder detection is enabled, the Supervisor can set the number of incorrect login attempts that can be made and how long an account is inactive after an intruder detection is reported.

- **Manage system login script.** Selecting this option enables you to view and change the system's login script. The system's login script is created by the Supervisor and contains mappings and other commands that are created at login for all users. It is stored as an ASCII file (NET$LOG.DAT) and resides in the PUBLIC directory. This option specifies the actions that occur when all users log in to a file server.

- **View the file server's error log.** This contains valuable information about server errors as well as server activities.

- **Create workgroup managers.** A workgroup manager is much like a user account manager; both are user accounts that have selectively been given the Supervisor privileges necessary to manage all users and group accounts assigned to them. These managers can only delete accounts assigned to them or created by them. Workgroup managers often are created to off-load some of the Supervisor's day-to-day management routines.

User Information

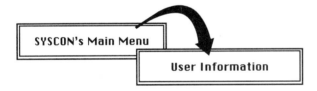

A list of users appears when you select User Information from SYSCON's main menu. For information on a user, highlight the user and press Enter. After selecting a user, a User Information menu appears. This menu shows different options depending on the user about which you are attempting to get information. A User Information screen appears when you try to get information about another user and you do not have supervisory rights. If you have supervisory rights or are attempting to get information about your own user account, the following options are available:

- Set account balances

- Specify account restrictions

- Change a user's password

- Indicate the full name of a user

- ♦ Assign a user to groups

- ♦ Determine intruder lockout status

- ♦ Create user login scripts

- ♦ Manage users and groups

- ♦ Create workgroup managers

- ♦ Gather "other" user information

- ♦ Set user security equivalencies

- ♦ Assign workstation restrictions

- ♦ Set user login time restrictions

- ♦ Grant trustee directory assignments (version 2.2 does not have this option)

- ♦ Grant trustee file assignments

- ♦ Set volume disk restrictions

Some of these functions may seem similar to those found under the Supervisor Options section of SYSCON's main menu; however, there is a difference. When these options are set under the Supervisor Options section of SYSCON, they become defaults. The defaults are used for any new user added; changes made in the Supervisor Options section have no effect on users already defined. To change existing users, the changes need to be made in this section.

See Also

FILER

NETUSER (NetWare 4)

NWADMIN (NetWare 4)

UPGRADE

The UPGRADE utility enables you to upgrade an existing NetWare 2.2 network to a NetWare 3.1x file server. To run the UPGRADE utility, type **UPGRADE** and press Enter.

NetWare 3.12 provides an in-place upgrade that upgrades a NetWare 3.1x file server to a NetWare 3.12 file server.

USERDEF

The USERDEF utility enables you to create templates for automating the creation of network user accounts. These templates enable you to set parameters and define login scripts which will then be applied to all newly created user accounts.

To run USERDEF, type **USERDEF** and press Enter. The USERDEF Available Options menu opens. This menu has three options:

♦ Add Users

♦ Edit/View Templates

♦ Restrict User

Add Users

Choose Add Users from the USERDEF Available Options menu to create user accounts using a USERDEF template. To create new user accounts using a template created with the USERDEF utility, choose Add Users, and then choose an existing USERDEF template from the list of templates. When the Users list appears, press Ins, type a username, press Enter, and then choose Yes when prompted to Create New Users Using Template name.

Edit/View Templates

Choose Edit/View Templates from the USERDEF Available Options menu to create new templates or edit existing templates. When you choose this option, a list of templates is displayed. From the list of templates, choose an existing template and edit its parameters, or press Ins, provide a template name, and then edit the Parameters for Template name options.

Restrict User

Choose the Restrict User option to set restrictions for user accounts.

VOLINFO

NetWare's volume information utility (VOLINFO) is a simple, convenient way to determine how much disk space you have left on a particular file server or volume. To start VOLINFO, type VOLINFO from a workstation that has rights to the Public directory. A screen appears that lists the servers to which you are currently logged in. Select a server, and a screen appears displaying up to six of the server's volumes. This screen provides you with the amount of space that originally was available on the volume as well as how much of that space is free. It also provides you with information on the volume's directories entries (see fig. 1).

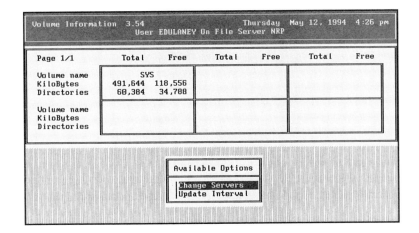

Figure 1
VOLINFO's Volume Information screen.

 The VOLINFO functions became a part of FILER in NetWare 4.10.

Change File Server

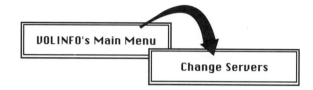

If you need to monitor a volume that is on a different file server, select the Change File Server option. A screen appears listing the file servers that you currently are logged in to. If the correct file server is not listed, press Ins. After selecting the new file server, the same volume information screen will appear listing the new server's volumes and their current status.

Update Interval

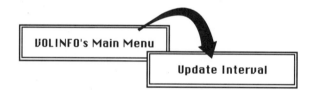

The only other option available in VOLINFO is Update Interval. This interval is how frequently VOLINFO checks the disks. Changing the interval to a shorter period of time (the default is every five seconds) will increase the load on the network. Using a short interval, however, will show the volume's dynamic nature.

VOLINFO can show only six volumes per server on one screen. If your server has more than six volumes, press the down or up arrow key to get to the following or preceding volumes.

Blinking numbers indicate that a volume's statistics are getting too low. If the amount of free disk space is blinking, then either you have less than 10 percent of the total disk's space left, or the free space is less than 1 MB.

"Directories" shows the number of entries that is allocated for the volume, and the number that is unused. When "Directories" is blinking, free directories are <=20 directories.

If a volume is removable (optical), an R appears next to the volume name. Removable volume names will appear and disappear as the volume is mounted and dismounted.

F2 toggles between kilobyte and megabyte formats.

Triangles indicate disk activity during the last update. If the tip of the triangle points down, disk space is being used. If the tip of the triangle points up, files are being deleted.

See Also

FILER

NETADMIN

NWADMIN

SYSCON

VREPAIR

VREPAIR, NetWare's volume repair utility, is a server console utility that can correct minor hard-disk problems on the volume without destroying data. VREPAIR also locates and adds new bad blocks to the bad block table on the disk.

VREPAIR is a server console utility that must be run after SERVER.EXE is loaded, but before the volume is mounted.

VREPAIR is an NLM for 3.1x and 4.10 and an EXE file for 2.2. As an NLM, VREPAIR runs on a server that is up and has the disk controller drivers loaded but the volume to be repaired is not mounted. The EXE is run on a 2.2 server that is down and at a DOS prompt.

VREPAIR can correct disk errors because NetWare stores two copies of the file allocation table (FAT): the primary FAT and the secondary FAT. Two copies of the directory table that contain critical information that the file server must have to locate directories and files also are stored.

If for some reason, the primary tables do not match the secondary tables, NetWare cannot mount the volume until the volume is repaired. To repair a volume, run VREPAIR. During the repair process, VREPAIR compares the primary tables to the secondary tables. If differences are encountered, VREPAIR attempts to restore the tables to their correct state. VREPAIR is not perfect, however. It simply compares the two tables and determines which table is the most correct. VREPAIR then restores the most correct table on top of the other table, thus causing the two tables to match.

Novell recommends that VREPAIR is run several times, until no errors are found. This could take 3 to 4 passes. VREPAIR should be run with caution.

VREPAIR's menu structure and mode of operation have not changed from one version of NetWare to the next, but its capabilities are different. Before running VREPAIR, take a moment to read the following note.

Running an older version of VREPAIR on a newer version of NetWare (a 3.x version of VREPAIR on a 4.10 version of NetWare, for example) can result in disaster as enhancements made to the file system cannot be predicted by older versions of VREPAIR. If, for instance, you run a 3.x version of VREPAIR on a NetWare 4 server with file compression turned on, the older version of VREPAIR will think that the compressed files represent corrupt data. It then will try to fix each compressed file and you probably will lose most of your data.

Because volume corruption can be caused by improper shut down of the server, a failing hard disk, a bad controller, or one of several other reasons, it is important to have the correct version of VREPAIR available for every NetWare server. When installing a server, store VREPAIR on the server's boot partition (so that you can get to VREPAIR even if the server's volumes cannot be mounted).

By default (in NetWare 3.x and 4.10), VREPAIR is stored on the NetWare SYS volume in the System directory. If your SYS volume will not mount, however, you will not be able to access VREPAIR. It is best to store the VREPAIR utility on your server's boot disk or on an emergency floppy. VREPAIR also can be found on the original NetWare System-2 disk.

VREPAIR

To start VREPAIR, the server has to be up, but the volume you are attempting to fix cannot be mounted. To start VREPAIR, type **LOAD VREPAIR** at the server's console, and the main menu appears (see fig. 1).

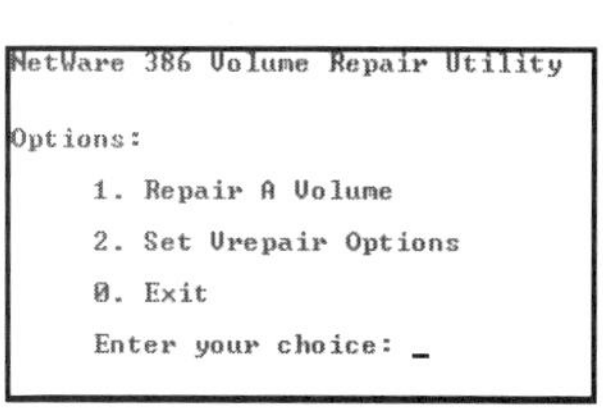

```
NetWare 386 Volume Repair Utility

Options:

    1. Repair A Volume

    2. Set Vrepair Options

    0. Exit

    Enter your choice: _
```

Figure 1
VREPAIR's main menu.

Repair a Volume

To repair a volume, select the first option in VREPAIR's main menu by pressing 1 and then Enter. VREPAIR checks the FAT, directory blocks, mirror mismatches, directories, and files. VREPAIR's progress is monitored and displayed on the server's console by periods that move across the screen (see fig. 2).

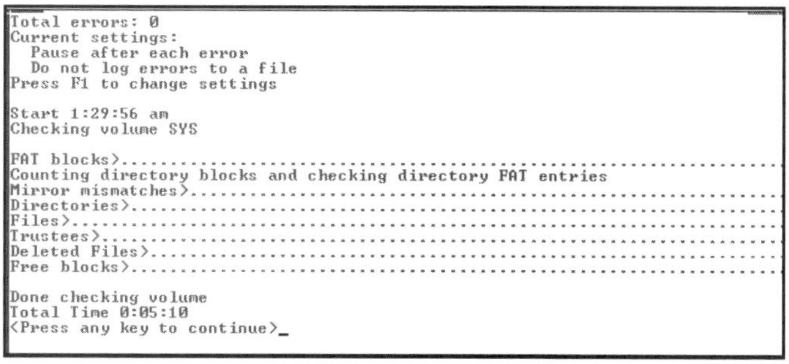

```
Total errors: 0
Current settings:
  Pause after each error
  Do not log errors to a file
Press F1 to change settings

Start 1:29:56 am
Checking volume SYS

FAT blocks>..................................................................
Counting directory blocks and checking directory FAT entries ...............
Mirror mismatches>..........................................................
Directories>................................................................
Files>......................................................................
Trustees>...................................................................
Deleted Files>..............................................................
Free blocks>................................................................

Done checking volume
Total Time 0:05:10
<Press any key to continue>_
```

Figure 2
A screen displaying VREPAIR's progress.

If VREPAIR finds any errors, you are asked if it is OK to write them to disk. By default, VREPAIR first attempts to write only the updated entries (the entries that have changed) to disk. If the volume still will not mount, run VREPAIR again. This time change the default VREPAIR option, telling it to write all changes to disk. (You might need to run VREPAIR several times.)

By default VREPAIR also asks you to confirm every change that it attempts to make. To change VREPAIR's default setting, see the following section on changing VREPAIR's options.

Set VREPAIR Options

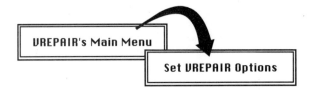

To change any of VREPAIR's options, select Set VREPAIR Options by
pressing 2 and then Enter. VREPAIR's Options menu appears (see fig. 3).

Figure 3
VREPAIR's Options
menu.

```
Options:
    1. Remove Name Space support from the volume
    2. Write All Directory And FAT Entries Out To Disk
    3. Write Changes Immediately To Disk
    4. Purge All Deleted Files
    0. Return To Main Menu
    Enter your choice: _
```

Each of these options (as seen in fig. 4) are "toggle" options. Pressing the
number changes the option. Pressing 3 and then Enter, for example,
changes the menu option from "write changes immediately to disk" to
"keep changes in memory for later update."

Figure 4
VREPAIR's Options
menu with all of the
options toggled.

```
Options:
    1. Quit If A Required VRepair Name Space Support NLM Is Not Loaded
    2. Write Only Changed Directory And FAT Entries Out To Disk
    3. Keep Changes In Memory For Later Update
    4. Retain Deleted Files
    0. Return To Main Menu
    Enter your choice:
```

Remove Name Space Support from the Volume

To remove name space support from a volume, select the first option by
pressing 1 and then Enter. A list of available name spaces appears. This
list differs depending on the version of NetWare and VREPAIR you are
running (for example, if you are using NetWare 3.12 or 4.10, the list
includes Macintosh, NFS, FTAM, OS/2, and NT). After selecting the
name space that you want to remove, return to VREPAIR's main menu
and run VREPAIR.

Only one name space can be removed at a time; each time you remove a name space, you must select the Remove Name Space support from the volume option and run VREPAIR.

To change any of VREPAIR's other default options, press the number of the menu item that you want to change, and then press Enter. Pressing the number of the menu option will toggle the option, and the menu item will reflect the change. One or all of the options can be changed; the menu line reflects the changes by showing the options that have been selected. Each line must be toggled separately. Figure 4 shows the Options menu with all the defaults toggled to the secondary option. After changing an option, return to the main menu and start VREPAIR.

Running VREPAIR in NetWare 2.2

The procedure for starting VREPAIR in NetWare 2.2 is considerably different than in later versions, as the utility is more DOS/command line oriented. The following steps outline the procedure for starting VREPAIR:

1. Down the server and reboot it with DOS.

2. Insert the SYSTEM-2 disk and type **VREPAIR**.

   A screen appears that lists the available drives. Those drives that are duplexed, or mirrored, appear as single entries. VREPAIR reports any discrepancies existing between the mirrors.

3. Select the drive that you want, and a list of volumes existing on that drive appears. From this list, choose the volume on which you want VREPAIR to work.

4. Answer the prompts as to whether you want:

   ♦ A report of any errors and corrections printed

   ♦ To test the volume for bad blocks

   ♦ To recover lost blocks not found in the FAT

5. Confirm your choices, and VREPAIR takes the appropriate actions.

VREPAIR checks the following items during the testing phase:

♦ SYS volume

♦ Directories

♦ Trustees

♦ Files

♦ Bad dir blocks

♦ Bad data blocks

♦ Mirror discrepancies

♦ The regular FAT

♦ The reserved FAT

♦ Bad FAT blocks

♦ Resource forks

♦ Resource fork consistency

VREPAIR also purges the salvageable files and recovers lost blocks. After it finishes, VREPAIR prints the report (if that option was selected) and then tells you to restart the file server. To do so, remove the SYSTEM-2 disk from the drive and power the server off then back on.

See Also

NETADMIN

NWADMIN

SALVAGE

Appendix A

Commands at a Glance

Commands					
	2.2	3.11	3.12	4.10	*Notes*
ABORT REMIRROR				X	
ACONSOLE		X	X		
ACTIVATE SERVER			X		
ADD NAME SPACE	X	X	X		
ALLOW		X	X		Part of RIGHTS in 4.x
ATCON				X	
ATOTAL	X	X	X	X	
ATTACH	X	X	X		Part of LOGIN in 4.x
AUDITCON				X	
BIND		X	X	X	
BINDFIX	X	X	X	X	Became DSREPAIR in 4.x
BINDREST	X	X	X		Became DSREPAIR in 4.x

continues

Commands, Continued

	2.2	3.11	3.12	4.10	Notes
BRGCON				X	
BROADCAST	X	X	X	X	
CAPTURE	X	X	X	X	
CASTOFF	X	X	X		Part of SEND in 4.x
CASTON	X	X	X		Part of SEND in 4.x
CD				X	
CDROM				X	
CHKDIR		X	X		Part of NDIR in 4.x
CHKVOL	X	X	X		Part of NDIR in 4.x
CLEAR MESSAGE	X				
CLEAR STATION	X	X	X	X	
CLIB		X	X	X	
CLS		X	X	X	
COLORPAL	X	X	X	X	
COMCHECK	X	X			
COMPSURF	X				
CONFIG	X	X	X	X	
CONLOG				X	
CONSOLE	X				
CX				X	
DCONFIG	X	X			
DISABLE LOGIN	X	X	X	X	
DISABLE TRANSACTIONS	X				

	2.2	3.11	3.12	4.10	Notes
DISABLE TTS		X	X	X	
DISK	X				
DISKSET	X	X	X	X	
DISMOUNT	X	X	X	X	
DISPLAY NETWORKS	X	X	X	X	
DISPLAY SERVERS	X	X	X	X	
DOMAIN				X	
DOS	X				
DOSGEN	X	X	X	X	
DOWN	X	X	X	X	
DSMERGE				X	
DSPACE	X	X	X		Replaced by NETADMIN
DSREPAIR				X	
ECONFIG	X	X			
EDIT		X	X	X	
EMSNETX		X			
ENABLE LOGIN	X	X	X	X	
ENABLE TRANSACTIONS	X				
ENABLE TTS		X	X	X	
ENDCAP	X	X	X		Part of CAPTURE in 4.x
EXIT		X	X	X	
FILTCFG				X	
FCONSOLE	X	X	X		Part of MONITOR in 4.x
FILER	X	X	X	X	

continues

Appendix A: Commands at a Glance   627

Commands, Continued

	2.2	3.11	3.12	4.10	Notes
FLAG	X	X	X	X	
FLAGDIR	X	X	X		Part of FLAG in 4.x
GRANT	X	X	X		Part of RIGHTS in 4.x
HALT				X	
HCSS				X	
HELP	X	X	X	X	
HOLDOFF	X				
HOLDON	X				
INITIALIZE SYSTEM			X		
INSTALL		X	X	X	
IPX			X		
IPXCON				X	
IPXPING				X	
IPXS		X	X	X	
JUMPERS	X				
KEYB				X	
LANGUAGE				X	
LIST DEVICES				X	
LISTDIR	X	X	X		Part of NLIST in 4.x
LOAD				X	
LOGIN	X	X	X	X	
LOGOUT	X	X	X	X	
MAGAZINE				X	
MAKEUSER	X	X	X		Part of UIMPORT in 4.x

	2.2	3.11	3.12	4.10	Notes
MAP	X	X	X	X	
MATHLIB		X	X	X	
MATLIBC				X	
MEDIA				X	
MEMORY		X	X	X	
MEMORY MAP				X	
MENU	X	X			Became NMENU in 3.12 and 4.x
MIRROR STATUS				X	
MODULES		X	X	X	
MONITOR	X	X	X	X	
MOUNT	X	X	X	X	
MSERVER				X	
NAME	X	X	X	X	
NBACKUP	X	X			Became SBACKUP in 3.12 and 4.x
NCOPY	X	X	X	X	
NCUPDATE				X	
NDIR	X	X	X	X	
NETADMIN				X	
NETBIOS		X	X		
NETSYNC3				X	
NETSYNC4				X	
NETUSER				X	
NLIST				X	
NMAGENT		X	X	X	
NMENU			X	X	

continues

Commands, Continued

	2.2	3.11	3.12	4.10	Notes
NPAMS				X	
NPATH				X	
NPRINT	X	X	X	X	
NUT				X	
NVER	X	X	X	X	
NWADMIN				X	
NWSNUT				X	
NWXTRACT			X	X	
OFF	X	X	X	X	
PARTMGR				X	
PAUDIT	X	X	X		
PCONSOLE	X	X	X	X	
PING				X	
PRINTCON	X	X	X	X	
PRINTDEF	X	X	X	X	
PRINTER	X				
PROTOCOL		X	X	X	
PSC		X	X	X	
PSERVER		X	X	X	
PSTAT	X				
PURGE	X	X	X	X	
QUEUE	X				
RCONSOLE		X	X	X	
REGISTER MEMORY		X	X	X	
REINITIALIZE SYSTEM			X		

	2.2	3.11	3.12	4.10	*Notes*
REMIRROR	X				
REMIRROR PARTITION				X	
REMOTE		X	X	X	
REMOVE	X	X	X		Part of RIGHTS in 4.x
REMOVE DOS		X	X	X	
RENDIR	X	X	X	X	
RESET ROUTER	X	X	X	X	
RESTART				X	
REVOKE	X	X	X		Part of RIGHTS in 4.x
RIGHTS	X	X	X	X	
ROUTE		X	X	X	
RPL				X	
RPRINTER		X	X		
RS232		X	X	X	
RSETUP		X			
RSPX		X	X	X	
RTDM				X	
SALVAGE	X	X	X		Part of FILER in 4.x
SBACKUP				X	
SCAN FOR NEW DEVICES				X	
SCHDELAY				X	
SEARCH		X	X	X	
SECURE CONSOLE		X	X	X	
SECURITY	X	X	X		Part of NETADMIN in 4.x

continues

Appendix A: Commands at a Glance

Commands, Continued

	2.2	3.11	3.12	4.10	*Notes*
SEND	X	X	X	X	
SERVER		X	X	X	
SERVMAN				X	
SESSION	X	X	X		Part of NETUSER in 4.x
SET		X	X	X	
SET TIME	X	X	X	X	
SET TIME ZONE				X	
SETPASS	X	X	X	X	
SETTTS	X	X	X	X	
SLIST	X	X	X		Part of NLIST in 4.x
SMODE	X	X	X		Part of FLAG in 4.x
SPEED		X	X	X	
SPOOL	X	X	X		
SPXCONFIG		X	X	X	
SPXS		X	X	X	
STREAMS		X	X	X	
SYSCON	X	X	X		Part of NETADMIN in 4.x
SYSTIME	X	X	X	X	
TIME	X	X	X	X	
TIMESYNC				X	
TLI		X	X	X	
TLIST	X	X	X		Part of RIGHTS in 4.x

	2.2	3.11	3.12	4.10	Notes
TRACK OFF	X	X	X	X	
TRACK ON	X	X	X	X	
UIMPORT				X	
UNBIND		X	X	X	
UNLOAD		X	X	X	
UNMIRROR	X				
UPGRADE		X			
UPS	X	X	X	X	
UPS STATUS		X	X	X	
UPS TIME		X	X	X	
USERDEF	X	X	X		Part of NETADMIN in 4.x
USERLIST	X	X	X		Part of NLIST in 4.x
VAP	X				
VER	X				
VERSION	X	X	X	X	
VOLINFO	X	X	X		Part of FILER in 4.x
VOLUMES		X	X	X	
VREPAIR	X	X	X	X	
WATCHDOG	X				
WHOAMI	X	X	X	X	
WSUPDATE	X	X	X	X	
WSUPGRD				X	

Login Variables

Following is a listing of variables that NetWare uses. These variables can be used for conditional execution in login scripts, or echoed to the screen with the WRITE command. Traditionally, variables are preceded by a percent sign (%), and written in capital letters.

Variable	Function
DAY	Shows the day of the month, from 1 to 31
DAY_OF_WEEK	Spells out Sunday, Monday, Tuesday, and so on
NDAY_OF_WEEK	Represents Sunday as 1, Monday as 2, Tuesday as 3, and so on
MONTH	Shows the month of the year, from 01 to 12
MONTH_NAME	Spells out January, February, March, and so on
YEAR	Shows all four digits of the year—1994, 1995, and so on
SHORT_YEAR	Shows the last two digits of the year—94, 95, and so on
HOUR	Shows the hour, from 01 to 12
HOUR24	Shows the hour, from 00 to 23
MINUTE	Shows the minute, from 00 to 59
SECOND	Shows the second, from 00 to 59
GREETING_TIME	Returns either Morning, Afternoon, or Evening

continues

Variable	Function
AM_PM	Returns one or the other, depending upon which is appropriate
FULL_NAME	Gives the user's full name
LOGIN_NAME	Shows the login name used
USER_ID	Shows the user's id
PASSWORD_EXPIRES	Shows how many days remain before the password expires
FILE_SERVER	Shows the name of the current server
NETWORK_ADDRESS	Shows an 8-digit hexadecimal number
DOS_REQUESTER	Returns the version of DOS in use
NETWARE_REQUESTER	Returns the version of NetWare in use
MACHINE	Returns the machine hardware in useOS Returns the operating system in use
OS_VERSION	Shows 3.3, 5.0, 6.2, and so on, for the operating system running
P_STATION	Shows the node address in 12-digit hexadecimal form
SHELL_TYPE	Returns the type of shell calling the login script
SMACHINE	Shows the machine name in short form
STATION	Returns the workstation connection number
ACCESS_SERVER	Returns a value of true if the server is functional
ERROR_LEVEL	If any error level is existing, its value is returned

Menu Key Functions

When inside NetWare menus, several keys are mapped to specific functions. Although these differ slightly between NetWare versions, the following is a list of the most common keys.

Key	Function
F1	Brings up the help screen
F3	Allows editing of the highlighted option
F5	Marks an item, or unmarks it if it was already marked
F7	Cancels the operation
Alt+F10	Exits the menu utility, regardless of how many layers deep you are
Ins	Inserts a new entry
Del	Deletes an existing entry
Esc	Goes back to the preceding menu
Bksp	Deletes one character to the left of the cursor
Enter	Accepts the current entry
Home	Moves the cursor to the left hand side of the entry
End	Moves the cursor to the right hand side of the entry
PgUp	Moves up one page

continues

Key	Function
PgDn	Moves down one page
Ctrl+PgUp	Moves to the beginning
Ctrl+PgDn	Moves to the end
Up Arrow	Moves up one line
Dn Arrow	Moves down one line
Rt Arrow	Moves right one space
Lt Arrow	Moves left one space
Ctrl+[la]	Moves right one word
Ctrl+[ra]	Moves left one word

Index

D

E

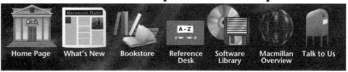

WANT MORE INFORMATION?

CHECK OUT THESE RELATED TOPICS OR SEE YOUR LOCAL BOOKSTORE

CAD and 3D Studio

As the number one CAD publisher in the world, and as a Registered Publisher of Autodesk, New Riders Publishing provides unequaled content on this complex topic. Industry-leading products include AutoCAD and 3D Studio.

Networking

As the leading Novell NetWare publisher, New Riders Publishing delivers cutting-edge products for network professionals. We publish books for all levels of users, from those wanting to gain NetWare Certification, to those administering or installing a network. Leading books in this category include *Inside NetWare 3.12*, *CNE Training Guide: Managing NetWare Systems*, *Inside TCP/IP*, and *NetWare: The Professional Reference*.

Graphics

New Riders provides readers with the most comprehensive product tutorials and references available for the graphics market. Best-sellers include *Inside CorelDRAW! 5*, *Inside Photoshop 3*, and *Adobe Photoshop NOW!*

Internet and Communications

As one of the fastest growing publishers in the communications market, New Riders provides unparalleled information and detail on this ever-changing topic area. We publish international best-sellers such as *New Riders' Official Internet Yellow Pages, 2nd Edition*, a directory of over 10,000 listings of Internet sites and resources from around the world, and *Riding the Internet Highway, Deluxe Edition*.

Operating Systems

Expanding off our expertise in technical markets, and driven by the needs of the computing and business professional, New Riders offers comprehensive references for experienced and advanced users of today's most popular operating systems, including *Understanding Windows 95*, *Inside Unix*, *Inside Windows 3.11 Platinum Edition*, *Inside OS/2 Warp Version 3*, and *Inside MS-DOS 6.22*.

Other Markets

Professionals looking to increase productivity and maximize the potential of their software and hardware should spend time discovering our line of products for Word, Excel, and Lotus 1-2-3. These titles include *Inside Word 6 for Windows*, *Inside Excel 5 for Windows*, *Inside 1-2-3 Release 5*, and *Inside WordPerfect for Windows*.

Orders/Customer Service   **1-800-653-6156**   Source Code   **NRP95**

New Riders Publishing   201 West 103rd Street ◆ Indianapolis, Indiana 46290 USA

REGISTRATION CARD

The Complete NetWare Command Reference

Name _____ Title _____

Company _____ Type of business _____

Address _____

City/State/ZIP _____

Have you used these types of books before? ☐ yes ☐ no

If yes, which ones? _____

_____

How many computer books do you purchase each year? ☐ 1–5 ☐ 6 or more

How did you learn about this book? _____

Where did you purchase this book? _____

Which applications do you currently use? _____

_____

Which computer magazines do you subscribe to? _____

_____

What trade shows do you attend? _____

_____

Comments: _____

_____

_____

Would you like to be placed on our preferred mailing list? ☐ yes ☐ no

☐ **I would like to see my name in print!** You may use my name and quote me in future New Riders products and promotions. My daytime phone number is: _____

New Riders Publishing 201 West 103rd Street ◆ Indianapolis, Indiana 46290 USA

Fax to **317-581-4670**   Orders/Customer Service **1-800-653-6156**   Source Code **NRP95**

Fold Here